IRISH EMIGRATION AND CANADIAN SETTLEMENT

Cecil J. Houston

William J. Smyth

Irish Emigration and Canadian Settlement: Patterns, Links, and Letters

UNIVERSITY OF TORONTO PRESS
Toronto Buffalo

ULSTER HISTORICAL FOUNDATION
Belfast

© University of Toronto Press 1990
Toronto Buffalo
Printed in Canada
Reprinted in paperback 1991
ISBN 0-8020-5829-9
ISBN 0-8020-6910-X

Printed on acid-free paper

Canadian Cataloguing in Publication Data

Houston, Cecil J., 1943–
    Irish emigration and Canadian settlement

    ISBN 0-8020-5829-9 (bound)   ISBN 0-8020-6910-X (pbk.)

    1. Irish – Canada – History – 19th century.
    2. Ireland – Emigration and immigration – History – 19th century.
    3. Canada – Emigration and immigration – History – 19th century.
    1. Smyth, William J., 1949– . 11. Title.

    FC106.I6H68 1990   305'.89162071   C90-093045-4
    F1035.I6H68 1990

This book has been published with the help of a grant from the
Social Science Federation of Canada, using funds provided by the
Social Sciences and Humanities Research Council of Canada.

For Lisa, Paul, Fiona, Sinéad, and Cathal

Contents

Acknowledgments

Brian Trainor, while head of the Public Record Office of Northern Ireland, encouraged us to start this volume. R.I.K. Davidson at the University of Toronto Press seconded the idea. The Social Sciences and Humanities Research Council of Canada and Erindale College provided funds necessary to the authors' transatlantic collaboration. Colleagues supported our efforts; we note especially Howard Andrews, Len Brooks, Deryck Holdsworth, Tom McIlwraith, Desmond Morton, and Ken Turner. Peter Toner was unselfish with unpublished results of his own research. Samuel Carrothers, Margaret Fallona, and Don Kerr provided family documents.

Great assistance was received from the staff of the Public Records Office of Northern Ireland, the National Archives of Canada, the Provincial Archives of New Brunswick, the New Brunswick Museum, and the Archives of the Catholic Archdiocese of Toronto. Pieces of drafts of the text and collections of emigrant letters were typed by Breeda Behan, Una Jordan, Geri McCullough, and Mary Wellman. Linda White put all the pieces together. Maynooth College Publication Fund contributed to typing costs. Anonymous reviewers clarified our interpretation. Jim Keenan produced the maps and graphs. Virgil Duff served as the editor. John Parry's skilful copy-editing improved the text.

Erindale College   St. Patrick's College
University of Toronto   National University of Ireland
Mississauga   Maynooth
Canada   Ireland

IRISH EMIGRATION AND CANADIAN SETTLEMENT

CHAPTER ONE

Introduction

They are rarely discussed now, except as people who were around in the past. In Canada, the Irish have disappeared and people can no longer point to an Irish township or an Irish block. It is curious that the Irish have become so unknown, so forgotten. Maps of Canada are not short of Irish place-names – Derry, Moira, Maynooth, Inistioge, Dublin, Boyne. Nor is the countryside short of symbols of Irishness – Catholic churches, Celtic crosses as gravemarkers, and Orange halls, although the latter are disappearing fast. Even the folklore surrounding Timothy Eaton, the Ballymena emigrant who rose to become Canada's pre-eminent merchant, has faded. Timothy's bronze statue in the Eaton Co.'s main department store in downtown Toronto has been moved from a ground floor entrance to a nook on the fourth floor and the right foot is again tarnished, no longer rubbed in reverence by grateful Irish immigrants. Like Timothy Eaton, the Irish have been shunted into the recesses of Canada's collective memory. In that memory only one event is vivid – the arrival of the Famine hordes in 1847.

In 1847 over a hundred thousand Irish emigrants were off-loaded from the converted cargo holds of sailing ships at Canadian quarantine stations. A large proportion of them were diseased, famished, destitute, or abandoned. Within a year a third of them were dead. They were the victims of the Great Potato Famine and in panic had fled Ireland. Their numbers and their misfortune left an impression on Canadian society that has not been dispelled, for as a result of the Famine the Irish in Canada have acquired a romantic and epic aura. In the popular imagination, the Famine, typhus, cholera, and involuntary exile have grown to be the primary image symbolizing the Irish emigration. The 1847 Famine episode has been generalized to represent a universal tragic beginning for the group. Recently, a private member's bill before the Ontario legislature sought incorrectly to have 1995 recognized as the sesquicentennial of the arrival of the first Irish immigrants in Canada.[1] It has even been said of Timothy Eaton that he was 'a victim of the Great Irish Potato Famine.'[2] The truth is otherwise.

The vast majority of Canada's Irish arrived before the Famine and not as exiles. From the mid-eighteenth century, safe passages, reasoned decisions, and fairly successful outcomes characterized an ongoing mass voluntary emigration. To be sure, it was not easy. This was a migration that preceded the era of scheduled steamship travel. The Irish arrived in the steerage of sailing ships usually employed in carrying timber, coal, slates, and other bulk goods. In coldly economic terms, the emigrants were a profitable, fare-paying ballast on trips of considerable risk. As a contemporary recalled of his experiences: 'A voyage across the Atlantic in those days involved many discomforts and privations totally unknown in these days of rapid steam navigation. Seven, eight, nine, and as high as thirteen weeks were not unfrequently occupied by sailing vessels on the voyage; and the consequent suffering experienced on such occasions, the news of which, when transmitted by the sufferers to relatives at home, had spread a universal dread of a trip to America.'[3]

Despite the universal dread, hundreds of thousands took the chance. British North America was close – the British colonial realm nearest Ireland – and the cost of passage was the cheapest of the various passages across the oceans. It was an attractive option, and as a consequence Irish fishing villages and lumbering and farming settlements emerged early in Canada and Irish skills and energy contributed much to the creation of a new country. In the nineteenth century the Irish comprised the largest immigrant group. They could be found across the country, and by their overwhelming prominence in some areas they even formed distinctive regional cultures. Fewer than half of them were Catholic, and the majority were Protestant; for both groups rural life was the norm. They were neither a minority nor unusual and they blended in with the rest of the Canadians. They became Canadians early in the creation of the country, and for that reason they have tended to disappear.

It is not the sort of story that fits the widely held stereotype of the Irish emigrant as a victim, uprooted by the Great Famine and immobilized in urban ghettos. Nor does it fit the earlier and alternate, frontier-America stereotype of Scots-Irish Presbyterian pioneers. Both these images come from American experiences and have been insinuated as primary myths into the backdrop of Canadian historiography.

The Scots-Irish myth depended on events in the eighteenth century. Presbyterians, kept from full participation in Irish society by proscriptive laws, emigrated in large numbers to New England and the 'Middle Colonies' of America in search of greater freedoms and easier economic opportunities. They migrated from Ulster, and their move to America has been interpreted as simply the second step on the way out of Scotland. The first step had been from Scotland across the North Channel to nearby Ulster, where they had spent a century. In American folklore, and especially in their own Scots-Irish legends, they were respectable farmers and tradesmen, God-fearing, industrious, relatively prosperous, and, above all, hardy frontiersmen.

Nineteenth-century American historiography developed another myth, based on the assumption that the hordes of poor fleeing to the United States in the Great Irish Famine of 1845–50 were all Catholics. That assumption has prevented any other pattern of Catholic Irish emigration from being recognized. The general view is that the Catholics did not become farm folk in the United States, although they came from a rural society, but rather were rural people caught in the great urban transformation of the Victorian era and relegated to life in the slums of cities. In contrast to the earlier Protestant emigrants, for whom a heroic image has been created, the Famine Irish have been typed as being lower class in origin, less entrepreneurial, boisterous, prone to drinking, and given to blarney.

However, neither version of the Irish stereotypes can be applied in the Canadian realm. In the Irish encounter with North America, the Canadian episode occurred between the two great American phases, overlapping with both the end of the eighteenth-century migrations and with the Famine exodus of the late 1840s. The outcome on opposite sides of the Canadian-American border was markedly different.

The Irish in Canada were inserted into an evolving political state that was ultimately the legacy of two great European empires, the French and the British. Settlers from these two sources are recognized as the co-founders of modern Canada, and from them originates a duality in Canadian life, juxtaposing a relatively homogeneous French culture with the various cultures of settlers from the British Isles. Within French Canada a basic cultural homogeneity was forged early. Direct immigration from France contributed fewer than 10,000 colonists in the century and a half before the British conquest in 1759–60, and by the time of the conquest, most of New France's 75,000 people had been bred from this small founding group. Subsequent growth would occur solely through natural increase, without immigration from France. As a consequence, French Canada's cultural character would contrast sharply with the multicultural origins of the other modern charter groups. English-speaking Canada was largely the result of nineteenth-century popular mass emigration from England, Ireland, and Scotland, which submerged a small eighteenth-century population base. Among the British migrants there existed a considerable cultural mixture. English, Irish, Scots, and Welsh immigrants brought with them their own distinctive outlooks and traditions, and their regional cultural backgrounds were transferred to become important characteristics of the new country's settlement geography.

Surprisingly, in a country that celebrates its multicultural heritage, the ethnic components of the migrations from the British Isles have been neglected of late. There has been general reluctance to think of the British peoples in ethnic terms, and instead they are lumped together under the 'non-ethnic' label of British. The present study attempts to redress some of this imbalance by examining the creation and development of the Irish presence in Canada. It explores the nature and timing of the Irish emigration and the subsequent pioneer settlement experience of those who chose Canada. Because the Irish arrived early, before Canadian towns acquired industrial characters, the study deals mainly with rural pioneering. Furthermore, the study gives little attention to the phases of cultural development faced by the emigrants' children, the second and third generations of Irish-Canadians. That topic, of immense importance in its own right, is beyond the scope of the present volume. Rather, the authors' emphasis is on developing both a general picture of Irish emigration (in part I) and of Irish settlement in Canada (part II) and a more particular picture of those epic events, as revealed in the lives and letters of four individual emigrants (part III). We trace the ways in which emigrants made their way to the New World and highlight the ways in which they created Irish regions abroad.

   Just twenty years ago this present volume could not have been written, so little was known about the role of the Irish in the history of Canada. At that time, there was only one work, Nicholas Flood Davin's *The Irishman in Canada*, that provided a detailed account of Canada's Irish settlers. It was written in 1877.[4] In the literary vacuum since then, stereotypes of the Irish, generally borrowed from US studies, were presented in lieu of accurate depictions and analysis. As a consequence, the Canadian Irish were generally, and often still are, seen to be mirror images of those stereotypes of Catholic Boston or Philadelphia or the Scots-Irish frontier counterpart – images that fail to fit Newfoundland's Catholic Irish fishermen or Ontario's Church of Ireland farmers.

The rousing of interest in the Irish experience in Canada dates to an article published by the sociologist Kenneth Duncan in 1965 on the impact of Irish famine immigration on Ontario's social structure.[5] That appraisal was added to in 1974 by John Mannion's geographical study of the retention and adaptation of material culture among Irish settlements in eastern Canada.[6] Mannion's study focused on three pre-Famine Irish settlements: Peterborough County, in Ontario; the Mirimachi Valley, in New Brunswick; and the Avalon Peninsula, in Newfoundland. This innovative study of material culture emphasized the transfer of tools, technology, and settlement patterns across the Atlantic. Mannion discovered that where the immigrants were confronted with an ethnically mixed and highly commercialized society, such as that of Peterborough, they rapidly abandoned their Old World material culture; only in the isolated, more subsistence-type economy of the Avalon Peninsula did transferred material-cultural traits survive the initial pioneering phase.

During the 1980s, other social and ideological aspects of Irish culture were explored. William Baker delved into the Canadian career of the Cork-born New Brunswick newspaperman and politician Timothy Warren Anglin.[7] The present authors examined the development and decline of the Orange Order in Canada and suggested that the transplanted values of Orangeism proved to be immensely durable and of widespread importance in Protestant Canada.[8] The historian Donald Akenson, in his analysis of the Irish in Leeds and Lansdowne Township in eastern Ontario before 1870, made a number of important points about the land settlement process and inter-group social mobility.[9] Bruce Elliott, in the most valuable recent original addition to the literature, has used his genealogical skills to present a fine historical study of the chain migration of Tipperary Protestant immigrants to Ontario.[10]

Shorter studies of the Irish have been carried out by local historians and genealogists, and primacy among these must go to Terence Punch's study of Halifax, which presents the background of the Catholic community of Halifax in detail.[11] Similarly, the work of Cyril Byrne[12] and

Brendan O'Grady[13] on Newfoundland and Prince Edward Island, respectively, Marianna O'Gallagher on the Quebec Irish,[14] and Murray Nicholson on Toronto[15] has contributed to an understanding of specific components of the Canadian Irish community. Peter Toner has dealt extensively with the New Brunswick Irish.[16] A recent two-volume work edited by Robert O'Driscoll and Lorna Reynolds has made accessible many essays on other aspects of the Irish experience.[17] The actual process of migration and its interlinkage with shipping and trading patterns have also received attention, significantly in the work of William Spray,[18] Deirdre Mageean,[19] and John Mannion,[20] all of whom have explored new sources and have generated new interest. Thus the study of the Irish in Canada possesses considerable vitality.

Despite major advances, the study of Irish emigration and settlement in Canada still lacks a national perspective and is frequently hampered by generalizations proposed for the whole country on the basis of patterns distinctive only in some regions. No single study has yet tackled the issue of the geographical distribution of the Irish throughout Canada, and it is impossible therefore to weight properly the many regional studies that have appeared. This study explores the geography of the Irish emigration to Canada. It argues the importance of pre-Famine events and the voluntary outmigration of those both alert to the worsening economic conditions of pre-Famine Ireland and sufficiently affluent to take evasive action. The Famine, far from being the primary causative force in Irish emigration to Canada, actually represented a late and most tragic spasm in that mass movement. The Irish were among the earliest settlers in English-speaking Canada, and for several crucial decades they were numerically predominant among arrivals from the British Isles. Consequently, they were a pivotal charter group in the settlement of the new lands.

The book also develops the facts that approximately 55 per cent of Irish settlers in Canada were Protestant, and predominantly Anglican rather than Presbyterian; that these settlers were drawn mainly from the northern third of Ireland – the nine countries of pre-1922 Ulster and the adjoining counties of Leinster – and from significant Protestant cores in Munster and south Leinster. Of the 45 per cent who were Catholic, as many as one-third were drawn from Ulster and the remainder from throughout the island, with a striking preponderance from Cork. Denominational diversity was reflected in the group composition of the emigrants. The oft-cited equations of Ulster origin with Protestant identity and southern-Ireland origin with Catholicism must be set aside.

They are quite incorrect. Neither has ever adequately described Ireland, and each is likewise erroneous in considering the Irish in Canada. The Irish in Canada, like the nation itself, were spread across a vast territory broken up into a disjointed series of settled places. A single identity would be impossible to create; a stereotype might represent a purely localized mythical circumstance.

Part One
Links in Emigration

CHAPTER TWO

Emigrant Origins

Irish emigration to British North America in the eighteenth and nineteenth centuries evolved within a new British empire. The conquest of New France and the loss of the thirteen colonies to the newly proclaimed republic of the United States of America concentrated the British colonial presence in the northerly lands. The maritime colonies of Nova Scotia, New Brunswick, and Prince Edward Island and the St Lawrence Valley colonies of Upper Canada (Ontario) and Lower Canada (Quebec) would in the course of the nineteenth century be added to by continued westward expansion, ultimately creating a Canadian Dominion stretching from Atlantic to Pacific.

In the eighteenth century, the British presence was minimal. Besides the garrison centres of Halifax, Fredericton, and Quebec City, and a scattered array of forts, there were only minor pockets of civilian settlement. Irish, English, and Scots settlers were to be found in the eastern colonies, where they augmented a small population of Empire Loyalists, also largely of British origin, who had fled northward in the aftermath of the American War of Independence. The English-speaking population in the east totalled only some 80,000 in 1791, roughly half that of the French-speaking population in Lower Canada.

That situation would be altered irrevocably by nineteenth-century immigrations. During the course of the Napoleonic Wars, Britain turned to her North American colonies in search of timber supplies, and the subsequent peacetime trade in timber, inbound to the British Isles, was counterbalanced by an outbound flow of emigrant settlers and manufactured goods westward to the colonies across the Atlantic: 'In the half century following Waterloo a significant anglophone society emerged in British North America. The small scattered remnants of the Second British Empire, anchored around the stronghold of Quebec City and Halifax, rapidly evolved from frontier fragility into complex colonial societies.'[1] Emigration was the principal demographic fact behind the creation of those complex societies, and apart from a significant number of Germans, the immigrants were from the British Isles.

EIGHTEENTH-CENTURY ANTECEDENTS

In the three decades between the Peace of Waterloo and the onset of the Great Irish Famine in 1845, half a million Irish travelled to British North America. They constituted 60 per cent of the total inflow. Scots and English made up the rest. The differential in the numbers reflected among the Irish their early tendency to see emigration as a solution to social and economic stress. From 1725, and interrupted only partly by the American revolutionary wars and the later Napoleonic conflict, there had been a steady outflow of Irish across the Atlantic. In the eighteenth century perhaps close to half a million people left for America, most to the middle colonies.[2] Philadelphia, Newcastle, in Delaware, and Wilmington, in North Carolina, were the principal ports of disembarkation. The Irish had been in the vanguard of voluntary emigration during the eighteenth century and continued that pattern in the nineteenth. The Scots were similarly mobile, but emigration was much less popular among the English, a characterization that extended from the eighteenth into the early nineteenth century. The propensity of the Irish to migrate and their relative group strength in the transatlantic movements permitted them to acquire disproportionate importance in the settlement of British North America, well before the Famine.

The eighteenth-century exodus from Ireland to North America not only established a tradition of emigration but also confirmed a regional dimension that influenced subsequent outflows to British North America. Nineteenth-century emigrants availed themselves of links developed by previous generations. The American exodus in the eighteenth century was derived mainly from Ulster and a few other regions, centred on the principal ports. Figure 2.1[3] depicts the extent of emigration to the North American mainland from Irish ports in the quarter-century before traffic was interrupted by the American Revolution. It is based on information derived from the researches of Lockhart and Dickson. Their data were assembled originally from newspaper reports

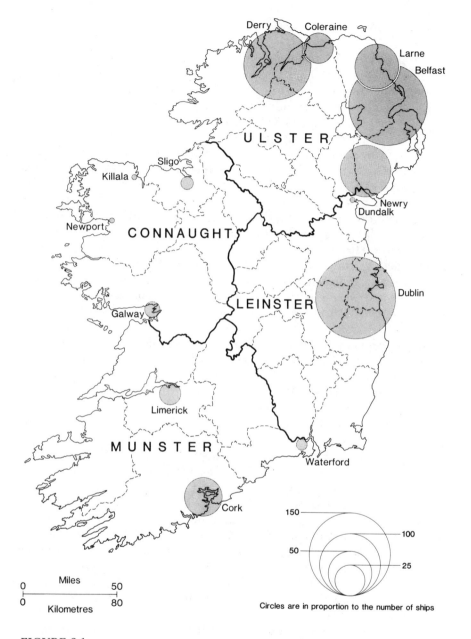

Miles
0 — 50
0 — 80
Kilometres

150
100
50
25

Circles are in proportion to the number of ships

FIGURE 2.1
Number of ships from Ireland to mainland North America, 1750–75; based
on data from Dickson and Lockhart: see chapter 2, note 3.

and probably underestimate the volume of shipping, but arguably the importance of the major ports relative to each other warrants serious attention. The data also do not include the flow of ships from southeastern Ireland to the Newfoundland fisheries.

The map shows that the major ports of embarkation were Dublin and the Ulster ports of Derry, Belfast, and Newry, the latter three ports linked to the middle colonies of America by, among other things, Ulster's demand for flax-seed. The emigrants went out to America on the returning voyages of the flax-seed ships. Cork and other ports, such as Galway, Limerick, and Waterford, were less important. In the eighteenth-century movements from Ulster, family emigration from rural areas was the norm, and most emigrants became pioneering settlers on the agricultural frontiers. A majority of the settlers were Presbyterian, from counties Antrim and Londonderry, the harbinger of what became known as the Scotch-Irish.[4] Anglicans and Catholics were also represented and were especially numerous[5] among those exiting through Newry and Belfast. The emigration from places outside Ulster had a different character. Participants were less likely to be organized in family groups, and more of them were rural labourers and single male artisans, quite often from towns and cities. A large proportion of these would have been Catholic.[6] They were often indentured to work on farms and in industry in the New World. However, regardless of region of origin, occupation, and religious affiliation, the Irish were headed for the same American destinations.

The eighteenth century saw also emigration to Newfoundland from southeastern Ireland, specifically from a hinterland within a thirty-mile radius of Waterford city. Waterford and the southeast, not being part of the trade in flax seed and linen,[7] had only limited contact with mainland North America. The emigrants' destination was the offshore colony of Newfoundland. Between 1770 and the 1830s, some 30,000 Irish settled there.[8] This particular emigration had originated in the late seventeenth century, with the seasonal migration of youths employed in the Newfoundland fisheries – almost 5,000 were leaving every year by the 1770s[9] – and it had evolved to include a fraction of permanent emigration.[10]

Waterford, New Ross, and Youghal, in the rich agricultural heartland of southeastern Ireland, were the centres of a provisions trade that supplied the fishing grounds off Newfoundland. The Irish merchants joined merchants in that trade from the West Country of England, who had throughout the eighteenth century been accustomed to calling at Waterford to take on flour, salted beef, and pork for New World markets, extending from Newfoundland on to Nova Scotia, New England, and the Caribbean islands. The merchant vessels carried, as well as provisions, young men recruited as indentured seasonal labourers for the cod fishery. Farmers' sons and village and urban artisans all participated, and in a unique regional pattern of confined interaction between New and Old worlds, the southeast of Ireland became bound to Newfoundland. Like the provisions, migrants were drawn mainly from counties Wexford, Kilkenny, Waterford, Tipperary, and Cork, specifically from the valleys of the lower reaches of the Suir, Nore, and Barrow. The Atlantic fisheries thus provided the first substantial Irish settlement in what would become Canada, and from that Newfoundland base many migrants moved secondarily to the maritime mainland of British North America and New England.[11]

In the 1830s the collapse of the southeastern provisions trade effectively terminated the Newfoundland migrations, and that fishing colony was henceforth isolated from subsequent Irish migration streams. The Irish settlements in Newfoundland, generated by the labour demands of the fishing trade and formed almost exclusively by emigrants from the southeast, were somewhat anomalous in the history of emigration to Canada, and their isolation helped consolidate their unique character. In its extremely localized nature, the relationship between southeastern Ireland and Newfoundland represented an even narrower set of linkages than that epitomized by Ulster's connections with the seaboard of colonial America.

In the mainland territories of maritime Canada, the initial magnet for Irish immigrants was land, and Nova Scotia saw the first efforts to promote agricultural settlements. There, in the aftermath of the French defeat of 1759–60, British authorities sought loyal populations with which to secure their new territories. The natural linkage was with New England, and New Englanders were prominent in the efforts to open new lands.

Among them, Alexander McNutt, probably of County Donegal origin, took a leading role. That entrepreneur in 1760 was promised a large grant of land from the crown on condition that he settle Irish people in the British colony. In May 1761 he advertised for recruits in the *Belfast Newsletter*. The advertisement, in the form of a letter from his office in Derry, read as follows:

Whereas the province of Nova-Scotia, the ancient right of Britain, is now settling, which will be a grand outlet and relief for all such industrious farmers and useful mechanics as may find themselves under difficulties in the mother country; and Colonel Alexander McNutt a native of the north of Ireland and who hath resided for many years in North America and is intimately acquainted with the said province having received a general grant of any the choicest lands therein which he shall think fit to settle upon; is now arrived here with a view to procure settlers and invite all such of his countrymen who it may suit to embrace the present opportunity of removing to this fertile country where each head of a family on arrival will be put into possession and have a deed forever; 200 acres for themselves and 50 acres for each child and servant (and the indented servant will be also entitled to other 50 acres at the end of his servitude) free of all rent for 10 years and after paying only a small quit-rent to the King of one Shilling for each 50 acres, and where they will be free of all tithes and have their civil and religious liberties fully secured. For further particulars he refers to a printed account by him published in the hands of the following gentlemen who will acquaint them with the method and means intended for their passage viz.

Mr. Joseph McNutt near Castledoe, Mr. Alexander Nesbitt, Merchant, in Rathmelton, Captain John McNutt and Mr. John Russell near Letterkenny, Mr. Neill Stephenson, Merchant in Raphoe, Mr. Samuel Moore, Merchant in Convoy, Mr. James McNutt in Faun, Mr. Thomas Short in Strabane, Mr. William Baxter in Omagh, Mr. James Elliot, near Maghera, Mr. George McKee in Castleblayney, Mr. Arthur Vance, Merchant and Captain James Moor in Londonderry who will acquaint them more fully with such matters as they may be desired to know of. Letters directed to the said Alexander McNutt to the care of said Mr. Vance, Merchant in Londonderry, shall be duly answered.

If a sufficient number of settlers should offer and engage in the Counties of Down and Antrim a vessel will be appointed to take them on board at the most convenient port as there will also be at Londonderry for those that contract on that side: and as the nature of their undertaking requires despatch persons inclinable to go must be speedy in their application.

If it should happen that a sufficient number do not offer in the Counties of Down and Antrim for a ship to take them on board at some convenient port in one of said counties, such as do so engage they take their passage from Londonderry; notice will be given in the *Belfast News-Letter* when a ship will be ready to sail from Derry to Nova Scotia.

Mr. McNutt would recommend it to such families as cannot be ready to go immediately, that they send one person out of their respective families to take possession of the lands forthwith and prepare matters for the more easy accommodation of the rest of their families as the lands are very fast settling by people coming from the neighbouring provinces. As to the passage the price will be the same as to Philadelphia and redemptioners and servants will be taken on the like conditions. Applications for further particulars may also be made to Mr. Thomas Greg of Belfast, Merchant.

Settlers having any quantity of hempseed to dispose of are desired to bring it to said Mr. Greg who will give a reasonable price for it. It is to be carried over and sown in Nova Scotia.[12]

The advertisement indicates clearly many aspects of the then established emigrant networks in Ulster. As with Philadelphia emigrants, provision was made for people to work their way across on redemption contracts as a way of securing passage. In Ulster, designated merchants provided information and tickets, being anxious not only to stimulate emigration but also to engage in a commodity trade, in this case hemp-seed. McNutt's use of the press and his terse description of the Nova Scotian destination testify to Ulster's familiarity with the New World. Significantly, too, although McNutt's scheme represented the first substantial connection with the lands recently taken from the French Empire, geographically it represented a simple northward, coastwise extension of the usual destinations of Irish emigrants in the middle colonies and New England.

In 1761 McNutt sent out about three hundred people,[13] Protestants drawn mainly from Donegal and Derry, the area best served by his network of agents depicted in Figure 2.2.[14] That map indicates areas of Ulster where Protestants made up more than half the population in the 1760s. McNutt's agents were confined mainly to the western section of the Protestant settlement and were conspicuously absent from the more Catholic areas. They were strategically located through the lowland areas of Protestant settlement in the Foyle Valley and eastern Donegal – the western sector of the emigration field whence many Presbyterians were going to the American colonies. McNutt was thus drawing his settlers from areas where a tradition of out-migration was established. In 1762 a further seventy emigrants followed, to join the first contingent. Those going directly from Ireland were augmented by Ulster Presbyterians coming from the New England settlements around Londonderry, New Hampshire.[15] Despite the initial effort, McNutt never fully realized his plan, because the English government resisted it, fearing depopulation of Protestant communities in Ireland. A government committee opined that 'however desirable an object the settling of Nova Scotia may be yet the migration from Ireland of such great numbers of His Majesty's

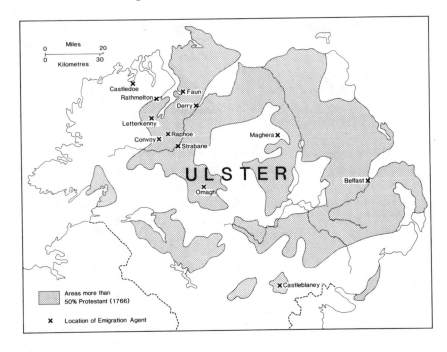

FIGURE 2.2
The location of Alexander McNutt's emigration agents in Ireland in 1761

subjects must be attended with dangerous consequences to that Kingdom. [We] do therefore hereby order that the Lords Commissioners of
Trade and Plantations do prepare a draft of an Instruction for His
Majesty's Governor or Commander in Chief of Nova Scotia requiring
him not to grant lands to, or permit any of His Majesty's subjects from
Ireland to become settlers in that Province, except such as have been
resident either in Nova Scotia or some other of His Majesty's Colonys
in America for the space of five years.'[16] McNutt's efforts signalled the
beginnings of the Ulster connection in the developing Canadian society,
but almost half a century was to pass before emigration to Canada took
root in the Irish popular imagination.

NINETEENTH-CENTURY MASS MIGRATION

Mass emigration from Ireland developed following the return of peace
in 1815 and the associated collapse of wartime agricultural prosperity.

The numbers leaving then far exceeded those of the preceding century and amounted to as many as 100,000 in exceptional years before the emigration haemorrhage of the Famine period. Large numbers went to Britain as seasonal harvest labourers. In 1841 alone, for example, more than 50,000 went for that purpose.[17] Many were tempted to remain as factory workers in the cities or as miners in colliery districts, and the census of 1841 registered more than half a million Irish living in Britain. The advent of regular steamship travel across the Irish Sea in 1820 had made Britain an accessible destination for the poorest of emigrants. Fares were only a shilling, and the journey took but a few hours.[18]

North America appealed to a different group. The transatlantic journey, with its much higher costs and almost incomparably longer duration, appealed more selectively to those with some capital. A landless labourer could acquire a one-shilling fare to Britain by a day's work, but saving the fifty pounds needed to take a family of four across the Atlantic was unrealizable. Arguably, those with capital – perhaps gleaned from savings, the settlement of family wills, or the sale of property – were at an advantage, and for them the Atlantic crossing beckoned early. As a consequence, the early-nineteenth-century transatlantic migrant was more typically to be found among the comfortable farming classes, who feared future loss of economic status, rather than from among those suffering from absolute penury, and he was destined, like the earlier settlers in colonial America, for life as an agricultural pioneer.

In the nineteenth century, a combination of colonial preference in trade, established shipping links, and cheaper fares directed a majority of Irishmen in the first instance to the ports of Quebec City and Saint John, New Brunswick, and a handful of other Canadian harbours. They went initially in small numbers, but as illustrated in Figure 2.3,[19] the trickle had reached flood proportions by 1830, when about 40,000 completed the journey from Ireland to North America. In 1831 over 60,000 made the trip. The rapid increase in the early 1830s provides an apparent contrast with the more gradual rise in numbers going directly to the United States and reflects primarily the cheaper passage via the timber trade to the British colonies. Figure 2.3, shows the duality of the flow to the two destinations. Nineteenth-century emigration to North America falls into two distinctive periods, the Canadian, in the first half of the century, and the American, in the second. Between 1825 and 1845, about 450,000 Irish went to British North America, and about 400,000 to the United States. For British North America, in these critical years, rural settlement was initiated and, in central and eastern Canada,

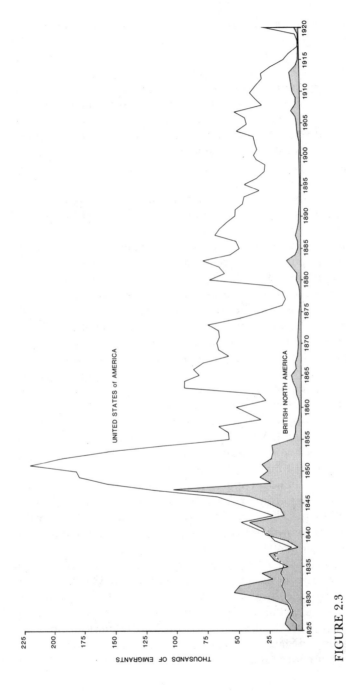

FIGURE 2.3

Irish immigration to British North America and the United States, 1825–1920

largely completed. During this settlement phase some of the best agricultural land in the country was appropriated, and the Irish far outnumbered arriving English and Scots and clearly established the pre-Famine era as definitive in the formation of Canadian Irish communities.

Canadian Irish settlements were created within a larger North American movement that saw many Irish arrivals in British North America continue on to US destinations. The cheap passage to Quebec City and Saint John led many to see British North America as a stop on the thoroughfare to the United States, rather than an ultimate destination. The advertisement in Figure 2.4 reveals the competitive nature of the transatlantic passenger trade. In the columns of the *Belfast Newsletter* of July 1818, Capt. Hardy maintained that an emigrant family bound for the US east coast could halve the cost of passage by going via Saint John, rather than proceeding directly to an American port. Sea transport southward from Saint John and St Andrews to the ports of New England was easy, for Boston was a major metropolitan centre for the whole northeastern seaboard region. Port records for Boston reveal that a very large percentage of the Irish arrivals in the American port had come via New Brunswick and, less occasionally, Nova Scotia.[20] From Quebec City, the most popular route inland was up the St Lawrence River to Lake Ontario, where transport to upstate New York or to the Ohio Valley could be obtained. Many of those who crossed into the United States had from the outset no intentions of settling in the British colonies but had intended simply to take advantage of the cheaper transport. Others, disappointed with their initial fortune in the British territories, altered their plans and migrated on to the United States. The Antrim-born immigrant James Reford wrote to his parents from Massachusetts in 1833, reporting that in the previous year 'we landed in Quebec on the 7th day of June. I went to work 35 miles above it at a place called Jacque Cartur at the Riva St. Lawrence. I had just got to work when the cholera broke out at Quebec where my family was, but thank God we all escaped the disease. I stopped there 16 weeks to the mill shut down, then I was obliged to proceed to the states.'[21]

It is difficult to determine the extent of through-migration to the United States because flows could vary enormously from year to year and from region to region. In addition, there were few means of monitoring those flows across a long border where crossing was easy. In 1826, A.C. Buchanan, later the official emigration agent in Quebec City, reckoned that the majority of Irish arrivals there remained in the Canadas.[22] His opinions suggest too that through-migration was

FIGURE 2.4
Advertisement, *Belfast Newsletter*, 1820

probably more prevalent in Saint John than in Quebec City.[23] In New Brunswick good land was in short supply by the 1820s, and although lumbering and shipbuilding offered alternative opportunities for work, those labouring possibilities were limited, and the region would soon display signs of a general pattern of high population turnover and out-migration.[24] By the time of the Famine, New Brunswick was largely incapable of absorbing Irish immigration. For example, of the 9,690 Irish arriving in Saint John in 1846, 4,500 were supposed to have gone on to the United States[25] right away, and an indeterminate number followed in subsequent years. Recent analysis by Peter Toner indicates that fewer than 10 per cent of the Irish who arrived in New Brunswick in 1846 remained there in 1851.[26] Even allowing for the high mortality of the late 1840s, the through-flow was massive and illustrates the role of Saint John as a transfer point on the route to the United States. Greater opportunities existed in the St Lawrence Valley, where Quebec City acted as the gateway to the open lands of Upper Canada. But even there the numbers continuing on immediately to the United States were very high – in 1847 at least a quarter of those reaching Quebec.[27] Neither the amount of land nor the scale of economic development in British North America was sufficient to provide the places needed to absorb the massive influxes of immigrants. The United States had far greater capacity.

The difficulty of determining how many arrivals in British North America remained there was acknowledged by contemporaries. As early as 1831, Governor Aylmer reported to Lord Goderich, the colonial secretary in London, that 'it would be extremely difficult if not impossible to ascertain the number of emigrants who actually settled in the Canadas: as of those who arrive at Quebec many pass into the United States, some of whom return from thence, and establish themselves in Canada, others return from Canada to the United Kingdom and some of those who emigrate to the United States from the United Kingdom come to settle in Canada. Perhaps after making due allowance for the circumstances above stated, it might be considered as a reasonable approximation of the truth, that the number of emigrants who finally settle and form part of the resident population do not fall very short of the numbers who arrive at the port of Quebec.'[28]

At this remove, it is difficult to evaluate Aylmer's conclusion. Some very approximate figures suggest that the governor was wrong. Upper and Lower Canada in 1842 had 122,000 Irish-born settlers, and all of British North America, perhaps 160,000.[29] In the previous quarter-

TABLE 2.1
Volume of Irish emigration during the
Famine period

| Year | Number of immigrants | |
	To BNA	To USA
1846	40,667	68,730
1847	104,518	119,314
1848	24,809	157,473
1849	33,392	181,011
1850	26,444	183,672

SOURCE: Data estimated using the tech-
nique of W.F. Adams, by D. Akenson,
The Irish in Ontario (Toronto 1984), 30

century between 350,000 and 400,000[30] Irish emigrants landed. Given
the few immigrants in the country before 1816, at least in comparison
to the next decade, British North America perhaps retained in 1842
about a third of the Irish emigrants who had arrived between 1816 and
1842. Of the other two-thirds, some fraction would have died, and the
majority would have left for the United States. These figures must be
treated with caution, but they suggest that net US flow-through may
have been almost as high as two-thirds of the emigrants. A similar
treatment suggests a comparably large flow-through for 1842–51: the
Irish-born population of Lower and Upper Canada increased by
roughly 100,000[31] while immigration to Quebec City amounted to about
300,000–350,000.[32] The shorter period would normally have meant
fewer deaths, but the unusual circumstances of 1847 would have had a
countervailing effect. These crude ranges indicate that while British
North America was the destination for a good proportion of the immigrants, the United States was the target of most. Nonetheless, the British
domain was a final destination for many Irish.

During the 1850s British North America gradually ceased being a
significant transatlantic destination, and the closing years of that episode
of emigration history were marked by the impact of the Great Famine.
The number of Irish arrivals peaked in 1847 (Fig. 2.3) with the landing
of some 70,000 in Quebec City and approximately half that number in
Saint John.[33] The arrivals of 1847 represented a 250-per-cent increase
on the previous year's influx (Table 2.1), and this difference of magnitude, combined with the obvious desperate condition of many of the

emigrants, stirred the contemporary imagination. The impact of 1847 was so great that writers subsequently have persisted in viewing Irish emigration to Canada in terms of that year alone, despite its anomalous place. Proportionately, the Irish immigrations of both 1831 and 1832 were just as significant. In those years, the annual migration was only half the 1847 complement, but the colonies' population was also only half the 1847 size. The effect of the Famine on British North America was limited mainly to a single year's inrush, and arrivals there in 1848 and thereafter fell to pre-Famine levels but continued to soar in the United States. The Famine's effect was further reduced in the British territories by increased through-migration.

Thus 1847 represented a temporary aberration in the long-established history of Irish emigration to British North America. Of the estimated 38,560 who got as far west as Toronto in 1847, less than 2,000 remained in the city. Supposedly, 1,100 others died and 35,650 were sent by aid agencies further westward, to smaller centres.[34] Many of those would necessarily have made their way south of the border. Comparable mobility would have applied in Montreal and Quebec City, too, and although all three cities experienced unusual expansion of poor Irish ghettos at this time, the dimensions of the problem were minimal in comparison with those of American neighbours.

Abrupt action by the colonial governments ensured that the experience of 1847 would not be repeated in British North America. Before the onset of the following shipping season, the Emigrant Tax was doubled from five shillings per head to ten shillings for arrivals at Quebec City, and additional punitive surtaxes for arrivals late in the season were put into effect.[35] For emigrants arriving after 10 September 1848, there was to be a levy of twenty shillings per person, rising to a prohibitive thirty shillings after 30 September. An additional 2s. 6d. per emigrant on board was to be levied for every three days that a ship was forced to stay in quarantine. In New Brunswick and Nova Scotia, comparable increases in taxes were enacted, and in all instances the new rates were to apply for 1848 and 1849. The legislation had the desired effect. The number of Irish arrivals in 1848 was a quarter of that of the preceding year and lower than that of the pre-Famine period. The extraordinary peak of 1847 was never to be repeated. During the next seven years the numbers arriving remained at pre-Famine levels and after 1854 drastically declined. Figure 2.3 indicates clearly that while the Famine had relatively little effect on British North America, the same was patently not true for the United States. The huge influx of Famine migrants there continued until 1852 and by its scale laid the 'Famine foundations' of communities into which subsequent generations of Irish immigrants were drawn.

The Famine immigration represented the conclusion of a British North American era of mass Irish emigration, but in the republic to the south it represented an originating force for a new phase of expansion of Irish communities. In that expansion, immigrant communication networks, in the form of letters home and remittance of prepaid passages, created a new dynamic that henceforth bound Irish emigration more strongly to the United States. The altered balance between the two North American destinations was regarded as inevitable. In 1851 the British Emigration Commissioners observed that this trend toward the United States,

which under any circumstances could not be long delayed, was probably accelerated by the increase and uncertainty of the tax on emigrants imposed by the Canadian legislature immediately after the disastrous emigration of 1847; and it has now been rendered permanent by the fact above alluded to, that the great bulk of the Irish emigration is conducted by means of prepaid passages, or of money sent home from the United States. The same affectionate feeling which prompts the settled immigrant to send home money to take out his relatives would naturally make him wish to repair to the same country as himself; and it is equally natural that persons emigrating under such circumstances should proceed to the country where their friends are settled and have prospered, rather than to a country where they would be strangers. We cannot, therefore, regard it as a matter of astonishment that so large a proportion of the emigrants from Ireland should proceed to the United States; nor can we think it probable that the stream of emigration could now be turned aside, even if it were desired, to our own Colonies.[36]

The emigration commissioners understood well the nature of the migration process and the role that each new emigrant played in establishing new transatlantic communication links. The importance of emigrant remittances, prepaid passages, and personal networks in directing emigration flows was not a new phenomenon. The same connectivity that bound post-Famine Ireland with the United States had previously directed emigrants to British North America.

By 1855 Irish emigration to British North America had slumped to a few hundred per year, and for the rest of the century it remained insignificant, relative to the flow into the United States. Figure 2.3

suggests similar periodicity of peaks and troughs in the flows to both destinations after 1850, reflecting the strong influence of economic conditions both within Ireland and within continental North America on the size of outflow in any particular year. Even short-term alterations in the Irish economy could generate a rapid response of increased emigration, for by this time the process of migration and its underlying supports of kinship links and monetary remittances were well established and could be called into play at relatively short notice. In 1860 a Canadian emigration promoter operating in Ireland noted: 'On my first visit to Ireland in the fall nothing appeared more unlikely than the "Exodus" to which you refer ... Even the Priests were quite unaware that it was about to take place. I think that the unusual severity of the winter and the loss of stock consequent thereon decided a great many who had friends in the States to appeal to them for means to get out. The sums transmitted for this purpose during March were fabulous.'[37] Similarly the Irish harvest failures of 1879 and succeeding years generated a rapid rise in emigration. Conversely, occurrences such as the American economic depression of the mid-1870s resulted in immediate slumps in emigrant numbers. The effect is particularly extreme during the late 1870s. Figure 2.3 seems to display a cyclical dimension, with twenty-year periods of heavy outmigration followed by lulls of upward of five years, reflecting perhaps generational pulses in the momentum of emigration.

The decline of British North America as a destination not only emphasizes the Famine's effect in severing connections but also reveals the economic limitations of the colonies in the second half of the nineteenth century. Most of the best land had been claimed by the time of the Famine, and large-scale urbanization and industrialization would not commence until the 1870s. At the same time, rural Canada itself became a major source of outmigration, leading to there being over one million Canadian-born us residents at the turn of the century.[38] Some increases in Irish immigration were associated with the opening of prairie settlements in Manitoba in the early 1870s and the subsequent building of the Canadian Pacific Railroad to Vancouver, but the effects were minor. It was not until 1905 that a concerted Canadian national effort to extend the agricultural frontiers in the prairie provinces of Saskatchewan and Alberta helped make Canada once again an important destination for the Irish. Unlike earlier eras of immigration, the Irish in the period 1905–14 were a minority beside the English, Scots, and other new arrivals from Europe, but socially and economically they were to form

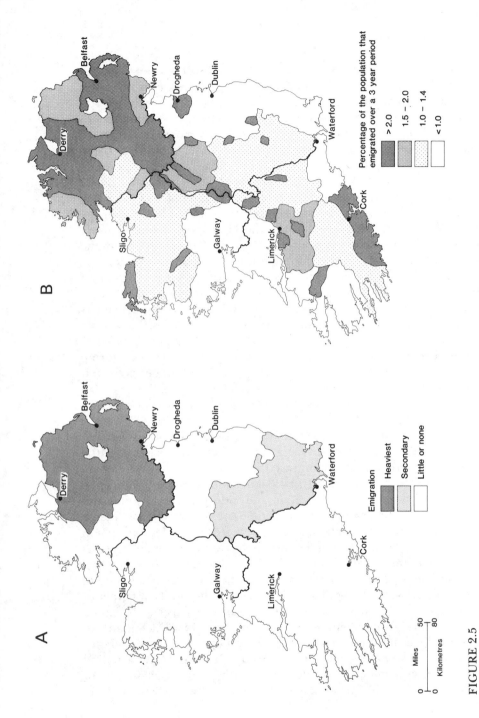

FIGURE 2.5

Emigrants origins, 1815–20 and 1830–5; after W.F. Adams, *Ireland and Irish Emigration to the New World from 1815 to the Famine* (New Haven 1932)

an extension of a much larger and earlier established charter group from Ontario and the Maritimes.

SOURCE REGIONS

With the renewal of regular transatlantic shipping in 1815, it was hardly surprising, given the significance of Ulster in the Irish emigration to North America in the previous century, that the early core area of recruitment of emigrants to both Canada and the United States was located in the northern province. Maps constructed over fifty years ago by Adams[39] (Figure 2.5) remain one of the better summaries of this regional pattern and indicate a changing geography of emigrant origins in the decades before the Famine.

In the first years of the emigration, central and eastern Ulster was the main centre, while in the south, the contiguous counties of Wexford, Carlow, Kings, Queens, and parts of Kilkenny constituted a secondary zone of outmigration. Both regions were endowed with a mature commercial economy and had well-developed trading links with Europe and North America. Their economies sustained a class of people with both the outward-looking mentality and the financial wherewithal to take the opportunity offered by emigration. As a consequence, the initial phase of emigration, in 1815, 1816, and 1817, selected a small core group of relative gentility and substance. Whole families and very often the extended families of three generations made the journey with all their capital. Those intending to be colonial administrators, those receiving compensation for service during the Napoleonic era, would-be speculators, the larger farmers, and larger farmers' sons could afford the high costs of the journey and contemplate not only the vital risks of passage but the economic risks of not emigrating. As fares were quickly and progressively reduced after 1817, the smaller tenant farmer–cum–weaver of Ulster could take advantage of the lower fares and follow in the wake of the better-off. Cheap passage to Britain opened avenues for even poorer emigrants and increased the ranges of classes contemplating emigration. This rapidly evolving pattern laid a foundation for subsequent emigration to British North America that favoured certain source regions over others.

By the 1830s emigration had extended from the Ulster core into the northern midlands and north Connaught; the configuration of the southern zone had been altered with the diminution of Wexford and the rise of Cork, Limerick, and isolated baronies and estate cores in south Leinster. Taken together, the maps of Adams in Figure 2.5 portray a gradual diffusion of an emigration mania from northern and central Ulster southward to embrace northern Leinster. Coincidentally, the migration fields were extended inland from Limerick, Drogheda, and Cork to their respective hinterlands. By the 1830s the earlier prominence of the southeast had waned and given way to the pre-eminence of Cork. The analyses of Cousens[40] and Fitzpatrick[41] support Adams's depiction of an Ulster and northern Leinster core of emigration, with an outlier in southern Munster.

Investigation of the location and relative importance of the ports whence the emigrants sailed further sustains the interpretation of distinctive regional bias in outflows. Not all parts of Ireland contributed equally. Figure 2.6 indicates the ports of departure of immigrants arriving at Quebec City in 1833 and 1834.[42] In the pattern, the north, the extreme south, and the east are prominent. Of the 40,800 who sailed directly from Ireland, the largest single group of 9,800 came from Dublin. Around 20,000 came from Ulster, which was served mainly by the ports of Belfast, Derry, Sligo, and Newry. Ulster, as indicated in Table 2.2, contributed almost half of the emigrants, although its share of the Irish population was only about 30 per cent. Cork and the other ports of Munster contributed 25 per cent. A slightly smaller proportion of the emigrants sailed out of Dublin and the few small ports of Leinster. Connaught's role was insignificant.

Among the Irish provinces, the ratio of emigration to population was highest for Ulster, a traditional source of emigrants. While Ulster's rate of emigration was well above the Irish national average, Leinster's was on a par, Munster's below, and Connaught's rate, relative to the all-Ireland level, minor. The pattern is based on information that does not include those Irish who embarked from the British ports of Greenock and Liverpool. Unfortunately, little is known of the Irish source areas of these groups, although Ulster probably contributed the bulk of the Greenock contingent and, together with eastern Leinster, most of the Irish leaving Liverpool. The importance of Greenock and Liverpool as second steps in the emigration then would only serve to confirm the leading role played by the northern and eastern half of Ireland in the Canadian immigration of the 1830s.

The map of emigration from the Irish ports suggests the regional character of emigration from the country. For most ports the hinterland from which emigrants were derived was no more than forty or fifty miles distant, reasonable walking or carriage distance. Only Dublin, the

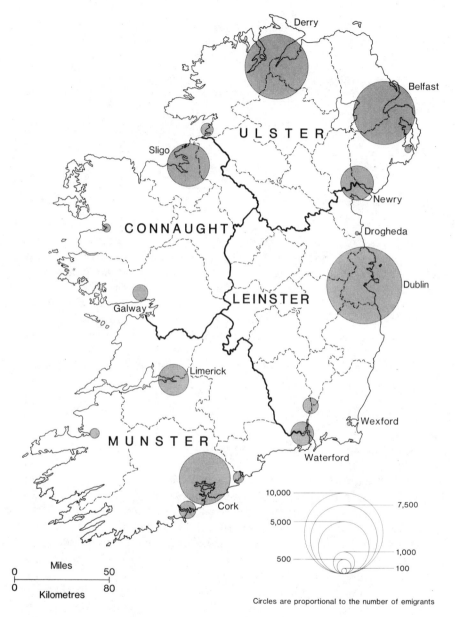

FIGURE 2.6
Irish ports of origin of emigrants arriving at Quebec, 1833–4

TABLE 2.2
Emigration to Quebec and Saint John, 1833–4

	Emigrants to Quebec and Saint John (%)	Population (%)*	Rate of emigration per thousand population*
Ulster	47.6	29.3	30.0
Leinster	23.7	24.4	18.0
Munster	25.2	29.0	15.8
Connaught	3.5	17.3	3.7
Ireland	100.0	100.0	18.4

*Population assumed to be average of 1831 and 1841 census counts

national metropolitan centre, could claim a wider hinterland because of its size and its better access to the wide area of the central lowlands. In the view of a contemporary observer, 'Dublin could scarcely be considered as giving forth the population of its own province so exclusively as those of the other provinces, being from its central position, and the convergence of roads and canals upon it, a common outlet for all.'[43] Few parts of Ireland were so remote from a port that potential emigrants would have been dissuaded by the distance overland. The regional character of emigration arises not solely because of different degrees of accessibility but because of divergent local economies and social propellants. The extent to which the Irish regions were linked to the overseas destinations was also a critical factor.

Trading links between Irish ports and the British North American colonies greatly affected the Irish outflow and forged in Canada a set of regions each with their own distinctive Irish regional ingredients. This is apparent in Table 2.3, in which the flows from Ireland in 1833 and 1834 have been separated into their Saint John and Quebec City components: while both ports received people from a variety of Irish origins, each had a distinctive set of links with Ireland. Derry and the ports of Cork and neighbouring Kinsale provided two-thirds of the immigrants arriving in Saint John. Derry's ties with New Brunswick had been particularly intense since the end of the Napoleonic Wars. Of the 29,000 people who emigrated through Derry in the decade 1816–26, almost 19,000 went to New Brunswick, only 6,000 to Quebec, and the remaining 4,000 to New York.[44] Derry's role was complemented by the major role of Cork, the two ports forming a striking bipolar pattern of

TABLE 2.3
Emigration to Saint John and Quebec
from the principal Irish ports, 1833–4
(%)

From	To Saint John	To Quebec
Belfast	11.4	18.1
Cork	19.0	10.2
Derry	39.5	11.0
Dublin	3.6	30.3
Galway	4.0	0.9
Kinsale	7.0	–
Limerick	0.8	5.4
Newry	4.3	5.3
Sligo	7.8	9.0
Waterford	–	3.8
Others	2.6	6.0
All	100.0	100.0
N	9,579	31,221

SOURCES: Quebec Emigrant Agent's
Report, 20 December 1840 (National
Archives of Canada), and Passenger
Lists, Saint John, 1833 and 1834
(Provincial Archives of New
Brunswick)

northwestern Ulster and southern Munster origins which contrasted
greatly with the pattern of origins of immigrants at Quebec. There,
Dublin was the principal single origin, and the relative combined inflows
from Ulster and Munster amounted to only half their contribution
to Saint John. Dublin's primacy for Quebec contrasts with its virtual
inconsequence for Saint John.

The remarkable difference between the origins of the immigrants to
the St Lawrence Valley and those to New Brunswick emphasizes how
well various Irish ports were tied to trading centres in British North
America. The timber ships used in the emigrant trade to Saint John
were controlled in large measure by Ulster companies in concert with
Greenock and other nearby Scottish ports and by Cork merchants.
Dublin was involved with Quebec but not with Saint John, and Liverpool, the largest English port and most accessible to Dublin and the
eastern seaboard of Ireland, was also not linked to Saint John. There

were practically no English immigrants to Saint John from the 1820s onward,[45] and the Liverpool–Dublin axis across the Irish Sea, so important in flows of both Irish and English to Quebec, was a minor part of Saint John's commercial arrangements. The Saint John pattern was much less diverse and its scale more limited than that of the St Lawrence port, and as a consequence Irish communities created in New Brunswick were less likely to encompass the full heterogeneity of the Irish emigrations than were those in the central Canadian settlements of Upper and Lower Canada. This regionalism in the transfer of Irish communities is further emphasized in the cases of Newfoundland and Halifax, which derived their Irish populations from an even narrower set of origins. The almost total dominance of the southeast of Ireland in Newfoundland's population has been discussed above; that regional emphasis can be interpreted as one particular linkage subdued within a larger pattern of rather diverse transatlantic trading connections.

The general regional pattern of emigration depicted in the port data for 1833 and 1834 is further refined in Figure 2.7, which illustrates the county origin of heads of Irish families relieved by the Montreal Emigrant Society in 1832. Relief was offered that season to 6,854 Irish who had landed at Quebec – about one-quarter of the Irish who disembarked at the St Lawrence port that year.[46] The bulk of the immigrants came from north of a line stretching from Sligo to Drogheda. Sligo and the Ulster counties were more important than any other Irish region, and the central Ulster county of Tyrone contributed the largest number. Cork's sizeable contribution was notable among the southern counties, further emphasizing its distinctive role, already exemplified above in Figure 2.6. The overall regional pattern confirms and elaborates upon that proposed by Adams (Table 2.3). The emigrants assisted in Montreal in 1832 may be considered representative of the poorer classes of Irish emigrants but did not arrive from the poorest Irish counties. Rather, they were drawn from those developed regions where economic stress and demographic growth had the greatest potential impact, specifically Ulster and adjoining counties, a region of agricultural and domestic textile production then undergoing structural change.

By the early 1840s the idea of emigration had diffused throughout the whole island. Worsening agrarian conditions and ongoing restructuring in the northern textile industry had combined with increasing demographic pressure to popularize emigration as a possible solution to social and economic stress. By the eve of the Famine most Irish counties were affected by emigration, although the older cores in the

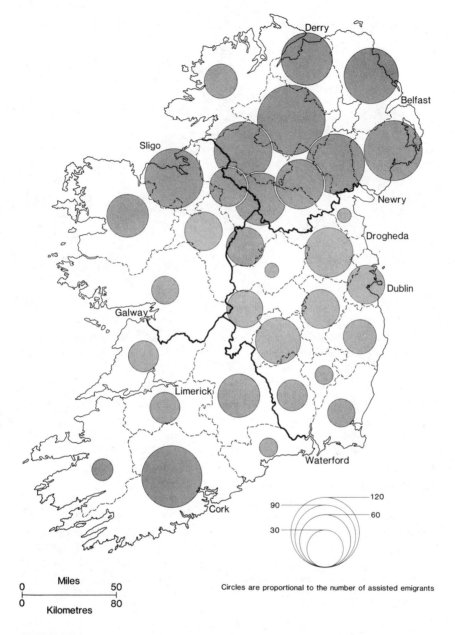

Derry

Belfast

Sligo

Newry

Drogheda

Dublin

Galway

Limerick

Waterford

120
90
60
30

Cork

Miles
0   50
0   80
Kilometres

Circles are proportional to the number of assisted emigrants

FIGURE 2.7
County origins of individuals and heads of households assisted in Montreal
by the Montreal Emigrant Society, 1832

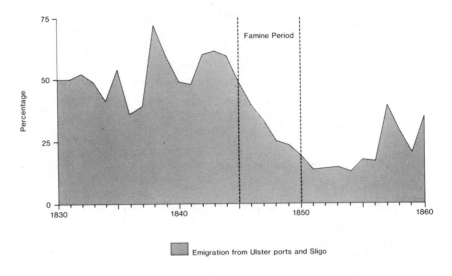

FIGURE 2.8
Emigration from Ulster ports and Sligo as percentage of emigration from
Ireland to Quebec, 1830–60

north and in Cork still predominated. In the 1840s the west-coast ports of Limerick, Galway, and Westport became more significant, and Limerick became especially well connected with Quebec. As suppliers of emigrants to Saint John, Cork grew in stature, whereas Derry and Belfast declined. Subtle shifts in origins heralded the development of a new geography in the years before the Famine.

During the Famine itself, the centre of gravity of emigrant source areas moved steadily westward, as reflected in the composition of British North America's Famine immigrants. Unfortunately, no record directly linking Irish county of origin with country of destination exists for this period, but once again the flow of emigrants to Quebec City from the various ports may be employed as a reasonable surrogate. Figure 2.8 shows the proportion of emigrants who sailed to Quebec City from Ulster ports and Sligo in selected years before the Famine.[47] Sligo served a hinterland that extended well into southwestern Ulster. During pre-Famine years these ports contributed approximately 50 per cent of the passengers who travelled directly from Ireland to Quebec. Their proportion declined in the mid-1840s, to 40 per cent by 1846, signalling the greater importance of ports formerly less involved in emigration. In the following year, 'Black '47,' the Ulster ports contributed only one-third of the arrivals. Worsening conditions had led to an increase in the absolute number of emigrants and simultaneously had consolidated emigration mania throughout the whole country. In 1847 Cork and Limerick shared the role as the leading ports of embarkation, and Munster replaced Ulster as the principal provincial source. Not until the end of the great Irish immigration phase in 1855 would the regional geography of emigration to Canada return to some semblance of its pre-Famine character.

The Famine introduced new elements to the geography of Irish immigration to British North America. Not only were the emigrants more likely to be diseased and destitute than their predecessors, but a majority hailed from source areas previously underrepresented. This alteration in the regions of recruitment was associated with other distinguishing characteristics. The arrivals of 1847 were drawn from much more remote areas, less integrated into the commercial economy. Their range of skills consequently was more limited, and most had virtually no capital, in keeping with their status as unfortunate refugees rather than as purely voluntary emigrants. Moreover, the emergence of new source areas meant that many arrived in the New World bereft of the social and kinship networks that had encouraged and facilitated earlier emigration. The arrivals of 1847 had another diverging characteristic, their religion. A far greater proportion of them were Catholic, and they thus represented a potential force for cultural change within their reception areas, which, outside Quebec, were preponderantly Protestant. Such Irish Catholic regions as the Miramichi Valley of New Brunswick, the Avalon Peninsula of Newfoundland, and even Halifax received practically no Famine emigrants. It fell to Saint John and its hinterland and places in central Canada to deal with the victims.

In all these ways the Famine emigrants differed from the earlier Irish complement. British North American reaction to the unfortunates was as much that of a surprised society as it was a defensive reaction motivated by fear of disease and social guilt. The emigration agent at Kingston described those emigrants who survived Grosse Isle and made their way to Upper Canada as being 'poor, lazy, dirty, shiftless, greedy, mean with money' and significantly added that 'fortunately for them a great many had friends and relations settled in the province who were able to render them assistance. But for this, the calamity would have been more severely felt.'[48] Had more of the unfortunates of 1847 been part of established immigration chains, coping in the colonies with the Famine exodus might have been even easier.

Although the Famine changed temporarily the geographical origins of British North America's Irish immigrants, its aberrant character meant that its impact was unlikely to be sustained. In its aftermath, the geographical sources of Irish emigrants contracted and re-emphasized traditional regions. This contraction meant the continuation of past patterns and old established linkages under the new conditions of greatly reduced immigration. With the possible exception of Cork, Ulster's links with British North America had been more intense and demographically more complex than those of the southern Irish centres, and as a result of this inheritance the northern province became in the post-Famine era the primary source area of Irish immigrants. That Ulster emphasis is demonstrated well in emigration during the 1880s and 1890s.[49] Figure 2.9 shows the proportion of people Canada-bound among all emigrants going to North America then. The vast majority were destined for the United States, but the Irish counties differed greatly in their links with Canada. Ulster was emphatically linked, as only from it did more than 10 per cent of emigrants choose the British Dominion. Fermanagh and Antrim were the most tightly bound, the latter because of Belfast's growing importance as a source of emigrants. Outside Ulster, only Dublin stood as a county of significance, perhaps because it was a national metropolitan centre.

Paradoxically, as the idea of emigration had come to characterize the whole island, the source area of emigrants to Canada after the Famine contracted territorially from its widest extent to become again a more Ulster phenomenon. The source areas of Canada's Irish immigrants were as spatially restricted in 1900 as they had been at the start of the mass movement in the 1810s. In 1900, 57 per cent of the Irish going to Canada originated in Ulster.[50] This pre-eminence remained during the 1900s and 1910s, when, as a response to the demand for agricultural settlers for the world's 'Last Best West' in Saskatchewan and Alberta, and coincidentally with the rapid rise of Toronto, emigration increased once more. Despite a fivefold increase in the annual volume of Irish going to Canada in the early twentieth century, Ulster retained its primacy, and in a few Ulster counties Canada was, as it had been a century before, a more attractive destination than the United States.

In summary, therefore, the principal phase of Irish emigration to

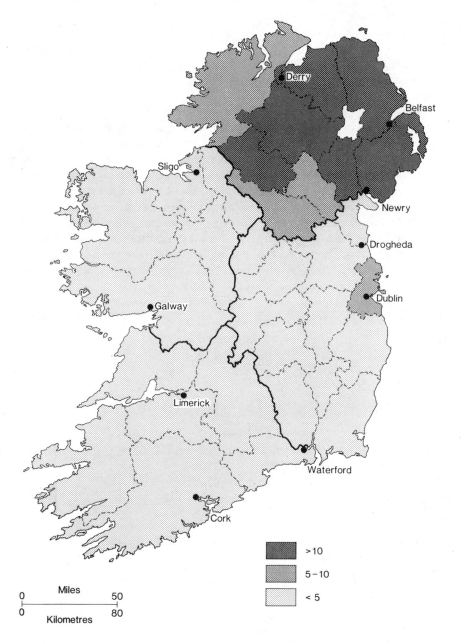

FIGURE 2.9
Emigration to Canada as percentage of emigration to North America,
1880–1900

Canada lasted but four decades, 1815–55. Subsequent migrations, smaller in scale and relatively insignificant within a much more global pattern of Canadian recruitment, did little to alter the character of the Canadian Irish established by the nineteenth-century pioneers. The pioneers had come primarily from northern Leinster and Ulster, and to a lesser extent Cork, and represented a much wider constituency than that indicated by the southeast's links to Irish settlement in New-foundland and Nova Scotia. Even so, not all parts of Ireland were well represented, and Connaught in particular provided relatively few emigrants. The migrations were selective, not only in regional but also in social terms, and nowhere in the new land was the breadth of Irish society replicated. The timing of the mass emigration thrust to Canada, its brevity, and its particular regional character distinguished it from that to the United States. Consequently, models developed in the United States for the study of the Irish abroad have only partial relevance for their Canadian counterparts. Geography and time set the two countries apart.

CHAPTER THREE

The Emigrants

The emigrants who left Ireland for Canada in the early part of the nineteenth century were not a representative cross-section of the Irish population. Willingness to emigrate had not been expressed by all classes, nor had it spread to all parts of the country. Those leaving in the first few years were most likely to have had modest capital, sufficient to sustain them in an adventure that few Irish had yet undertaken. The first emigrants were also without the social support that they themselves would provide for subsequent arrivals and were in the full sense pioneers. Most of them, like the earlier emigrants to colonial America, were Protestant. The high cost of passage selected emigrants of higher socio-economic status, and the Protestants of Ulster and the scattered southern enclaves formed a disproportionately large fraction. In short, the earliest immigrants were derived from among the better-off, and only in time would poorer elements be added to the mix.

The end of the wartime agricultural boom in 1815 initiated a protracted period of economic adjustment in rural Ireland. The eighteenth century had been a period of economic growth and expansion, characterized by the development of great landlord estates, market towns, and commercial agriculture. The agricultural economy, with its growing emphasis on export of grain, meat, and butter, had prospered, and the English demand for provisions during the Napoleonic Wars gave the Irish economy an increased stimulus. After 1815, sharp reductions in the price of grain and higher profitability of livestock triggered a change in the use of land from tillage to pasture in many parts of the country. The disadvantages of the new economy were felt most by medium and

TABLE 3.1
Distribution of farm size,
County Armagh, 1841

Size of farm (acres)	Percentage of farms
30+	2.7
15–29	8.7
5–14	39.8
1–4	48.8

SOURCE: Census of Population,
Ireland, 1841

small farmers, those with less than twenty acres and thus least likely to benefit from grazing. Among the larger farmers, fewer were now willing to subdivide their family holdings among their sons, and as a consequence the maturing generation of the better-off was displaced. Similarly, agricultural labourers encountered fewer opportunities for work and became increasingly redundant and impoverished. Demographic conditions compounded economic difficulties. Ireland had just entered a period of rapid family formation consequent upon the rise in the birth rate in the previous century. Increasing demographic pressure had further constricted opportunities. For the very poor there was little to do but survive as they might; those with some means could emigrate. Thus the relatively better-off, born in the high-fertility years of the 1780s and 1790s, constituted the first wave of emigrants and inaugurated the modern phase of mass emigration from Ireland.

In Ulster, where even by Irish standards land holdings were extremely small, adaptation to the new economic and demographic conditions was proportionately more difficult. Population growth was rapid, and emigration, while it provided a release for thousands, failed initially to relieve the economic stress and pressure on agricultural land. Land hunger could not be satisfied. For example, in County Armagh, in 1841 only 3 per cent of farms were greater than thirty acres in extent (Table 3.1) and almost half the farms were less than five acres.[1] That remarkable pattern of minuscule farm-size does not take into account the large number of gardens and patches of half an acre and less that provided the vital potato ground for labourers and weavers. Places like Armagh's Kilmore parish, whence Wilson Benson, a weaver, emigrated in 1841, had a population density of 750 per square mile in the year of his departure.[2]

The economic situation in Ulster was complicated by its rural domestic linen industry, and much of the rural population depended on a combination of labouring, farming, and linen production. The degree of participation by a small tenant farmer's family in the linen industry varied from season to season, and the age and sex of members dictated their tasks, but all were intensely involved. In times of harvest and spring cultivation, the adult males would be full-time farmers or agricultural labourers; for the remainder of the year they would operate their heavy domestic looms. Women and children performed the lighter task of spinning. Families thus relied on a composite income from farming and weaving, and from the 1820s that was under threat not only from changing profit margins in agriculture but also from structural reorganization within the linen industry.[3]

Spinning had been technologically revolutionized, becoming the preserve of a few large factories in eastern Ulster, and throughout much of the province female and child labour in the industry became redundant. Family incomes dropped. Simultaneously, reorganization of the weaving process contributed to the growing pressures on family income by reducing the traditional independence of weavers. Increasingly, they became piece-workers, employed by owners of spinning and bleaching firms. In that manner, the weaver Wilson Benson had managed to prevail and save passage money for himself and his wife. Economic change in both the domestic linen and agricultural production spheres, together with increasing population pressure, limited opportunities to maintain existing levels of prosperity. In Ulster the stimulus for emigration was thus more intense.

The effect of these economic and demographic forces was filtered by the socio-religious character of the country. Protestants were potentially more prone to respond to the disruptions by emigrating. More of them had the means, and geographical mobility was more significant in their recent traditions. Throughout the seventeenth and early eighteenth centuries there had been a sustained immigration to Ulster from Scotland, overlapping slightly with the start of the eighteenth-century transatlantic exodus of Ulster Presbyterians to colonial America. This tradition of mobility was augmented by an ongoing process of internal migration and population redistribution within Ireland. The expansion and relocation of Protestant communities were also ongoing in southern Ireland, where landlords, seeking to consolidate isolated Protestant communities, offered attractive leases to encourage Protestant settlement. In south Wicklow, north Wexford, Carlow, Tipperary, Kilkenny, Cork, and Limerick, this Protestant expansion was most apparent.

Unlike in Ulster, however, the southern Protestant settlements were rarely contiguous but were formed of isolated pockets of better-off tenant farmers and the commercial classes in towns. Constructed under artificial conditions and in a period of economic prosperity, these Protestant enclaves felt the full impact of the nineteenth century's economic recession. Their inhabitants also lived as minorities among Catholic neighbours, whose hostility had peaked in the sectarian and political bitterness of the 1790s. Their power and position were under threat, and like their counterparts in Ulster their response included emigration.

By way of contrast, the history of Catholic communities in Ireland was marked by a greater sense of rootedness and attachment to land. The Catholic population's stronger sense of place was derived from its native identity, its never having known another place, and the limitations to movement imposed by the system of landholding. Opportunities for Catholics for internal migration were few – and even fewer because of their generally lower social and economic ranks. More of them were in poverty. The possibility of emigration in the Catholic community was thus smaller than for Protestants, and a differential between the two became evident in the very first migration streams to British North America.

Funds to finance emigration were obtained in many ways and were required not only for passage but also to maintain immigrants on arrival in the new country, to get land, and to settle. Despite falling fares, the cost of emigration and resettlement for intending settlers rose, especially after free (but difficult to obtain) grants of land were phased out in Upper Canada in 1825 and in New Brunswick in 1827.[4] Many early Irish settlers bought prime cleared land from the earlier established residents, but most moved to the frontier in search of cheaper, uncleared lots. Their purchases were often financed by a little money brought with them. This imported capital could have been acquired from savings, the sale of property prior to emigration, or partly by remittances and aid from relatives who had emigrated earlier. The sale of tenant right, that is, of the "goodwill" value of a farm in Ireland together with the right to renewal of the lease, provided capital for some. Tenant-right sales could raise more than £10 per acre for a fortunate tenant,[5] and even on a ten-acre holding this would have amounted to a sizeable sum, but it is unlikely to have been the source of funding for more than a minority of emigrants. To sell the family's rights to its acreage was too final. It was the last step in leaving the land. Besides, where the lease of the family farm passed to only one son, the other, propertyless sons had no recourse to funds from the sale of tenant right, as no exchange of the leasehold interest had taken place. For example, four sons of William Carrothers left their home in County Fermanagh in the 1830s, and the tenant right was retained in the hands of the remaining son, who inherited the farm. A financial settlement from the will of their father may have financed the emigration,[6] but no sale of tenant right was involved. Carrothers and a very great many Irishmen probably had, from various sources, money sufficient to get a start on the other side, despite the image that has been created over the years of an exodus of indigents.

Given the cost of passage and associated land settlement expenses, the earliest emigrants to Canada probably had a modestly comfortable background; as the decades unfolded and emigration became increasingly more popular, the numbers leaving from the lower ranks may have correspondingly increased. In the relative absence of government and private assistance schemes, most emigrants went on their own initiative and dependent on their own or their family's wherewithal. The only major British government funds allocated were those expended in Peter Robinson's schemes of 1823 and 1825, which moved more than 2,000 landless labourers and impoverished tenant farmers from the Blackwater Valley of Munster to crown lands in Upper Canada.[7] Some Irish landlords contributed to the removal of tenants from their overcrowded estates by providing free passages to the colonies, but they spent virtually nothing on resettlement. For landlords seeking to introduce improved husbandry and more efficient production, the few pounds invested in fares for a surplus tenantry were a small cost. This subsidy, however, was extended to only a very small fraction of those emigrating.[8]

Apart from other occasional measures undertaken by a few notables or local charities, the vast majority of emigrants, even the poorest, received little aid. Assistance in the form of prepaid passages from family members already abroad was of greater significance, and in the 1830s, for example, perhaps half of those going through the port of Derry were funded in this way.[9] For the poorest, it was probably the only way. Among families, resources were obtained and pooled to finance one departure, in expectation that fares for subsequent departures would be paid from the American side. By such family-oriented and voluntary means, the mass migration from Ireland was funded.

Although we cannot say just how many of the emigrants to Canada were rich and how many were poor, the specific social and economic

TABLE 3.2
Occupation of heads of Irish emigrant households
assisted from New York to Upper Canada by James
Buchanan in 1817

27 farmers	2 shoemakers	1 apothecary
11 labourers	2 manufacturers	1 machine maker
6 blacksmiths	2 masons	1 surgeon
6 weavers	1 batter	1 butcher
4 tailors	1 clerk	1 printer
3 carpenters	1 quarryman	1 wheelwright
2 sawyers		

SOURCE: Passes signed by British Consul, New York,
for emigrants from Great Britain, March 1817
(National Archives of Canada)

background of many emigrants can be reconstructed from a variety of documents. One of the earliest detailed listings of emigrants is that compiled by James Buchanan, British consul in New York. Among his activities was promotion of secondary emigration from the United States to Upper Canada. Between 1817 and 1820 he provided transportation expenses for upward of three thousand Irish emigrants from New York City.[10] A fragmentary record of 236 of his Irish emigrants in 1817 contains details on names, occupation, family structure, and county of origin.[11] The record reveals that Buchanan assisted a wide range of people, as if he were deliberately trying to create a complete community, with a full spectrum of occupations. A summary of those occupations is given in Table 3.2. Members of the largest single group described themselves as farmers, and most of them had families. Labourers were the second largest group. The remainder were skilled workers, artisans, and professionals. In all, the emigrants by their occupations were very representative of the craft industries and farm economy of rural Ireland at the time. There were a few single artisans and a number of skilled, and possibly entrepreneurial, millers and sawyers. Significantly, there was a surgeon and an apothecary. Just as significantly, Buchanan did not assist single women or servants; his people were meant for a rough new frontier. There is no indication about the amount of money carried by the immigrants, but it might be surmised safely that they were not entirely impoverished. They were assisted only after arrival in New York, not because they were poor but because they were needed to consolidate the British presence in the colony after the War of 1812.

Eighty per cent of the people Buchanan sent in 1817 were from Ulster; the remainder were drawn from southern counties with significant Protestant populations. That distribution is evident in Figure 3.1. In that map, the Ulster emphasis is most evident, but the counties of Dublin, Limerick, Waterford, and Wicklow were also represented in a minor way. In acknowledging the regional background of the settlers, Buchanan arranged that some of their land grants be located in townships called Cavan and Monaghan.[12] The places of origin and the family names suggest an almost exclusively Protestant group, in line with Buchanan's own strongly held religious views and his membership in the Orange Order.[13] His people were being added to a community in Upper Canada already composed largely of Protestants. In the Kawartha Lakes districts, where many of them settled, they joined with the half-pay officers – yeomanry demobilized after the Napoleonic Wars – and other privileged settlers. It was one of the first colonization districts designated by the colonial authorities after the Napoleonic Wars, and free grants of land were readily given. In that region Robert Reid and William Stewart from Bushmills, County Antrim, were granted 2,200 acres of land in 1822.[14]

This area was also the site of Peter Robinson's assisted settlement in 1823 and 1825, the best-known experiment in government-assisted emigration to British North America. In all, the British government shipped two and a half thousand Irish, mainly from the Fermoy region of County Cork, to Upper Canada, and helped them settle on free grants of land (Figure 3.1).[15] The logistical details and arrangements were undertaken by Robinson, brother of the colony's attorney general, and the emigrants were also selected by Robinson as part of an effort to clear unwanted tenants. In this sense the emigration was relatively unusual. Unlike most emigrants, dependent on their own or their family's resources, each of Robinson's emigrants received free passage, tools, some livestock, seeds, and money for provisions, and a rough cabin was prepared on the allotted lands. The cost of the scheme was approximately £12 per person or £60 per family.[16] Although the venture proved successful, such costly arrangements were never repeated[17] and practically all emigrants to British North America depended on their own means or on remittances and other forms of family assistance.

Non-government organized group settlement of emigrants was also rare in the annals of Irish emigration to Canada. The Talbot group-migration of Protestants from north Tipperary is an example of one such scheme.[18] Richard Talbot, unable to find military commissions for

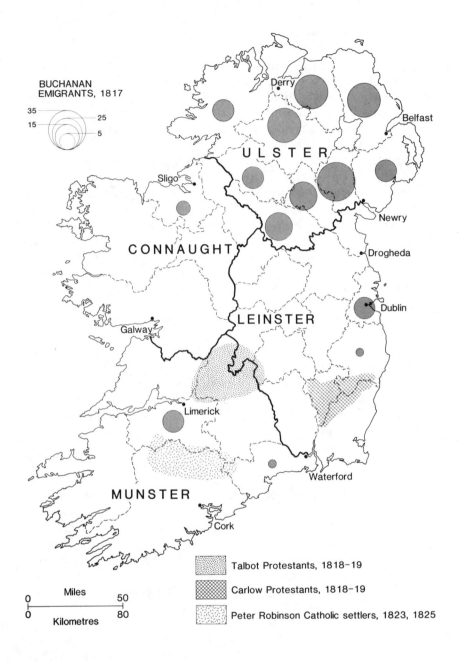

FIGURE 3.1
Origins of some early immigrants to Upper Canada, 1817–25

his sons, decided on the family's emigration to a crown colony. A subsidy was sought from the British government, and under an existing land-granting scheme Talbot was offered one hundred acres per adult male emigrant willing to settle on the military frontier of Upper Canada. From among his neighbours and acquaintances in north Tipperary, Talbot selected thirty-eight families with whom he proceeded to the New World. By any standard, the Talbot settlers were of substantial rural stock and representative of the Protestant classes leaving southern counties in Ireland. Half of the families were farm people quitting small leaseholds. A dozen were tradesmen from principal trades: shoemaking, weaving, blacksmithing, and carpentry. A few families were of gentry origins. All of them had funds, generally more than £50, all were literate, and all could have just as well taken part in the emigration as independent single families. The group scheme may have helped reduce costs (some participants thought otherwise), but its real value was in the social familiarity and security that a group emigration represented at a time when the overseas networks of reliable kin and countrymen were just being initiated.

Many independent emigrants from Ulster in the early phase of nineteenth-century emigration were as well off as Talbot's selected group and were of a similar respectable farming background. The Irish emigrants in the 1820s were adjudged by A.C. Buchanan (James Buchanan's brother), emigration agent in Quebec, to be 'generally of a superior description, from the north of Ireland, from Tyrone and Fermanagh; they were men generally possessing a little property, and in anything but a distressed state.'[19] That situation continued into the next decade. Among groups of immigrants coming from a wider Irish set of source regions in 1831, Buchanan noted that there persisted a recognizable component of better-off farming classes. 'Very many respectable and wealthy farmers came out this year from almost every portion of Ireland, but more particularly from the counties of Armagh, Fermanagh, Cavan, Leitrim, Mayo, Sligo, Tyrone, Dublin, Limerick and Wexford.'[20] During the 1820s Ulster and the southeast of Ireland had been sending out large numbers of respectable farmers, but subsequently the proportion of emigrants who were poor steadily rose.

The Carrothers of Fermanagh are a good example of displaced members of the better-off farming classes, and the farm they left represents the type of environment from which many of the Irish emigrated. Four members of the family left the home farm of forty-two acres at Farnaght in 1835. Their farm was located in Ulster's drumlin belt but

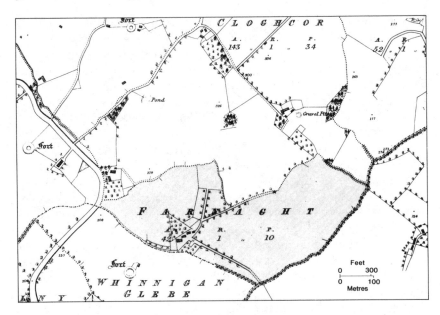

FIGURE 3.2
The townland of Farnaght, County Fermanagh; Ordnance Survey Six Inch
Map, first edition, 1834

outside the main central and eastern linen regions of the province.
Their house, built in 1815, and still recognizable in the fabric of the
present-day dwelling, was by its dimensions and its fine eighteenth-
and early-nineteenth-century furniture, the homestead of a modestly
comfortable farming family. In Figure 3.2, the Ordnance Survey Map
of 1833 depicts well the farm on which the brothers lived. The farmstead
consisted of two occupied houses, a barn, and a byre in a cobbled yard.
It was sited on the south side of a drumlin and away from the main road
to which it was linked by a private, beech-lined lane. The laneways to
the haggard – the storage area for stacks of hay and oats behind the
house – and the lanes elsewhere were lined with ornamental tree plant-
ings. An orchard to the rear of the dwelling houses and a large vegetable
and herb garden in front completed the ensemble of a well-appointed
farm. Most of the land was arable, there being but a few acres of marshy
bogland running along the base of the drumlin. The surrounding district contained many similar farms, and the landscape, with its scattering

FIGURE 3.3
The farm-house in which William Hutton lived at Grangefoyle, County Tyrone; photograph by authors

of Iron Age ring forts, testified to more than a thousand years of agricultural settlement and improvement.

The Carrothers were not unique, and large parts of Ireland were not by European standards poor. Successful farming and industrial development attest to that. In addition, a surprising amount of cash existed among the farming classes.[21] Guineas and sovereigns were passed on as inheritances and often stored for major eventualities such as provision of dowries for daughters, purchase of a tenant right for a younger son, or, more likely in the nineteenth century, subsidizing of an emigrant passage.

An even more striking but unusual case was that of William Hutton, who was able to finance his settlement abroad in 1834 by a loan of £700 from his parents.[22] His home at Grangefoyle in County Tyrone, represented in the photograph in Figure 3.3, was a clear landscape expression of wealth. The two-storey Georgian residence was elegant and of the same form as many a fine town-house in Dublin. The down-stairs storey, partially hidden by the garden, was meant to appear submerged. There were located the kitchens, scullery, and servant area. Upstairs were the parlour, sitting area, and bedrooms of the family. The house and its courtyard of late-eighteenth-century farm outbuildings articulated an impression of gentry farming.

William Hutton was born in Summerhill, Dublin, in 1801.[23] As a younger son of an apparently wealthy Unitarian clergyman he was sent to Agricultural College to acquire an education suitable for an untitled and propertyless gentleman. Applying his education to good use, he became leaseholder of a large farm of about 350 acres in the Foyle Valley, ten miles south of Derry.[24] Hutton's attempt at farming in Ulster proved a financial disaster. Falling prices, high rent, and a certain unwillingness to engage himself in manual labour took him into debt and prompted his seeking an agricultural career elsewhere. He contemplated emigrating to England where he had relatives, and getting a farm there, but finally decided on North America, where he arrived in 1834.

Although few among the emigrants would have had a comparable standard of living or access to such large amounts of money as Hutton, most of the early emigrants were not poverty stricken. People with sums of fifty, one hundred, or two hundred pounds were common. For example, Timothy Eaton, founder of a Canadian retailing empire, having ended his apprenticeship to a shopkeeper relative in Portglenone, County Antrim, left in 1857 to join his brothers and sisters with £100, a new suit of clothes, and a silver watch, compensation for his years learning the shopkeeper's trade.[25]

Besides the farmers, there were people of higher station, for the requirements of colonial societies demanded that an educated élite be transferred from Britain. Administrators were needed for Colonial Office functions and for a plethora of other positions, from judges to customs commissioners and surveyors. Without these administrators, rapid settlement in Britain's colonies would have been impossible. Many of those chosen to serve in British North America were Irish, often graduates of Trinity College, Dublin. Ecclesiastical administrators and clergy were likewise required, and again Irish institutions, such as Trinity College and the seminaries at Maynooth and later All Hallows, Dublin, supplied many of the needs. The latter two, as the major Catholic seminaries in the British Isles,[26] played a critical role for Catholic emigrants. For the

Catholic community too, nuns, one of the few groups of educated female emigrants, were also supplied from Ireland.[27]

In the pioneering phase, most of the educated had to be brought in from abroad. Ireland, with its tradition of colonial service and its well-developed educational system, played a pivotal role in staffing British North American colonial administrations. Innumerable individuals of substance and Irish origin played significant roles in the foundation and cultural life of the new country: the Protestant Corkmen, Francis Hincks and Robert Baldwin, Upper Canadian prime ministers; the County Armagh Protestant landlord Lord Gosford, lieutenant-governor of Lower Canada; the Catholic Corkman, newspaper publisher, and politician Timothy Anglin; the Catholic politician D'Arcy McGee from County Louth; Ogle R. Gowan, Wexford Protestant and founder of the Canadian Orange Order; William McMaster, merchant from Tyrone and founder of the Bank of Commerce; and Robert Workman, Montreal merchant industrialist from County Antrim. After Canada became a confederated Dominion in 1867, the office of governor-general was occupied by such Irishmen as Lords Dufferin, Lansdowne, and Lisgar. Ireland was both an important source and a fruitful training ground for officers in the British North American colonial service. The Irish coming to Canada represented a wide range of an advanced mature society. They do not bear easy stereotyping.

The stereotype of the Irish emigrant has been that of the indigent labourer. An example was Wilson Benson, a native of Bottle Hill, County Armagh, who arrived in Canada in 1841 and whose story is preserved in his autobiography, published in 1876.[28] Benson, the son of a weaver, spent his youth in a society of few opportunities. The townland of Bottle Hill, illustrated in Figure 3.4, contained two hundred acres of medium-quality land on which two hundred and forty people lived. Most of the land was in tillage, potatoes being the principal crop. Settlement was concentrated along the main road, and so great was the population density that the linear line of houses formed a virtual village. The enclosed landscape of small fields outlined by hawthorn hedges was rarely more than two acres in extent and devoid of trees, except for small orchards near the farm-houses. The residents were weavers, flax spinners, and farmers working as piece labour in the domestic linen industry. The nearest village was Kilmore, which in 1841 had fewer than twenty houses.

In this society, apprenticeship at basket-making and weaving was as

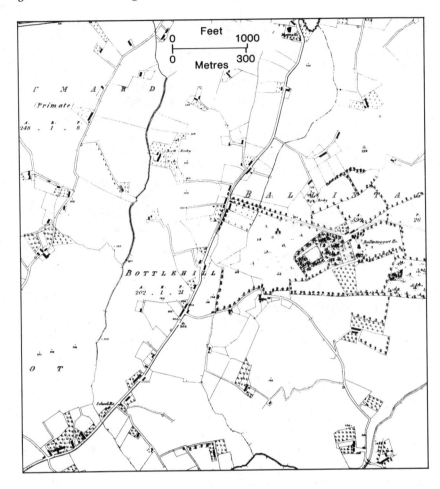

FIGURE 3.4
Bottle Hill, County Armagh; Ordnance Survey Six Inch Map, first edition, 1833

much as Wilson might aspire to. It was not enough, and so he tried emigration to Scotland, where his sister and her husband had already settled and were prepared to offer him assistance. His hopes for Scotland were not realized, as there, too, he was relegated to a life of menial labour. Many Ulstermen, particularly those like Wilson with few means, went across to Scotland as seasonal and/or permanent emigrants. Wilson's place in the migration steam was like that of any of the other thousands of agricultural labourers who flocked across with their sickles and sharpening stones or spades and forks.[29]

Labourers were the core of the mass movement to Canada. In the first few years after the Napoleonic Wars, they were a small proportion, but as economic conditions in Ireland worsened, cheaper passage, augmented by increasing flows of remittances, enlarged the range of people able to respond to the transatlantic lure. The British North American timber industry was often a draw for young men, and public investment in canals and roads, as well as the construction of towns, created demand for casual labourers. Single Irish labourers, bound for work as navvies, became increasingly important in the outbound flow. Teams of them, often grouped by region of origin – Corkmen, Monaghanmen, and the like – moved from project to project, becoming a common feature of the new colonies' work-force.[30]

These labourers carried with them regional and parochial loyalties, forged first in their Irish homeland, and in the rough and rowdy labourer's life in frontier shantytowns, fractiousness and violence were not rare. Wilson Benson witnessed one such outbreak near Cornwall, on the St Lawrence River: 'A riot occurred on the [Beauharnois Canal] between the Cork and Connaught Irishmen. The former, being the most numerous, obtained the mastery. News of this reached the Cornwall works; the Connaught men here, who were most numerous, determined to avenge the cause of their party, and drove the handles out of their picks, and with other bludgeons fell upon the Cork men with an energy which would have done credit to a better cause ... Two men had their brains beaten out ... the wives and children of the murdered men rendering the air with their piercing shrieks while the bloody butchery was being enacted ... My countrymen earned for themselves an unenviable notoriety, and produced an impression, especially among the rural population of Canada at that time, that the Irish, one and all, were "hard cases".'[31]

Among adult male Irish immigrants arriving in British North America in the 1830s, the labouring classes predominated, as might be expected

TABLE 3.3
Occupations of adult male Irish immigrants (%)

Occupations	Assisted in Montreal, 1832	Disembarking at Saint John, 1833
Labourer	72.9	73.0
Farmer	5.9	12.7
Weaver	6.1	1.9
Other occupation	15.1	12.4
Total	100.0	100.0
N	1,083	1,286

SOURCES: Montreal Emigrant Society, Passage Book
for 1832 (National Archives of Canada); Passenger
lists, Saint John, 1833 (Provincial Archives of New
Brunswich)

in a mass exodus from a largely rural society. Table 3.3 summarizes the
occupational characteristics of immigrants arriving in Montreal in 1832
and Saint John in 1833. The information for Saint John, based on
passenger lists from ships, provides an unparalleled record of the emigration.[32] Labourers made up almost three-quarters of the arrivals,
indicating the widening appeal of North America in Ireland. About an
eighth of the arrivals were farmers, representing a displaced younger
generation of that class. A very small number were weavers, and among
the rest were shoemakers, carpenters, tailors, and blacksmiths, the same
sort of people as those directed by James Buchanan from New York
fifteen years earlier. Occupations included apothecary, lawyer, bleacher,
stonecutter, and whitesmith.

The Saint John arrivals of 1833 were comparable in occupational
range and in emphasis on the labouring classes to those Irish newcomers
recorded as having received assistance in Montreal in 1832. In that
cholera year, the Montreal Emigrant Society aided emigrants by giving
them tickets to continue inland and in a few cases getting them jobs in
Montreal.[33] As with Saint John, almost three-quarters of the adult males
were labourers. Farmers were less prominent, as might be expected,
given the circumstances for which the information was recorded. Weavers made up a larger proportion in the Montreal group, but occupational patterns were similar. Notwithstanding the unique circumstances
that led to the recording of the Montreal information, those migrants
assisted at Montreal may have been fairly representative of the mass of

TABLE 3.4
Amount of money carried by
emigrants from parishes in
County Antrim, 1835–9

Amount (£)	Number of emigrants
100–200	4
50–100	6
20–50	16
10–20	26
10	277
None	49
Total	378

SOURCE: Ordnance Survey of
Ireland, Memoirs, County
Antrim (Royal Irish Academy)

Irish immigrants disembarking at Quebec in that year. The people assisted included a quarter of all the total Irish arrivals at Quebec for 1832.

The prevalence of labourers among the immigrants does not mean that the people were also indigent. Labouring classes going abroad were known to have had some funds. For example, among the Ordnance Survey Memoirs for County Antrim there is an incomplete list of emigrants who left several parishes there in the late 1830s; more than 80 per cent carried some money with them (See Table 3.4).[34] Four individuals carried in excess of £100, and 329 of 378 carried at least £10.

For a day-labourer, savings of £10 would have represented the equivalent of nine months' gross income. Passage would have cost the gross returns for two months of labouring. For a single labourer, £10 would have represented in net terms the savings gleaned from several years' work. Had he also paid for the passage of his wife and family, his savings would have been an even more striking indicator of the unusual effort required to emigrate. Savings of £10 in excess of the direct cost of migration reflected a concerted, deliberate plan to move beyond the circumstances of rural Irish life. It was the effort of a person with hope and forethought. Furthermore, the sums indicated in Table 3.4 are, if anything, an underestimate. Official surveys of contemporary personal wealth would scarcely have revealed the complete truth. For the emigrant labourer, especially the poorest, emigration was an investment of unusual proportions, and its significance cannot be conveyed in purely monetary terms.

There were, of course, indigents and unfortunates among the emigrants, many in extreme destitution. Many were forced to seek assistance from public charities and emigrant aid societies. Receipt of benevolence, however, did not mean that one's resources were at a complete end, and recourse to public assistance did not necessarily indicate final, dispiriting impoverishment. Many emigrants, informed by friends who had already made the journey, knew full well the type of assistance available in ports along the way and availed themselves of it, often when not in dire need. Many of those in absolute need were only temporarily bereft of means and sought support only to sustain them through a bad spell.

Some of the anguish and hardship that public assistance was meant to ameliorate is illustrated in Table 3.5. That list, prepared by the Prescott Emigrant Aid Society in Upper Canada, includes destitute emigrants who received assistance (free passage to parts farther west) in 1835.[35] It contains a litany of woe and personal tragedy but shows that many of those assisted were en route to join relatives already in the colony. Sarah Henry was going to join her son in Toronto, Ellen Barrett to rejoin her husband after a two-year separation. Misfortune and geography may have separated recipients from their eventual destinations among friends and relatives. But the nature of emigration, built around a set of transatlantic information networks and chain-like migration, ensured the possibility of relief from the untoward vagaries of penury and bad luck. Most emigrants were enclosed within the comforting chains forged by prior emigration.

Even the greater misery of 1847 must be kept in context and remembered – not as the linchpin, but as an anomaly – in the pattern of Irish emigration to Canada. In their formative period, the colonies had attracted better-off emigrants, and even in the midst of the Famine such classes continued to arrive. Indeed, the immigrants of 1847 were composed of two groups, the usual mix of labourers, farmers, and artisans and a large proportion of Famine victims without means. The former group included two individuals whose correspondence is related in this volume, Joseph Carrothers and Jane White. Such Famine emigrants tend to be overlooked in the descriptions of the trauma. Attention has been given almost exclusively to the unfortunates and the reactions of British North American communities beset by an influx of the dis-

TABLE 3.5
Immigrants assisted at Prescott, Upper Canada, 1835

Name of family head	Number	Origin	Destination	Remarks
Bernard McMahon	9	Ireland	Hamilton	a discharged soldier
Nelly McDermott	2	"	"	a widow to join a brother
Martha Palls	3	"	"	a very old woman with 2 grandchildren, to join a brother of hers at Streetsville
Michael Culkeen	8	"	Port Hope	a very old man having a son in Mariposa
Ann Dennison	6	"	Toronto	to join her husband
George Bridges	3	England	Hamilton	a discharged solider with very sore eyes, to go to his father
Sarah Henry	4	Ireland	Toronto	to go to a son residing on some part of Yonge Street
Patrick Murray	4	"	Hamilton	has been hurt on the canal at Long Sault
John Rodgers	1	"	Niagara	a boy to go to his father in law and mother
Margaret Gallagher	2	"	Toronto	a very old woman, say 70 years of age, to join her son
Nancy Grames	5	"	Kingston	to join her husband
Mary Culkeen	1	"	Belleville	had a daughter who died in hospital here and was herself sick, to join the rest of her family
Ruth Walker	2	"	Toronto	a girl and a boy
John Strachan	4	"	"	a discharged solider from the 9th Reg't of Foot
William Langdon	5	England	"	one of his legs very bad, has relations in Toronto
Joseph Rodgers	2	Ireland	"	Wife lately dead, has a sister in Toronto, to whom he is carrying his infant daughter
Elizabeth Murray	2	"	"	to go to a brother living in Oakville
Margaret Pew	1	"	"	has been sick in hospital here
Ellen Barrett	8	"	Niagara	to join her husband, who has been out 2 years
James Read	1	Scotland	"	has had very bad feet
Nancy McGivern	1	Ireland	Toronto	to join her husband

TABLE 3.5 – continued

Name of family head	Number	Origin	Destination	Remarks
Niel McKearne	8	"	"	an elderly man
John Armstrong	6	"	Port Hope	has been hurt at the Long Sault Canal, has relations in the town

NOTE: Document entitled 'Return of passages furnished at the public expense to destitute emigrants at Prescott, Upper Canada, from the opening of the navigation, to the 31st August, 1835, inclusive.' Prepared by Prescott Emigrant Aid Society. The list also includes thirty-six Irish emigrants 'wrecked in the Wm. McEwen on Scataree Island' and sent on to various destinations.
SOURCE: National Archives of Canada, c-6887, Upper Canada Sundries

eased and destitute. The pathetic year will remain in Canada's history as the primary symbol of pauper immigration – a deserved distinction. But the Famine came near the end of mass Irish emigration to Canada, unlike in the United States, where it heralded a new Irish era. Access to British North America was severely restricted after 1847, and the country's limited economy further inhibited the absorption of great masses of pauper immigrants.

Following the aberration of the Famine period and the subsequent rapid decline of immigration in the 1850s, British North America was forced to recruit immigrants actively. The natural immigration inflow had slackened as emigrants perceived a comparative disadvantage in opportunities in British North America relative to those in the United States. The collapse of the Canadian wheat economy and the hiatus in trade brought on by the Crimean War diminished immigration. Lack of expansion in New Brunswick's timber industry meant few emigrants would be going to that region after the Famine. Movements to Nova Scotia and Newfoundland had largely ceased even before the Famine.

As uncertain economic fortunes resulted in only the merest trickle of immigrants, active recruitment of manpower was increasingly seen as a necessary part of colonial settlement policy. In 1856, after a thirty-year gap, free grants of land were again offered in Canada West. This time they were located not in prime areas but on the marginal land of the rocky and barren wastes of the Canadian Shield, north of the settled agricultural zone. Those poor lands were made accessible by the construction of colonization roads, and settlement along them was supervised by the Bureau of Agriculture, under William Hutton. The conditions of the grants were quite liberal: 'On these roads, free grants not exceeding 100 acres each, will be made to settlers of 18 years of age and upwards, on condition that they take possession within a month, put 12 acres into cultivation within 4 years, and build a log hut 20 by 18 feet, and reside on the lot.'[36] This marked a return to pre-1825 colonization policies, but this time the offers – 100 acres of marginal land on the granite wastes of the Canadian Shield – had little real potential to absorb and sustain a large agricultural population. The scheme had little appeal for Ireland's farming families and none for its industrial labourers, both of which groups were now much more aware of and tied to opportunities in American cities. The land's appeal was greatest for Canadian residents, who saw in the schemes the chance of quick speculative profits.

British North America's attraction for the labouring classes of Ireland after the Famine was not great. Potential immigrants were being deflected toward the United States, where urban economic opportunities and the networks created there by the massive Famine migration had created a new dynamic in the Irish emigration process. The need for unskilled labour in Canada was also small. In 1869, Ontario's provincial government conducted a survey of all the mayors, township wardens, and reeves in the province in order to establish the region's labour needs. The result was a reported demand for only 15,125 agricultural labourers, 1,448 mechanics, and 6,576 female servants.[37] Twenty-three thousand jobs, to be distributed among not only Irish but increasingly larger contingents of Scottish and English arrivals, was a very small number. In addition to these openings for immigrants, the Ontarian immigration agent in 1870 indicated a demand for a 'goodly number of tenant farmers, with more or less capital at their disposal, who will settle on partially cleared farms in the older townships of the province.'[38] This mix of a few better-off farmers and a large number of agricultural and industrial labourers and female domestic servants characterized the occupational pattern of Irish immigration for the rest of the century. An increasing proportion came from the towns of Ulster, particularly Belfast. The total number arriving, however, was insignificant in comparison with the rural influx in the pre-Famine period. Even the opening of prairie lands did not alter the inertia in the emigration pattern.

In dealing with the emigration's demographic characteristics, research has been beset by very poor information. Manifests of ships, which provide listings of passengers, their age, sex, and other pertinent social information, have rarely survived. In most cases they were not required until the 1860s. As a consequence, records of the Irish emigration to British North America, the critical period of which was 1815–55, are less than adequate. Only two sets of useful manifests, for ships arriving in Saint John in 1833 and 1834, have been uncovered,[39] and they provide little more than a starting-point for pursuit of demographic and social questions about the nature of the emigrants. No comparable set of data exists for Quebec and other ports of entry before 1860. Although the Saint John passenger lists in 1833 and 1834 provide a valuable record of single years and single ships, they cannot give a full depiction of emigrant demography. In particular, they underestimate the family nature of the emigration: families fractured by the departure of individual members were generally reconstituted on the North American side over a protracted period. A husband may have gone out in one year to be followed by his wife a couple of years later. Or brothers could have gone out at different times, to be reunited later with their siblings. As a consequence, passenger lists record only glimpses of the emigration, greatly exaggerate the importance of individuals, and thus conceal the underlying and fundamental demography, in which connectedness between people and especially within family groups was central. Keeping in mind the discontinuities that the passenger lists emphasize, we may still suggest a few critical elements about the demography of the emigration.

The earliest set of information that may be employed with confidence is that pertaining to the emigrants assisted in 1817 by James Buchanan in New York. The extant records of the 233 people whom Buchanan assisted from New York to Upper Canada reveal the dominance of men – 60 percent of the adults in the group were men (Table 3.6). Thirty-four males travelled as unaccompanied single men, but even though Upper Canada was a primitive frontier in 1817, thirty-nine of the male emigrants were married and accompanied by their wives. The six single women in the group included three elderly widowed mothers and three sisters travelling with married siblings. There were no unaccompanied women. In total, 94 per cent of the immigrants migrated as part of family groups, and the role of nuclear families is striking.

TABLE 3.6
Irish emigrants assisted to Upper Canada by
James Buchanan in 1817

	Number	Percentage
Single men	34	14.6
Married men	39	16.7
Married women	39	16.7
Single women	6	2.6
Children	115	49.4
Total	233	100.0

SOURCE: Passes signed by British Consul,
New York, for Emigrants from Great Britain,
March 1817 (National Archives of Canada)

This sort of emphasis on family migration is also apparent in the early Protestant emigrations from Tipperary to the Ottawa Valley and London regions of Upper Canada,[40] and among Peter Robinson's settlers from Cork in 1823 and 1825. Undoubtedly, these cases are too few to allow generalizations, but the data suggest strongly that the Irish pioneering experience in British North America was not the prerogative of single men. For Newfoundland's fisheries and New Brunswick's timber industry a prevalence of men was more likely, but wherever permanent agricultural settlements were to be built, Irish emigration flows were either based on family or directed at that objective.

The predominance of families is suggested also by the emigrants who sailed into Saint John in 1833, despite recent work on New York that challenges the family orientation of the emigration. A pyramid of their age and sex characteristics (Figure 3.5) illustrates the population's male and youthful elements. Sixty per cent of the emigrants were male, and even more in the principal migratory age groups, 20–29 years. A sex imbalance of the same proportion has been indicated by Mageean's analysis of Irish emigration to New York in 1830–1 (Figure 3.5). However, in New York, the excess of males was most pronounced in the younger age groups, 15–24 years. Mageean's profile, emphasizing greater youthfulness than in Saint John, is more typical of a population dominated by single men. For Saint John, the presence of families is also indicated clearly by the higher proportion of children under 10 and adults over 30 years of age. Fifteen per cent of Saint John's immigrants were children, compared with 9 per cent in New York, and adults

FIGURE 3.5
Age-sex structure of Irish immigrants arriving at Saint John, 1833, and New York, 1830–1; New York data from Deirdre M. Mageean, 'Nineteenth-Century Irish Emigration,' in P.J. Drudy, *Irish Studies 4. The Irish in America* (Cambridge 1985)

over 30 represented 21 per cent in Saint John, but only 12 per cent in New York. On the basis of her evidence, Mageean has concluded that the pre-Famine 'emigration was characterized by mainly young unattached males,'[41] thereby challenging the interpretation that families were the core of the movement. Her analysis may have been affected by the small size of her sample. She had available the age records of only 593 people – a minuscule proportion of total New York arrivals.

The present analysis of the Saint John data, based on a much larger sample, of almost 3,000 individuals, does not sustain such a challenge to family orientation, at least in Canada's case. As late as 1840, the New Brunswick emigrant agent at Saint John, Alex Wedderburn, reported to his government 'a peculiar feature in our emigration which in my humble view indicates the most healthful character of it both for the individuals and the Country. It is the relative division of adults and minors.'[42] Wedderburn provided numbers: children comprised 20 per cent of the emigrants, adult women 23 per cent, and adult men 57 per cent. The pattern was virtually identical to the situation there in 1833. Wedderburn's information is about those arriving. The demographic composition of those who settled could be very different and could in theory have an even more pronounced family orientation. The nature of making a living on an agricultural frontier selected family migrants.

The emigrants assisted by the Montreal Emigrant Society in 1832 belonged almost exclusively to family groups and were perhaps selected for assistance because of the children. Regardless, those assisted comprised 20 per cent of the total number of Irish disembarking in Quebec that year.[43] Eighty-one per cent of the assisted individuals were members of nuclear families; 16 per cent were members of single-parent families. Only 4 per cent could be identified as single adults, although the way in which the information was recorded does not rule out the possibility that they too belonged to a larger family unit and were simply temporarily estranged from it. Notwithstanding the weaknesses inherent in the data, at least 20 per cent of Irish emigrants arriving in central Canada in 1832 did so in family groupings. It is inconceivable that all Irish immigrant families required assistance, and consequently the Montreal Society's records indicate the very minimum proportion of the emigration that families constituted in that year.

RELIGIOUS COMPOSITION

Recent research has done much to document the specific denominational background of Irish immigrants – an issue of significance, given the social character of Ireland. However, much of the research effort has been concentrated on Irish communities in Atlantic Canada and almost invariably identifies Irishness and Catholicism. Certainly, the Irish of Newfoundland were Catholic. Mannion's studies have shown that the origin of the majority of Newfoundland's Catholic Irish was an area within a forty-mile radius of the port of Waterford. As such they were less than typical of the much larger numbers of Irish who settled in the mainland regions. Even the regional origins of the Halifax Irish were extremely confined in comparison with the overall pattern, and it is arguable that some Irish communities of the Atlantic region were somewhat unusual. But that could be claimed as well for the Presbyterian districts that McNutt had started in Nova Scotia. The apparent distinctiveness may well be simply the consequence of dealing singly with small Canadian regions that had only a few, perhaps only one, supply region and overlooking the composite of rather distinctive places that constituted a very different and more varied whole. In reality, the Irish immigration to Canada was as much a Protestant as a Catholic event. The forces of regionalism operating in both Ireland and British North America conspired to create a complexly varied geography of new Irish communities in British North America, and the model of Catholic Irish settlement in Atlantic Canada, like the American model

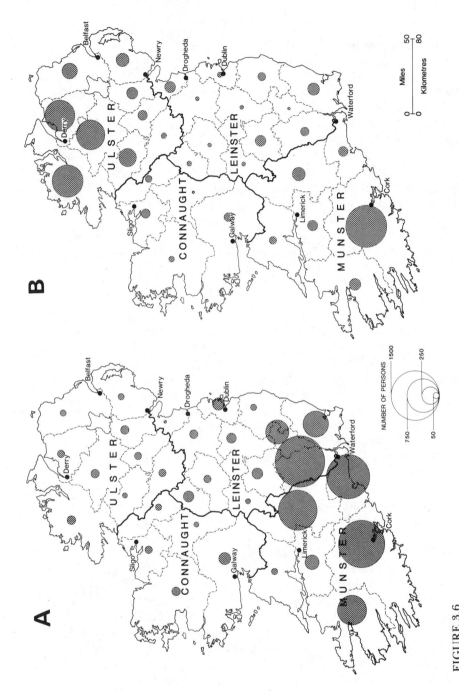

FIGURE 3.6
County origins of immigrant Irish Catholics: (A) those who died in Halifax, 1825–1903, based on data from Terence Punch; (B) those resident in New Brunswick, 1851, as determined by Peter Toner

of the Irish,[44] does not explain the religious pattern of Irish immigration to Canada.

The Catholic Irish of Halifax, so meticulously recorded by Terence Punch,[45] afford a prime example of a community drawn from a limited regional source in Ireland and also help to underline the problems inherent in extrapolating from the local to the larger Canadian situation. Punch's study shows that the majority of the Halifax Irish originated from southeastern Ireland. He employed burial and marriage records to determine the number who had come from each county, and his findings are presented in mapped form in Figure 3.6. Every county in Ireland had contributed some people to Halifax, but the extreme south provided an inordinate share, the small numbers from central and northern counties being glaringly evident. Punch's conclusions were that 'it is possible to make a generalization that south Kilkenny, Waterford, south Tipperary and east Cork – adjacent areas in a band about 75 miles east to west and thirty miles north to south – were the major sources of the Irish in Halifax.'[46]

The Halifax pattern would not fit Irish Catholics outside Halifax. For Newfoundland, source regions were even more restricted. The central and northern Irish counties were even less represented, and Cork's role was also less significant, with Waterford, Wexford, south Tipperary, and Kilkenny being the only major sources of Irish Newfoundlanders. In Saint John, the Halifax pattern also did not apply, as the counties of Londonderry, Donegal, Fermanagh, Cork, and Limerick were primary suppliers of Catholic emigrants. These counties, except Cork, are not important in Halifax's case (Figure 3.6). The researches of Peter Toner for New Brunswick have shown that clearly, and they are summarized also in Figure 3.6.[47] The contrast between source regions of the Catholic Irish immigrants of New Brunswick, focused on the northern and southern extremes of Ireland, and those of Halifax is obvious and cautions against generalizing for Canada from local regional circumstances.

Toronto was strikingly different from the Atlantic Canadian examples, in that the regional origins of its Irish Catholic community were more heterogeneous. Figure 3.7 summarizes the origins of Irish Catholic immigrants married in Toronto during the 1850s. It is based on information from Brian Clarke's study of Catholic voluntary associations in Toronto.[48] The map exposes a wide constituency, with every county in Ireland except Louth being represented. Given the period involved, 1850–9, the pattern illustrates the sources of supply of those migrating around the time of the Famine. It reflects a wide set of supply sources

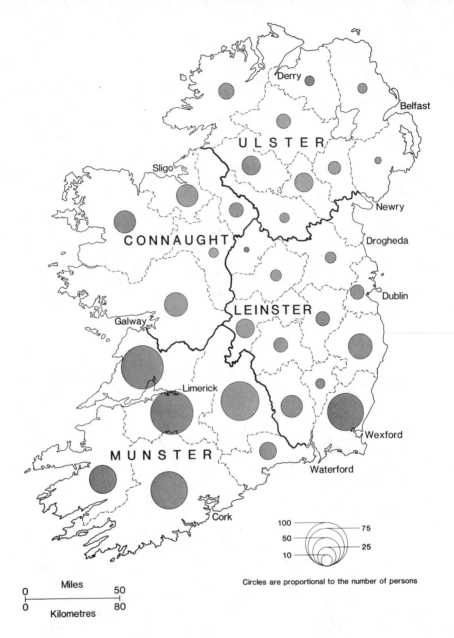

FIGURE 3.7
County origins of Irish Catholic immigrants married in Toronto during the 1850s; based on data from Brian Clarke, 'Piety, Nationalism and Fraternity: The Rise of Irish Catholic Voluntary Organizations,' PhD thesis, University of Chicago, 1986

for immigration into central Canada. The southern areas were the main sources of immigrants, but that emphasis was much less extreme than in Halifax. The Halifax and Newfoundland examples portray a narrower regionalism. The Toronto case was also less geographically emphatic than that for New Brunswick. Furthermore, the counties identified by Punch as responsible for virtually all the Halifax community provided less than a quarter of the Irish Catholics in mid-nineteenth-century Toronto. Each Canadian region had its own distinctive set of Irish source regions, and none constitutes a Canadian model.

Less than half of the Irish in Canada in 1871 were Catholic, even though Catholics constituted slightly more than three-quarters[49] of Ireland's population at that time. The situation in Canada differed markedly from that in the United States, where a very large majority of nineteenth-century Irish immigrants were Catholic.

In part the distinction reflects the difference in timing of the two migrations. Emigrants bound for British North America were associated primarily with the pre-Famine decades, and the first ones were more likely to belong to a Protestant class better able to migrate than the mass of the Irish population. Pre-eminent source areas included the religiously mixed province of Ulster and the scattered Protestant districts in southern Irish counties. While Ulster provided the bulk of these Protestant emigrants, it was not, contrary to popular belief, the sole supplier. Southern Protestant communities not only offered a significant mass of emigrants but also contributed a large component of Irish leadership in the colonies. Popular leaders such as Baldwin and Hincks had come from Cork, and the early organizing effort behind Canadian Orangeism was provided by Thomas Hopper, from among Talbot's Tipperary emigrants and, more significant, by Ogle R. Gowan from Wexford. There were also the Protestant weavers of County Cork and the Protestant élite of Trinity College. The stereotypical image of northern sources for Protestants, and its mirror image of southern sources for Catholics, must be dismissed in order to comprehend the full diversity of the Irish emigration to Canada.

The denominational characteristics of emigrants to Canada were well known to contemporaries. In 1826, A.C. Buchanan informed a British Select Committee investigating emigration: 'You can almost tell, from the counties they come from, what persuasion they belong to.'[50] Of the 30,000 emigrants who had sailed from Derry to Canada in the previous ten years, the majority were Protestants: 'The Catholic peasantry of the

TABLE 3.7
Denominational characteristics of County Londonderry emigrants, 1833–5

	Percentage of whole population	Percentage of all emigrants	Percentage of emigrants to			
			Quebec	Saint John	New York	Philadelphia
Presbyterian	46	61.7	59.9	60.5	46.9	74.6
Catholic	39	28.8	25.2	30.0	44.1	20.6
Anglican	15	10.5	13.9	9.5	9.0	4.8
All	100.0	100.0	100.0	100.0	100.0	100.0
N		(1774)	(817)	(210)	(374)	(373)

SOURCES: Emigrant data from Ordnance Survey of Ireland, Memoirs, County Londonderry (Royal Irish Academy); denominational data from J.H. Johnson, 'Population Movements in County Derry,' *Proceedings of the Royal Irish Academy* (Sec C), LX (1959–60), 141–62

north of Ireland have not the means to emigrate. I should suppose that three-fourth were Protestants and Dissenters, and about one-fourth Catholic.'[51]

Data collected by the Irish Ordnance Survey in County Londonderry in the early 1830s indicate that among those who emigrated, Protestants were the larger proportion by far. Summaries of these data are given in Table 3.7. Catholics in the outflow from County Londonderry at the time represented almost 30 per cent. Presbyterians were the largest component, and the Anglican group was small. Relative to the denominational character of the county's population, the Presbyterians were apparently overrepresented; Catholics and Anglicans were underrepresented.

The denominational composition of the outflow was further refined by choice of destination. In comparison with the average outflow, Quebec attracted fewer Catholics and more Anglicans. Saint John most closely approximated the average condition. The American ports exhibited greater deviation from the expected. For Philadelphia, Presbyterians were overrepresented; for New York, Catholics were disproportionately in excess. These patterns suggest a selectivity in the migration process, the explanation of which is quite beyond the scope of this study. The peculiar denominational characteristics of ports' hinterlands and the selective pull of North American destinations on migrants make it difficult to generalize about the detailed denominational composition of the Irish emigration to Canada. We are certain, however, that, unlike in the American case, the relative weight of Protestants was great.

Given the Protestant character of the early outflow, it was scarcely surprising that James Humphrey from Moneymore in County Londonderry should report the July 12th parade that the emigrants had held on board his ship in mid-Atlantic in 1824: 'On the 12th of July there were twenty six Orangemen dressed themselves and walked three times around the deck and gave three cheers for old Ireland and went and bought four gallons of rum and parted in peace.'[52] That simple event and the proliferation of Orange lodges in British North America from the time of the earliest Irish arrivals testified to the weight of Protestantism among the migrants, especially in New Brunswick and Upper Canada, where they were actively creating new Irelands, loyal and defensive.

During the 1830s and 1840s the proportions of Catholics among Irish emigrants to British North America rose as the hinterlands of recruitment expanded beyond the initial cores to embrace eventually, at the time of the Famine, all of Ireland. The increased numbers sailing from more southern and western ports helped to alter the religious balance among the immigrants. Despite this, however, the proportion of Catholics did not overwhelm established patterns. In Upper Canada, the great tide of Famine immigration failed to change that colony's Protestant base or upset the character of the Irish settlement there. The proportion of Catholics in the Upper Canadian Irish population remained virtually static between 1842 and 1871,[53] indicating that greater-than-average out-migration among the Catholics to the United States had diminished a potent force for change in the religious structure of the colony. The rapid through-migration of Famine Catholic arrivals reduced the possibility of the emergence of a self-perpetuating mechanism that would have encouraged further large-scale emigration of their co-religionists. However, in Saint John, Quebec City, Montreal, and Toronto, Catholic immigrants from the Famine period did significantly augment Catholic Irish communities. Earlier Irish Catholic communities in Nova Scotia, Prince Edward Island, Newfoundland, and the Miramichi area of New Brunswick were largely avoided in the Famine emigration. The development capacity of those regions and their ability to absorb immigrants had been already exhausted. There, Catholic communities, like the Protestant ones elsewhere, remained as the consequences of a pre-Famine movement.

Post-Famine emigration tended to preserve and even refine the geographical and religious attributes of the early-nineteenth century migrations. Only Montreal and the cities of Upper Canada – a limited field – could absorb large numbers of immigrants. Compared to the immigrant potential of the United States, British North America in the 1850s and 1860s had little appeal. There was no opportunity for absorbing a mass influx comparable to that which characterized the pre-Famine period. Given, too, that emigration was conservative and that continuity in the movement was maintained by ongoing kinship links, the likelihood of a major Catholic influx was negligible, because in Upper Canada two-thirds of the Irish population was already Protestant. Further immigration would follow established patterns. In addition, the Protestant image of Upper Canada, built through generations of Loyalist, British, Scots, and especially Protestant Irish emigration, offered little appeal to an Irish exodus, now largely Catholic.

In the last third of the nineteenth century, Canadian officials, at levels ranging from the prime minister down to emigration agents, all tried, mostly in vain, to broaden the appeal of the country to Catholic Irish. Indeed, the demise of Irish Catholic emigration was welcomed by some members of the Canadian Catholic hierarchy. Bishop Lynch of Toronto circulated in 1864 a printed letter to each of the four archbishops of Ireland enumerating the problems and moral delinquencies that were the lot of unfortunate Irish migrants in large cities in Canada and the United States.[54] 'In visiting the [Toronto] jail, a few days ago, we found that two-thirds of the bad women confined there were Catholic,'[55] he reported, and he argued that no more helpless emigrants should be thrown into the same situation, for 'the Irish come without leaders, entirely defenceless and the majority impoverished. They find before them the Protestant religion and infidelity in the ascendant. No wonder, therefore, that a vast number of the youth have been absorbed into the pores of this society, through the medium of mixed marriages, common schools, living with Protestant employers, the great scarcity of priests to attend their spiritual wants and the innumerable associations with the Protestant and infidel element of the country!'[56] Lynch's address was published in newspapers on both sides of the Atlantic and was probably instrumental in shaping the Irish hierarchy's subsequent policy of not overtly encouraging emigration.

Notwithstanding the displeasure of the hierarchy, the Irish continued to flee their homeland in the tens of thousands, but few made their way to Canada. Lynch's refusal to encourage Irish emigration extended to his opposition to attempts at diverting already committed emigrants from their chosen US destinations. He spurned in 1864 a request from an official in the Department of Crown Lands that he should support Irish settlement on the vacant lands of the Canadian Shield. Those lands were the same that William Hutton had promoted in the previous decade. Pragmatically, the Canadian government official had argued that the Irish could be enabled by the government to settle together on the frontier in Catholic communities, which would be morally superior to the Irish ghettos of the American cities.[57] The bishop declined to support such opportunism, refusing to lend his name to the project.

Lynch maintained his opposition to Catholic emigration, despite growing interest among the leading Irish-Catholic laity in Canada, who wished for a larger population of co-religionists from which they could draw political support. In 1873 Lynch declined an invitation from John O'Connor, a Canadian Irish Catholic politician, to lecture in Ireland on emigration. This refusal earned Lynch, by then an archbishop, a rebuke from another Catholic politician, Frank Smith, who observed in a letter to him: 'There is quite a number of our people who think some of our Clergy are not inclined to encourage emigration to this country because we are under the British Flag and that is one of the reasons we are loosing ground. Now if our clergy would only encourage emigration, it would benefit the Church as well as themselves. There is something wrong when we are loosing in population or at least we are not increasing. There were as many Catholics in Toronto fifteen years ago as there is now. If your grace would look into this you would see we are losing in proportion to others.'[58] The political motives of Smith and O'Connor were clearly at variance with the archbishop's concern for the welfare of his flock and his belief that urban life spelt moral ruin for the immigrant Irish. But even if Lynch had consented to support the two politicians' ambitions, he could have done little to alter the migration pattern. The momentum of the post-Famine movement continued to favour northeastern US cities.

The ongoing imbalance between emigration to Canada and that to the United States continued to concern the Canadian government, which was anxious to attract settlers to Manitoba and the new frontier of the North-West. In 1881 the prime minister, John A. Macdonald, communicated with Cardinal Manning in London, England, and with Archbishop Lynch, on the possibilities of Catholic settlement in the west.[59] Lynch's opposition to Irish emigration persisted, and in July 1881 he effectively blocked an agreed statement prepared by Archbishop Hannan of Halifax on behalf of the Canadian Catholic hierarchy. That draft statement read as follows: 'We the Prelates of the Catholic

Church in Canada having ourselves a knowledge of the Irish people and of their needs desire affectionately to draw their attention to the appended statement which shows in brief the resources of our Canadian land and the favourable position insured by its laws to the Catholic population. We do not desire to draw away from the Old Country one man or woman or child who may happily live there. On the other hand we do desire where men have themselves determined to seek another home beyond the seas they may be placed in possession of facts which may tend to widen the area of their choice.'[60] Lynch immediately rejected the proposed statement, and in his reply he emphasized the lack in Canada of any organization and funds capable of helping the immigrants: 'We are troubled every day with applications for help, emigrants as well as others in want of work or bread. People are leaving now for the States. Machinery displaces labourers even in the harvest fields. To encourage the poor Irish then to come to the towns and cities is to betray them and the disappointed emigrant will complain and charge us with all their disappointments. As a Prelate of the Church I would not like to undertake the task of being the cause of bringing emigrants without being able to present them with such advantages as the Catholic Colonization Societies of the United States, with the Bishops and very influential Catholic gentlemen at their heads.'[61] Lynch understood well the geographic reality of immigration to Canada in the early 1880s, and his archdiocese would have had to accommodate the immigrants. At that time none was arriving in Hannan's Halifax archdiocese, and the majority of those arriving in Canada were most likely to settle in Ontario in general, particularly in Toronto. Lynch feared the unfortunate consequences of further Irish emigration to his city.

Toronto was beginning to develop its industrial base, and migrants from rural Canada competed for jobs with immigrants. Industrial development, however, was too small to absorb the influx, and us cities drew off the surplus. Lynch comprehended that situation and was reluctant to exacerbate the condition of poor Catholic immigrants who would have gravitated eventually to the American cities. The attraction of the newly opened lands of the Canadian North-West had but a limited appeal in a society altering under the pressures of urban industrialization. Archbishop Lynch maintained his opposition to emigration until the closing years of his episcopacy, but in 1882 he finally succumbed to pressures from the prime minister and lent his support to a colonization scheme aimed at creating Catholic Irish farm communities on the western prairies.[62] Such plans, however, were never fulfilled.

The disproportionately small number of Catholic Irish coming to Canada was often linked to the opposition of Protestant Canada to Catholics. In 1873, the Ontario emigration agent in Dublin, C.J. Shiel, a Catholic, had written a confidential letter to a leading Catholic politician in Ontario, John O'Donohoe, seeking greater community co-operation for the encouragement of Irish Catholic immigration. Shiel referred to the Ontario government's recently announced plan to employ locally based immigration societies to attract suitable immigrants. The plan, Shiel conceded, was good in principle, but he feared that it would in practice continue to inhibit Catholic Irish immigration:

Who are to *compose* these Immigration Societies in different sections of Ontario? I answer, Englishmen, Scotchmen and Orangemen, – Every class but Irish Catholics, – unless Irish Catholics wake up and either join them or form similar societies composed of their own creed. From what I know of the sort of immigrant that arrived in Ontario during the past year or two, and from what I have learned since I came here, unless Irish Catholic employers of labor throughout Ontario take some interest in this immigration movement they will not receive a fellow countryman or Co-religionist under the auspices of these societies. Ontario is being filled up with Orangemen, from the North of Ireland, and why? simply because Charles Foy and Capt. Madden, the Dominion Government's agents, are working like beavers to get every man of their 'brethern' to go there and make a second Belfast of the whole province ...[63]

Shiel, as a Dublin-based agent, was an interested participant in the emigration process, frustrated with the poor local response to his recruitment efforts. He would have been extremely sensitive to the composition of the emigration flow. His identification of a lack of organization among Irish Catholics in Ontario was perceptive: the small community and its dispersed parts made links among Catholic settlements in Ontario and with Ireland much weaker than the more cohesive relations among their Protestant Irish countrymen. Catholic momentum propelling further emigration was correspondingly weaker.

The main thrust of emigration from Ireland was not to be influenced by the Catholic hierarchy, either in Ireland or in Canada. Momentum in the system, instigated by economic forces and further ordered by personal networks, was too great. Most emigrants continued on their way to the United States, and in the trickle settling in Canada after the 1850s, Protestants formed the larger proportion. The mass movements of emigrants to North America in the post-Famine era did not alter the basic demographic balances within Canada, for, by and large, those movements avoided the northern country. Redirection in the migration processes toward the United States at the time of the Famine had been fully consolidated.

CHAPTER FOUR

The Emigration Process

By 1900, millions of Irish had emigrated to Britain, its colonies, and the United States, leaving at home a society in which virtually every family had close relatives overseas. Few countries in the world have ever experienced such rapid, intensive, and long-lasting demographic upheaval. Notwithstanding this upheaval and the implicit social separations, the Irish emigrations were not a haphazard process. The decision to emigrate took place in a social circle of kin and neighbours. Destinations were carefully chosen on the basis of knowledge gathered through the successive migrational experiences of other kin and other neighbours, and those accumulated experiences were firmly entrenched in local lore. Districts of Ireland were reproduced in the New World as microgeographies of home, and the connections tended to be self-perpetuating and long-lasting.

The migration process revolved around an interactional system of information flows. Once initial links were established with a New World destination, by whatever means, a natural conduit for subsequent information flows was in place. Merchants and trading systems were often the founding link in the eventual chain. The garrisoning of soldiers abroad, their payment in kind by land grants, and official government settlement schemes could all constitute similar originating links. Laudatory reports of the attractions of the new areas were spread among contacts in Ireland, entered the folklore, and made familiar formerly unknown geographies. Letters home from pioneering emigrants, occasional newspaper reports, pamphlets, and lectures delivered by emigration agents all clarified and embellished these geographies. This diffusion of information combined with deteriorating social and economic conditions in early-nineteenth-century Ireland to generate an emigration fever. In the early stages of that fever, British North America was promoted as the optimum destination.

TRANSATLANTIC TRADE

Some colonies of British North America had been open for immigrants since the 1760s, but apart from small-scale movement from a few regions of the British Isles and larger influxes of Loyalists fleeing the new American Republic their potential for settlement had been barely tapped by the beginning of the nineteenth century. It was at that time that Britain, shut off from its Baltic supplies of timber and naval stores, turned to the North American colonies in search of replacement sources. The subsequent development of the transatlantic timber trade emerged to make necessary and facilitate mass transatlantic emigration. For the next forty years forest clearance was bound with agricultural settlement, and timber boats served dual functions as passenger vessels and cargo ships. Timber and emigrants were the inseparable commodities in the exchange between Britain and British North America. Irish merchants were heavily involved, as the ports of Belfast, Derry, and Cork were conjoined with those of Quebec City, as well as Newcastle, St Andrews, and Saint John in New Brunswick in this transatlantic movement. Another staple, codfish, provided the economic rationale for a similar set of linkages with Newfoundland and a comparable emigration process.

The significance of Irish trade in North American immigration has yet to be explored, with the notable exception of John Mannion's work on the role of Waterford in Newfoundland's provisions trade and fisheries.[1] To expand on that effort we have chosen to exemplify the functioning of the timber and emigrant trade between Ireland and the British colonies as demonstrated by the case of Derry. Derry's role in the emigrant trade was established in the eighteenth century. The Rev. Mr Vaughan Sampson, writing in his *Statistical Survey of the County of Londonderry* in 1802, noted how the American trade in goods, capital, and people formed part of Derry's history. He wrote: 'A considerable trade is also carried on with the northern states of America; flaxseed, tobacco, tar, white oak, plank, and staves, are among the articles of most general commerce. During the [food] scarcity of the late years, Indian meal was imported to a large amount, and was of the greatest service; wheat may be imported under regulations; wheaten flour is also imported. In return, we export partly money, partly linens, 3–4ths wide, unbleached, and of a low price; we also export the most valuable of all products, the human race. In former years, I have heard that this export rated at from four to five thousand annually, from the port of L. Derry.'[2]

In the early nineteenth century Derry's links with British North America were an accidental consequence of occasional landings in Nova Scotia of ships bound for New England and Pennsylvania. A formal connection with Canada was attempted in 1808: a ship intending to sail from Derry to Quebec City and Montreal had advertised for passengers, but there being too few interested in going to British North America, the vessel sailed for New York.[3] The attempt was premature. However, in the post-1815 disruptions and readjustments of the Irish economy to peacetime and through declining fares, the passenger trade was reinvigorated. Hesitant initially, and probably more dependent on timber and other goods than people, it quickly expanded, as agricultural exploitation overseas demanded pioneer lumbermen and farmers. There seems to have been no voyage from Derry to mainland British North America until 1817, when a ship from the port landed passengers in Shelburne, Nova Scotia,[4] but in that season shipping links were forged with Saint John. By the following spring, ships seeking passengers to New Brunswick were frequent at Derry's quays. The upsurge in the numbers of people wanting to leave was made possible by the reduction in fares but also occurred against the background of a local famine and economic disruption in the 'Dear Summer'[5] of 1817.

In 1818, at least eight ships from Derry were recorded as having arrived in Saint John with almost 1,600 passengers. Four arrived from Belfast and three from other ports. The records of those arrivals are reproduced in Table 4.1, and the distinct duality of westward-bound passengers and eastward-bound timber from the port of Saint John is well represented. All the ships went out with passengers; all went back with timber. The records indicate that while Derry was by far the most important port of origin for emigrants to Saint John that year – it sent 1,584 of the 1,864 passengers recorded – it was relatively unimportant as a market for timber. Only two of the eight ships from Derry to Saint John returned to that Irish port with timber. The other six returned with their cargoes to other destinations. The *Prompt* returned to Greenock, the *Draper* to Cork and Liverpool, and the *Sarah* went to a 'European' destination. The *Lord Whitworth* and the *Halifax Packet* (Figure 4.1) returned with their cargoes to Liverpool. Timber was being shipped

TABLE 4.1
Ships Calling at Saint John, 1818

Ship (in order of arrival)	Arrived from	Returned to
Prompt	Derry with 251 passengers	Greenock with timber
Thomas Henry	Derry with 335 passengers	Derry with timber
Integrity	Workington with 60 passengers	Limerick with timber
George	Belfast with 90 passengers	Greenock with timber
Lord Whitworth	Derry with 235 passengers	Liverpool with timber
Sarah	Derry with 156 passengers	Peticodiac for timber for Europe
Draper	Derry with 114 passengers	Cork and Liverpool with timber
Alexander	Derry with 150 passengers	Milford with timber
Neptune	Belfast with passengers	Waterford with timber
General Brock	Norway via Ireland with 186 Irish passenger	[not known]
Ganges	Belfast with 43 passengers	Aberdeen with timber
Martin	Belfast [cargo unknown]	Cork with timber
Jeffie	Drumfries with 70 passengers	Dumfries with timber
Bartley	Derry with 130 passengers	Derry with timber
Young Halliday	Dublin with 67 passengers	Liverpool with timber
Nile	Dumfries with passengers	Dumfries with timber
Halifax Packet	Derry with 213 passengers	Liverpool with timber

SOURCE: Extant issues of *City Gazette*

to a wide array of Irish and British ports, yet Derry was serving as the emigrant source. The trade was reciprocal in only the most general sense. While the resource economy of the timber staple interlinked the British and Irish ports with the overseas colonies, it was the unique rise of emigration in Ireland and its regional particularism that funnelled westward-bound ships through Derry more frequently than through any other port. Ships going out for timber provided the passage; conditions in Ireland provided the passengers.

The emigrants travelled in the steerage berths of cargo ships going out for loads of timber and thus helped finance the return leg of the voyage. As the volume of transatlantic shipping increased, there was subsequently greater demand and competition for passengers, prompting merchants to reduce the cost of passage. In 1816 a single passenger fare cost £16,[6] and these high costs confined emigration to the relatively well-to-do. By 1827 the fare had dropped to £4 for the Derry-to-Saint-John trip,[7] while the voyage to New York was £5.25.[8] The reduced fares had been prompted initially by pressure from Ulster shipping interests

First Ship.—*Now in Port*.

FOR HALIFAX AND SAINT JOHN'S,

New Brunswick,

THE FINE NEW SHIP

HALIFAX PACKET,

BURTHEN 500 TONS,

JOHN CLARK, Master,

To sail first of March.

For Freight or Passage apply to Mr. J. Buchanan, Omagh; Mr. Gerard Irvine, Strabane; or

ROBINSON & BUCHANAN.

Londonderry, 5th January, 1818.

N. B. The Ship ALEXANDER BUCHANAN,
Captain Clements, 500 Tons Burthen, will sail
hence for New York 10th April; for Freight or Passage, apply as above.

FIGURE 4.1

Advertisement, *Londonderry Journal*, 13 January, 1818. The *Alexander Buchanan* was lost in July 1818 off Cape Sable, Nova Scotia; the crew and passengers were saved. Courtesy Alan Roberts, Librarian, Magee University College, Derry

seeking advantages over American shippers.[9] Reduction of fares was also inevitable, given the larger number of small operators vying for custom. The Derry trade, until the mid-1830s, was dominated by small companies using sailing ships of less than 300 tons, able to make only one or two sailings a season.[10] In 1833 the port could boast of an Atlantic fleet of fifteen vessels belonging to seven owners,[11] although the trade was shortly afterward to be rationalized and confined to two main companies, McCorkell and Cooke.[12] Cheap passage and the easy availability of ships were sufficient to tap the emigrant outflow, which in turn was directed to sister ports across the Atlantic, where timber was available. Through the merchants and through the information that returning home crews passed on to local society, parts of the New World were made very familiar to parts of the Old.

The shipping of Derry passengers and British North American timber was only part of Derry's wide commercial operations with Britain, Europe, and, of course, the United States. Given the poor sailing conditions on the Atlantic during the winter and also the difficulty of settling emigrants abroad in the depths of that season, the emigrant trade was inserted into the context of a greater annual cycle of trade and transportation. Passengers were generally taken overseas in the spring and summer; timber was brought back in the summer or fall. Winter Atlantic weather was avoided. In winter, the ships plied the Irish, North, and Mediterranean seas before setting out again on the Atlantic journey in the spring.

Figure 4.2 displays how a Derry brig, the *President*, spent five years, 1828–32.[13] The ship, built in 1824, probably in Lower Canada, displaced 105 tons, and was wrecked off the Wicklow coast of Ireland in 1833. A third of her time 1828–32 was spent in port, loading, unloading, being repaired, and sitting out storms. The rest of her life was spent carrying cargoes – timber and passengers being the most important in terms of time spent on the seas. Passenger journeys to Saint John took up a great deal of the outbound journeys. However, more time was spent going with ballast to British and European destinations. The *President* had few exports to carry besides emigrants and some agricultural produce. Derry's hinterland supplied oats and potatoes to Liverpool, some linen went to Saint John with the passengers, and Derry merchants supplied their own salt and barrels for herring that they imported from the Orkney Islands fisheries. The *President* brought, in addition to the salt herring imports, timber from Saint John and Norway; barilla soda and fruit, probably oranges, from Spain; flax-seed from the Netherlands;

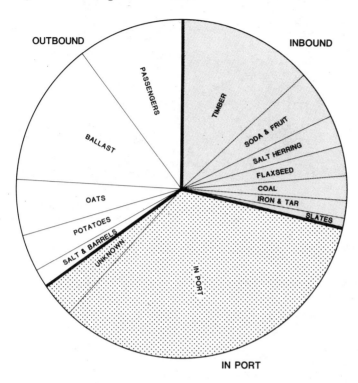

OUTBOUND

INBOUND

PASSENGERS

BALLAST

TIMBER

SODA & FRUIT

SALT HERRING

FLAXSEED

COAL

IRON & TAR

SLATES

OATS

POTATOES

SALT & BARRELS

UNKNOWN

IN PORT

IN PORT

FIGURE 4.2
Time budget of the Derry brig *President*, 1828–32

coal and slates from Britain; and iron and tar from Sweden. Expansion of the linen industry demanded seed, and the barilla was needed for bleaching. Building materials helped the city and surrounding towns cope with a boom in construction spurred by rapid urban development. Between 1820 and 1830, Derry's population doubled to 20,000 and nearby tributary towns were similarly affected. Emigration and local development were coincidental processes conjoined through the trade undertaken by such ships as the *President*.

The recruitment of emigrants for British North America was not left completely to chance. From the onset of emigration, Derry shippers had networks of agents, often shopkeepers, abetting the process. They continued a tradition begun in the early eighteenth century and well exemplified in the network employed by Alexander McNutt in his efforts

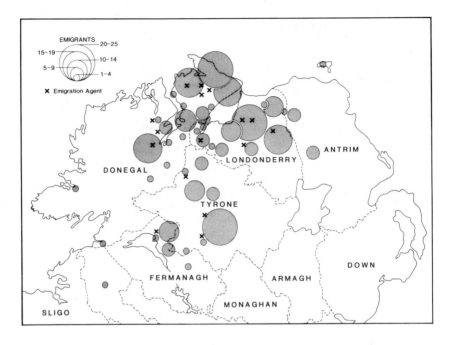

FIGURE 4.3
Origins of the passengers and locations of the agents for J. and J. Cooke's
vessel *Lord Maidstone*, bound from Derry to Saint John, March 1848

to promote Nova Scotian settlement in 1761. Local merchants, on a
commission basis, sold passages and touted emigration. The Derry network was extensive in Ulster west of the River Bann and extended
southward through the Foyle Valley of Tyrone and Donegal and
well into County Fermanagh. That geography is illustrated in Figure
4.3,[14] which maps the locations of the ticket agents and the passengers
on the *Lord Maidstone*, which left Derry for Saint John on 23 March
1848.

Passengers were drawn from within the network of agents that the
Derry owner, J. and J. Cooke, operated in major market towns up to
fifty miles from the port. Agents provided information on sailings and
kept ticket-holders informed of dates of departure while at the same
time keeping shipowners aware of the mood for emigration. They could
also arrange for transfer of the intending emigrants to the port of

embarkation, and in some cases they might even accompany the passengers to the port and see them well on board. Joseph Carrothers described how his family was helped from his home to his ship in 1847: 'With respect to our Enniskillen agent, Mr. Primrose, he has done everything agreeable to our wishes and we will be benefited by his coming to Derry with us ... Mr. Baird came with me from his office and took me through the ship and recommended a berth to me and sisters family Capt. Hancock his Agent spoke to him to do something for me as I was a decent man this was uncilicited he is a very nice man and treated me very kindly.'[15]

The emigrants were just as likely to find the same company's agents on the other side of the Atlantic. There, the shipping firm's representatives who gathered the timber and arranged the cargo contracts had the knowledge of local conditions that emigrants needed on arrival to get work, housing, and transportation inland. The merchant's North American agent knew where the timber was being felled and what districts offered not only work but land, and it was he who had the commercial responsibility to ensure that an immigrant's arrival in British North America would mean subsequent emigrant departures from Ireland. He communicated news of their safe arrival to his employers and ultimately to the emigrants' relatives in Ireland. Writing in 1839 to his agent in Saint John, the Derry shipper J. Cooke requested: 'As soon as you receive this letter send me a few lines advising me of the arrival of the vessel and what news you have by the very first ship for this country as the friends of the passengers are anxious to hear of their arrival out.'[16] Cooke was also anxious that the next season's vessels be filled with friends of those safely abroad. The complementarity of the timber and passenger trade was firmly established, and each successful voyage ensured another subsequently.

Derry's involvement with the British colonies included much more than mere shipping interests. The activities of a local family, the Buchanans, brought imperial politics and loyalist motives to bear on the trade and helped direct emigrants into the Canadian realm. Several members of that landed merchant family were intimately engaged in the trade and in transatlantic affairs. Their operations included establishments on both sides of the Atlantic and combined timber, grain for both milling and brewing, and, of course, passengers. In 1817 the shipping company of Buchanan and Robinson had been among the first to trade with Saint John, and its associates included the Gaults of Strabane,[17] probably the same family from which immigrant sons would eventually go on to found the Sun Life Insurance Co. of Montreal. Family members also served as Irish agents of the Canada Co.,[18] which owned huge tracts of land in Upper Canada and offered them for sale abroad. Beginning in 1822, and later in conjunction with the Canada Co., William Buchanan and Co. operated chartered ships regularly on the Derry-to-Quebec route.[19] The trading business involved their cousin A.C. Buchanan's milling interests in Lower Canada and was augmented by the American activities of his brother James Buchanan, who from 1816, as British consul in New York, had been recruiting settlers for Upper Canada from among loyalist groups and recent immigrants.

An example of James Buchanan's influence on the emigration process is given by the case of a Lisburn emigrant, James Stephens, whose reminiscences record how the consul convinced Stephens's father in New York to go to Upper Canada instead of Ohio. Stephens wrote: '[My father] was offered an Agency by a Company who owned large tracts of Land in Ohio ... He was on the eve of accepting it. (Pity he did not) Mr. Buchanan the new appointed British Counsul for New York. They knew each other in Ireland. Allso a Baptist advised my Father to go to Canada ... [Mr. Buchanan] spoke glowingly of the country and urged upon my Father to make Canada his ultimatum. [He] intimated that Canada was allmost a second Canane ... This decided my Father. The Die was cast. Ho for Canada was now the Watch Word. [Subsequently, in Montreal, Buchanan] introduced [Father] to Peter McCutner afterward the Hon Peter McGill and to the President of the Montreal [Bank]'.[20]

Buchanan was indeed well connected, and given that Stephens was one of thousands directed north, the effort devoted to promoting the British colonies was formidable and potentially formative. In 1817 he had convinced the Molson family of Montreal to provide better terms for immigrants travelling inland. The *Londonderry Journal* printed the following report from the *Montreal Herald*: 'We are truly gratified to learn, that Mssrs John Molson and sons proprietors of the first Steam Boats used in the St. Lawrence, have, upon the application of his Majesty's Consul for New York, liberally agreed to afford accommodation to such settlers as may in future arrive at Quebec, transport on the most easy terms to Montreal, with a view to proceed to Upper Canada. We understand that each settler will be allowed to take nearly 200 lbs. baggage, instead of only 60 lbs. allowed to travellers: and that the whole expense for each grown settler will be 30s from Quebec to Kingston, and 1s 3d more to York [Toronto]; children half price.'[21]

By such arrangements and persuasion Buchanan influenced the Irish emigration to Canada and helped channel a select group to the British colonies. He knew the Montreal merchants. One of the emigrants he convinced to leave New York and go instead to Toronto was William McMaster, who, like Leslie Gault, was a merchant from Strabane, just up the River Foyle from Derry. McMaster arrived in 1833 and would eventually rise to prominence as a banker and founder of the Bank of Commerce and of McMaster University.[22] Buchanan was instrumental in many other such diversions, for his personal network was wide and his period in office was long. As Buchanan himself noted in a letter to the Irishman Lord Gosford, lieutenant-governor of Lower Canada, in 1838: 'Above twenty two years residence in my official capacity here, has made me intimately acquainted with all the leading men, having any share in the Government of both [Canadian] Provinces, and having sent vast numbers to settle in upper Canada, has led to much intercourse with the several Governors who have resided there both open and confidential.'[23] From 1816 to his death in 1843, Buchanan perceived part of his consular function to be that of Canadian immigration agent in New York.

The Buchanan connections were extended in Quebec and Montreal through James's brother, Alexander Carlisle, who emigrated from Derry in the mid-1820s. Alexander Carlisle Buchanan established himself as a sawyer and miller[24] outside Montreal and, because of his family knowledge and associations with the emigrant trade, assumed the role of an emigration specialist there. In 1827 he was appointed the emigration agent for the Colonial Office at Quebec City, to oversee the landing and through-passage of every immigrant arriving in the port. His nephew, a son of the consul in New York, and also named Alexander Carlisle, joined in the work, and when the elder retired in 1838, the nephew succeeded to the post.[25] James Buchanan noted how his personal connections provided the two Alexander Carlisles with the opportunities to be chief emigration agents. In a letter of thanks to Lord Gosford in 1828 he observed: 'We are truly grateful to Lord Glenelg for having nominated my son to succeed my Brother as Emigrant agent at Quebec. Your Lordship's kindness [in suggesting his name to Glenelg] is duly appreciated, by, my Lord, your faithful grateful and humble Servant.'[26] In the office of emigration agent, the younger Alexander Carlisle remained until his death in 1868. Throughout the main Irish phase of Canadian immigration, the Buchanan family was intimately involved in key positions, and the full extent of its influence on Canadian settlement can only be imagined.

As with most Irish ports, Derry was not linked to all parts of the New World, and accordingly emigration was confined to those destinations with which regular trade was maintained. Saint John and Quebec, the two principal timber ports, were the main destinations of Derry ships in the British colonies. Very few Derry ships plied the routes to the Miramichi or to Nova Scotia, and none went to Newfoundland. A few went to Prince Edward Island, in the Gulf of St Lawrence. Belfast's sister ports in British North America were basically the same as Derry's, although Belfast appears to have been more involved with Quebec, and Derry with Saint John. From Saint John, passengers often went on to St Andrews, as a first step to the United States, or northward through the Bay of Fundy toward Sackville or Windsor, Nova Scotia. Digby, across the Bay of Fundy from Saint John, offered another point for getting into Nova Scotia. Ships from the Cork region were linked to the same ports, but the southeastern harbours of Ireland, Waterford and Youghal, had a more geographically restricted set of contacts. They were engaged in trade with Newfoundland, Nova Scotia, and Quebec, and although voyages were undertaken occasionally to other harbours, most of the southeast's interest was directed, through fisheries and provisions, more than timber, to the Atlantic coastline and St Lawrence mouth. It was noted in chapter 2 how Dublin was not part of Saint John's network but was significant in the St Lawrence ports. Likewise, the west of Ireland was most closely linked with the Quebec City entry to Lower and Upper Canada. There was in the geography of Irish trade a set of constraints that funnelled emigrants from particular origins to particular destinations. That geography represented a bias that researchers are only now beginning to document, and its effect on the nature and extent of emigration from Irish regions remains to be understood.

EMIGRANT LETTERS AND REMITTANCES

While the merchant trade provided the opportunities and some information for willing emigrants, the most critical element directing people to the New World was to be found in the information and support system represented in letters home to relatives and friends. The emigrant letter was at once symbol and memorial of the process of emigration and causative force in that process. It served to convey knowledge about jobs, cost of produce, risks and expenses of settling, profits to be expected from farming, and countless other issues. Not infrequently, letters included passage money for the outward journey of a relative.

In 1847, Mary Duggan, a Catholic maid in the home of John A. Macdonald in Kingston, Upper Canada, wrote to her sister in Dungiven, County Londonderry: 'Dear Sister, I understand by your letter that you are willing to come to America if you had the means of coming. I send you in this letter four pounds sterling which is quite adequate to bring you to this country. I hope you will take care of it and lay it out to the best advantage ... You will find a check in this letter for four pounds sterling, go to any bank and they will give you four pounds for it.'[27]

Such letters facilitated emigration and created in the minds of family members remaining at home a distinctive, if personalized geography of British North America. They removed the mystery and alien character of the far-away place. Comments about familiar topics such as soil fertility, climate, crops, and animals bonded farming families on either side of the Atlantic. Information on social conditions was imparted and the emigrant's progress charted. The progress, too, of other friends and acquaintances who had emigrated was often communicated, and requests were made for similar information about those left behind.

From the earliest trickle of emigrants the chains linking Ireland and the colonies started being forged. When James Humphrey, his brother, and his brother-in-law arrived in Quebec City on 29 July 1824 with their families, they had before them already a known network of friends spread from Quebec City to Fort George at the western end of Lake Ontario. In a letter home, James noted thirteen of those whom they had met:

We stopped two days in Quebec. It has a black appearance. There are full fine stores in it. I saw John Egnew, he was very kind to us. I saw James McCana, he is very well and is going home. He and Edward McAnaway, they were very kind to us. We then took a steamboat to Montreal and stayed two days there. Mr. Richardson went to Benjamin Workman and left the letter for Robert Workman. He told us he was there about two weeks ago and that he would be back in about eight days and that they were well and doing well. We went and hired a wagon and went out nine miles to Lachine and there took a steamboat one hundred and fifty miles to Prescott. The first I saw was my sister Mary and she took us to her house and we stayed all night in her house and then we took the steamboat sixty miles to Kingston and we stopped there six days. You may let James Baylen know that I went out and saw George and he is well and he told us he would send his mother six pounds. Kingston is a good town and is very rich. Mr. Twig lives five miles out of the town and William and I were out and he has a beautiful place. You may let Mrs. Johnston know that her brother Will Cranis is well and has a full fine shop. We went and got a steamboat and sailed to Fort George and found John and Robert Gilmore there and they were all in good health when I saw them. It is a beautiful place, the Yankees are on one side and the British on the other and the sentries about eight perches apart. John Humphrey's Joseph is dead, he lived but two days after he landed at Fort George. The steamboat stopped about eight hours and then we went away to York. We landed on the 25th of August and went to John Richardson's place. He has 200 acres of good land and a house on it about two perches from the road. Two days after Margaret had a young daughter and it lived three weeks and I called it for my mother. I took a house three miles from their place and set up a tavern.[28]

Humphrey was writing in 1824, just as the mass emigration was getting under way, and yet could mention thirteen links in his own immigration network. They epitomized the early-established dynamic of the emigration process.

The existence of networks known in advance of emigration indicated the intensity of communication and the role of chains of migrants in the mass exodus. New emigrants followed in the wake of information sent home by the earlier leavers. In the House of Lords' Enquiry into the State of Ireland in 1825, the critical formative role of chain migration was recognized. At the inquiry, testimony about Protestant emigrants noted that 'there was a colony of the friends of the Protestants of Ireland, settled in America, and there was a constant coming of letters from their friends, inviting and encouraging them to emigrate. Almost every Protestant family in Ireland, has his friends before him in America; they consider it as merely going to visit their own relations.'[29]

Bruce Elliott's study of the emigration of 775 Protestant families from Tipperary between 1818 and 1855 has demonstrated clearly the intensity and significance of such chain migration.[30] The chains were formed of links created by family, neighbourhood, and religion and were sufficiently strong as to extend over the generations, across the Atlantic, and though North America. Through the genealogy of these families, Elliott has uncovered an elaborate emigration history, the value of which is unrivalled. The same pattern could have been claimed for the Catholics going to the Miramichi or to Prince Edward Island, and by the end of the Famine it could have been applied to every nook and cranny of Ireland.

Emigrant letters conveyed a surprisingly large amount of detail and often inadvertently displayed hidden feelings and emotions. As personal documents they carried great weight for their readers, and invitations to join the emigrants overseas would have been seriously considered. Letters were to be relied upon because there was no commercial profit at stake. Families' well-being and future prospects hinged on the emigrant's accurate evaluation of the potential of his New World home. Likewise, warnings to delay emigration, or to abandon hope of it altogether, would have been given serious consideration. The significance of such emigrant correspondence is emphasized in the case studies of chapters 8–10, below.

A remarkable feature of the personal correspondence was the frequency and duration of contact and thus the long-standing and ongoing possibility for retention and use of links created by the first migrant. The Carrothers, for example, maintained contact for thirty years with their brother in Fermanagh, and in the case of the Kirkpatrick family of Craigs, County Antrim, regular correspondence was maintained for more than half a century.[31] In other families the correspondence was limited and confined to times of crisis or petered out after a few years. However, all the correspondence ensured that the Canadian letter (often bearing a Liverpool postmark, having been brought across the Atlantic in the bulk mail of the Canada Co. or some other trading company) was a regular and recurrent feature of life in Ireland.

The longevity of this directional influence is hardly surprising. It was self-perpetuating, with each new emigrant reinforcing older existing bonds and simultaneously extending the networks. At another level, however, the survival of linkages was embodied in the long lives of many of the original pioneers. The second generation, although it often maintained some kind of nominal contact, rarely wrote to emigrant parents' home places. Although letters were a single-generational conduit of information, many settlers' lives were long, and Canada was a relatively young country. Even in 1900, Canada could count numerous 'pioneers' in its population. The Kirkpatrick family kept in contact with a surviving relative in County Antrim from 1815 to 1881, and links with the Erskine Mayne family of Belfast were maintained from 1841 to 1897[32] and those of the Carrothers family from 1839 to 1870. Contact through letters to parents was sometimes succeeded by contact with uncles and aunts and with brothers and sisters, and thus links could be maintained until the death of the emigrant correspondent.

Letters kept the bonds between friends intact and provided the most personal and immediate information system on which potential emigrants could depend. They encouraged and directed subsequent emigration, reinforced connections between places, and created a geography of movement that was to persist. In 1827, A.C. Buchanan, about to be appointed emigration agent in Quebec, reported to the British Government Enquiry into emigration that he could usually predict the level of emigration one year in advance: 'It depends upon the success that the emigrants met with in the preceding year; they write home letters and if the season has been favourable, if there has been any great demand for labour, like the Western Canal, that absorbs a great many of them, they send home flattering letters, and they send home money to assist in bringing out their friends.'[33] Letters could just as well have contained warnings to prevent emigration. Sampson Brady, writing home from Montreal in the cholera year of 1832, advised: 'Health is very bad here in general. The poor Irish at home thrive far better on potatoes and milk and stirabout than we do here on the best ... I would rather prefer the States to any part of Canada, being quite a superior country altogether.'[34] Similarly, in 1842, Capt. William Mitchell took the time to write his wife in Derry that his ship had arrived safely in Quebec: 'The times is very bad in this part, even worse than in Ireland. The labourers has only 2/6d per day currency.'[35] That wage was better than in Ireland, but less than half what Mitchell and other Irishmen expected on the Canadian side.

The effectiveness of the letters in conditioning the flow of emigration was well demonstrated in 1838. Rebellion had erupted the previous year in Lower and Upper Canada and, combined with severe economic depression in the United States, dampened for one season the outflow to North America (see Figure 2.3). From Derry, J. Cooke wrote in March 1838 to a fellow shipowner in Scotland that he would not be seeking additional chartered tonnage that season 'in consequence of the late disturbances in British America having rather frightened emigrants from going out this spring and what will be going will be later than usual.'[36] The episode clearly indicates the rapidity with which information flowed across the Atlantic and affected emigration decisions.

Emigrant remittances and prepaid passages consolidated the links between source areas of emigrants and destinations by paying the way for subsequent emigrants. Cooke's agent in Saint John collected from settlers monies which he remitted to the company's office on the Derry quays, and there passage vouchers were issued to named recipients who came forward to collect. Every Cooke ship to Saint John carried passengers under the remittance arrangement. It was only a small part of an extensive network of banking and other commercial relations designed to facilitate the flow of money from the colonies and the reciprocal flow of emigrants from Ireland.

Between 1843 and 1846 the Canada Co. forwarded from Upper Canada to Ireland almost 2,000 remittances (Figure 4.4), most of which were no larger than £4[37] – just sufficient to pay a passage. They were directed mainly to immediate family relations, and such aid could have permitted the reconstitution of families in British North America or the repayment of a passage debt. In 1839, Nathaniel Carrothers, living in London, Upper Canada, surrounded by his brothers and cousins, invited his mother-in-law, Mrs. Kirkpatrick, of Lisbellaw, County Fermanagh, to join the family: 'I take this opportunity of letting you know that I sent you the sum of £11. this money we gave to a merchant that was going to Newyork to get a check on the bank of Ireland ... hoping that you have received it; and thinkes well of coming out to this country in the spring by quebeck is the cheapest way it cost Eliza £6 to come to London ... you have acquantance in nearley all the towns you pass trough in Canada who will give you free quarters for anight and when you come to Toronto there you will have Mr Rutledge.'[38] Once landed, Mrs Kirkpatrick would have felt right at home, and her experience would have been quite like that of a great many migrants, dependent on remittances from friends and supported by networks created by those who had emigrated before.

EMIGRATION PROMOTION

In the early nineteenth century, travellers provided an important source of information about the new lands in North America. Their descriptions frequently romanticized the far-away place and conveyed images of excitement and adventure. Niagara Falls was known widely for its spectacular nature. Indians, wolves, and bears were added to the lore. Among the earliest influences on the popular imagination was the Irishman Thomas Moore's romantic ballad, *The Canadian Boat Song*.[39] Recited and sung in the parlours of Dublin and throughout the British Isles, it became synonymous with Canada. With its images of river rapids, oars keeping time, and the 'Uttawa tide,' however, it hardly represented a settler's dream. Other travellers journeyed through the wilds and recorded more prosaic impressions of vegetation, soil quality, climatic conditions, and economic prospects. Their pamphlets and lecture tours

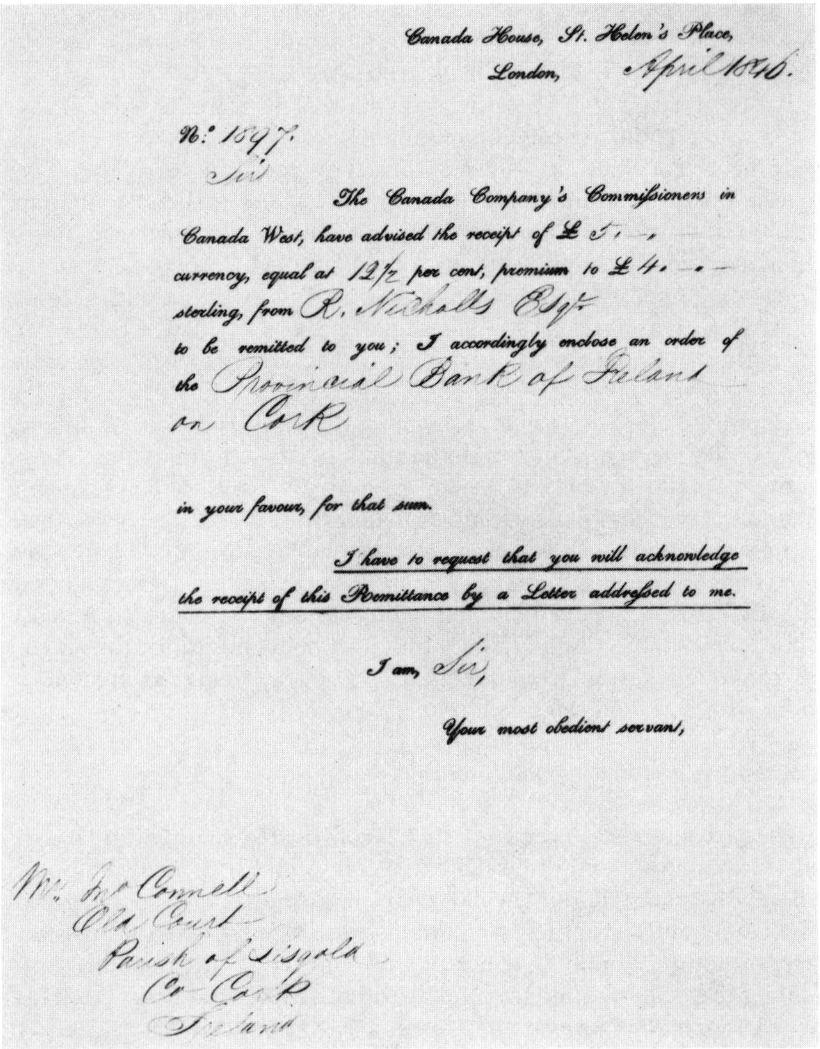

Canada House, St. Helen's Place,
London, April 1846.

No. 1897.

Sir

The Canada Company's Commissioners in Canada West, have advised the receipt of £ 5. – currency, equal at 12½ per cent, premium to £ 4. – sterling, from R. Nicholls Esqr.

to be remitted to you; I accordingly enclose an order of the Provincial Bank of Ireland on Cork

in your favour, for that sum.

I have to request that you will acknowledge the receipt of this Remittance by a Letter addressed to me.

I am, Sir,

Your most obedient servant,

Mr. Jno Connell
Old Court
Parish of Lisgold
Co Cork
Ireland

FIGURE 4.4
Copy of a remittance document used by the Canada Co. in the 1840s. The remittance was sent by R. Nicholls, an agent of the company, on behalf of an unnamed immigrant in Upper Canada, to a Mr Connell in the parish of Lisgold, County Cork, April 1846. Archives of Ontario

in Ireland and Britain popularized both the notion of emigration and the image of opportunity in the British colonies, thus contributing to the emigration fever that eventually erupted.

Professional agents and governments augmented those beginnings. Their promotional techniques included pamphlets, public lectures, and newspaper advertisements. Subsidized passages and free grants of land were also used as inducements. James Buchanan's travel assistance was an example of private initiative being combined with official function. Alexander McNutt's schemes, while needing state approval, were motivated by entrepreneurial opportunism more than imperial design. The only full-scale colonization schemes that the British government funded were Peter Robinson's settlements in Upper Canada. Free grants represented a way of moulding emigration, but they were ended in the mid-1820s. They had instigated regional cores of settlement, but the policy ended too soon to allow the mass of immigrants to benefit from it. At least a fifth of the Irish who settled in New Brunswick arrived before the end of the free grants in that colony.[40] It is hard to say what the comparable proportion might be for Lower and Upper Canada, but the pioneer nucleus of most Irish districts there at mid-century included settlers who received free grants. By the mid-1820s and in the 1830s and 1840s there seemed to be no end to the number of people willing to emigrate, and consequently inducements were not needed. Governments let the markets in land and labour decide who would get access to the country.

Private land-colonization companies and their agents were also a significant part of the emigration promotion. For such companies, rapid settlement of vacant lands was a priority, and they needed agents on both sides of the Atlantic to spread information about the advantages of their land and also seek emigrants willing to take the risk of buying some. These companies, through their control of large territories, helped create distinctive micro-geographies of settlement. The Canada Co.'s operations for Upper Canada, for example, included sales and information agencies in Dublin and Derry and a bureau for remittances that served as a conduit to potential emigrants.

In Lower Canada the British American Land Co. performed a role analogous to that of the Canada Co. (Figure 4.5), and through its company structures and promotional activities it created for itself an important niche in the emigration process. Formed in 1833 in London, the company had obtained rights to 300,000 acres in the Eastern Townships, fifty miles south of Quebec City. The company's first schemes

EMIGRATION TO CANADA.

THE BRITISH AMERICAN LAND COMPANY, incorporated by Royal Charter and Act of Parliament, have
for sale One Million Acres of Land, in Farms of 100 Acres and
upwards, situated in the healthy and fertile Eastern Townships
of Lower Canada, distant from 50 to 100 miles from Montreal,
Three Rivers, and Quebec. Prices from Four Shillings to Ten
Shillings currency per Acre, payable one-fifth cash down on
the higher priced lots, one-fourth on the lower priced lots, and
the balance in six annual instalments bearing interest. Money
remitted to Canada through the Company's Office, in London,
on favourable terms.

For Prospectuses, with particulars, (gratis) application may
be made to WILLIAM M'CORKELL & Co., Londonderry, who
will also furnish information as to Passenger Ships, or to the
Subscriber, at the Company's Office, No. 4, Barge Yard,
Bucklersbury, London.

JOHN REID, CLERK.

March 4, 1835.

FIGURE 4.5
An advertisement in the *Belfast Newsletter* (1835) promoting land of the
British American Land Co. in the Eastern Townships of Lower Canada

included a plan to settle poor English families[41] in Bury township, in
the hope that the newcomers' success would entice others with more
capital to follow in search of land. In Bury, the company built some
houses and at a number of crossroads erected churches[42] as nodes for
new communities and to give a sense of development progress. However, it could not get settlers to follow in the wake of the initial wave
of pioneers. Many of the first comers, in despair at their primitive
circumstances, simply wandered off.[43] In Victoriaville, only one person
remained in 1838 out of an original three hundred[44] – hardly the

endorsement the land company needed. Nonetheless, efforts in the British Isles and North America to promote the land continued, and some emigrants did venture into the territories.

In the 1840s the company's speculative interests aligned with those of railway developers. The railroads needed immigrants as paying passengers and, especially, as labourers and pioneers to encourage development of industrial centres and farming districts along their routes. In their turn, land companies needed the railways to stimulate the industrial and urban development that might give the promise of appreciation in land values and the possibility of access to urban markets for the pioneers' produce. Together, their futures were bound.

The St. Lawrence and Atlantic Railway was the primary venture involving the British American Land Co. and its territory (Figure 4.6). The stimulus for that railway project had been generated in the American port of Portland, Maine.[45] Merchants there had encouraged the idea of extending a railway northward into the Eastern Townships in an effort to capture a commercial hinterland. In the Eastern Townships, the citizens of the principal town of Sherbrooke, with eyes on their own futures and year-round access to both American and overseas markets through Portland's ice-free port, added their support. Among these citizens were the British American Land Co. representatives, Sherbrooke being the centre of the company's operations. To complicate matters, a group of Montreal developers and speculators, fearful of Portland's separating Sherbrooke from Montreal's market area, entered the discussions. A plan was proposed to link Lower Canada and the Atlantic seaboard by a railway passing through Sherbrooke and the lands of the British American Land Co. In 1845 the land company 'voted £20,000 to promote the development of the railway. One of the railroad depots was to be within ten miles of the land Company's estates of nearly 100,000 acres, all of which was for sale.'[46] The decision had been easy to make, the directorate of both companies being largely one and the same group of London-based financiers.

Another piece was added to the corporate arrangement in the late 1850s. At the time, the Allan brothers in Montreal had secured the contract for shipment of mail between Britain and Canada.[47] Steamships of the Allans Montreal Ocean Steamship Line sailed weekly with mail and immigrants from Liverpool via Derry, to Montreal in the ice-free period, and to Portland, Maine, during the winter. From Portland, the mail, goods, and immigrant passengers were forwarded to Montreal on the St Lawrence and Atlantic Railroad. The railway, the Allans, and the

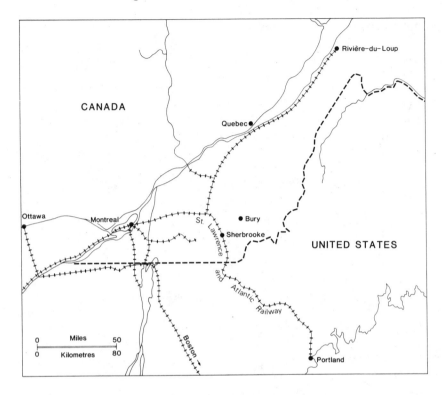

FIGURE 4.6
British American Land Co. connections, 1860

British American Land Co. reinforced each others' interests. Steam, rail, and ship transportation lashed together settlement and immigration in an economic combine that structured the geography of transatlantic migration in the way the timber sailing ships had done before. Together, they depended on the promotion of emigration and a continuing flow of emigrants.

In an effort to promote its lands and recruit immigrants, the land company, in 1859, appointed John Cummins as its agent in Britain and Ireland. Cummins, the son of a respectable Cork mercantile family and formerly land agent to Lord Mountcashel in both Ireland and Canada, actively employed his social connections to further the recruitment drive. A set of his business correspondence that survives in the Public

Archives of Canada demonstrates clearly the planned strategy of recruitment that he pursued over a year and a quarter and illuminates this major element in the process of emigration and colonization.

Cummins's strategy was direct and multifaceted: 'My first action should be through the medium of the press, to point out the many and great advantages which the Company's territory offers to emigrants and to invite those contemplating to become such, to meet me at the Cork or Queenstown offices of my Cousins.'[48] From Cork, Cummins planned to travel to the other Irish ports associated with the passenger trade to Canada – Limerick, Galway, Donegal, Sligo, Belfast, and Dublin – but he centered his activities on the hinterland of Derry. There he was able to employ to maximum advantage both his personal standing and his knowledge of the local land-holding system. County Londonderry, from the early seventeenth century, had been subdivided into a series of large estates owned by London guilds and administered by local agents. Cummins systematically contacted the administrators of the estates of the Ironmongers, Grocers, Skinners, Salters, Fishmongers, Mercers, Drapers, and Clothworkers, ascertaining the length of term remaining on the leases of tenant farmers and obtaining approval from the companies for his recruitment drive. He hoped to entice tenants whose leases were about to end, but he found few. For example: 'Mr. Barnes the agent of the Mercers considered that their estate had not a man to spare but promised all the influence which he could exert in the event of their people leaving to determine them towards the Eastern Townships in lieu of the United States.'[49] Cummins next visited Templemoyle Model Agricultural School at Eglinton (Figure 4.7), near Derry, where he sought emigrants from among the students, 'being anxious to induce well trained farmers to settle on the lands of the British American Land Company.'[50] In addressing the school he carefully stressed the suitability of the new land for growing crops familiar to his audience: 'Every cereal known either in Ireland or in any part of America, flourishes in the Eastern Township [and] aftergrass in our Townships affords as good pasture as in Ireland.'[51] By such means did Cummins seek to stir interest among and reassure his potential recruits. Unfortunately for him, the era of mass Irish emigration to Canada had ended by 1859, and much of his effort was in vain.

In response to the dwindling number of new settlers, the Canadian government also became directly involved in recruitment. The entrepreneurial efforts of private companies and the activities of government agents, who hitherto had merely facilitated emigration flows, were now

FIGURE 4.7
Templemoyle Agricultural School – a pioneer in practical agricultural
science – and farm nestle in a glen above Lough Foyle in County
Londonderry. Its work was reported in Canadian newspapers of the 1850s;
John Cummins sought emigrants there in 1860. Photo by authors

replaced by government bureaux, replete with large budgets and networks of agents based in Europe. Free grants and subsidized passages
slowly reappeared as inducements to settle the remaining marginal land
in Upper Canada. In the 1850s William Hutton was involved in efforts
to extend settlement northward by opening roads to unsettled districts
in Upper Canada and offer free grants along their fronts. Usually,
however, such land was taken by wily locals interested in the timber,
and the emigrants who came after had to pay dearly for partially cleared
properties.

When the Canadian Confederation was created in 1867, there began a
period of intense emigration promotion, partly because of the perceived
shortage of immigrants but partly also because of the need in the new
political arrangements to work out the limits of provincial and national

jurisdiction. In 1869 the government of Ontario authorized $10,000 for the production of a forty-page pamphlet outlining the 'Free Grant and Homestead Act' and containing a map showing the free-grant townships and colonization roads.[52] Thirty thousand copies were published and distributed, mainly in Britain, and almost immediately second and third editions were produced in print runs of 20,000 and 50,000. Ten thousand copies of a poster in English and 2,000 in German were also distributed to further support the drive for immigrants. Ontario also appointed a 'special commissioner of emigration' to represent the province in the British Isles. In 1870 the federal government went one better, appointing Charles Foy and J.G. Moylan to emigration offices in Belfast and Dublin, respectively. Three years later the Ontario government assigned two agents to Ireland: C.J. Shiel for the south, and John McMillan for the north. This federal and provincial duplication of effort was terminated in 1875, when the Ontario agents in the British Isles were withdrawn, and thenceforth recruitment of immigrants fell solely to the Dominion government's agents.[53] The principal focus of their efforts was to be the promotion of settlement on the remaining marginal lands of Ontario and the new frontier of the western territories.

Emigration pamphlets and posters were key devices in the promotional activities.[54] In 1820 a traveller in a remote upland region of County Londonderry observed the presence of emigration posters in local houses. He wrote in his journal that 'in several cabins we observed printed notices stuck up of ships about to sail for America and found that a great many are going from time to time though not so many as some time ago.'[55] Most emigration pamphlets conveyed a distinctive tenor of boosterism through exaggerated claims of soil fertility, climatic salubrity, and accessible wealth. In general, they sold an idea of material and moral progress to a literate audience, often with means, the type of people whose example would be emulated.

Such were the objectives of pamphlets written by William Hutton, Dublin emigrant, farm manager, and Canada booster. In 1854 he produced an extensive guide, *Canada: Its Present Conditions, Prospects and Resources, Fully Described for the Information of Intending Emigrants*, and had it published in London by Stanfords. It met with a ready sale, a second edition was distributed, and he reported from Quebec to his brother-in-law in Ireland: 'The emigrants on board ship coming to Quebec are in possession of numbers of copies and I have had several letters of capitalists led hither by it.'[56] Hutton's pamphlet extended to some 120 pages and had an image of official authenticity, coming as it did from the pen of a perceived pioneering agriculturalist, by then secretary to the government's board of statistics. Its detailed tables relating to prices, crop yields, and settlement costs, together with its advertising of the recently approved free land grants along colonization roads running northward into the Canadian Shield, all seemed impressive. Hutton's claim as to the extent of its influence was probably not an idle boast.

Hutton had shown an inclination to pamphleteering when he emigrated in 1834. His observations on first reaching North America were sent off as letters home to his brother-in-law in County Tyrone and were subsequently published in the *British Agricultural Magazine*. From a trip through New York State and Upper Canada he reported on 'the details of the information I have procured during the ten weeks that I have been spending in this country – the result of accurate observation, and the best enquiries from the most respectable sources.'[57] Aimed specifically at British and Irish farmers with capital, Hutton's letters home were designed in the genre of emigration pamphlets. In 1857, under the direction of the Bureau of Agriculture and Statistics, Hutton produced a second pamphlet, published this time under government aegis in Toronto.[58] He had access to a great deal of basic information and knew the Canadas because of his daily routines in the bureau. He had overseen the Canadian census tabulations in 1851 and was in a fine position to contribute the informational appendices to an edition of Catherine Parr Traill's book *The Female Emigrant's Guide*,[59] one of the most famous publications of its type because of its 'do-it-yourself' emphasis in explaining the modes of existence in the New World. Hutton's rather dry, factual appendices, however, were not included in subsequent editions. Mrs. Traill's prose was more appealing alone.

Charles Foy, the Canadian government agent in Belfast, continued these traditions in his pamphlet *Dominion of Canada: Emigration to the Province of Ontario*, published in Belfast in 1873.[60] Unlike most of the pamphlets, which were designed for general audiences, Foy's material seems to have been calculated to appeal to a regional audience – Ulster's Protestant community, then the main source of Irish emigrants to Canada. Foy included letters from emigrants to their families and friends at home and thus played on the intrinsic personal elements of the emigration process. Allegations about the authenticity of the published letters appeared in the pages of the *Belfast Newsletter*, and the considerable opposition of Ulster leaders against emigration was directed at Foy.

Although the letters Foy published received his editorial attention, there is no reason to believe his detractors' claims that the letters were complete forgeries.[61] Too many details about family connections and too much specific information regarding names and addresses were included for Foy to have forged letters destined to be distributed throughout Ulster's parochial society. Rather, the problems and controversy were likely of sectarian origin. The narrow appeal of Foy's pamphlet clashed with the aspirations of Canadian Catholics for widening the sources of immigration to include more Catholics. Their objection to Foy's emphasis found support in Belfast from among those who branded Foy's pamphlet a lie.

The true issues were more akin to those expressed in private by C.J. Shiel, Ontario's agent in southern Ireland (see above, p. 77). Shiel, a Catholic, was convinced that Foy was an Orangeman bent on recruiting none but Orangemen and thus inimical to the Catholic community in Ontario. Shiel insisted that Catholics in Ontario should combine their efforts to encourage more Catholics from Ireland to choose the province as a home, to offset the Protestant bias in the recruiting system. Shiel especially feared that Protestant county immigration societies in Ontario would unduly influence the selection of immigrants to be assisted to Ontario.

Shiel's allegations about Foy may not have been far from the truth, but they were never substantiated. Given the previous history of emigration from Ulster to Upper Canada, and the importance of Protestants among the early contingents, it would have been surprising if most of Foy's recruits had not been Protestant and Orange. That section of the community had the best-developed set of personal connections with Ontario, and recruitment efforts expended among them were likely to bring the best results. Foy was making use of the natural elements and information channels of the emigration process. None of the letters he reproduced came from Irish immigrants whose origins were outside Ulster. His purview and his intentions were narrow and confined to Ireland's northern province.

Some of the letters that Foy published had distinctive appeal to Ulster Orangemen, and the tone of the letters suggests Protestant bias. For example, in one of the letters, an Ulster settler located in Tyendenaga township wrote to his brother: 'This township is twelve miles square, and the Indians have three miles by twelve in the front of it. As they do not like farming they rent it all. They are all civilised and Christianised; they are the Mowhawk tribe; splendid men, and everyone of them an

Orangeman. They gave Mr. Johnston M.P. for Belfast, a beautiful crown, when he visited Shannonville.'[62] In this letter the Orange content was quite clear (Johnston was Ulster's most colourful Orangeman). It was also indicated in other material. One young emigrant writing from Lambton County, Ontario, advised his brother-in-law in Ballinderry Upper, County Antrim, to bring out 'a good black thorn stick and a Ballykilbeg pipe'[63] – both items were necessary accompaniments to a Twelfth of July parade, and Mr Johnston, M.P., was Ballykilbeg's best-known resident.

The letters published by Foy contained a wealth of information on wages and opportunities for servant girls, labourers, and tradesmen. 'Should any of your friends think of emigrating,' advised one writer, 'you had better advise them to come to Canada, particularly to Ottawa, as wages for tradesmen are very high; lots of work, and living cheap.'[64] These were the classes of immigrants most sought after by the Canadian and Ontario governments in the later nineteenth century, and the repeated insistence that wages were good would have appeared attractive. Likewise, the letters extolled the virtues of farming, especially if one had capital to invest, and argued by way of comparison 'that you could do better in this country by begging than in Ireland on a small farm.'[65] The differential in living standards between Ireland and Ontario was a recurring theme promoted by the pamphlet's letters.

Besides the economic concerns, Foy's pamphlet, like similar publications, stressed the potential for unfettered progress toward independence and social equality. Such progress was to be the reward for hard work, temperance, and strict moral behaviour – values common to both Ontario and Ulster society. As expressed by one of the writers in Foy's pamphlet: 'Come on, here is the road to independence. Keep clear of Mr. Damnation Whiskey and you must become independent. We have none of the 'haw-haw,' would be gentlemen you have in Ireland, who are ashamed to confess that they ever were poor, or their fathers before them. I am sure you will agree with me, that any man who could rid the old sod of these brainless, lisping idiots, would be doing as much good as St. Patrick, when he rid Ireland of snakes. The total absence of such in Canada is one of the great charms of the country for me.'[66] The social and moral progress advertised as awaiting the immigrant in Ontario implied considerable change for the better. That change was also to be realized within a society containing many friends and relatives, familiar institutions and culture. For the readers, the pamphlet's references to the presence of family members, encounters with 'many an old

County Cavan man in your travels,' and indications of friends from Ireland living nearby would all have been reassuring. They provided confirmation of Ontario's being a familiar community in which the Ulster emigrant was welcome.

The success of the agents, both private and governmental, is difficult to measure. Their activities formed part of an accumulative process whereby millions crossed the Atlantic. It is unlikely that the Irish agents initiated emigration; their role was more in propagating an idea of British North America and contributing details to be added to existing folklore about the new land. They were but part of a well-functioning information system that incorporated imperial, mercantile, institutional, and family interests. This system, operating within the context of relative economic distress in Ireland and potential prosperity in the New World, fluctuated according to short-term economic changes on either side of the Atlantic. In times of emigration fever, the conduit provided by the agents functioned and they could influence the direction of flow, but at other times the agents were hard pressed to attract recruits. The system was total, and they were but one intrinsic part of it.

THE JOURNEY

Irrespective of why people emigrated, all had to undertake a journey that until well into the second half of the nineteenth century represented a dangerous and often traumatic experience. They knew a great deal about the potential suffering and perils before embarking. They knew what sort of ships they were going on, what conditions they might expect on board, and potential dangers.

Until the mid-century advent of regular and cheap steam-passenger shipping, emigrants from Ireland journeyed on timber ships, forming a human ballast on the return trips to North American ports. Voyages could last six to ten weeks, depending on the weather, and most were undertaken in the months of April through September. At best a ship could make only two round trips before the onset of winter, when it might be relegated to cargo shipping closer to home.

Although conditions on board were regulated by official passenger acts,[67] they rarely exceeded minimum standards. Shortages of clean water and food, as well as cramped quarters and pestilence, often made the journey a misery. William Campbell, in a letter to his father in 1839, noted the severe shortages: 'It was well [the Captain] was not tossed overboard by the passengers. There was a general scarcity of sea store. I saw a shilling offered for 1 lb. of meal and a penny for a noggin of dirty water say 10 weeks old.'[68] Better conditions were obtainable only at the behest of the captain, and the reputation of both captains and vessels formed part of the information relayed to intending emigrants. Campbell warned: 'I would advise everyone in coming out to be particularly careful what ship's captain they come with.'[69] Wilson Benson had been unsettled by the captain on his ship: 'Captain Lowe was a strict disciplinarian, but his general demeanour both to seamen and passengers was brutal in the extreme; indeed, on some occasions he seemed to be partially insane ... The vessel was lost on her return voyage, but the crew were saved, and the captain died of brain fever afterwards.'[70] Joseph Carrothers was pleased that he had 'the best ship that sailed from Derry and the best Capt. it is said by all that I have hear speak of her.'[71]

As the century passed and steamships replaced sail, the small contingents of post-Famine emigrants were able to avail themselves of safer, more comfortable passage. For passengers able to afford cabins, conditions permitted a degree of comfort and privacy denied to those travelling in the open steerage. Mrs Forster, an emigrant travelling from Dublin to Quebec in 1869, had many creature comforts denied to the mass of emigrants and dined regularly with the ship's captain. However, she could not avoid the smells around her:

We went on board the Lady Seymour to sail for Quebec on our way to Upper Canada on the 5th of April 1869 at 1/2 past 8 in the morning. We settled our berths, turned our heads in the direction the stewart advised, uncle Ian gave great help and nailed up all our odds and ends tidly, we were all very cheerful and anyone who felt otherwise kindly hid their feelings, we dined at 2 had soup, roast beef and rice pudding, had tea at 6 with soup and pudding made of mashed potatoes, minced meat, onion and other savory condiments, this I liked particularly, one way or other there was a deal of merriment, Ian and I danced like a pair of country people and Mrs. Hopson played, the time of parting came at last and then came the dulness and sense of loneliness ... We all went to bed, the berths are most comfortable and the little door opening on deck is a great comfort, the frequent supply of fresh air gained in that way is more refreshing, I do not know what we should do without it. I should be smothered. In spite of our care, the odors are sickening and I w'd recommend friends to have at hand each one in their berth some aromatic vinegar or other pungent refresher, I longed much for some strong peppermint losenges.[72]

For all passengers, however, the vagaries of the weather continued to present dangers. Lord Dufferin, on his way from Derry to become governor-general of Canada in 1872, was awakened in his stateroom by passengers fearing for their lives in the midst of a severe storm and hoping that he could do something to relieve their anxiety.[73] Forty years later the pride of the Belfast shipyards, the *Titanic*, sank off Newfoundland, a salutary reminder of the dangers of the Atlantic passage.

The early ships were small and may have carried as few as ten passengers, although complements of two hundred or more were common. The ships were intended to carry cargo, and for each voyage out from Ireland they had to be refitted as temporary passenger boats. The refitting involved putting in a platform to cover the ballast and erecting thereon rows of bunks between the decks in a space rarely exceeding six feet in height. This steerage accommodation contrasted with the odd private cabin on the deck above.

In 1828 William McCorkell, in outfitting the *Anne* for emigrants, estimated the following materials and costs: 'We can give plank three inches thick and nine inches broad at 3 1/2d. per foot, each plank will be sufficiently strong with one deep cut for the laying of the deck and two deep cuts in each plank for berthing. The expense of carpenter work for laying deck and berthing would be about £2 10 0. Water casks containing about 100 gallons and pipes 120 would be got from 14/- to 18/- each, the quantity of water for each passenger would be at least 45 gallons. The ANNE if here by the 1st of March would be in good time as passengers do not offer freely before that date.'[74] Cooking facilities had to be constructed on deck from brick tied with iron straps, and on arrival in North America these cooking cambooses, the berths, and even the water casks would be dismantled to make room for the timber cargo on the homeward journey. As part of the colonial trade, the dismantled pieces were sold. In 1837 Cooke's agent in Saint John, Samuel Thompson, was directed that 'the water casks you can have shaken and sent home by first opportunity for Derry. The iron hoops on the casks cost 2s.6d. per cask and if you can get half price for them sell them. If not send them home with the casks. There is a good deal of iron and brick in the 2 cambooses. I hope you will get as much as you can for them and credit me with it.'[75] Part of the outfitting expense was thus recouped by selling the dismantled brick and metal components in the colonies, where, in the early years, manufactured goods were at a premium.

The emigrant's journey to the new land began with the leave-taking at home. Wilson Benson recorded that the 'customary preparations' involved the gathering of 'messages from friends in Ireland to friends in Canada.'[76] They meant, too, preparation of provisions, a packing that could have amounted to almost 200 pounds of goods per adult. From Upper Canada, Mary Duggan gave her sister Eliza in Ireland a detailed list of necessary provisions for the trip and approximate prices. The list[77] included

3 st oat meal [42 lbs]	9s od
1 20 lb pork halm	5s od
1/2 lb tea	2s od
4 lbs sugar	2s 6d
2 bushels potatoes [120 lbs]	5s od
3 lbs soap	1s od

It weighed in total 189.5 lb. Eliza benefited from her sister's experience and was thus not alone in her journey but rather, with her emigrant sister, part of a familiar process.

Then could begin the trip to the port of embarkation. Walking, or riding in carts and coaches, families and single individuals would have left home on notification that their ship had arrived in port and was being fitted. Outfitting the ship took time, and intending passengers were informed through agents and newspapers of an approximate date of departure, (Figure 4.8). In 1820, an English traveller recorded the trek of emigrants to Derry: 'In passing over the moor we observed a cluster of twenty or thirty persons walking in a body across the moor, two or three small carts carrying their luggage, and on enquiry were told it was a convoy of persons conducting some of their friends who were going to take ship for America.'[78] Congregating in quayside hostelries, emigrants faced a potentially expensive waiting period if the ship's departure were delayed, and delays were common. Provisions could have been purchased at this point for the journey, and, as Joseph Carrothers indicated of his stay in Derry in 1847, 'It left us with lighter purses.'[79] As the century went on, technological change eased the trip to the port. In 1863 Edmund Letson of Glenavy, County Antrim, boarded a train in Belfast for Derry: 'We went through Antrim, Ballymena, Randalstown, Coleraine and a great many stations. We stopped nowhere but at Coleraine till we reached Derry. There was nearly 300 emigrants on the train. When we arrived at Derry there was omnibuses waiting to take us to the several hotels we had sixpence a piece for taking our luggage to the hotel. I along with about 60 others went to Dogherty's Hotel and stopped all night. We had three shillings and sixpence to pay

NOW IN PORT.

NOTICE TO PASSENGERS.

Those Persons who have taken their Passages by the First Class Coppered Ship

SUPERIOR,

CAPTAIN MASON,

FOR QUEBEC,

Are required to be in Derry on TUESDAY, the 13th of JULY, pay the remainder of their Passage Money, and go on Board, as the Vessel will sail first fair wind after that date. A few more Passengers will be taken, on moderate terms, if immediate application is made to

Mr. DAVID MITCHELL, *Dungiven,* or the Owners,

J. & J. COOKE.

Derry, June 28, 1847.

☞ The Cargo of the SUPERIOR, just arrived, from *Philadelphia,* consisting of Indian Corn, Indian Meal, Flour, &c., for Sale, on moderate terms.

BUCHANAN, PRINTER.

FIGURE 4.8
Announcing the departure of the *Superior,* bound from Derry for Quebec, this poster was circulated in the Dungiven area of County Londonderry by the Derry shipping company J. and J. Cooke. Public Record Office of Northern Ireland

for our bed and board.'[80] By rail and steamship, Letson's voyage was easier than that of most.

The journey was dangerous. Death rates on board ship in the first half of the nineteenth century averaged about 8 per 1,000 passengers,[81] a rate about five times higher than that of the people remaining behind. In the Famine period, mortality levels in the order of 150 per 1,000 passengers were not uncommon.[82] The average shipboard death rate in 1847 was 57 and on a few ships the rate was as high as 330 per 1,000 passengers.[83]

Under normal circumstances, fire, disease, and storms were the main hazards, and offshore ice was an additional peril. John and Eliza Anderson's boat spent a harrowing time locked in pack ice off Newfoundland in 1832. They recounted thankfully in a letter home that '3 days and 3 nights we were in the ice and for 2 days and 2 nights we had to walk the deck with oars and other pieces of timber to defend the vessel we had to let down logs of timber with chains and ropes about the vessel to keep her from being wrecked with the ice, I saw more ice on the banks of Newfoundland or rather the northern coasts nor if I had lived in Ireland to the age of Methusalem and for size we had it from the smallest piece to the largest hill in Knockaduff.'[84] Jane White observed in 1849: 'A great number of ships have been lost in the ice here early in the spring. One was wrecked in the Gulf of St. Lawrence here during the gales. It contained four hundred passengers who all perished except one child who was picked up by a vessel passing the spot.'[85]

The gales that swept the Atlantic terrified passengers, most of whom had never been on a boat before. When William Campbell, a doctor from Templepatrick, County Antrim, was emigrating in 1839, his ship encountered a violent storm:

The storm was truly dreadful, our cordage and canvas was torn to tatters and I too [?] rags, the women of course screamed (thats natural) the Captain's countenance looked blue. The sailors behaved like jolly stars and most of the passengers. There was one however that I could not but remark, when the storm was at the worst he was upon his knees with his hands clasped around the mast beating his breast and vociferating with religious fear, 'Hail Mary! Sweet Mary! Mother of God Save Us.' I gave him a kick on the posterior and ordered him up to assist, told him there was no time to be lost in praying upon such an occasion, he turned round with a face, shade of Hogarts Whether art thy fled! The face that would have made a complete frontispiece to the Book of Lamentation, and sung out 'Sweet Mary Save Us.'[86]

Even without horrific weather, small boats tossing on a swell were stomach-wrenching. James Humphrey, travelling in a fair wind in 1824, watched as practically everyone around him fell victim to chronic seasickness: 'At four o'clock on Saturday morning the 12th of June we weighed anchor and had a fair wind. The next morning we took our departure from Derry Mountains and saw land no more. We had one hundred and seventeen passengers. They were almost all sick, only myself and a few others. Margaret was sick for three weeks, my mother-in-law was sick for two weeks, and my father-in-law had not had an hour's sickness since he left home and is quite mended of the old complaint. Samuel was but a few days at sea until he got well.'[87] New problems could arise, as water and food reserves became depleted en route, and the passengers' troubles would have continued throughout the trip until the shelter of Saint John or the St Lawrence was reached and contact with land made.

The emigrant's feelings on sight of land are hardly imaginable. Most were not recorded, but letters home frequently noted the wonder of the impressive landfall vistas. The settled landscape of the French shores of the St Lawrence was inspiring, and strikingly different from the Irish landscape left behind. Jane White from County Down described it on her arrival in 1849: 'The scenery on the banks of the river is delightful especially at this season of the year, hill and valley and beautiful towns and villages slooping to the river's edge together with fertile islands, form the most beautiful landscape I ever saw. The houses are of wood and very white. The inhabitants are mostly of French descent and speak the French language. The Roman Catholic religion is established here.'[88] Wilson Benson had been similarly impressed and, despite claiming an inability with words, managed to portray the scene: 'The grandeur of its natural scenery, and picturesque beauty of the many charming villages which stud its banks, and the glittering tin roofs of the houses, in the effulgent rays of an April sun, forms a panorama not readily forgotten.'[89] Lord Dufferin resorted to even more elaborate literary devices to convey his wonderment: 'Ones first view of a new continent is always as an epoch in ones life. What struck me most were the primaeval woods which covered the hills at Gaspe for miles and miles through the interior. One felt one saw what the first red Adam and Eve first opened their eyes upon.'[90] No one could fail to notice being in a new place, and closer contact with the new environment would soon be forged as the immigrants made their ways inland by riverboat and on foot.

Irish emigrants disembarking on the quays of Saint John or Quebec

City in the summer or early fall would certainly have been struck by the strangeness of the destination, but the sense of alienation and isolation would have been mitigated greatly by the social supports that pervaded the emigration process. These new arrivals were not encountering the whole continent, only those parts of it that had already been settled and made ready for them by those who had come earlier in the emigrant chain. Arriving immigrants sought to make contact with former friends and acquaintances, easing the alien quality of the new country and consolidating and confirming the social network to which they belonged. Temporary accommodation, advice on how to proceed, and an updating of the conditions and location of other friends and relatives could all be provided. Letters and messages from friends in Ireland were passed along and reported back home. For those without friends and short of funds, work had to be sought immediately, and the ports were often clogged with such temporary residents. Agencies such as the Montreal Emigrant Society or the Commissioners of the Poor in Saint John worked to prevent hordes from accumulating and sent them on to places where work might be obtained. A.C. Buchanan, as emigration agent in Quebec City, implemented this policy there, and great sums were spent forwarding immigrants inland.

The risks and hardships normal for most of the emigrant period were indescribably intensified in cholera years, especially 1832, and during the worst famine year, 1847. Sampson Brady, from Graystones, County Antrim, encountered cholera in Montreal in 1832. He wrote home: 'This town and Quebec has suffered very much. There is one large pit or grave in the French burying grounds here which contains three thousand dead bodies which died of the cholera, besides many other pits and graves where some thousands more are interred. The disease is greatly abated. God grant it may continue as long so. I am sorry poor Ireland has suffered greatly by the disease.'[91] Death and disease afflicted tens of thousands more in 'Black '47,' and the unprecedented emigration panic then brought into the passenger trade boats and captains of inferior quality and skills. Commercial avarice compounded the misery of famine and fever. The names of Partridge Island at Saint John and Grosse Isle in the St Lawrence became synonymous with migrant hells. The two islands served as quarantine stations, isolated and secure from the mainland, and there the boats arriving were checked for diseased passengers.

Even relatively well-to-do emigrants were not immune to the ravages of disease. Joseph Carrothers's friend George Scott was removed sick

from the boat, and his own sister Jane died near Lachine, outside
Montreal. His daughter Margaret died on arrival in Westminster township in Upper Canada, having 'been worn out on the journey and up
the country in the boats and the wagon the most fatiguing of all.'[92]
Joseph, aged fifty, convalesced for a month recovering from the journey.[93] The Famine period marked the end of the most horrific episodes
in the journey to British North America. Subsequently, steamships
replaced sail. A few years later, in the mid-1850s, William Hutton could
undertake a holiday visit home to Ireland[94] without trepidation, and
future immigrants would realize that their decisions to leave Ireland
were not irrevocable. Return migration would be easy, but few would
take up that option. Furthermore, the interlinking of transatlantic passenger services with railway connections regularized travel and removed
much of the gamble.

The emergence of new transportation links was critical, because the
earlier conveyances virtually disappeared when the timber trade col-
lapsed in the 1850s. That collapse did not end Ireland's shipping connections with Canada, but subsequent immigrants came generally on
regularly scheduled voyages. From 1870 the Allan Line of steamers,
which had the Canadian government mail contract between Canada,
the United States, and Britain, called at Derry every Wednesday and
Friday on the outward voyage from Liverpool. The inclusion of Derry
reflected that city's proximity to the North Atlantic shipping lanes and
affirmed the early role played by it in the migrations to British North
America.
   The Allan Line's virtual monopoly focused subsequent Irish emigration: Ulster now possessed the only regular and frequent link from
Ireland to Canada via Halifax and Quebec City, and thereon to Montreal
and Toronto. By way of contrast, southern Ireland had much more
limited access to Canada-bound ships. In 1872, the Allan Line, after
petitioning by an Ontario emigration agent based in Dublin, agreed to
include Dublin on its Glasgow – Montreal route. However, in its first
year of operation, 'owing to the great rush of emigrants at Glasgow,
there were no vacant berths left for [those hoping to board at] Dublin.'[95]
The same situation pertained when Queenstown (Cobh) was included
in the Allan Line's Liverpool – Montreal route. In comparison with the
United States, Canada was much less accessible for potential emigrants
living in southern Irish countries. In 1874 the Cork-based Ontario
emigration agent despairingly reported: 'Agricultural labourers and

TABLE 4.2
Emigrants from Irish ports of
embarkation, 1895–1900

From	To USA	To Canada
Queenstown	137,534	9
Derry	29,033	3,728
Galway	2,875	0

SOURCE: Department of Agriculture, Ireland, *Emigration Statistics*, 1895–1900

their families come to Queenstown, the great port of embarcation, and can chose from 11 to 12 vessels a week to American ports, whereas if they desire to sail from Queenstown to Quebec, they are accommodated with about six ships in the year, and one every two weeks to Halifax.'[96]

The great passenger liners sailing from Britain called at Ireland en route to North America, and the shipping lanes firmly established a geography of the diagonal: Derry in the northwest and Queenstown in the southeast were endowed with a virtual monopoly of the emigrant trade. Table 4.2 shows that by the end of the century the Irish emigrant trade with Canada was channelled exclusively through Derry, although even there the flow to the United States predominated. Emigration to Canada was less than 2 1/2 per cent of that to the United States. From Queenstown, and from Galway, practically none went to Canada. Only these three ports were engaged in the transatlantic business, and the inordinate position of Derry in Canadian movement represented the persistence of the Ulster link with Canada and the closing of the circle with the earliest emigrations.

Throughout the nineteenth century, emigration entailed creation of chains of new emigrants following the paths of early pioneers. Safe arrival of the early leavers provided at once encouragement for others to follow and a New World network of which subsequent emigrants could avail themselves. Many of the areas to which emigrants headed had been first made familiar by merchants trading in fish and timber. A few other earlier arrivals had been encouraged to go as part of group schemes, but by and large the decisions to emigrate were independent, family choices. In the nineteenth century, for the first time, popular mass emigration seized the Irish imagination and ordinary people went off to new places on their own accord. They went against the will of government at first, but increasingly they left with government sanction and even encouragement. They were armed only with some cash, the addresses of a few friends or relatives who had left earlier, and the knowledge that something new but nonetheless familiar was being created on the other side. Their emigration to Canada was simply an extension of, not a break from, their Irish lives.

Part Two

Patterns of Settlement

CHAPTER FIVE

Settling In

'It is very fine land but grown with immence timber' was Joseph Carrothers's view of his new country in 1847.[1] 'Nightland' was how Wilson Benson described the virgin forest in which he hoped to make a farm.[2] Shafts of sunlight pierced through apertures left in the dense canopy of treetops and generally failed to illuminate the ground. Except in swamps, marshes, and beaver-meadows, trees towered over all, enclosing the new settlers and obscuring the horizons. But not for long. In their own generation Benson and Carrothers would witness the retreat of the forest. In thirty years the bush would be largely gone and the sun would scorch grassy earth or glint from acres of shadowless snow. Only stumps, wooden rail fences, and scrubby forest would remain to remind them and other pioneers of their first encounter with the magnificent 'nightland.'

The emigrants experienced an encounter without sentimentality, for making a living was the issue, survival the objective, and a cleared farm the final outcome. In New Brunswick, the forest did not give way to the same extent as inland but remained the vital second element of an economy based on the seasonal pursuit of lumbering and farming. In Nova Scotia, farming was combined with fishing. In Newfoundland the process of settling in was of a different order. Conquest of the land was neither feasible nor desired, except for the creation of garden-scale cultivation on that rocky island. Trees were poor relatives of their magnificent mainland counterparts and of use generally only for fuel, construction, and small boats. Fish was the principal resource staple, and the focus of life was the sea. To the west of Lake Superior, on the open prairie grasslands, agriculture predominated as the initial resource activity. At the Cordilleran edge of British Columbia, the far horizons of the prairies were truncated and replaced by limited vistas in valleys among the mountains. In that Pacific province agriculture was of minimal significance and the staple economy was founded on fishing, mining, and forestry.

Thus from the Atlantic to the Pacific the Irish in Canada encountered a broad range of economic opportunities and physical environments, and the associated variations in adjustments were further complicated by the length of time over which the emigration occurred. Most of the Irish immigrant experiences were those of eastern Canada in the first half of the nineteenth century, and there the encounter with forest, land, and sea was engaged in by independent settlers operating at the level of family enterprises.

OBTAINING LAND

The Irish immigrants before the Famine arrived in search of land and the opportunity to re-create a rural life. Their chances depended on personal circumstances, the fertility of the farm lot that they pioneered, and the economy of the region in which they settled. Their collective experience was indistinguishable from that of the other immigrants arriving at the same time from Scotland, England, and the United States to settle the same set of places. The first step on the road to fulfilling their hopes was to obtain land, and a surprisingly large number succeeded in doing so. The land was rarely free. Even when land grants were available, the cost of the fees and legal steps involved and the acquisition of tools and supplies meant a sizeable monetary outlay. In part, this capital could be gained by temporary paid employment in the New World, but modest funds brought from Ireland were critical. In the early phases, as noted in chapter 3, most farm pioneers had cash sufficient to make a start.

Before the arrival of settlers in a district, surveyors had traversed the territory blazing the lines – that is, marking the routes – that roads would eventually follow and marking the outer corners of rectangular lots that would become farms. William Hutton, writing from Upper Canada in 1834, graphically described the planned outline of rectangular lots and straight roads intersecting at right angles:

Nearly all the farms in Upper Canada are of either 100 or 200 acres. The land is divided into districts, counties, townships, concessions, and lots: neither districts nor counties are any fixed size; the townships are about nine miles by twelve; the concessions one mile and three-eights long, and a quarter of a mile wide; each lot contains 200 acres, but some of them are divided by the original purchasers; there are also what are called broken fronts, i.e., pieces left after running the *concession* lines straight; and gores are pieces left after running the *township* lines straight. The fronts are sold to the person holding the lot adjoining, and the gores are thrown into the last lot of each township, and there is a county road laid off between every second lot, so that every man holding a full lot has his farm in a ring fence, and a public road, or an allowance for one, the whole length of his farm. It is beautifully surveyed, and most advantageously for the farmer.[3]

A cartographic rendering of the type of survey arrangement applying to Upper Canada is provided in Figure 5.1. The geography of settlement was determined at the outset, even before settlers arrived. The prior survey was meant to ease access to property and keep to a minimum the possibilities of settlers locating on the wrong lots or coming into conflict with neighbours. In New Brunswick, the Eastern Townships of Lower Canada, and especially the prairies, this geometry encased the land. For the Irish it must have been quite a shock to come face to face with such an arrangement of straight, unnatural lines, cutting contrary to the sweep and slopes of the natural landscape. The reasons for it were, however, well within their ken.

Lots could be obtained from the government directly if the settler were on the spot early enough and aware of the legal steps. William Richardson arrived with his brother-in-law James Humphrey in 1824 and immediately petitioned for a free grant of land. His petition to the lieutenant-governor, Sir Peregrine Maitland, asserted his claim: 'The petition of William Richardson of the Township of Scarboro Yeoman Humbly showeth That Your Excellencys petitioner is a native of Ireland Emigrated to this Country during the last Summer has a wife and five children has taken the Oath of Allegance and being desirous of Cultivating Land humbly pray that Your Excellency will take his case into consideration and grant to him such portion of the same as to Your Excellency may deem meet.'[4] With that petition Richardson also provided a letter of reference of good character from his parish rector in Ireland: 'We Certify that William Richardson, of the Parish of Balinderry, and County of Londonderry: is an honest, Industrious, and well conducted Young Man; having from his Infancy been generally consid-

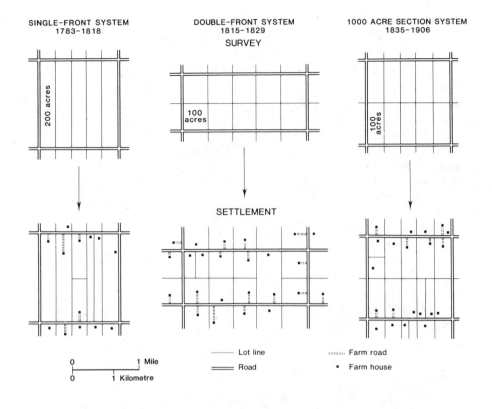

SINGLE-FRONT SYSTEM
1783-1818

DOUBLE-FRONT SYSTEM
1815-1829

1000 ACRE SECTION SYSTEM
1835-1906

SURVEY

200 acres

100 acres

100 acres

SETTLEMENT

0   1 Mile

0   1 Kilometre

——— Lot line   ······ Farm road

=== Road   • Farm house

FIGURE 5.1

Principal survey systems and settlement patterns in Upper Canada; after R.C. Harris and J. Warkentin, *Canada before Confederation* (Toronto 1972), 124

ered, as Possessing an Unimpeachable Character, and is beside descended of honest, Creditable Parents.'[5] After receipt of such documentation, a 'location ticket' was issued (Figure 5.2).

A location ticket gave the bearer the right to try to make a farm. Certain settlement duties were required before a patent giving legal title could be obtained. The duties called for improvements – destruction of the forest – that showed the settler's intention to remain permanently on the land, engaged in making a farm. In 1800 a settler's duties on a lot in Upper Canada included clearing and fencing five acres, building a house, and planting a crop.[6] Fifty years later, Wilson Benson was required to indicate his desire and ability to be permanently on his land grant simply by 'either immediate settlement' or 'to be and appear once in each month on the said premises.'[7]

Alexander Robb's requirements in British Columbia in 1868 included both improvements on the land and an acreage fee. He wrote home: 'According to the land laws of this country any British subject may take up 160 acres of land in any place in the country by merely paying the registration fees which is only ten shillings and settling on it. After he has done a certain quantity of work on it you get what is called a "certificate of improvement" which is in fact neither more nor less than a government title to the land. This you may sell or otherwise dispose of as if it were your own land. In fact it is so only that when the land comes to be surveyed (which may not be for years) you or your successor have to pay government one dollar per acre for it.'[8] Alexander thought the land granting system a great boon, even a liberating force: 'There is a wonderful difference between this and paying twenty pounds or so per acre for leave to farm a patch of hungry land from which one may be turned out by the mere caprice of a landlord.'[9] The granting system, while designed to encourage settlement by people of small means, also encouraged speculation by those with capital – and often debt for those without it. Alexander Robb himself had acted as a proxy pioneer, hired by a friend speculating in free grant lands.[10]

Even early in the history of the colonies, men with capital and the right location benefited greatly in the speculative venture of claiming, improving, and selling land. They hired choppers and labourers as proxies and agents to complete settlement duties, or simply in many cases did nothing in the way of clearing the forest and lied that the duties had been rendered. Land acquired for a pittance could be resold for a sizeable sum to a settler able or willing to mortgage his lot. In 1834 William Hutton noted the high cost of land in Upper Canada: 'The

LOCATION TICKET.

The Bearer *William Savage* — is allowed to settle and cultivate *Lot Number* — *in the Emigrant District of Westmorland*

Two Hundred Acres
At the expiration of the time limited by the Royal Instructions, he is required to take out a Grant of the same ; otherwise the said Lot, with all the improvements made on it, will be forfeited to the Crown.

_____ Surveyor General.

Surveyor General's Office,
Fredericton, May 21. 1822.

By Command of His Excellency the Lieutenant Governor.

FIGURE 5.2
Location ticket of William Savage, who settled in the Tormentine Peninsula of New Brunswick in 1821; courtesy New Brunswick Museum, Saint John

usual method of purchasing farms in this country, is to pay, in annual instalments, for five or ten years; thus the purchaser of a farm at £500, pays £50 per annum for ten years, or £100 per annum for five years, according to the bargain, without interest. It is quite possible to purchase one hundred acres some ten or twelve miles from town, with twenty acres clear and a small house upon it, for £200, payable £40 per annum for five years. Here then, an industrious man who can work with his own hands, if he have £100 to begin with, can support his family upon the twenty acres that are clear, and clear as much more every year as will pay the necessary instalment.'[11]

It was not a venture for a poor labourer or a farmer without some capital. Property appreciated rapidly during the early pioneering phase, and immigration kept the land market buoyant. The unending stream of immigrants meant that the speculator's role would not be diminished, and the cost of entry into the land market rose. William Hutton again reported 'that the properties purchased in Canada, during the last twenty years, or more, have increased in value to an almost incredible extent: for instance, in the town of Belleville, the half-acre building lots, which were sold nine years ago at £7. 10s. are now selling at £100.; farms which could be had three years at 50s. per acre, are now £5. Wild lands, that were two years ago 30s. per acre, are now 60s.; and further off, those that were 5s. are now 15s. per acre, and this is the same case wherever I have been; thus, you see, a purchaser has every prospect of realizing a handsome profit, in the gradually increasing value of the lands in this most rising country.'[12] Speculation, in the hope that time would allow a handsome profit from little effort, had established the wealth of many British North Americans. It also severely limited the types who could get access to the land.

British North America was not the place for the impoverished. Free land grants were few and virtually non-existent during the height of Irish immigration between 1825 and the 1850s. Land in the colonies had to be paid for, and each year that passed made the possibility of being a pioneer more remote. Nathaniel Carrothers told his brother in 1853: 'The land is getting dear in this section of the Country it is worth from 20 to 30 doullours an acre and I would not take even that amount for mine; there is no chance for a poor man getting a farm in this neighbourhood he will have to go back to some of the new townships where he may get it from 2 to 5 doullours an acre; Dear Brother if you had onley plucked up courage and come to America a few years agoe and got a good farm in this part of the country before the land got dear you would have had not cause to rue it and I ame sure your children would ever bless the day that the came to Canady.'[13] Youthful settlers in a young territory were, Nathaniel believed, those most likely to succeed, but the need for capital was clearly recognized.

Temporary work in the colonies could provide immigrants with the possibility of acquiring cash for investment in land. Carpenters could get five shillings per day in the 1820s and 1830s, and demand for them was good. The shipbuilding and timber enterprises employed such people in New Brunswick, and inland house building, canal building, and such endeavours as building the fort of London paid similarly.[14] Canals and other public works projects were employment outlets, and at times great numbers were engaged in these ventures. It has been estimated that in New Brunswick a farm labourer could earn upward of £25 plus room and board per annum in the 1830s, when uncleared land cost from 4s.6d. to 12s.6d. per acre and was usually purchased in 100-acre lots.[15] The cost of a farm would be between £20 and £60. The case of County Fermanagh emigrant John Macguire demonstrates the pattern. He went out to New Brunswick in 1841 and spent three years lumbering and saving before bringing out his wife. In 1845 he paid £40 for a farm near Woodstock and in the following year had his mother-in-law join them.[16] However, for the many emigrants who travelled as family groups, retention of wages would have been more difficult, and their families would have required support in the interim. Paid employment for these, the main group of agriculturalists, served to augment, not to replace, modest capital.

Even when free land became available in the west, settlement was still not possible without capital. Alexander Robb, who had obtained a free grant in British Columbia in 1868, still estimated the outstanding capital requirements to be substantial. He thought 'a man with a small amount of capital saved from £500 to £1000 could make himself independent in a very few years by raising stock for which this country is peculiarly adapted.'[17] Alexander, not having the savings, went into debt in order to commence the farming of his free grant and felt the chain that binds those without capital: 'You need not think dear father, that I had money enough to buy these cattle and what implements we require besides food for a year without going into debt. So anxious however was my partner that I should go in with him (he being a blacksmith and not knowing much about farming) that he lent me money enough to pay my share and promises to wait for it until I can pay him. It is the first time I ever have owed a dollar in this country and I hate the idea of it as bad as I hate poison but I am so heartily sick and weary of working for other people that I am willing to take my chance however desparate so that I may get quit of it.'[18]

Robb was not alone in facing the financial difficulties inherent in pioneering. Joseph and Nathaniel Carrothers also arrived at farming indirectly, from their trade as carpenters. Joseph started working in Upper Canada 'with a waggonmaker learning to make waggons at 20 dollars per month'[19] before taking to farming part-time. In a letter to his brother, he noted: 'I have been advised to not mind settling on wild land and Thomas gave me an acre of land sowed in wheat on the 5th concession (that is the name the Government roads has that is laid out in survey of the lands it is the principal road from the east to London) and to try to live by the trade as the prospect is good in so thriveing a township. Opposite my House a Mr. Rutlege owns 200 acres of land and he gave me the liberty of it for 8 years until his son is of Age, to Clear and crop and pasture as I please for the time. I had better than half an acre of very fine pitatoes in Thomas' land.'[20] Despite his opportunities, Joseph did not come to own land or have a farm. Carpentry continued to be his livelihood. His brother Nathaniel, who had preceded him to Canada by twelve years, had bought land immediately on arrival with money brought from Ireland and spent another nine years carpentering before being able to take up farming full-time.[21] Nathaniel had worked and also speculated on building two houses. What monies he brought are not known, but he would have needed more than £100. By contrast, William Hutton was extravagant in his requirements: in 1834 he spent over £600 of borrowed money on an established 165-acre property at Belleville, Upper Canada; in 1850 he was still paying off the debt to his family in Ireland.[22] Wilson Benson spent nine years as a pedlar and a cook on Lake Ontario steamers before getting his chance to farm a piece of wild land, formerly part of an intended endowment for the Protestant churches.

Choosing the location for a farm in wild country presented many difficulties for immigrants. An element of luck was involved in the process, as many settlers put down their money for land sight unseen. Even when inspected, the ground was so obscured by the forest as to prevent accurate imagining of soil fertility and agricultural potential. Evaluation of raw land was difficult, and as Wilson Benson probably believed, a lottery was as good a method as any to choose one's land:

[In 1851] the Toronto line through the County of Grey being then recently surveyed, and the reports of the new settlers representing it as a second Garden of Eden, I with many others came to see it. The prospect was lovely; where the surface was not covered with ground-hemlock, there was an abundance of wild nettles, cow cabbage, wild onions (leeks), &c., which certainly gave the virgin forest a luxuriant appearance. The black flies and mosquitoes assailed one in myriads, coming through the Township of Melancthon, especially; but even these torments seem frivolous when you 'get used to it.' There were three of us in company when we started to select a farm apiece. The three of us had made up our minds as to possessing *two* lots, and the difficulty arose how to decide. I agreed to 'cast lots,' but one of my companions refused to accede to that proposal; hence my other companions and myself became the possessors of the coveted lands – not that they turned out to be superior to thousands of acres in the same Township of Artemesia.[23]

Land turning out to be no better than other land could have been said of untold thousands of situations.

William Hutton trusted less to chance in his choice of farm. In seeking an already cleared piece of land, Hutton undertook a methodical search through upstate New York and much of Upper Canada in 1834. He traversed a two-hundred-mile stretch of the Lake Ontario north shore and also travelled inland to the Peterborough settlement.[24] His search was undertaken as an exercise in the contemporary location theory propounded by Ricardo in Britain. Ricardo had introduced the significance of distance and transportation costs to economics, and for agriculture he had developed the notion of transportation costs per acre, which permitted comparisons between products whose yields and prices varied but whose transport costs by weight would be equivalent. Distance to market was the critical variable to be considered.

With this method Hutton evaluated the relative merits of farming districts. Location relative to markets was his primary concern, and he could use both theory and his Irish experience to support his judgments:

Having experienced how great a drawback it is from the Irish farmers' receipts to defray the expense of exporting surplus produce to Liverpool and Manchester, even from ports where there is great competition amongst the merchants, and, of course, every thing of that kind done at the least possible expense, I kept steadily in view the necessity of being as near Montreal, which is the outlet, as soil and climate would allow me. I am aware that even from Ireland to England, where freight and wages are low, the expense of transport is, almost everywhere, 12 per cent upon grain, and 18 per cent upon live stock. With this fact staring me in the face, you will not wonder at my avoiding the evil as much as possible, and warning my friends to do so likewise, if any of them should bend their steps this way.[25]

Hutton searched deliberately and methodically, analysing the potential of every district. He objectively assessed distance to markets, quality of markets, price of goods, possibilities of local economic improvements, quality of harbours, locational and environmental advantages of American competitors, availability of firewood, quality of soil, enterprise of residents, and so on. He took 'ample notes, being determined to trust as little as possible to memory,'[26] and the effort led him to select a farm in the Moira River Valley, near Belleville. However, a man who worked this farm with horses described it as 'rib-breaking ground.'[27]

The real value of Hutton's farm was not in its agricultural potential but in its speculative value, arising from its location at the edge of the town of Belleville. In time, the town expanded to incorporate Hutton's homestead. As a farmer, Hutton fared no better than Wilson Benson and Nathaniel Carrothers, whose land had been chosen much less scientifically.

MAKING A FARM

Creating a farm from the wilderness could mean unremitting toil, discomfort, danger, and isolation. Trees had to be felled and cleared away, crops cultivated, animals bred, and buildings erected. Tasks that had taken shape over many generations among people 'at home' had to be accelerated in the New World and compressed into less than a single lifetime. Strong arms, strong backs, stamina, and willingness were the prime prerequisite for pioneering. All successful settlers knew the simple secret: 'It is quite clear, that in a new and not thickly-settled country, manual labour is what is most required.'[28]

Labour was the key, and the more of it the settler could organize within his own family the greater his chance of prosperity. The newcomer would have to keep away from impetuous decisions and unfamiliar pursuits and be willing to work, just the characteristics the immigrant farmer had in abundance. He had the energy, but what he had been short of at home was the land on which to apply it. In the New World, where land-labour ratios had been reversed, a relative abundance of land offered him the possibility to liberate his strength.

In the eastern half of British North America, felling the forest took precedence in the settler's endeavours. Some clearing was generally needed right away to provide both open space and suitable logs for a shanty and wood for the fire, and to allow sunlight to get through to the ground. The sharp bite of the axe was the signal of settlement: 'The process of clearing land is this: first, the underbrush (or small bushes) is cut and piled, then the large trees are cut down about three feet from the ground, (all smaller than six inches diameter are cut close to the ground, so as not to interrupt the harrow) then the trees are cut into eight or twelve feet, then the tops are cut off and piled with the brush-wood; when dry, all the brushwood is set fire to, and burns very rapidly, the fire generally spreading over the ground, and burning the dead leaves and long grass, and often even the hut and shanty, if in the way. Then the large logs, if not required for firewood or railing, are drawn together by oxen, and piled about five feet high.'[29]

Besides willingness to labour, settlers needed skill with a team of oxen and dexterity with an axe. The work was awkward, and awkward men only compounded the pain and danger of their toil. A novice such as Wilson Benson often came afoul of his own inexperience: 'The first chopping I attempted was on my new farm, and while underbrushing cut my foot severely, which laid me up for six weeks.'[30] Danger and fear often caused newcomers to hire skilled choppers, an army of whom worked side by side with the agriculturalists pushing back the edge of the forest. Choppers were usually longer-time residents proven at the task. They had spent their lives bringing down trees and could read the subtle weakness of any species, quickly calculate the balance in the crown, and fell with ease:

The rapidity with which a Canadian can cut down the forest is almost beyond the comprehension of one who has never witnessed it. On whichever side he wishes it to fall, he cuts the trunk about six inches lower than on the opposite side, and before you suppose he has done with it, the axeman leaves it, and inflicts some severe wounds upon its neighbour; presently you hear a great creaking noise, and then comes the dreadful crash, which sounds to an immense distance through the woods: a novice can do nothing at this business. Then at cutting the timber into lengths, they are equally dexterous: they make incisions into the two opposite sides, leaving the log not quite cut through, but in such a way that the oxen, when their chain is fastened to the end to remove it, break it off with great ease.[31]

These skills were valuable. William Hutton placed a value of £3 per acre on them.[32]

As the axe was the primary instrument of the clearing process, the felled wood was the primary material, and it served the settler in innumerable ways: 'The timber that is intended for saw logs, they cut into lengths with a cross-cut saw; that for fencing, they cut into twelve-feet lengths; and that for firewood into four feet. The twelve-feet lengths they split into rails for fences with surprising quickness now using the axe and now the wedge; they must all be four inches diameter, and ought to be five, to make a stout fence. A large log will frequently give eighty rails; these they pile in the fences to the height of five feet or six, forming an angle with each, thus, resting one upon the other: there is a good deal of ground lost in this way when the field is in grain, but land is not so valuable here as at home.'[33] Wood was used for housing, fencing, heating, tools, implements, utensils, bowls, and whatever. Even when burnt it had value: ashes could be watered to yield potash (lye), a primary export of the primitive North American economy. Potash was likely the farmer's first commercial product and thus represented the first chance to defray some of the expense of pioneering.

There was no chance to avoid expenses and start with nothing. Critical items had to be bought. The axe, a spade, maybe a hoe, a bit of rope, seed, and a store of food comprised the essentials of survival, and much more was needed. Wilson Benson noted the extent of his preparations: 'I had brought with me a year's provisions, which lasted me till the growth of my own crop the following summer. I also brought a yoke of steers, two cows, a heifer, and some pigs. Fodder was almost out of the question, and I barely succeeded in purchasing two hundred pounds of straw, giving each animal a small handful night and morning, the rest of their subtenance depending entirely on browse.'[34] Wilson had been well prepared. In the previous year he had gone to work on his virgin lot on thirteen occasions and had managed to erect a dwelling and clear a few acres before taking his family there from the relative civilization of a cleared settlement forty miles back from the frontier.

Others would have had much less time to secure their survival – a summer season at most. Wilson had been only too aware of the dangers: 'In summer many families eked out an existence in a very precarious manner. In the early part of the summer, wild leeks and cow-cabbage, wild nettles, etc were a valuable substitute for a more substantial meal.'[35] Even recourse to supplies of wild food was at times inadequate. Jane White, well fed and comfortable in the town of Goderich, noted the incidence of famine less than thirty miles away, in the newer settlement districts. Jane wrote to her friend Eleanor in Ireland: 'The crops last year were a failure owing to the dryness of the summer. The people in Huron and Bruce are starving in hundreds. Bruce is worst being a new settlement. Some of the Highland Scotch up at Kinloss who depended on the cultivation of the new farms are subsisting on roots gathered in the bush.'[36]

At best, three or four acres could be cleared in a year,[37] and as soon as a patch was ready a rough garden and a field crop would have been planted in between the stumps: 'The wheat is harrowed in – about one bushel per acre; there is no occasion to plough, and if there were, it would be impossible, owing to the roots of the trees not being decayed.'[38] A fence was needed to keep animals out of the 'fields.' Ploughing of the ground could be five or more years away, when the roots were sufficiently rotted that stumps could be levered out. When the roots were finally removed, the pock-marked surface required levelling. Ten years would not have been too long a time between felling trees and seeing a surface fit to be ploughed in straight furrows and harrowed and seeded with comparative ease. In the mean time critical skills were being learned, and an appreciation of the weather and planting dates was being acquired.

Cropping experience from home was applied with great caution. Winter grains were risky and in some places impossible. In Nova Scotia and New Brunswick, oats, hay, and root crops predominated, but in Upper Canada wheat was adopted early as a commercial crop. The crops were familiar to the immigrants, but new modes of cultivation had to be developed, usually being copied from the patterns of earlier arrived settlers. For example, leaving potatoes and root crops in the ground until needed, as was possible in Ireland, was disastrous in British North America. In the depth of winter, frost could reach −20°c regularly, and snow on the ground might accumulate to a depth of four feet or more. It had to be learned that planting could not be rushed, despite the spring warmth, and had to await the time when the trees were in leaf. A North American cycle of husbandry was required. No season was free of work, and no season easier than another.

Shortages of cash added extra pressures, and farming one's own lot might be enmeshed with labouring elsewhere. Free time on the farm merely provided time for work in the woods. A contemporary observer in New Brunswick noted that poor immigrants from Britain had been 'compelled occasionally to hire out and get lumber until their land was sufficiently cleared to live on.'[39] In Upper Canada, Wilson Benson and his neighbours spent summer periods, between the planting and the harvesting of their own crops, in the older settled areas, working as farm labourers.[40] 'Myself and many of my neighbours went to the older settlement in haying and harvest, returning before our own crop was ripe. A portion of our earnings had to be carefully hoarded to meet the taxes, for it was next to impossible to obtain a cash market for farm produce [nearby].'[41] Part-time work off the farm was common and necessary, and nowhere was it possible for the ordinary farm pioneer to use his time other than in productive work.

The climate was always of interest to the immigrants. Among farmers it could not have been otherwise, and great attention was given to its extremes. In letters home, severe heat and cold, drought and flood, were always thought worthy of mention. The continental extremes of dry, hot summers and long, frozen winters marked the distinctiveness of the climate, and for people in Ireland news of extremes in the weather was tantalizing. In an effort to convey the distinctiveness of the climate, some writers grossly exaggerated the effects of the Canadian winter. Alexander Robb wrote from British Columbia: 'We have had a very severe winter here this year. It set in nearly a month earlier than usual and we have had more snow and more cold than I have seen for these last three years. On Christmas day the thermometer was down to 31 degrees below zero. You cannot fancy what such cold is, but it may give you an idea when I tell you that at 15 degrees lower mercury will freeze and strong brandy will become as thick as syrup.'[42] Other settlers insisted on greater credence in their reporting. Nathaniel Carrothers opined that 'you have hard so much about our summer heat and winter cold that I need say littel and that is that the are not near so intence as the are generely represented.'[43]

Even for Irish immigrants not engaged in agriculture the climate was worthy of note. The North West Mounted policeman Ernest Cochrane was more uncomfortable in the heat of the prairie summer than in the deep cold of the continental winter. In 1897 he wrote home to County Antrim: 'We are having our hot weather spell; and with the thermometer at between 90° and 96° *in the shade*, times are not pleasant, as they give us no summer uniform to wear.'[44] Yet the prairie winters, which Cochrane termed 'the almost never ending season of frost and snow,'[45] were also severe and uncomfortable. At his barracks in Calgary he recalled: 'There is no fire in my bedroom and I have to go to bed cold and have to break any washing water in the morning with an iron boot-jack. Over half an inch of ice during the night.'[46]

Winter was severe, but its severity was also of benefit. Frozen ground, rivers, and lakes offered possibilities for transportation by sleigh in areas where in summer movement was impeded by broken tracks and swamps. Roads, if they existed at all, were rutted, always irregular, and nowhere free of obstacles and hindrances. In early spring, 'just after the breaking up of the ice and melting of the snow, the roads were almost impassable; the horses being frequently above the knees in mud, and the ruts so deep that land travelling was really dangerous.'[47] In summer, clay tracks were hard-baked and excruciatingly rough, making the strain on hubs, spokes, and axles extreme. Once winter came, a blanket of snow filled in holes, evened out contours, and buried the usual stumps. Timber could be skidded to the mill or stacked in riverside piles, where it remained until spring thaw permitted it to be floated downstream. Grain could also be moved off the farm to the markets on sleighs, and journeys were often taken with relished abandon: 'The people like deep snow for it gives good slaeing and the drive like fury with all kins of loding.'[48] More realistically, the 'slaeing' was still a chore, and despite the ease that winter brought to moving goods, it did not bring safety. Wilson Benson and three neighbours came near death while taking their teams back from an eleven-mile trip to a grist-mill:

The snow was between four and five feet deep, and towards evening the cold became intense. Our oxen were exhausted, and if one team remained ten minutes behind another, the track was filled up, the snow was falling so fast. What with breaking the road ahead of the oxen and the exertion required to wade through the deep snow, I was in a perspiration when we reached the Toronto line, where the road was much better. The slow pace of the oxen prevented me taking sufficient exercise to keep up warmth, and I became chilled, then benumbed, and finally, when I reached the foot of the hill on which Mr. John Allan's hotel stands, I was unable to walk, and crawled on my hands and knees most of the way up the hill. I was taken into Mr. Allan's and kindly cared for. I was compelled to remain two days before I was able to set out for home. My companions were nearly in as bad plight as myself.[49]

The dangers were recognized, and the hardships became folklore.

If anything, the weather and climate were gauged less in negative terms and more often in terms of benefit – a boon to health and longevity and distinctly preferable to the bronchial dissipation of old country damp. On this practically everyone agreed: they judged the climate to be healthful. British Columbia's climate was rated highly by Alexander Robb in a letter to his sick sister: 'How I wish I could transplant you here for the next six months or as much longer as I could prevail on you to stop. Besides the comfort it would be to me to have you near me, I am satisfied that a few months in this high altitude and dry climate would completely restore your health, diseases of the chest being a thing almost unknown here.'[50] Ironically, tuberculosis claimed the lives of Robb's two brothers back in Ireland, and he returned home to take over the family farm in County Down.[51] In Upper Canada, Nathaniel Carrothers was also convinced of the healthful qualities of the climate: 'I forgot to mention that we had got six children 3 boyes and 3 girls the two eldest ar boyes and the next two are girls and the youngest is a girl we have had none that died for none of them has had any sicknes we never lost an our of sleep with them yet I belive Children are fare more healthey in general than the are in Ireland.'[52] Fewer bronchial disorders, life as long as or longer than at home, and less sickness among children were important and weighty advantages brought by emigration to a so-called harsh environment.

Good health was held not only to be part of the climatic bounty but the consequence as well of clearing away the forest, the source of a fever or so-called ague. William Hutton noted that as 'the country becomes cleared, it becomes more healthy; thus, then, it is very important to be located in an old settled district ... Persons ... who go into the woods, seldom escape the ague, but it is not dangerous; they also suffer much from the mosquitoes, which seldom venture into the full blaze of day; they are very little larger than a gnat; many are severely affected by their bites, the parts swelling considerably, whilst others allow them to bite away, without suffering any inconvenience.'[53] The swamps and forests of the wilderness were perceived to be the source of ague, and thus unhealthy, and clearing was deemed to be good. Ague in fact was the fever symptom of malaria, brought on by parasites living in mosquitoes, but the science of the time was ignorant of the link between mosquitoes and malaria. Rather, educated opinion then had it that the ague was caused by the forest. The incidence of ague declined as the forest was pushed back, but the logic of the time placed the forest at fault, not the mosquitoes.

Clearing the forest was believed also to improve the climate by somehow lessening the extremes, but Wilson Benson thought otherwise: 'The tendency of frost during the later years of settlement in this country is somewhat singular, as it is the general opinion that as a country becomes cleared, the frost decreases; but the history of this section of country proves the reverse.'[54] He had noted how howling winds and drifting snow had not been a feature of the forest he had come to clear. The changes suggested to him that removing the forest served to expose the land and its occupants to the worst of winter's chill. He had no scientific evidence of temperature change, but his intuition and the aches of broken bones told him that it was getting colder.

MATURING SOCIETY

Inexorably, the forest retreated, and the landscape lost the look of the wild. Progress at clearing was slow, and except for the social warmth of family and neighbours, life was primitive: 'Every necessary of life was provisable only at an enormous sacrifice of toil and privation.'[55] Year after year the work went on. Some families gave up and left to become pioneers again or wage labourers, quite often elsewhere in the New World. Some, including Alexander Robb, returned to the Old. Some went mad. George Carrothers was put 'in a delicate state ... broke down by his former hard labour.'[56] Wilson Benson was broken physically also, by the fly-wheel of a steam thrasher, but his spirit was undaunted.

As society matured, settlers' efforts were directed less and less toward environmental conquest and physical survival and more to completing the farm and getting ahead. To fulfil their dreams, they cleared more land and, when possible, bought more land. It was also a matter of pride to have solid indicators of wealth that folks back home could understand and appreciate. Every acre over what had been left behind in Ireland constituted another step on the road to success. Every acre held free of rent or free of mortgage magnified the growing social distance from what the emigrant had been and what he might have been had he not emigrated. Edward McCullom wrote: 'I thank God who directed my steps to this land of peace and plenty. I have nearly four hundred acres of land mine own – no bailiff to visit me; a good village property – two good stores doing a good business. This is my experience, and I would like Lord Lisgar, "or any other man," to prove to me how I could have done as well had I remained in the County Cavan.'[57]

Canadian success meant fulfilment of the emigrants' objectives of acquiring not only for themselves, but for their children, assets that might ease their lives. It would not be much – few but dreamers desired to become rich. Rather, settlers were content to have their own lands to work as they saw fit and a modest income to raise their lives above the level they had left. It meant too that their children's lives should be better than their own. Providing opportunities, especially for sons, had been a factor in the original decision to emigrate, and improvement of their children's lives continued to be a principal goal. William Hutton expressed the hope for the children: 'There is some hope, however, that the farmer, *who can put to his hand*, when he has his farm free of rent, and you may say of taxes, will be able to provide the necessaries, and even the comforts of life; and if I am to judge by what I see around me, I think some little may be accumulated for a rising family ... There is ample room for your children to succeed around you. No profession is crowded here; there is plenty to do and good pay for all, and you need be under no uneasiness about their settlement in life.'[58] Accumulation was thought to be possible, and a secure future attainable.

The emigrants had left Ireland at a time of growing reluctance to subdivide holdings by partible inheritance. Fragmentation was to be avoided, and emigration was a route to that objective. In British North America the reluctance to subdivide persisted. Holdings were usually left to one son, and his siblings would remove from the farm and, as their parents had done before them, migrate in search of opportunities. When sons coming of age could not be accommodated on the family farm, possibilities existed on the frontier, where land was cheaper because it was uncleared. For sons willing to pioneer and repeat what their parents had undertaken, there was sometimes opportunity relatively close by, especially in Upper Canada, but much less so in New Brunswick and Lower Canada.

For some families, generational change meant locational change and a new family geography. Joseph Carrothers saw his newly wed son William move on to occupy unimproved land to the west: 'My son William got married last year a Miss Willsie, her Father gave her eight Hundred Dollars, he has removed last month to the Township of Bosanquet 54 miles from this place Land being cheaper than here. Land is selling in this place for 40 to 50 Dollars per Acre as it is improved, and some above that price.'[59] Once the newlyweds left, others, including Joseph, followed. His brother Nathaniel wrote: 'Brother Joseph has moved a way from hear, his son James has bought a farm in the same township that his son William had settled in and close by and James was determed to go on it last spring so the all moved to it; and I had a letter from him last week and the were all well and he said his health was very good.'[60] Nathaniel's own children also moved with the expanding frontier in Upper Canada and eventually crossed the continent to British Columbia. Brothers Joseph and Nathaniel were split by their children's need to move on and seek their own independent livelihood. In the process, some family links were strained, others secured, still others widened, but, as indicated by the Carrothers's letters home, the links were not sundered. Only geography had been stretched.

LANDSCAPE CHANGE

Within a generation, immigration and settlement revolutionized the visual appearance of the New World. In formerly forested regions, farming land was enclosed within field boundaries and farms were carved from the wilderness. On farms, stumps began to disappear, and inconvenient boulders were moved to piles in the middle of fields or into the corners, between the bends in snake-rail fences. Straight furrows in fall and smooth harrowed surfaces in spring created new ground textures and seasonal colours. In the areas best suited for agriculture, the forest had been cut back most evidently, but nonetheless, even there, woodlots, intervening unoccupied lots, and stretches of unsuitable land retained a second growth of scrub bushes and trees.

To Irish eyes the cleared landscape still would have appeared as infinitely more tree-clad than that left behind, and it would also have been deemed untidy and incomplete. In New Brunswick and Nova Scotia, where farming, lumbering, and fishing continued to coexist, farmsteads in the Irish areas were often little more than isolated clearings. Among the Appalachian foothills of the Eastern Townships, the rural landscape was similarly disjointed. Some environments could not be overwhelmed. Common to the immigrant settlement experience throughout central and eastern Canada was the continual struggle to maintain and to increase the area of cleared land. The battle was easiest where land and markets were good, but in marginal zones the encroachment of nature was always a threat and often realized. Some areas reverted to the forest within a generation, and some, even though they had been cleared, never felt the point of a plough.

By 1860, 'the universal shelter of the forest'[61] on his hundred-acre lot in Artemesia township was in retreat for Wilson Benson, who in the previous decade had cleared away thirty-two acres of trees. In the following decade he cleared another thirty-three acres, and thus within twenty years of settlement he had removed two-thirds of his forest.[62] His neighbours had done likewise on their lots, opening the land virtually to the limits possible. The portions uncleared, one-third of the hundred acres in Wilson's case, were there to provide the annual necessities of firewood. Within twenty years most of his free timber was spent and his fields had been squared, his fences straightened, wood-frame houses built, and a timber-frame barn and a log stable raised. Twenty years was all it had taken for Wilson and his pioneering neighbours to alter the look of the land that nature had taken aeons to create.

The landscape began to acquire a gentility and a husbanded aspect as more and more labour was wrought. Survey lines – initially no more than an untidy procession of rows of axe scars on the sides of trees – had been given man-made forms as almost straight roads and fences. In southern Ontario a rectilinear geometry was engraved on the land in fields, farms, concessions, and townships. The farm rectangle was focused on the farm-house, the barn, and other outbuildings.[63] The house of the Irish immigrant William Graham (Figure 5.3) faced out to the main road, and, amid expanses of cleared land, it stood as the sentinel of agricultural victory and pioneering success. It was also an architectural copy of an American pattern-book sketch and thus clearly removed from any Irish cultural format. Offset to one side were the farm buildings, respectably distanced from the house, and out in front an orchard. From the road a lane led up past the side of the house and on to the barn. Behind it all, at the back of the lot, were the cut-over remnants of the former forest. Orderly, neat, geometric, established, and respectable, the farm's arrangement bore some similarity to the larger Georgian farmsteads of Ireland. The exceptional could become common.

Nathaniel Carrothers's farm yard might be imagined from what he said about it in his letters home. He considered the house he built in 1845 'a good deacent frame house deacentley fineshed,'[64] revealing his pride through the use of the word 'decent,' applicable to houses and people alike. He built it himself, on a slight rise made from ground dug out for the cellar. The house was a one-storey affair, a basic timber-frame cottage with lapped wood siding. He also built his barn of timber frames, clad with vertical planking, in the style depicted in Figure 5.3: 'The barn is 50 feet long by 30 feet wide and 16 feet high in the side; in this i store my grain as it comes of the harvest field this saves a grat dale of trouble in the stacking.'[65] There was no need for a haggard around the back of the house as in Ireland, but because of the climate and larger herd there had to be a large barn. The scale of Canadian barns was much greater than that in Ireland, and in their size they came to symbolize the farm landscape of the new country.

Step by step Nathaniel effected the same changes as most pioneers, bringing his buildings to the number and size needed to store all his

RES. OF **WILLIAM GRAHAM**, CON.10, LOT 6, HUNGERFORD TP. ONT.

FIGURE 5.3
A stylized rendition of the Ontario farm of William Graham, Irish
immigrant; H. Belden and Co., *Illustrated Historical Atlas of the Counties of
Hastings and Prince Edward, Ontario* (Toronto 1878), 65

produce and organizing them to suit a rather mixed agricultural system.
Nearby he had an orchard – the mark in Ulster of a respectable farming
family – and also a garden for both flowers and vegetables, which he
had started at the outset of his pioneering life: 'I planted out about an
acre with fruit trees such as apples pears plumes peaches cherries these
all do as well in this country as I ever saw them in Ireland if not better
our verieteys are very good the trees groo quick and bear soon I have
had about 60 bushel on mine this season I allso carry on a flour and
vegible garden all of which do well in this country we have a great many
kinds of both that would not grow in Ireland.'[66] It was a place very like
that of his neighbours on the sixth line of Westminster township, and
in the detail of its gardens and orchards it reflected elements common
to his home in Fermanagh.

The similarity of landscape tastes was not just reflected in the design
and inclusion of gardens and orchards but also extended to the settlers'
choice of plants and shrubs. Settlers often brought plants, roots, and
seeds with them on their journeys and later received seeds and roots

clandestinely and ingeniously sent through the mails. Joseph Carrothers wrote home just after his arrival in Canada: 'You will oblige me if you will make it your business to get some of the seed of the Balm of Gilead & the Annagalis you will send them in your next letter. You will fold your letter first and then open it again and rub a little paste in the crase and stick a row of seeds in it and fold it up. I have sent seeds to Paul [in Australia] in that way. I gave plants to Miss Armstrong you can get some of them put in to a corner of a newspaper by my Friend Mr. J.C. do not neglect it.'[67]

Letters transmitted more than news and views! They were also a conduit for the dispersal of species to the New World. Canada's famous Red Fife wheat was developed from seed sent through the transatlantic mails. Some of the seeds sent over were for ornamental purposes, but others were definitely sought for economic motives, as part of the determination of what might grow best. Nathaniel Carrothers was willing to experiment a great deal, and by the type and range of grasses he asked his mother-in-law to bring out he showed the skills and efforts involved in making agricultural improvements:

I want you to get me some gras seed one kind I want which I dismember the name of but it is the softest and lightest of all the gras kinds I remember us to have it sown on the narrow strip of meadow below the kill the have it in many parts of the country I think Andrew Mongomery can eisley get it for you only one pound of it I want let it be very Clean it is jenerly sown on bottoms so you cant mistake it; it produces very soft and light hay I want you to try the seed shopes in eniskilen if the have got any of the Italian rye grass seed and if the have get me a point of it likewise it is sown and cultivated in england and scotland and far preferible to any other gras; gather me allso a pound of common gras seed of your own stabel loft letting it be clean possible marking the name of each kind on the enclouser we have the timethey and rye gras here the grow well but I don't like them as the dont produce any after groth and send them by hur and you will oblige me very much.[68]

Landscape copying could be carried to extremes. Nathaniel's brother Joseph built his house not only in the shape but in the actual form of an Irish masonry cottage, because he wished to have nothing to do with a 'good deacent frame house,' Canadian timber construction having no appeal for him: 'I have a dislike to the timber Houses the are very cold in winter and very hot in summer and are allways sinking and twisting.'[69] He chose to build his house in the cottage format of the home farm in

Ulster: 'Dear Willy I have been very busy this summer building a house and I am living in it now i have a neat Cottage House 30 feet by 20 the out walls 10 feet high of mud and inside walls of Brick It is well thought of in this country (stones is very rare in this place) ... I got help from Brothers and Cosins but I was Brick layer and Carpenter my self the wondered I done the fireplaces so well.'[70] The structure described is a common mud cottage with end chimneys; stones were not available in the rich farmland of Westminster, but clay for mud walls and brick was, in abundance. The building would not have been odd to his Irish immigrant neighbours, but for the fact of its being in Upper Canada.

Building a house was often a settler's first mark of permanence on his lot. Generally the first dwelling would be constructed of logs, a crude single-storey structure with an open fireplace and rude chimney. Despite all the draughts, its two rooms made it a definite improvement over a shanty or tent. New skills were needed to construct it, and because of the size of logs involved and the height of wall to which logs had to be successively raised and laid in place, the building of a good cabin generally involved more than one man. Ideally, four men, two handling the logs and two others notching the log ends that dovetailed together to bind the corners, could do the job efficiently. That meant sharing labour and exchanging expertise. It was a pattern of co-operation that mitigated the individual settler's isolation. A wood frame-house with clapboard siding, as built by Nathaniel, would have represented a further improvement on the original crude log structure and was generally as much as could be undertaken in the first, immigrant generation. Elaboration on the basic designs by the incorporation of pattern-book styles and industrial materials such as brick and prefabricated windows and doors was more likely to be done by the better-off, especially by the Canadian-born generation. Changes in the design and construction of housing reflected the growing wealth and sophistication of society and the integration of localities into a larger regional culture.

Rural localities acquired the look of permanence when churches, schools, and community halls were built. Initially, church meetings and worship had been infrequent or occasional, as there were too few people and too few permanent church mission stations. Most denominations sent their churchmen on missions that involved a circuit, taking as much as a month to complete. As population increased, services could become more frequent and a church could be built. For Protestants, Orange halls were the landscape indicators of their particular Irish outlook. Often the Orange lodge had a building before the church congregation did. Orangemen were drawn from all Protestant denominations, and their lodge halls served in many localities as churches and even schools.

Schools and churches represented the case of local social organizations integrating families from disparate backgrounds and binding large fractions of the community into a set of overlapping and interacting collectivities. In rural localities they might be found facing one another across the intersection of two roads, the church on one corner, a school on another, and perhaps a general store on yet a third. They added to the landscape a visible symbol of community in an area where the dispersed, isolated farmsteads might otherwise suggest an area of individualists, remote from one another and without a collective identity.

The picture Wilson Benson painted of his Protestant district in 1876 represented a world vastly changed from the scene he described on coming into the settlement area. On his arrival he claimed: 'The prospect was lovely; where the surface was not covered with ground-hemlock, there was an abundance of wild nettles, corn cabbage, wild onions (leeks), &c., which certainly gave the virgin forest a luxuriant appearance. The black flies and mosquitoes assailed one in myriads.'[71] A trip along the same route in 1876, as depicted in the contemporary map in Figure 5.4,[72] would have been for him into terra incognita – a strip of cleared land marked by junction towns and a regular spacing of schools, Orange halls, and churches. On both sides of the Toronto and Sydenham Road (Figure 5.4) the ground hemlock and trees had been relegated to unimproved wet ground and protected woodlots. Practically every 100-acre lot worth cultivating was occupied by a farming family, although the map here records only the names of those willing to subscribe to its publication and sale. Where the Toronto and Sydenham Road entered Artemisia township, at lot 190, a school-house was now located, serving a local community of Irish, Scots, and native Canadians. Further north, the swampy bottom ground and slumped valley banks made it impossible to keep the road in a straight alignment past the Moore farms. Into a corner of lot 179 the hall of LOL 244 was tucked, attended by fathers and brothers of the children attending school down the road. The Moores were in the lodge. Johnathan Moore had taken out the warrant in 1850.[73] A mile on was another school, and another mile further the town of Flesherton lay along the east bank of the Boyne. Grist mills, saw mills, and numerous small craft and factory industries shared the urban place with a school and Anglican, Presbyterian, and Methodist (but no Catholic) churches.

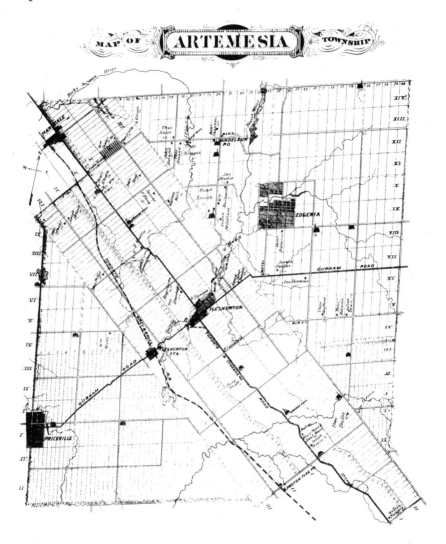

FIGURE 5.4

The vicinity of the Toronto and Sydenham Road in Artemesia township c. 1880. Wilson Benson's farm is indicated by the cross-hatched area to the east of Markdale. H. Belden and Co., *Illustrated Atlas of the County of Grey* (Toronto 1880), 24

Across the Boyne were more farmland and farmers. Samuel Cunningham had come from Ireland. Francis Beattie had come from Scotland and with his son Andrew farmed 200 acres.[74] The younger children went to the Orange Valley school beside the hall of LOL 509. Beyond this, on lot 115, Orange Valley Presbyterian Church, which the Beatties and Cunninghams attended, had been erected, and a burying ground created beside it. Across the road lived William Irwin, the minister, an Ulsterman. His brother lived two lots away, and between them a rough hillock of lot 114 served as the Methodist burying ground. Practically at the end of the colonization road in the township, a bit on from Wilson's old farm on lot 110 east[75] (marked by cross-hatched lines), the town of Markdale, named after Mark Armstrong from Fermanagh, had sprung up.

Wilson was living there in 1876, keeping a shop and resting the broken body that no longer allowed him to farm. There, he could hear factory whistles and the steam blasts from the Grey and Bruce Rail Road engines and contemplate the progress made. Genuinely thankful that he had been part of it all, he noted that 'it is a source of extreme gratification to me, as it no doubt will be to all the pioneers of my early days, that their sacrifice of worldly comforts and exposure to toil and suffering so largely contributed to the development of our country and the welfare of succeeding generations.'[76]

The countryside, marked by increasingly permanent residential, farm, and social architecture, was punctuated here and there by urban centres, the real marks of economic development and maturity. These might range from small, almost completely rural-based hamlets, providing milling, handling services, and implements to farmers and shop goods to their families, to industrial towns. Cannington was described by Richard Braithwaite of County Antrim in 1849 as 'a lively place. There is a grist mill and saw mill and distillery and four merchant shops and 2 schoolhouses at the place and the English Church one mile and a half from it.'[77]

That sort of place would have been familiar to all Irish immigrants. Cannington's status of farming village meant that settlers there had reattained the type and level of local services they had left behind in Ireland. In County Fermanagh, the village of Lisbellaw, which Nathaniel Carrothers had left in 1835, was at the time of his departure a well-developed market centre (Figure 5.5). The village was already complete, and its stone churches, mill, houses, and other structures offered a semblance of settledness and permanence that Nathaniel and his neigh-

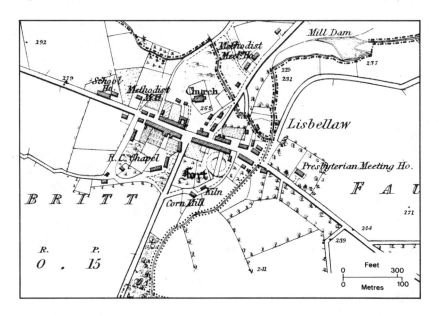

FIGURE 5.5
Lisbellaw, County Fermanagh; Ordnance Survey Six Inch Map, first edition, 1834

bours in Upper Canada had to re-create. In 1839 Nathaniel told his brother in County Fermanagh that 'bisnes of every kind is good London is nearly as large again as when I came to it [in 1835].'[78] Fourteen years later he remarked: 'London has become a large and fine place since we came to this Country there is a great many fine Churches, and merchant shops and whole sale ware houses all of breek.'[79] Mercantile prosperity and population growth framed a new existence for those who had pioneered.

Growth of towns marked the maturing phase of Canadian settlement. For example, Orangeville was a 'hamlet of houses'[80] when Wilson Benson visited it in 1850. By 1875 the town had 4,000 people and boasted railway links and the finest market street in rural Ontario. Steam-power and railways heralded the transformation of merchant centres and crossroads corners into new central places. In 1876 Benson noted: 'Things have changed – a market at our own door – the sound of railway and steam whistles, of mills and manufactories, where a few short years ago resounded the howl of the wolf. Innumerable villages, containing mills, manufactories and general stores of merchandize now mark the spot which was overgrown by dense forest trees fifteen or twenty years ago. The stride of prosperity made by the County of Grey, and indeed the country at large, has been gigantic.'[81]

Jane White understood how her own life had been integrated into a larger national, even North American network:

The railway [to Buffalo, New York] is completed about two months ago or more. There were great excursions to Goderich of both Yankees and Canadians. On the celebration on the 8 July at the opening of the line the town was so thronged many had to leave same day because they could not be accommodated with lodgings, so many thousands persons. There were two brass bands up from Stratford and Brantford. The firemen's torchlight procession was pretty. The fireworks were very inferior to expectations. The Governor General Sir Edmund Head was up. There was dinner and ball. The town was decorated with flags, such a number I have not seen before. There were triumphal arches decorated with green mottoes such as "success to the railway", "Welcome American friends", "Reciprocity etc.". The plank sidewalks were finished for the occasion. There was a flag to be hoisted on the courthouse, a dangerous place from its great height. A man went up and did it for the sum of 3 15s.od. so that money was no object that day. The Signeaw [] came by the Lake. Goderich is bound to be a stirring place being a terminus but I hear that the towns down along the line are nearly ruined, the trains passing through spoils business.[82]

Railways heralded the rise of an urban phase and the decline of a rural-dominated pioneering phase. With the stimulus of trade, the pioneer centres gave way to other towns in centralizing economic networks. In announcing the arrival of industrialism, the railways also signalled the virtual end of pioneering in central and eastern Canada and coincidentally the end of the great Irish emigration to Canada.

The maturation of Canadian society is well exemplified in the transformation of a lumber town into Ottawa, designated Canada's capital in 1857. Lord Dufferin, arriving in 1872 from Ulster as governor-general was a witness to the transition:

Ottawa is not an inviting town. It is just in that stage which is so characteristic of a new country. A collection of small wooden houses, scattered higgldy-piggldy all over the place but interspersed with new built or half built stores, shops and residences of considerable pretensions. The disjointed articulation of the city,

however, are rapidly drawing into an organised mass, the whole being sur-
mounted by a lofty group of public buildings of Gothic architecture comprising
the House of Commons, Senate House, and the very fine ranges of Government
offices, – well situated on an eminence overlooking the river. This pile is really
very fine, the architecture is good and the outlying groups well together. The
interior of the Senate house is quite beautiful, – the House of Commons scarcely
inferior to it, both being in better taste to my mind than our own Chambers.[83]

Mrs Woodburn, a native of Belfast, had lived through various stages in
the new capital's development, and toward the end of the century she
recounted the city's achievements with affectionate pride:

Bytown [Ottawa] in '41 had about 4000 inhabitants, and now the figure is
53,000 – and as you are doubtless aware our City is the capital of the Confederated Provinces of British America – half of a continent, leaving the small province
of Newfoundland, which has so far kept out of the Union. Ottawa is really now
a very progressive little city and is not a bad place to live in, altho' when
compared with your Queen city of the North, our Washington of the North is
but a small place. One feature of progress, however, we lead you in – that is,
the general use of electricity. Most of the houses are lit by that light, our street
cars run all over the city, and much of our mill and shop machinery is driven
by that subtle power. Thanks for this to the Great Chaudiere Falls on the Great
Ottawa river, which flows by the city.[84]

Arriving before the Famine, Mrs Woodburn, like many other Irish
pioneers in Canada, had lived to witness the creation of a nation and
the onset of the electrical age. By 1875 the first wave of pioneering was
done. The next would involve extension of Canadian society into the
prairies and British Columbia, but in the settlement of these new lands
the Irish would never predominate as they had in central and eastern
Canada. Similarly, they were underrepresented in the immigration that
fuelled the urban expansion of the late nineteenth and early twentieth
centuries. The principal Irish contribution had been in the rural, pioneering phase. In the subsequent urban and industrial phases the Irish
contribution was effected mainly by the Canadian progeny of the Irish
pioneers.

CHAPTER SIX

Social and Religious Life

Coming to grips with the new environment in British North America meant more than adapting skills and adopting new procedures. Old ways of organizing social life were redefined to suit the Canadian context. Little was lost except for a few forms of behaviour based on the social distinctions inherent in the more rigid arrangement of Irish society. Most forms of behaviour seemed to fit the new place exceedingly well. Religion received as much attention in the New World as it did in the Old, and this was as true for Catholics as for Protestants. All denominations transferred their churches, but for the transplanted communities the politico-religious identities were best summarized by the Catholic church and the Protestants' Orange Order. The cultural division of Ireland was in essence transferred intact, and much of Irish Canada became a New Ireland unchanged.

Socializing and conviviality were carried on in traditional ways and thus also complemented the institutional similarities of the New and the Old. Families tried to live close to kin, and friends were drawn from the local community. Sons and daughters born in Canada married into neighbouring families and frequently, like their parents, migrated on. In some respects family bonds assumed a new importance in a place of many more strangers. Survival and economic opportunity were a family strategy, and mobility formed a major part of the effort. These themes – the increased importance of family ties, the continuing search for new opportunities, and the transfer of traditional institutions, virtually unadapted – are the subject of this chapter.

FAMILIES AND MOBILITY

Newcomers to British North America, especially in the nineteenth century, have become known for their geographical mobility. They seem to modern observers to have been always on the move, putting down stakes in a place only to uproot them and move on again. *Transient* has been the term most often used to describe the apparent mobility, and the study of transiency has become a focus of modern attempts to understand the changeable and, for some, unstable character of pioneering society.[1] Transiency, as discussed among modern observers, has been identified with rootlessness and aimlessness, but this is an incomplete and misapplied depiction. The movements of many pioneers in North America were purposeful, deliberate, and directed at achieving eventual permanent settlements. In British North America the mobility of many of the Irish was purposeful, with a strong social and economic motivation, and the attraction of the neighbouring United States made it more intense. They did not move just for the sake of moving. Only a minority were transient – lacking a base in life and the social ties that create and provide a home. Perhaps the best indicator that the mobility of the Irish in British North America was not aimless is given by the geography of their settlement. Whole regions of Irish were created and maintained, and the longevity of these regions (and those of other peoples as well) challenges the notion of widespread rootlessness.

Society did move. After all, the large forested and wild territories of half a continent were being taken over by a farming and lumbering society, and the process required more than a generation to effect. What immigrant parents accomplished in one place might be attempted in another by their children, or at least some of their children. Failure in one place could entail a subsequent attempt to succeed in another. Economic change was omnipresent, letting no place just be. People adjusted, and some did so through moving – to cancel debts, to seek new opportunities, or to join their friends. To move was to be part of the New World. To move was simply the consequence of deciding to become part of that world.

Wilson Benson is the best-known example of mobility in pioneering Canada, and his itinerant years, 1836–50, have been used as the centrepiece of a recent study of transiency.[2] But Wilson, while he did travel a great deal, spent his last sixty years in the same place.[3] Born in Belfast in 1821, he was taken shortly thereafter to Portadown, County Armagh. At the age of twelve, he was led by family circumstances to be hired out to work as a weaver apprentice, and for the next several years his life seemed an unending series of moves. Figure 6.1 depicts the places among which he moved. He emigrated to Scotland in 1836 at the age of fifteen to join his married sister. There he passed three years in odd jobs. He worked as a pedlar, as a hand in a cotton mill, and as a seasonal harvest labourer. He returned to Ireland in 1838, signed on as an apprentice weaver in Bottle Hill townland in Kilmore parish, County Armagh, served some time as a weaver in Mullatine townland, a mile away, and after about two years married and left for British North America, where he had a brother-in-law near Kingston.

Arriving at Brockville in Upper Canada in 1841, Benson would spend the two subsequent years in a variety of poorly paid jobs. At first, he wove woollen cloth. He chanced his hand at ploughing, but his ineptitude was soon discovered, and he then tried hotel portering, baking, shoemaking, and eventually labouring in a farm implements factory. In 1843 he entered a phase of seasonal work that lasted six years. Each summer he shipped out for the season on Lake Ontario steamers, generally as a cook, and each year, when the ice closed shipping, he took to keeping a shop or peddling. He reported in 1843, after the end of the boat season: 'I rented a house on lot 24, Stewartsville, Kingston, where I opened a small store, stocked it with groceries and other miscellaneous articles suited to the trade of the locality, and was tolerably successful.'[4] He later gave up that store, in subsequent years tried two others run by his wife, and in the non-shipping season concentrated on peddling. At various times he peddled oysters, whisky, millinery, and his own potent alcohol cure for ague. Misfortune, accidents, and petty crooks darkened his life, and he seemed at the whim of people and forces more certain than he was.

His seasonal regime continued until 1849, when the chance alignment of three events led him to become a pioneer. A shop his wife kept in Toronto burned down and 'immediately after quitting the schooner, a brother-in-law of mine, who lived in the immediate vicinity of Orange-ville, came to see me, and from his representations of the benefits of farming, I sent my wife up with him to ascertain from her how she liked the place. I sent a barrel of whiskey with him to sell for me. Soon after this I received a letter informing me of the death of my father, in Ireland, which hastened my departure from Toronto to Orangeville.'[5] His brother-in-law had asked him to consider farming because of the fire. The death of his father in Ireland broke his primary kinship bond and familial ties to Ireland, and the possibility of land offered a more

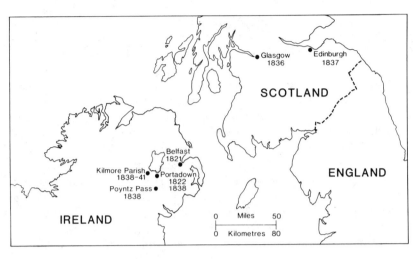

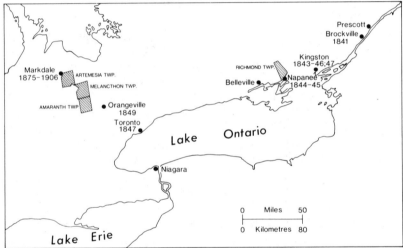

FIGURE 6.1
The travels of Wilson Benson in Ireland and Scotland (above) to 1841 and
in Canada West / Ontario from 1841

permanent form of both work and connection with his new homeland. In 1849 he ended the to-ing and fro-ing of an itinerant life and at the age of twenty-eight started farming. Wilson had spent three years in Scotland, two years in Ireland, and eight in Canada in a transient existence, but that time had not been spent without purpose. He had tried numerous jobs and acquired a range of skills. He was only twenty-eight when he went to pioneer – by no means aged – and by all accounts at the right stage of life to encounter the wilderness. He had a family, his outlook on life allowed him to cope with misfortune and adversity, and his links with Ireland were weak. He was no longer a juvenile greenhorn.

Despite the appearance of excessive mobility, Wilson's early adult life had not been entirely rootless. After his marriage he had always maintained a home for his wife and his children and always returned to the family base. Each location represented another effort to settle permanently. His houses had also been shops, the ideal sort of venture for a young man with a family who had little capital, no recognized professional skill, and apparently no willingness to be a manual labourer. Wilson's home was also anchored by his wife's relations in the country. Two of her brothers were there, one in Richmond township, near Kingston, where Wilson built his first 'snug house' and opened a shop, and another northwest of Toronto, in Amaranth township, where Wilson acquired his first farm lot in 1849. Wilson's life was one of apparently extreme mobility, but even in his movements the social and economic elements in his life were constant, and his objectives, set within the family milieu of needing and wishing to provide, were fixed. He would find eventually a place of permanence. In 1850 he sold his land in Amaranth and left for Artemesia township, where he started again to farm on a lot in virgin forest. That bush lot he made into a respectable farm, but he was forced to leave it in 1873 or 1874, after a serious accident rendered him physically incapable of farming. He retired to be a shopkeeper in the local village and died there in 1911, sixty-one years and one mile from the farm he began to pioneer in 1850. Sixty-one of his ninety years had been spent in one place. His fifteen-year period of mobility was simply a life-cycle transition from adolescent dependence to independent adulthood.

If part of Wilson Benson's life was mobile, the life of Nathaniel Carrothers was by comparison static. Nathaniel made only two moves. The first took him in 1835 from the house of his birth at Farnaght, County

Fermanagh, to a house he built on King Street in London, Upper Canada.[6] The second move took him but five miles, to his farm lot in Westminster township in 1844. Nathaniel was virtually a single-step emigrant and wanted it that way. He had emigrated at the age of thirty-two, much too late, as far as he was concerned. 'I am sorry at nothing as much as that I did not come sooner to it,' was his view.[7] In 1853, seventeen years after arrival, he felt the same: 'I never was sorry for coming but ever shall be that I spent so many of my days in Ireland.'[8] He remained throughout his life an inveterate supporter of his new country. His conversion was complete from an early stage, and he appears not to have had any desire to move on, or any need to. Being content with his life, he had no reason to alter it. Probably he never went much further from his farm than the five miles to London or the sixteen miles to his furthest-off immigrant friend from Fermanagh. His family ties in the locality were numerous, and he felt good in the knowledge of his family being about him.

Most of his family was nearby; few were back home. The families of two brothers lived right beside him, as well as the families of eight immigrant cousins (Figure 6.2). In Westminster township in 1860, the Carrothers lands amounted to 1,200 acres, all adjoining. Some Carroth-erses also lived in nearby London, and others lived to the west, in Bosanquet township, and far to the east, in the Ottawa Valley. In Upper Canada in 1858 the Carrotherses 'came up to 90 in name and number.'[9] There were only half a dozen in Ireland. Emigration and mobility had established a new permanence for the Carrothers kinship group. Nathaniel had worked to ensure that parts of the family remained close. He reported how he had managed to buy neighbouring lots for his sons and thus complete a task that would have been impossible for him in Ireland. There had been four sons on the home farm at Farnaght before he left, and only one could be accommodated on the forty-two-acre holding. Emigration for Nathaniel was liberation and independence, for he managed to create in the New World all the social strengths of the Old without the economic disadvantages that limited opportunities for his children. He told his brother William, who retained the home farm at Farnaght: 'I have been thinking had you come to this country when you were thinking of it with such a family of sons how wel of you woud have been and how well it woud have been fo them besides toiling all their dayes in Ireland.'[10] William was the only Carrothers of the line left in Ireland.

The family ties that bound Nathaniel to his place tore his brother

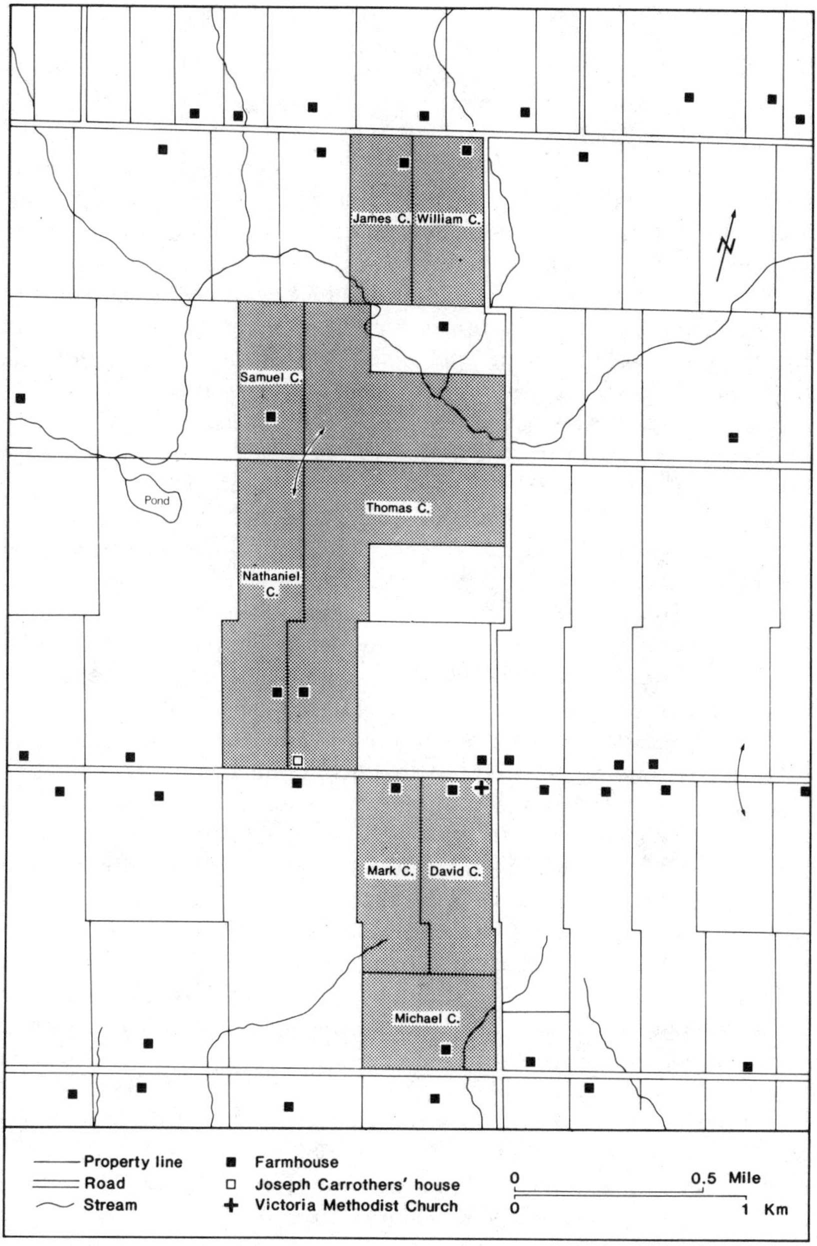
James C.
William C.
Samuel C.
Pond
Thomas C.
Nathaniel C.
Mark C.
David C.
Michael C.
Property line
Road
Stream
Farmhouse
Joseph Carrothers' house
Victoria Methodist Church
0
0.5 Mile
0
1 Km

FIGURE 6.2
Carrothers lands, Westminster township, 1860

Joseph from his. Joseph was a reluctant emigrant at the relatively old age of fifty, forced along by the needs of his sons and family. He and his sister and their families left Ireland in June 1847, in the midst of the Famine, and although they suffered they were not Famine victims as such, simply late departures caught up in the unexpected. Joseph Car-rothers and his family had some degree of freedom to choose. They left with cash, in a well-planned move. Escorted to the boat in Derry by the local agent for Daniel Baird's shipping line, they stayed overnight with friends. They purchased supplies for the trip. On the British North American side relief societies did not have to come to their aid: The family bought a wagon and team to transport itself inland.

Joseph was a hesitant emigrant and did not relish being uprooted. He made every effort to reconstruct his life on the model of his Irish days. He built a mud and brick cottage in the fashion of the family stone cottage in Ireland, and alongside the house he duplicated in large measure his family's Fermanagh garden.[11] By these actions Joseph sought to diminish the impact of emigration. His discomfiture with his new surroundings was apparent. Nathaniel noted: 'Brother Josef seemed to be discontent when he came and to murmer after I knew not,'[12] and when Joseph was asked his opinion of the new country, his unenthusiastic reply was, 'It is a place of hard labour both summer and winter.'[13] Pioneering was hard for him to accept, and he had a need to be close to his home, to cling to threads of familiar acquaintance. Age may well have been an unsettling factor, for at fifty he was unusually old for an emigrant. At sixty-nine he was forced to move once more, this time with his sons James and William, who had moved fifty miles to become pioneers on Canada Co. lands in Lambton County. Joseph was still with his family, but he had the pain of having to start over again, to try once more to duplicate his corner of the Old World in the New. In his last letter home, and presaging his own death, Joseph wrote: 'You will oblidge me by sending me (perhaps the last time) if convenient the following plants.'[14]

The stages in life-cycles and family formation were critical factors in the emigration process. Nathaniel and Joseph Carrothers and Wilson Benson were all impelled by life-cycle evolution, their time in history, and some circumstances beyond their control, but they did make their own decisions firmly within the context of family needs. Family was paramount, and the mobility of populations can be seen largely in reference to the working out not of individual lives but of complexes of lives of families, ranging from those of the extended groups to nuclear families with their children and those without. Wilson Benson and his wife had gone as a childless couple, and consequently both were able to enter the employment market and were potentially footloose. Nathaniel Carrothers went out with his brother Thomas, both of them unmarried, but Nathaniel's betrothed was to follow. Joseph went out with his spinster sister and his family. Two unmarried sons of William went out to join their uncle Nathaniel, but William remained at home. The Carrothers cousins from Bracky had gone out together, unmarried. Practically every possible combination was to be found, but the most common involved people linked by marriage, kinship, and other less formal bonds.

Alexander Robb's migration represents a different pattern of mobility but again highlights the significance of family ties in determining the extent to which emigrant mobility represented rootlessness and social disorientation. In his case, emigration took him half-way round the globe in search of gold. He found none, and with his savings gone he turned to labouring and farming. Eventually he returned home. Robb had left his comfortable home at Dundonald near Belfast in 1862, bound for the gold rush in the Cariboo Mountains of British Columbia. He set off with thirteen other local boys, full of enthusiasm and boundless spirit to cross the Atlantic and the American continent in search of fortune and adventure. They crossed at the Panama isthmus, sailed north along the Pacific coast to Victoria, and finally reached Fort Yale on the Fraser River in British Columbia. From there Alexander and his friends stumbled and strained for four hundred miles through the valleys and ranges of the western Cordillera to Antler Creek in the Cariboo Mountains. (See Figure 6.3.) They found little gold.

His savings exhausted, Robb was forced to return back downriver two hundred miles to take up work as a labourer on a gang cutting out a mountain road near Lytton. Over the next five years he engaged in labouring, lumbering, and mining. He would go up to the mines and the diggings in summers and go downriver in the fall to wherever work was available – journeys of two and three hundred miles. He was not alone in this itinerancy, for booms in the mining districts meant streams of men arriving each year in search of their fortunes and just as surely leaving, disappointed. But even in this volatile, transient society, there were groups of permanent residents. Many like Robb laboured, using their experience and contacts to survive. A few, like his acquaintance from Ireland Alexander McWha, kept a store and prospered on the

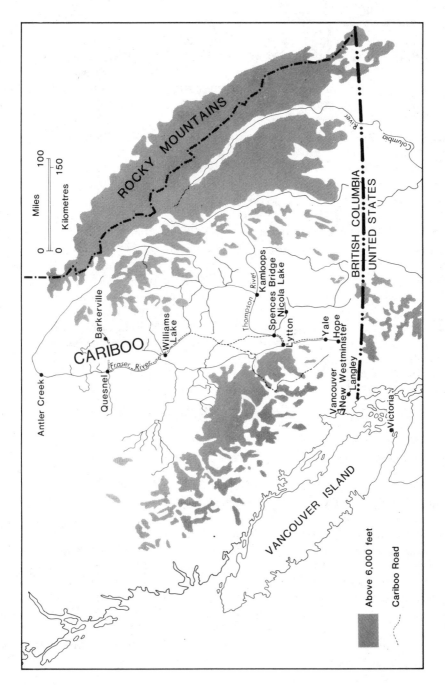

FIGURE 6.3
British Columbia in the mid-1860s

greenhorn's misery. Some others, like his English friend Edwin Dalley, tried farming. In fact Dalley managed to survive as a farmer for four years near Spence's Bridge, until he realized that the frequent water shortages he suffered there could not be remedied.[15] John Clapperton lived and worked there, too, but at what no one recorded. Clapperton, from Queen's County, Ireland, and Dalley had come out together from England in 1862,[16] a month after Robb, and the three had met that season in the Cariboo. For five years they formed part of a band of men sojourning in the valleys of British Columbia, going up and down to the mines, victims of goldlust, moving from job to job, from opportunity to opportunity.

In the winter of 1867–8 Clapperton and Dalley decided to take up free land for cattle ranching in the Nicola Valley.[17] Robb was hired by Clapperton to fulfil the settlement duties, and in the spring he and Dalley claimed the first two lots and commenced settling – the first white men to take up residence there. Four months later Robb staked his own claim to a lot.[18] After six and one-half years of unsettledness in British Columbia, Robb, scion of a middle-class Protestant Irish family, had finally found a full-time job as a pioneer rancher in a remote corner of the British Empire. In May 1868 he wrote to his sister that to visit his nearest white neighbour: 'I would have to travel as nearly as I can judge (for the track has never been measured) between 45 and 50 miles. I have heard indeed that two men have settled about eight or ten miles from here, but I have never seen them.'[19] So rapid was settlement that by the end of that year he could report that 'quite a number of settlers have located in the valley making it more pleasant and safe to live in.'[20] However, a ranch in the sparsely settled Nicola Valley in 1868 hardly offered an easy livelihood. Slowly and unhappily Robb came to realize that the choice was bad.

The valley was dry, and, like his friend Edwin Dalley before him, Alexander was slow to comprehend the risks in dry-land ranching. Grass that he perceived at first to be luxuriant and boundless turned out to be seasonally sparse, coarse, and tough. He learned the need for irrigation and acquired the requisite techniques, but his knowledge was worthless when the water ran out. Helpless, he grew disappointed. The market for his butter was small and distant. A trip there with a butter-laden pack-horse was a dangerous expedition of six days. His disappointment became disenchantment. He hoped for a road to a market, but neither road nor market materialized. He was elated by the prospect of economic growth from British Columbia's joining the Canadian Confederation and having the promised railway pass near his ranch. Neither economic growth nor railway brightened Alexander's realm. He prayed for a woman and asked his family in Ireland to send one – none arrived. He prayed for water, only to see his pastures wither and find himself forced to go up again to the Cariboo gold fields to labour in the diggings. He saved money for passage home but took sick and could not go. Immobilized, he hung on, catching at straws. Through all his darkness, his family in Ireland sustained him with newspapers, letters, and love. Happily, probably in 1874, he managed to escape, selling his ranch for $4,000[21] and returning home, where he was needed to relieve his aged father on the family farm.

Robb, the Carrothers family, and Benson provide examples of the mobility possible in the new society. William Hutton, who was away from home and family most of the time, could just as easily have been used as an example. He was continually on the move through Upper Canada and in the 1850s alternated between Quebec City and Toronto as part of his many jobs as bureaucrat in local and colonial governments. But even for him, mobility was purposeful and disguised an underlying permanence. Hutton's life was rooted in the family's farm, which he had first settled on arrival in 1834 and still owned when he died in 1861. Moves in the New World were responses to family considerations, economic opportunities, and an overwhelming desire for stability.

SOCIAL RELATIONS

Social life also revolved around family and the immediate neighborhood and in some respects did not differ from its Irish form. Convivial occasions were quite frequent, and, especially in the early pioneering phase, alcohol flowed at public gatherings of men. But most convivial activity centred around visits to neighbours. The focus of social activity was the home, where friends and especially kin could congregate and exchange news and gossip. Meetings in kitchens mirrored those known before but may have been less frequent, with distances between neighbours being greater and work and weather being seasonally more intense on the Canadian side. Participants would have been the same as in Ireland. Women would have been at home, and the visitors would have been men on their way somewhere. Neighbouring children, sent along with messages and requests, would have been major afternoon frequenters.

Hospitality was given freely and ungrudgingly, even to distant acquaintances chancing to drop in. It would have been easy to drop into the Carrothers's house. It would have been open to the world. Wilson Benson's too. Alexander Robb would have given his right arm for visitors. In contrast, Hutton's house would have been approached by his neighbours reluctantly, perhaps mainly by invitation and with some degree of formality.

Kin were frequently part of the visiting rounds. Chain migration made it possible for blood relations to be on the Canadian side, often nearby. Remittances, letters, and the reinforcing tendencies of the emigration process conditioned that possibility. If letters home were at all favourable, someone from the Old World would be encouraged to join the New World relatives. How close newcomers were able to locate would depend on countless circumstances – whether there was work, capital to buy nearby land, or strength in the bonds of affection. Given the scale of settlement, and density of population, it was possible to live close to emigrant kin. The Carrothers kin group in Westminster township showed that it could live as close as in the Old World, making allowances for differences in size of farms and population density. Nathaniel, Robert, and Joseph, and Mark had farms beside each other. They saw each other frequently, and all the dwellings were clearly visible one from the other. Other members of the group were nearby. Wilson Benson's nearest relative was about forty miles away, but he had helped Wilson establish his first farm. Wilson's best friends were his wife and his neighbours. William Hutton relied on his cousin Francis Hincks,[22] eventually premier, for patronage for himself and his son. Alexander Robb in British Columbia was almost entirely alone: 'It is true that I have got lots of friends, as the world calls them, and I believe I may say without any vanity that I am generally regarded as not a bad sort of fellow but I do thoroughly believe that there is not within some thousands of miles of where I sit tonight one solitary individual who would care two straws if I were dead and buried tomorrow.'[23] Robb's experience was exceptional, the consequence of emigration on a youthful whim – at a time when emigration from Ireland to British North America was quite minor, and to an area where settlers were few. Migrants without the company and support of fellows could be lonely, but most of Ireland's agricultural pioneers had ample company from among their own kind.

News and gossip were the mainstays of casual visits. News on prices at the markets was primary, and items on remedies, new techniques, and new crops were exchanged. News from home could be relayed within the social networks. Letters from home containing news of mutual acquaintances would have been discussed, and their requests for news of friends fulfilled. Irish newspapers would have been exchanged and knowledge of events at home updated and refreshed. As the Belfast emigrant Mrs Woodburn said about her life in the 1840s: 'Letters and papers were exceedingly welcome, for when we came to Canada newspapers were few and letters "from home" a luxury. We lived in a new country where the people lived generally a mile apart, separated by great forests and unimproved roads. Not one family in perhaps twenty ever got either letter or paper, and the Belfast Newsletter and Northern Whig were loaned and read in the whole settlement.'[24] News from home was also one-sided, confined to situations known before emigration and the fate since then of those left behind. Joseph Carrothers inquired of his brother William in Fermanagh in 1848: 'Let me know if any of my old acquaintances came out this last season and any Deaths that you would think I would wish to know of.'[25] In 1855 Joseph asked after an old friend: 'Let Mr. Hugh Lunny know I am living and well let me know if he is alive.'[26] His brother Nathaniel in 1867 asked to know who among his friends was living: 'I want you or some of the boyes to write me a long letter with the account of all the friends and neighbours that you can think of: there has been no deaths among the friends of mine on any side but that of [my son] Joseph since I last wrote to Yo.'[27]

Death was an important issue. News of births was much less important, because it represented a new generation being created. One's own generation would die, and by the death of compatriots and acquaintances one's own life could be measured. Death of a friend back home was all the more affecting because of the distance emigration had put between the dead and the living. Normally, people expected to be at the funerals of their friends, to reconfirm the life they had shared and the lives that remained. Emigration prevented that, and the absence of emigrants made the home circle of mourners incomplete. The separations were signalled and exaggerated. Ellen Dunlop, writing from Canada in 1881 about her aunt's correspondence to relatives in Ireland, conveyed the strength of the bonds transcending the space and time between emigrant and home. The aunt's letters 'kept alive the loving interest my ailing mother lived on for all those years of separation from her loved country and loving friends. Could you see the letters written to her from 1822 till 1872, so steadily received and so horded up till the last, they are now in my care, I look at them with the greatest admiration and wonder, – feeling no one could ever have had such steady friends.'[28] Deaths of friends at home were almost the final steps of the emigrant's journey.

Although the former social networks at home had been disturbed by emigration, emigrants had also entered a world of far wider contacts and complications. They were now confronted with the task of making new friends and associates while the old-country ones rested in abeyance. They were also now an intermediary between the old and the new. Immigrants newly arrived from the Old Country locale would be likely to seek them out, having been given their name and address before departure. Established settlers were the focus for new arrivals' transition from the old to the new society. Advice could be given, work suggested, food and accommodation provided. From the other side, news would be brought, along with gifts and necessities. Emigration of others was thus a conduit in the information system, and as long as emigration continued the conduits functioned. Once emigration waned, as it did from the mid-1850s, Irish communities in Canada were progressively cut off from the land of their birth by both the cessation of traffic and the death of their friends.

Social relations in the New World, although containing many of the persons and social forms of the Old, were subtly modified, becoming more open and egalitarian. William Hutton had noted the significance of a 'democratic feeling' when he arrived in 1834. He commented on how much narrower was the social distance: 'But indeed we have not many gradations, all appear pretty much on a level, and, except in cities, there is little or no aristocracy. The servants, except amongst the farmers, do not sit down at the same table with their master and mistress, but they will allow of no difference in diet, nor will they bear the terms which I have just used. In speaking of their master, they call him Mr. so-and-so; and it is surprising how soon the poor Irish pick up this democratic feeling, even though they have all their lives been accustomed to use, "your honour" and "your honour's honour."'[29] Alexander Robb, feeling the sensitivity of his new society to landed titles and titled status, let it be known what it meant to him: 'P.S. Whoever directs my letters in future will please not put Esq. to my name. It appears to be so very ridiculous.'[30] Margaret Carrothers suggested that some differences in status were lessened by the purchasing power of the lower ranks: 'You would see more silks worn here in one day than you would see in Maguiresbrige in a lifetime and could not tell the difference between the Lady and the Servant Girl as it is not uncommon for her to wear a Silk Cloak and Boa and Muff on her hands and her Bonnet ornamented with artificial flowers and vail and can well afford it wages is so good.'[31]

For some emigrants the adjustment was uncomfortable, their old traditions putting them at odds with their new society. Jane White commented to her friend in 1856: 'I do not have much society with the exception of some young ladies'[32] and went on to rail against the reduction of local politeness because of her area's contact with American society: 'Indeed I must say Goderich is as much changed lately as could well be imagined. It is becoming an abominably Yankiefied place being so near the States and such a remote place in Canada all the correspondence of any importance is with the States. The more we approach the manners of the old country either British or Continental it is the more conciliating mild and gentle, whereas the other is the reverse. I used to hear the Yankees were nice people but I don't think so now. This proud mean aristocracy of money is very revolting especially when they do not care how or in what low way it is obtained so as the steam is kept up. Down about Hamilton, Toronto and further down the manners of the people are quieter and more polished'[33]

The absence in the colonies of clearly rooted deference, of obsequious behaviour by lower ranks, and of the detached aloof regard from upper ranks was used by the emigrant agent Charles Foy in his efforts to encourage Ulster emigrants. A large proportion of the emigrant letters used in his pamphlet pointed out the advantages of living without "their honours." "Democratic feeling" was increasingly attractive, and men like Foy knew the value of exploiting the looser, less apparent social differences between Canadian groups. Foy implied for his readers that an end to deference was a consequence of leaving Ulster. He promised them freedom from rank and social typing.[34] In Canada the façade of gentility had been eroded; the ordinary citizen did not have to face the agents of the aristocracy. Worth in the new society was to be measured in effort and application, not in inherited status and wealth: 'It is not money that makes a man to be respected in this country; no matter what his position is, if he is sober, honest, and industrious he will be as much respected as the richest man in the land.'[35] (See Figure 6.4). It may not have been entirely true, but it was perceived that way.

FIGURE 6.4

'Sober, honest, and industrious': In Orillia, Ontario, c. 1908, Samuel Kerr, his wife, Margaret, and their three daughters and eight sons prepare to eat their Christmas dinner. Note hard, stained hands and bandaged fingers, spotless Irish linen, and formal flatware. Home-packed preserves, chutney, purées, boiled vegetables, potatoes, gravy, bread, and butter accompanied the bird. The spoons indicate a main course between soup and dessert.

Samuel Kerr, born in Crossgar, County Down, in 1827, emigrated with his parents to Upper Canada in the cholera season of 1832. They settled near the Peter Robinson immigrants in the Perth district. In 1856, Samuel married Margaret Vandervoort, a Canadian of Loyalist stock, and a few years later the family migrated to Otonabee township in Peterborough County. There, they lived beside a group of Robinson settlers, in a district renowned for its Irish character. In 1878, they moved to Orillia, where Samuel died in 1909. Courtesy Samuel's grandson, Donald P. Kerr, Toronto

THE ROLE OF THE CHURCHES

Kin and neighbours were linked by letters and remittances in a dynamic process of emigration. Those parts of the system dependent on personal contacts were reinforced by the wider links created by familiar social institutions functioning on both sides of the Atlantic. Institutions served to ease the emigrants' entry into new communities and their transition to North American modes of social life, as well as setting and maintaining standards of acceptable social behaviour. The main institutions were the churches, primary among which were the Catholic, Anglican, Presbyterian, and Methodist.

The churches' roles were played most effectively at the local level, but initially their impact on immigrant life was limited by weak infrastructure, shortage of cash, and dearth of personnel. Nonetheless, their missionary and pastoral activities were impressive. In Ireland, All-Hallows College in Dublin was founded to cater expressly to the education of priests for overseas dioceses. The sizeable influence of the clergy helped in maintaining transatlantic ties, especially in the early period of settlement, when most of them were emigrants themselves, sometimes from the same districts whence their lay brothers and sisters came.

This regional and social linkage applied equally to Protestant churches. For example, in the Streetsville area of Upper Canada, the local Anglican Irish community was first served by the Rev. Mr James McGrath, sent out from Dublin by the Society for the Propagation of Christian Knowledge in 1819.[36] A successor, the Rev. Mr S.J. McGeorge, was likewise an emigrant clergyman, sent out because of his knowledge of the emigrant community. McGeorge was appointed to Streetsville in 1841 because, in the words of his superior, Bishop John Strachan, 'the village and neighbourhood contains a great number of church people, many of them Orangemen recently from Ireland, a class with which Mr. McG has been in the habit of dealing with in Glasgow.'[37] Well into the mid-nineteenth century, Irish clergymen continued to arrive. Jane White reported to her friend Eleanor of Newtownards, County Down, in 1859: 'We have got six clergymen out from Dublin lately, some of them very talented men, one who is placed at Clinton comes up to preach sometimes, the Revd. James Carmichael. He is very young and very enthusiastic.'[38] Some clergymen came not to administer to parishes but to collect funds and seek support for religious projects back in Ireland. Joseph Carrothers noted in 1855: 'Dawson Dane Heathers visited London in his tour through Canada raising money to support the reformation in Ireland he got 120 pounds in London, I heard, I was in town soon after he arrived, his arrival not been made publick I had not the plesure of seeing him he had good success in all the towns he visited he returns on the 20th of this month from Ireland.'[39] Such activities as Heather's demonstrated the degree of establishment of the Irish communities in British North America by the 1850s and the strength of the organic links binding Irish communities at home and abroad.

Through their pastoral activities, the churches served to consolidate and develop communities. Significantly, however, they played a much wider role as ethnic agents. The Protestant churches acted as forums for ethnic fusion. In their congregations they interlinked the Irish with Scots, English, and American settlers. The Methodists, with the energy of a newly created institution and the objective of spreading the gospel to the frontier, were especially successful in that role. In the New World some Irish were significant promoters of Methodist ideals, which proved appealing to people of many ethnic and denominational backgrounds. Through conversions and the emigration of adherents, Methodism spread rapidly through the new colonies. None of the Protestant denominations acquired an exclusively Irish identity. By way of contrast, the Catholic church in English-speaking Canada was virtually synonomous with Irish Catholicism and as such stood as a focus and defence of a distinctive Irish identity.

THE CATHOLIC CHURCH

On their arrival in British North America, Irish Catholics encountered a church that was already functioning well. The religion of New France was Catholicism, and following the British conquest that reality was recognized in Quebec by a de facto and subsequently de jure accommodation reached between the church and the British authorities. In the Atlantic colonies, however, the English penal laws proscribing Catholicism and restricting the access of Catholics to official position were applied. Nonetheless, early immigration to Newfoundland resulted in an episcopate being raised there in 1796. Elsewhere in the Atlantic region, the base for creation of a non-French Catholic church would await the immigrant influx of the post-Napoleonic era. In the nineteenth century, the immigration of Catholics, partly from Scotland and Germany but overwhelmingly from Ireland, altered North American Catholicism, pushing it into new territories beyond its base among the

French settlements of the lower St Lawrence and prompting the creation of dioceses, parishes, mission stations, and churches. The unfolding settlement frontier was the primary stimulant to the development of the church, and in the wake of voluntary migrations the church created the necessary institutional infrastructure. As the church evolved, immigrant Catholics found not only religious solace and guidance but also strong support for their community consciousness and a vibrant symbol of their ethno-religious identity.

Initially, Irish Catholics found themselves a double minority.[40] As Catholics they were a minority element in an immigration that was predominantly derived from the Protestant populations of the British Isles; as English-speakers they were a minority within a predominantly francophone Catholic church. Their history was in part, therefore, the story of a struggle to attain greater autonomy within that church and to acquire a clergy drawn from their own ethnic group. In Montreal and Quebec, in the communities of the Ottawa Valley, and, much later, in Manitoba, tension within the church between the Irish and their French co-religionists was very apparent. But where Irish Catholics arrived in virgin territory, they were able to attain a degree of autonomy and ethnic identity.

The clearest sign of the autonomy of the Irish Catholic church was given by the establishment of episcopacies in the Atlantic region. A separate episcopacy for Newfoundland was created in 1796 and James Louis O'Donel was consecrated bishop, twelve years after he had first taken up his duties as prefect apostolic on the island.[41] On arrival in St John's, O'Donel had found the scattered Catholic communities of the Avalon Peninsula served by a couple of itinerant priests of dubious standing, and he immediately set about creating a more orthodox church structure. In Halifax, Catholic clergy had ministered since 1785 with the blessing of the Quebec archdiocese and the connivance of Nova Scotia's colonial government. By 1790, ten priests – Scots, French, and Irish – were at work there, but it was not until 1817 that Halifax was erected into a vicarate-apostolic within the Quebec archdiocese. Increases in the immigrant population prompted the creation in 1829 of a separate diocese centred on Charlottetown and including both Prince Edward Island and New Brunswick. Further subdivision was undertaken in 1843, when New Brunswick was elevated to a separate diocese, with Fredericton, and later Saint John (1852), acting as the episcopal seat. The resulting diocesan administration embraced most of Atlantic Canada, was separate from the French-Canadian administration, and was led by Irishmen.

In Newfoundland, there was forged from an early stage a unique amalgam of clergy and laity based on their local Irish origins. As has been indicated earlier, the Irish population of Newfoundland was almost totally Catholic and largely derived from a single region in southeast Ireland. In its early years, the Newfoundland church was served by priests and bishops drawn from the same area. The first bishop, O'Donel, a Franciscan friar, was a native of Knocklofty,[42] four miles north of Clonmel in County Tipperary. His successor, Bishop Lambert, was a native of Kildavin, County Wexford, and he in turn was succeeded by his nephew Bishop Scallan, a native of Ballymore, County Wexford.[43] Scallan was followed in 1829 by Bishop Fleming, who had been received into the Franciscan order at Wexford in 1808. Thus for more than half a century the leadership of the Catholic church in Newfoundland was derived from the same region as the laity.

The localism represented in the Newfoundland hierarchy was found also among the clergy. Until late in the nineteenth century the island's parochial clergymen were drawn mainly from Kilkenny, Tipperary, Waterford, and Wexford, and many of the nuns and Christian Brothers who staffed Newfoundland's convents, monasteries, and schools were selected from the same regions.[44] This seemingly all-pervasive regional identity was unique to Newfoundland in the North American Catholic church. It reflected the island's limited resources and its almost total dependence on cod fisheries, which in turn were exploited by only a few English and Irish merchants, the Irish being from a single region. The narrow confines of that cod fishery similarly confined the emigration process. Newfoundland's small Catholic population – some 15,000 in 1804[45] – and the scarcity of priests available to serve it permitted the perpetuation of the intimate ties between them, as did the special role of southeast Ireland within the church. The area contained the large farms and prosperous farming communities from which the Irish Catholic church drew most of its clergy in the early nineteenth century. It was the major source of the Irish clergy and the only source of the Irish in Newfoundland. That unusual geographical coincidence conspired to forge a unique form of Catholicism in Newfoundland.

The regional association between clergy and laity was both a strength and a weakness. Many of the Irish in Newfoundland, being from the southeast, were native Gaelic speakers and could communicate easily in that language with O'Donel and with their priests. However, the regional association permitted many Old World grievances of family and territorial groups to spill over into the ecclesiastical realm. Newfoundland retained much of the traditional rivalry between Leinster and Munster men – between Kilkenny and Tipperary men in particular. Such rivalries often assumed quasi-tribal character, frequently leading to public brawls and ongoing private feuds. One of the earliest difficulties Bishop O'Donel faced with his priests stemmed in part from their identification with opposing Leinster and Munster factions transferred to the outports of Newfoundland.[46]

The church in Newfoundland was faced also with almost insuperable problems posed by the geography of settlement. Scattered populations in isolated outports along the Avalon Peninsula taxed an already stretched ecclesiastical administration seeking to establish churches and parishes. Small hamlets tucked into coves, distant from each other, and largely isolated from outside contacts, compounded the difficulties of pastoral work. Larger centres such as Ferryland and Placentia received permanent churches early, but in the traditional Irish manner, in which mission stations served remote places, masses in the smaller centres were usually celebrated in homes when a priest chanced to come by. Travel among the faithful was hazardous, for the priests had to brave the sea in small open boats. In 1795 O'Donel wrote to Archbishop Troy of Dublin lamenting his exhaustion: 'in this dismal & dreary country, where I can't visit any of my fellow labourers, nor they me, but in open boats at the manifest risk of being drowned. I went to Ferryland only 14 leagues from this place last June; was blown of to sea 3 days & nights; during the nights we could not distinguish the froth of the sea, from an island of ice with which we were entirely surrounded. Who would wish for anything short of heaven, to be condemned to such dangers & drudgeries.'[47]

The social and environmental peculiarities of Newfoundland notwithstanding, the lot of a priest in pioneering days was invariably difficult and hazardous.

In Upper Canada, to the west of the French settlements on the St Lawrence, a diocese was not created until 1826, and Kingston was selected as the episcopal see. A highland Scot, Alexander Macdonell, was appointed the first bishop, but he could call upon only seven priests to help administer a territory stretching over four hundred miles, from the Ottawa River in the east to the Detroit River in the west. Subsequent population growth and accompanying development of the territory prompted division of this huge diocese. In 1842 the church created the diocese of Toronto, stretching from the Newcastle district westward to the Detroit River. It had a rapidly growing population of 50,000 Catholics – and thirteen priests,[48] under Bishop Michael Power, a native of Nova Scotia. Over the next fifty years the two original Upper Canadian dioceses were subdivided, and new episcopal territories were created around London, Peterborough, Ottawa, and the original Scots territory of Alexandria, in the eastern corner of the province.

While the cultural homogeneity of Newfoundland Catholicism was obvious, the church on the mainland dealt with greater degrees of social and ethnic hetereogeneity. At the outset in Upper Canada, Bishop Macdonell served from a core community of Catholic Scots. Of his seven priests, two were French Canadian, two Irish, and three Scots. That mix reflected the early ethnic diversity of his diocese. Increasingly, however, the Irish came to dominate the church by virtue of their numbers and growing clerical power. But even within the emerging Irish communities there was no regional identity comparable to Newfoundland's. The Irish immigrants in Upper Canada and their priests came from all parts of the country. This was especially clear when Toronto became a diocese in 1842: of the nineteen priests serving under Bishop Power, eleven were Irishmen – two each from Cavan, Dublin, and Galway and one each from Counties Clare, Limerick, Queen's, Roscommon, and Tipperary.[49] None of these men could claim a congregation representative of his own Irish region of origin.

Faced with a rapidly growing population, Power encountered what became a chronic problem – a shortage of priests.[50] The situation was made more severe with the arrival of the Famine immigrants, a disproportionate number of whom were Catholic and who settled mainly in Toronto and the growing cities of southwestern Ontario. The number of immigrant priests did not match the secular inflow, nor was it adequate to deal with the miserable conditions created by the Famine. Few Canadian-born Catholics became priests, and successive bishops of Toronto were forced to appeal, generally unsuccessfully, to Ireland for help. In 1857 Dr O'Brien, bishop of Waterford, informed Bishop Charbonnel of Toronto: 'I spoke to our students of your Lordship's wishes to receive them on the Mission of Canada West, but none of them had zeal enough to offer himself for that purpose.'[51] Seven years later Bishop Lynch, ordained in Maynooth in 1843, and the first Irish-born bishop of Toronto, informed the Irish hierarchy of the difficulties of getting clergy, especially men who would match the character of the laity:

There is another feature in this emigration where so many people have left their homes, whole parishes must have been nearly depopulated; yet it is a very remarkable fact that few, very few priests, have emigrated with them. Bishops of various origins remark this feature when speaking on the subject, and their strictures sum to question the vitality of the former missionary spirit of the clergy of Ireland. Some students, indeed, come, but generally those whose future prospects at home are not of the brightest shade. Many having tried in vain to procure a place in their native diocese ... There are many Irish congregations directed by French and German priests, whilst Ireland certainly can furnish enough of priests for the wants of the people. Some of these congregations number from ten to sixteen, to even twenty thousand, and have only two, sometimes only one, sometimes a foreign priest to administer to their spiritual wants.[52]

The dependence of the archdiocese on immigrant Irish clergy continued until the end of the nineteenth century. In 1890, of a total complement of fifty-two secular clergymen serving, only nine had been born in the archdiocese and twenty-eight were natives of Ireland. The Irish birthplace of two is unknown, but nine were natives of Munster, eight were from Ulster, five from Leinster, and four from Connaught.[53] The diversity of origins fitted well with the diversity of origins among the Toronto Irish at the time. However, by then such regional identities were less important among the laity, which was largely Canadian-born. Nonetheless, the church remained clearly an Irish institution, serving a largely Irish archdiocese.

The emerging identification of Catholicism with Irishness in English-speaking Canada often generated tensions within the church administration, especially so in the contact zone of the lower Ottawa Valley, where Irish and French-Canadian communities were juxtaposed.[54] As French Canadians migrated across the Ottawa into southeastern Ontario in the 1840s, they came into increasing competition in both secular and religious affairs with the recently arrived Irish. Competition for land among the laity and rivalry between priests of differing ethnic backgrounds characterized the cultural conflict. It only increased as populations were enlarged and the strength of the Irish church grew. Matters were brought to a head in 1874, when Father O'Connor of Ottawa sought the aid of Archbishop Lynch in promoting a division of the metropolitan powers of the archdiocese of Quebec, claiming that 'we long to be separated from Quebec and placed under Toronto.'[55] The reason for the dissatisfaction centred on the fact that within the archdiocese of Quebec, 'while there is not an Irish priest in charge of any French parish, that there are several French priests in charge of parishes which are in a great majority Irish and in some which are, I may say, altogether Irish.'[56] A common creed was insufficient to contain the tensions arising from strongly established ethnic identities. Those tensions remained until the 1950s, when the arrival of European Catholic immigrants created a more multicultural image for what had been a French and Irish church.

Given the sprawling Catholic dioceses throughout British North America and the few priests available to serve them, it is scarcely surprising that the formation of parishes and the building of churches failed to keep pace with the needs of the growing numbers of immigrant Irish Catholics. In general, the church, without state recognition and dependent on the financial support of its parishes, followed, rather than led, its congregations. Churches were erected only where and when populations could provide for a priest. The sparsely scattered populations were served by priests who might visit an area only once or twice a year, saying mass in the home of some of the locals. Even when churches were erected, the scarcity of priests frequently precluded the establishment of a resident clergy, and a new building in an outlying part of an extremely large parish might be given the status only of a mission station or a chapel of ease. In general, the development of parish churches was a slow and hesitant process, and not until the 1840s was a significant network of churches established in the mainland English-speaking regions. Then the structures built were of modest proportions. The strikingly triumphalist architecture of many present-day Irish Catholic churches in Canada was created in the last quarter of the nineteenth century and represents, for the most part, the third generation of church building at those sites.

The slow, hesitant process whereby a network of parishes and churches was created may be illustrated by the case of Upper Canada, in general, and the archdiocese of Toronto, in particular. When the diocese of Upper Canada was established in 1826, only six parishes and churches existed in the territory,[57] concentrated overwhelmingly in the eastern corner. There were parishes at Richmond, Perth, Glengarry, and Kingston, but no resident priest in the 150-mile-long lakeshore tract between Kingston and York (Toronto), where St Paul's Church had been built in 1822. The most westerly church was located at Sandwich, 200 miles from York.

During the next fifteen years, Bishop Macdonell sought both land for churches and priests to staff them. The early church sites were acquired through either purchase or the gift of private individuals, often within a circle of Macdonell's friends, which included members of the Tory elite in the colony. For example, in 1827 John Galt donated a block of land overlooking the new settlement of Guelph.[58] A few sites were granted by the government, but because of the disability under which the Catholic church was working in the colony the grants represented only a token acreage. Reserves of land for support of a clergy were available only to the Church of England, and lands other denominations might get were dependent entirely on the niggardly goodwill of colonial authorities.

Between 1789 and 1833 the Church of England in Upper Canada received from governments a total of 22,345 acres as glebes for its clergy, the Church of Scotland 1,160 acres, and the Catholic church 400.[59] Between 1834 and 1838, the Catholic church received several grants of land, largely through the sympathetic offices of the lieutenant-governor, Sir John Colborne. They included the site of St Michael's Church in Toronto and the country township parish centres of Tyendinaga, Fenelon, Trent, Toronto Gore, Adjala, London, and Moore. Some were 200 acres in extent and thus sufficient to provide both the farm needed to sustain priests and the space for a church, school, cemetery, and other parochial institutions. Colborne's grants created a set of parochial centres for a scattering of already settled Catholic localities and in turn acted as foci for subsequent settlement.

The Adjala settlement, some forty miles northwest of Toronto, illustrates well the creation of these Catholic parish centres. The eastern half of Adjala township was predominantly Catholic, one of the very few such districts in Upper Canada. Many of the first settlers had come in the 1820s by way of a secondary migration from Albion and King townships, immediately to the south. Some arrived early enough – by 1825 – to receive free grants. Subsequently, other Catholic settlers gathered in the neighbourhood of the first arrivals. In 1829 two local small merchants and millowners, Messrs McLaughlin and Keenan, organized a committee to raise a subscription to support a priest. Keenan was a native of County Tyrone and married to the sister of the president of Maynooth College.[60] McLaughlin was probably also an Ulsterman, and as the primary merchants, the two men were obvious leaders in a pioneering Catholic community.

Through Bishop Macdonell, approaches were made to the government, which led to the church being granted lots 10, 11 and 13 of the 8th Concession of Adjala. The terms of the grant stipulated that the lots were to be kept 'in trust for a church and school house'[61] and thus effectively assigned the land for ecclesiastical purposes in perpetuity. St James Church was built there in 1833 and became the centre of the hamlet of Colgan, but it was not assigned a resident priest for more than a decade. There was a shortage of clergy in general, and the local parish, despite its expressed desire to have a priest, was unable to provide for one. In 1842 a visitation from Toronto found the church and the community still in a primitive condition: 'a small log building falling fast to decay. A large quantity of land covered with a few graves. Closely adjoining the church is a small log house intended for the residence of the priest, but not finished, consequently badly secured against the winter. No out offices of any description attached to it. No furniture in it. No house of public entertainment nearer than 9 miles and very few, if any, private families in the Mission prepared to receive and board a priest could be found.'[62]

The fortunes of the church in Adjala were not unique; life in pioneering communities was harsh, and scattered, mobile congregations were precarious supports for a resident clergy and ecclesiastical infrastructure. In the neighbouring Methodist mission of Mono, the Protestant settlers were likewise ill able to support their church. The missionary there reported in 1846 that 'the people are poor, generally speaking, and those that are not poor are very close.'[63] The circumstances of pioneer existence made institutional progress very slow.

It was scarcely surprising that the Catholic church usually awaited evidence of strong local community support and definite financial commitment before granting permission for a frontier church to be built. During the 1840s the maturing Catholic communities of rural Upper Canada made many requests to the diocesan authorities, seeking permission to erect churches. An address to Bishop Power from the Catholics of Adelaide township in May 1844 was especially revealing of the decision-making process. The bishop had expressed concern about the possibility of both support for clergy and space for a church. In an appropriately formal letter,[64] the settlers sought his permission to raise a parish and a church. The letter contained maps providing elaborate details about the social geography of the settlement and the alternative sites available for a parochial centre:

Adelaide May 27th 1844

My Lord,

The long promised maps of the township with the names of the heads of the Catholic families, the numbers in each family and the lots on which they reside I have made out and which I hope your Lordship will find satisfactory. It is as correct as possible. Your Lordship desired that I would make out from the heads of the families how much they w'd contribute towards the maintenance of a resident Clergyman or how much they would contribute to a Clergyman for twelve visits in the year or how much for six visits. I cannot inform you on this point as I could not find one out of three at home in going round the township, so that I w'd suggest to your Lordship that the only way to ascertain this w'd be to call a meeting and to give a fortnight's notice. At which meeting Mr O'Dwyer would attend and it w'd then be seen how much each w'd contribute. Your Lordship also wishes to know the number of vacant lots in the village plot of Adelaide. You will see by referring to the within diagram of the village plot your Lordship could procure an acre or two I think we w'd be able to put up a church as I have a subscription list in my possession these two years past and to which I am sure many Protestant families of the township w'd contribute. I made different applications myself for the site of a Church but could not procure it.

> Wishing your Lordship many happy years
> I remain your Obd' servant
> Patrick Mee.

The map attached to the letter (Figure 6.5) revealed the scattered nature of settlement and thereby also highlighted the efforts of these Catholics to become New World pioneer farmers. Although most of the settlers were not at home when the petitioner called, he was able nonetheless to complete what appears to be a full census of his co-religionists. Catholics in the township represented a minority, about a tenth of the population and about a sixth of the Irish. They were scattered around the township among the much larger Protestant population, and the location of some of them along the main settlement road from London suggests that the community was there from the outset of settlement. They arrived coincidentally with their Protestant neighbours. A careful reading of the names and numbers given in Figure 6.5 and an interpretation of relative locations will also suggest both the family nature of pioneering and possible chains in the migration process. Despite the

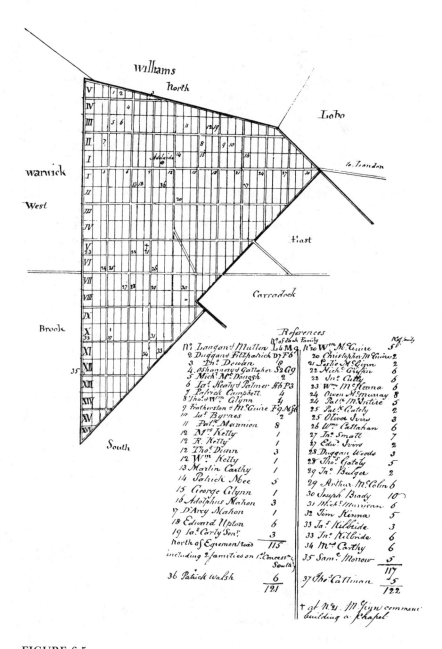

FIGURE 6.5
Patrick Mee's maps showing the location of Catholics in Adelaide township,
Canada West, May 1844; Archives of the Catholic Archdiocese of Toronto

small numbers, there were the denominational and social foundations for a local community. On Concession v South, a Mr McGinn had begun building a chapel for the congregation, although the bishop's preference was for one in the village, where a church was ultimately built. Relations with local Protestants appear to have been amicable, and people had land on which to secure a livelihood. The basis for a parish and parochial centre was there.

Through evaluation of many similarly local requests, the Catholic church gradually came to develop an infrastructure whereby it could serve the scattered settlements of Irish Catholic immigrants. Eventually the successful church sites became the foci of Catholic communities, and, with their adjoining schools, church halls, and, frequently, taverns, there was established the core of many a rural hamlet. In the initial stages of these developments the church had played the cautious role of a bureaucracy intent on conserving the short supply of priests and allowing only what might be guaranteed success. As a consequence, the Catholic churches in Canada were not simply the by-product of spontaneous local demand. Indeed, in that way too, spontaneous extension of Catholic populations into new districts was probably hampered, and the consequent geography of Irish Catholics was restricted.

The growing infrastructure of the church depended on the financial and religious support of the laity and increasing numbers of clergy serving growing populations. For the most part the Catholic church suffered from a perennial lack of clergy, a problem even in the homeland before the Famine, and in provision of churches and creation of parishes it was required to follow rather than lead its immigrant lay members.

THE ORANGE ORDER

In Canada, while the Catholic church summarized a major part of the Irish identity, the Orange Order embraced a large part of the remainder, although not all Protestant Irish supported Orange ideals. Reformist elements and liberals often stood opposed. However, the Orange Order was central to the social life of the Protestant communities among which it operated, and it enunciated a basic cultural identity. The Order derived from an oath-bound secret Irish society, and it espoused a politico-religious philosophy which sought to defend both Protestantism and the British constitutional monarchy. These ideals were carried from Ireland to the British North American side by emigrants and there attained a comparable, uncompromising reputation. The mid-Atlantic

Orange parade that James Humphrey witnessed on the decks of his emigrant ship in 1824 provides a metaphor of the overseas Orange emigration – further steps in the imperial march of Britain.

So successful was the Order in British North America that it moved beyond its ethnic roots: by the end of the nineteenth century about one-third of all English-speaking Canadian adult men belonged to it. Three nineteenth-century prime ministers, John A. Macdonald, J.J. Abbott, and Mackenzie Bowell, were members, and among the Orange ranks were also members of Parliament, premiers, members of legislative assemblies, countless mayors, reeves, wardens, and councillors. Many of them were Irish or sons or grandsons of Irishmen, but an Orange affiliation in British North America did not require Irish origin. Witness the Scot Macdonald, the Englishman Bowell, and other Canadian Orange noteworthies such as John Hillyard Cameron and Oronhya-tekha, a Mohawk chief. Scots, English, and, to a lesser extent, Germans were included, but the Irish identity was primary.[65]

Members of the Order arriving in British North America had ready-made access to a circle of contacts wider than that provided by their family group. Membership provided a character reference for someone far from home and frequently smoothed the path to acceptance in society. Jobs, aid, and even knowledge of legal procedures for land applications[66] could all be obtained, and the widespread network meant that the emigrant could travel well beyond the points of disembarkation with reduced uncertainty. An Orangeman in Ireland, on leaving his lodge, was given a transfer certificate (Figure 6.6) asking Orange organizations 'throughout the universe' to recognize his fraternal qualifications, and acceptance into the overseas network was automatic. Parting from the native land was a sad occasion, but the destination was somewhat known. Verses of 'The Orange Emigrant's Lament'[67] relate those circumstances:

'Tis a sad thing to part thus for ever,
My Brethren, my dear Orangemen;
'Tis a sad thing that thus we should sever –
Oh ne'er to commingle again.

They tell me I go to a nation,
Where I'll meet Orange brothers sincere
Who glow with as strong a pulsation
As beats in the hearts we have here.

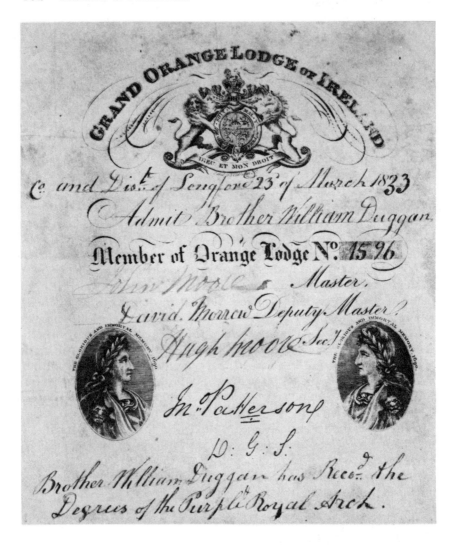

FIGURE 6.6
Orange transfer certificate (1833) of William Duggan, an emigrant from
County Longford to York (Toronto); Orange Archives, Toronto

To be an Orange emigrant was to have in the colonies a ready-made introduction into the new society.

For its members, the Orange Order constituted a steadfast and staunch garrison, defending the monarchical and parliamentary traditions of imperial Britain. Americans were regarded suspiciously, and French Canadians, being non-British and non-Protestant, doubly so. Apparent threats to the colonial identity evoked a vociferous response from the self-appointed defenders. Challenges to authority perceived to come from the American or French-Canadian quarters, as in the rebellions of 1837, 1870, and 1885, entered Canadian and loyal Orange folklore. The war of 1812–14 did too, despite the few Orangemen in the country at the time. In 1866, the quixotic Fenians invasion from the United States confirmed the Orangemen's view that the dangers faced by Ireland were shared by the British North American colonies. The Protestant destinies of the two countries were common, and the fraternity that regarded itself the defender of the advantages of Protestantism in Ireland insisted that British North America was to be likewise preserved.

The Order's image in British North America, as in Ireland, was replete with political and sectarian passions. So ingrained were Orange notions and so significant the Orange body in Toronto that the city acquired the appellation 'Belfast of Canada.' The Order's reputation was replete, too, with the lore of faction fights and sectarian skirmishes on either 12 July or 17 March. However, to stress the open physical violence would be to focus on the unusual. One-third of all Protestant Canadian adult men were not on the streets annually fighting with Catholic neighbours. Officially, the Order frowned on violence and imposed sanctions on members who engaged in unruly behaviour during Orange celebrations.

Orangemen could be found across British North America from Newfoundland to British Columbia. In Protestant communities, once or twice a month local men would gather in lodge meetings to confirm their ideals and consolidate their relationships. A sombre ritual meeting would take place around an altar draped with a Union Jack and on top of it an open Bible. New candidates would be proposed, and those proposed the previous month would be initiated into the mysteries and credo of the fraternity and take their place among the members. Formal proceedings would be followed by chit-chat and discussions on the affairs of the day. Help could be arranged informally for the sick, the widowed, and the orphaned, and later in the century the Order provided its own insurance scheme. The latest political manoeuvring could be assessed, and the results of the latest election debated. Most of the talk would be common, mundane, and neighbourly – on the state of the crops, the chance of work, or the price of salt cod.

The social role of the organization was very much to the fore. In the early phases of pioneering, lodges were known for their hospitality, some seemed to exist just to get up 'a right good jollification.' In Leslie-ville, Ontario, on 3 April 1839, the local lodge consumed its typical one and a half gallons of whisky and two pounds of brown sugar.[68] On 1 May there may have been a guest at the lodge, because the usual fare was complemented with three quarts of beer, at 5d per quart. On 6 November the consumption of whisky amounted to two gallons, and the lodge treasurer soberly noted in his accounts the purchase of half a pound of candles to keep the room lit. Clearly, having a good time was an important part of being an Orangeman in the new colonies of British North America. The lodges provided conviviality and socializing and allowed men of varying character and demeanour to discuss their lives without the usual impediments to social mixing. Wexfordmen found their commonality with Derrymen, and Canadians could join with their immigrant parents' people. The lodges linked members of different Protestant denominations and mixed together the generations, the in-firm and the healthy, the well-off and the not so well-off. They were local community centres.

Socializing was a prime function of joining a lodge, and the great social occasion was the annual twelfth of July festivities, when Orangemen celebrated William III's 1690 'Victory over James at the Boyne, in Ire-land, by assembling with [their] brethren.'[69] They would meet at their lodge room after daybreak on the twelfth and commence a meeting, but instead of finishing their proceedings in the usual way, they would proceed in 'open lodge' to meet other lodges for a massed parade. They might have to march across their township to get to the event, and few locals could have failed to notice their arrival. Flute bands and booming Protestant drums that had been warmed up for weeks before were the unmistakable sound of the twelfth.

Most Protestants (and many Catholics) would come out to watch the affair. By their presence and the scale and colour of the proceedings, Canadian Protestants of all origins made the twelfth a public holiday and often the social highlight of the year. The parade through the main part of a settlement was led by a lodge brother on horseback, playing the part of King Billy crossing the Boyne, followed by a member carrying the lodge warrant and a chaplain bearing an open Bible – sign of the lodge being in session and symbol of Reformed (Protestant) faith. After them came the lodges in the order of date of foundation. The men wore Orange sashes – indeed anything orange, perhaps boutonnières or lilies plucked from the roadside. Each lodge usually carried a large banner depicting an equestrian King William, the name of the community it represented, and the particular Orange motto it supported. The banners revealed that the brethren considered themselves a chosen lot: Sons of William, True Defenders, Purple Heroes, Ulster's Chosen Few, and Cocks of the North. The twelfth was their day.

Orange lodges maintained the solidarity of Protestants locally – in the countryside, in the villages, and in the towns – at the same time as they linked the local community into a larger constituency – national, Protestant, and ultimately imperial. Orangeism and Irishmen were especially suited to British North America, for a society was being created there in the image of a British colony, not an independent, separate state. Britain's first colony had been Ireland, and out of that tradition of colonial connection Orangeism had emerged. In creating the rules for life in the new environment the tried and proven Old World models of behaviour and organization were the prime points of reference, the main source of inspiration – loyalty, Protestantism, and conservatism. Orangemen found on the new frontier reasons to continue and deploy their colonial Irish ideals. They were not there to create or to allow a republic. In their view, Canada would be Protestant and British, would fear God, and would Honour the King, (or Queen).

Just as the ideals of Orangemen enmeshed with those of the colonies, so the lodges' functions and the Order's form also suited the settling realm. Lodges could be social garrisons of frontier settlement. Step by step across the country, through the areas to which Protestant Irishmen went and later through the areas to which their Canadian-born sons migrated, the Order moved as part of the settlement process. As the first Orange settlers arrived in a district, lodges were created. All that was required were five Orangemen to band together, and such a requirement could be easily met. The lodge was often the first formal institution to be organized, the first to bring together and provide social connections and a community focus for strangers arriving in a strange place. It was well suited to new settlement, as it could provide for social interaction and create community cohesion. In the New World, communities created by migration lacked the normal social reference points and traditions that characterized established communities in Europe. The fraternal model for social cohesion was useful in such settings. It was an ideal framework for introducing and bonding strangers in the New World.

To a large extent, the Protestant component of Irish emigration to British North America was Orange. The Order was very recent, formed only in 1795, but it had taken hold in practically every Protestant part of Ireland by 1810, just before Irish emigration to British North America had become significant. The Protestant Irish emigrants going to the New World in the 1820s, 1830s, and 1840s were from Ireland's first Orange-born generation. They left Ireland knowing full well the possibilities of meeting fellow Orangemen on the other side of the Atlantic, and they arranged for that eventuality by leaving their home lodge 'on certificate.' Fraternalism suited the settlement process because of its voluntarism. It could spread at the grass roots by simple migration of ordinary members and word of mouth.

Orangemen from Ireland were welcome in the new settlement areas of loyal colonies. In providing their own resolute brand of imperial fervour, they could be seen not as anomalous exceptions but rather as proponents of many of the ideals of British North America. Orange ideals were similar to the developing ideals of the young country. The Order did not conceive of emigration from Ireland as desertion or loss, for the organization's self-perceived role was that of keeping not merely Ireland, or British North America, but the empire loyal and Protestant. It favoured emigration as a means of extending the loyal domain. As early as 1818 the Order in Ireland sanctioned the formation of overseas lodges. In 1848 the Grand Lodge of British North America, meeting in Toronto, passed a resolution that Upper Canada 'offers a safe and quiet retreat for our brethern at home; and that more better opportunities would be afforded them were they to emigrate to this colony, than is afforded by any other Colony under the British Crown.'[70] What action could be taken to implement this resolution is unclear, but the statement does represent a formal commitment by a body that was numerically and politically strong.

At the very least, the message was heard clearly on the Irish side. Ten years later the Grand Orange Lodge of Ireland, in welcoming a visiting delegation of Canadian Orangemen, noted: 'The connection of a great Colony with a realm of England is mainly, under God, to be attributed to the loyalty and union of the Orangemen of Canada.'[71] In 1870, after a trip to Canada, Stewart Blacker, deputy grand master of the Irish Grand Lodge, reported to his Irish brethren in Dublin: 'All these scenes and experiences inspired us with admiration of the magnificent country, in which we saw a fine opening for emigrants who, if wanting means of progress in the Old Country, might be disposed to try their fortune in a foreign land, and we doubt if, in the whole extent of the British Empire, there is a spot where honesty, industry, and sober intelligence, will meet its due reward, sooner than in ... [Ontario].'[72]

The Orange Order's interest and prominence in the emigration process were made possible by the fact that it arrived with the first immigrants to the colonies, and in conjunction with the expanding frontiers of settlement new local lodges were speedily created and officially sanctioned. The Order grew with the immigrants to Canada, matured with them, and eventually, through them, became Canadian. It established itself remarkably well, and by 1900 there were more lodges in Canada than in Ireland.[73]

For the Orangeman going to lodge and the Catholic going to a parish function, there was a semblance of continuation in the Old World social patterning. The demands of family and kin still focused their lives, and many of their cultural values persisted. Their new lives, however, were worked out within a new physical and economic milieu, and adjustments had to be made. Opportunities and demands unheard of in Ireland conjoined with the need to work out their lives in a society composed of other groups from different cultures. In addition, the geographical diversity inherent in the continental expanse of Canada complicated the adjustment process and ensured that the experience of the Irish in the new land would assume a diversity dependent on myriad regional situations. No single Irish 'type' was created in Canada.

CHAPTER SEVEN

The Geography of Settlement

By the mid-nineteenth century the Irish had become the principal English-speaking ethnic group in British North America, because of their large share of early immigration. They maintained that numerical predominance until the last years of the century, as the name Canada was taken from the St Lawrence colonies and applied to a new nation that stretched from Atlantic to Pacific. Their social prominence lasted even longer, despite the collapse of emigration in the mid-1850s. Although immigration waned for the Irish, other ethnic groups were similarly affected, and natural increase of the resident population meant that the Irish could hold their position as the primary group. By the 1870s, they had had time to create two generations of native-born Canadians, the first in the late 1840s and early 1850s, and the second in the mid-1870s. With these generations the Irish not only increased their numbers and maintained their relative strength but also completed the settlement of the immigrant districts. Subsequent migration would focus on the west, the rural districts of the prairies and British Columbia, and a few critical eastern cities. It would do little to affect the Irishness of much of the rural east. Thus, left alone with those Scots and English with whom they first arrived and without the competing influence of newly arrived immigrants, the rural Irish became rural Canadians and helped constitute the conservative and colonial identity of large parts of the country.

When the first census of the Dominion of Canada revealed the cultural character of the new nation in 1871, the 850,000 Irish amounted to a quarter of the national population – second only to the three-tenths that the French charter group constituted. They were strongest in New Brunswick and Ontario (and in Newfoundland) – about 35 per cent of the population. In Prince Edward Island, soon to become a province, the Irish represented probably 20 per cent of the population, and in Nova Scotia, 15. In Quebec, where the majority of French Canadians lived, the Irish were only 10 per cent, but this low figure concealed some districts where they amounted to a third of the residents. The Irish were not as numerous as the French in Canada, but among the rest of the population, almost exclusively from the British Isles, the Irish were the primary group: English and Welsh represented one-third, Scots one-quarter, and the Irish fully two-fifths.

Although the 1871 census revealed quite variable proportions of Irish from province to province, it also revealed striking commonalities. As in the Canadian population as a whole, the majority of the Irish – three-quarters of them – were rural, hardly unexpected, given the primitive level of urban development achieved by the time of the major Irish influxes in the 1820s and 1830s. In the 1830s, only the port cities of Quebec, Saint John, Halifax, and Montreal were significant urban centres, yet they could not absorb the tens of thousands of immigrants crowding to their quays each year. Places such as Toronto and Fredericton were little more than frontier outposts. Derry in 1831 had 20,000 residents, Toronto fewer than 3,000. Waterford in Ireland was as large as Quebec or Montreal, Canada's primary ports. Belfast was almost twice their size, Cork three times larger, and Dublin's population of 205,000 in 1831 would not be achieved by a city in Canada until the end of the nineteenth century.

In British North America rural areas constituted not only the main but often the only destinations and opportunities for ordinary Irish newcomers. By the time of the Famine, urban centres had grown and correspondingly offered scope for immigration to cities, but throughout the 1840s, 1850s, and 1860s the primary destinations continued to be lumbering and mining regions and new farming districts. The Irish continued as the main set of immigrants. By the 1870s increasing proportions of all immigrants headed to city jobs, as centres such as Hamilton, Toronto, and Montreal began to receive the economic stimuli of industrialization.[1] In this urban development the Irish, because of the hiatus in their emigration to British North America since 1855, were a much diminished component. In the last quarter of the nineteenth

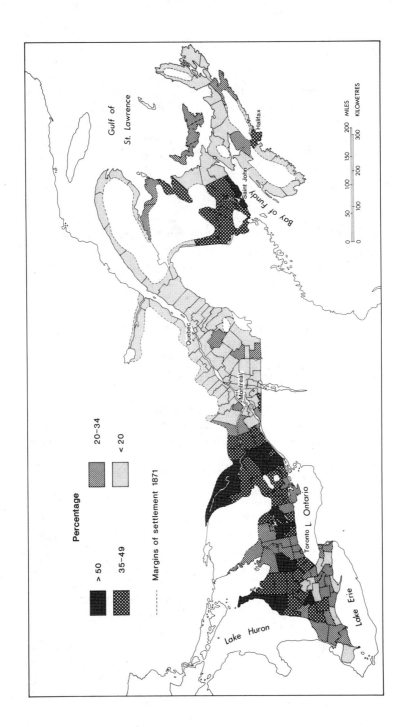

Percentage

> 50

35–49

20–34

< 20

- - - - Margins of settlement 1871

FIGURE 7.1

Percentage of Canada population claiming Irish origins, 1871

century a significant influx of English and Scots immigrants added to existing urban populations and took its place alongside Canadian in-migrants from the surrounding countryside, many of them Irish in origin. In rural districts of central and eastern Canada, largely settled before 1870, the new immigration had little impact. The Irish and the other early immigrants – the new Canadians – kept control of the land and local society.

Figure 7.1 indicates the geographical concentrations of the Irish across the country in 1871. The map is based on census counts of those who claimed to be Irish or descended from Irish stock and thus provides a summary of the results of Irish immigration and settlement in the previous century. Two poles of considerable Irish development are apparent: New Brunswick in the east and Ontario in the west, separated by Quebec. The Irish were less important in Prince Edward Island, and in Nova Scotia, as in Quebec, they were isolated in a few significantly Irish districts and scattered thinly in most. The southern half of the Avalon Peninsula in Newfoundland (not shown) was almost exclusively Irish. In Canada, New Brunswick and Ontario were the principal regions of Irish rural settlement.

The patterns depicted in Figure 7.1 are the results of the interplay of temporal and regional change in Irish emigration, the variable role of trading links between Old World and New, and the different possibilities for fishing, lumbering, and agricultural settlement before the Famine. Irish settlement occurred first in parts of the Maritime colonies in the 1760s, but after 1815, when the mass movements began, it took place on several regional fronts – eastern Nova Scotia, the Gulf of St Lawrence region and the Saint John Valley of New Brunswick, the St Lawrence and Ottawa valleys of Lower Canada, and the southern peninsular Upper Canada.

Immigration to the Gulf of St Lawrence area had virtually ended by the mid-1830s. Shortly afterward, movements into the Saint John Valley had also slowed. By the time of the Famine there was virtually no immigration to the seaboard regions, except to Saint John and its imme-diate hinterland – the last stage of Irish emigration to the Maritimes. Migration after the Famine was focused inland, especially on Upper Canada, where after 1855 the formerly great migration stream was reduced to a trickle. As destinations in British North America shifted, the regions of origin in Ireland had also been changing, and as a consequence the Irish communities of British North America had estab-lished quite different characteristics from region to region.

The earliest and most distinctively Irish region in North America was created in Newfoundland, particularly on the Avalon Peninsula, the North American point closest to Ireland and because of its fisheries a natural target for European merchants. A singularly homogeneous Irish community grew out of the specific and limited regional dimensions of those fisheries and the long-standing maintenance of an immigrant recruitment field in the Barrow, Nore, and Suir valleys of southeastern Ireland.[2] From the late sixteenth century, migratory fishing fleets containing Irish sailors had crossed the Atlantic to the rich fishing grounds of the Grand Banks, which became known in the Irish vernacular as 'Talamh an Eisc.' Eighteenth-century Gaelic poets celebrated this 'fishing ground' far to the west, and in the communities of southeastern Ireland there were many men who had served a season or more in the Newfoundland fisheries. That seasonal migration was the precursor of a more permanent emigration from the same source region, and beginning in the 1760s permanent Irish fishing settlements were apparent onshore. The emigration lasted until the 1820s and eventually involved more than 30,000 emigrants.

In the imperial drive for resources, the Newfoundland cod fisheries became Britain's first great staple in North America. Irish merchants from Waterford and Youghal would join their English counterparts across the St George's Channel in Bristol, Poole, and Weymonth in exploiting the resource. Mercantile competition led to the creation of discrete spheres of commerce in Newfoundland, where certain bays and long stretches of coastline came to be recognized as English or Irish shores. The fishing villages along them acquired similarly an English or Irish identity, the merchants tending to settle people from their home region. The fate of the Irish communities was intimately bound up with the role of the Irish merchants and their transatlantic empires. In most instances it was the merchant who had recruited the settlers, sailed them across the Atlantic in his ships, provided work, and monopolized the market for the fish they caught. The role of the merchant was evident also in the cessation of emigration. The collapse of the fisheries and provisions trade and a reorientation of mercantile interests in the 1830s attenuated the links between Ireland and 'Talamh an Eisc.' Ten years before the Famine, the migration outflow from Ireland to Newfoundland ceased.

The Newfoundland Irish community matured largely in isolation from the direct influences of other cultures and remained quite distinct from the other major ethnic group on the island, the English of the southwest. Transferred Irish material and oral folk culture, music, and in some instances the Gaelic language were preserved virtually intact. Fisheries provided the principal economic reason for the settlement: the island's agricultural resources were meagre, giving rise to little more than spade cultivation. Even in those areas where alluvial stretches of ground allowed small farms to be taken from the forest, agricultural pioneering was very slow,[3] difficult, and rarely brought the pioneer above a subsistence level. In the harsh and isolated conditions of the settlements, the essence of southeastern Ireland's culture was protected from the challenges of other cultures. The Irish population was small, confined by the narrow source region of its origin and by the bonds of kinship maintained by that origin and the Catholic faith. Settlements were scattered along the southern shores of the Avalon Peninsula and a few bays to the north, in a series of isolated coves and inlets, and kinship links were made intense by geographically restricted marriage fields. The Catholic faith was also a formative force in the transplanted cultural identity. The exclusive bond between the Newfoundland Irish laity and its clergy was both a symptom and a further reinforcing element in the culture of the Newfoundland Irish. Continuity and stability were guaranteed, and an unusually homogeneous cultural region was created and maintained.

Elsewhere in Atlantic Canada Irish settlers were drawn by different economies and from a wider set of regional origins, and two other major emigrant geographies were created. The provisions trade that interlinked a small core region in southeastern Ireland with Newfoundland was extended gradually to include a larger British North American realm centred on the Gulf of St Lawrence (Figure 7.2), including Newfoundland, Prince Edward Island, Nova Scotia east from Halifax, the north shore of New Brunswick, and the valley of the Miramichi River. The home region involved was also extended well beyond the Waterford core to include Cork and other ports in Munster. In contrast, a quite different set of geographical linkages bound the Bay of Fundy as well as the Saint John and Kennebecasis valleys to the Irish ports of both Ulster and south Munster. Cork, Derry, and Belfast were the principal ports involved. The timber trade provided the dynamic for the Bay of Fundy's connections with Ireland but the local potential for agricultural settlement was also much greater than elsewhere in the Atlantic region.

The distinctions between the Bay of Fundy and Gulf of St Lawrence

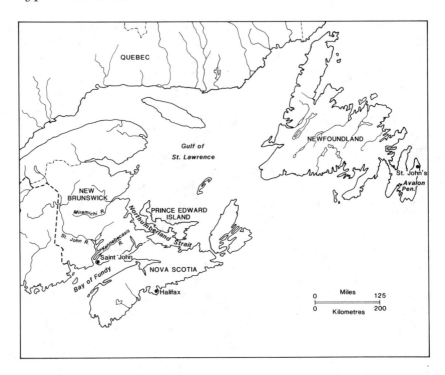

FIGURE 7.2
The Maritimes region

regions were further complicated by their economic development occur-
ring in different, though overlapping phases. The Gulf of St Lawrence's
regional economy peaked in the period 1760–1835 and failed subsequently, as structural changes in the international provisions trade saw
the merchants of southeastern Ireland turn away from the region in
favour of greater involvement with Europe. That shift took place while
the Bay of Fundy region was still undergoing considerable development,
its strongest ties with Ireland being created in 1815–55. Growth of the
Irish communities there followed to a large extent the sequence of developments not in the Gulf region but in the valley of the St Lawrence.
There the fishery was not important, timber being the main initial
pursuit, and Irish trade was directed from a geographically wider set of
merchant ports. A different Irish emigration resulted. The timing of

emigration from Ireland and its changing geography enmeshed with shifts in the settlement geography of the Atlantic realm to produce two quite distinct Irish regions there. The Famine also complicated that regionalism.

The main base for Irish rural settlement in Nova Scotia was the district surrounding the Minas Basin at the head of the Bay of Fundy (see Figure 7.2). This area was the earliest significantly Ulster base in British North America, the meagre result of overblown colonization schemes designed by Alexander McNutt in the early 1760s. McNutt's attempts to make his fortune speculating in land and plantation schemes, not only in Nova Scotia[4] but in Prince Edward Island[5] as well, are the most celebrated of efforts at organizing settlement from Ulster. His designs to acquire millions of acres of Nova Scotia would have made him and his associates the largest land consortium in the colony, but in the end he acquired perhaps only a thousand acres for himself. The scheme ended because of McNutt's own mismanagement and personality, combined with the British government's unwillingness to promote a movement that might lead to the depopulation of Protestants in Ulster.[6]

Nonetheless, McNutt's legacy consisted of the Presbyterian districts of Londonderry and Onslow on the Minas Basin shores of Nova Scotia. It was a legacy that also owed much to Ulstermen moving north from New Hampshire, the Bay of Fundy being simply a northern extension of New England's coastal seas. The American Ulstermen, travelling by way of a two-stage migration, and the 500 Donegal men (and probably Derrymen) whom McNutt organized in 1761–2 formed cores to be added to later by demobilized troops and small numbers of emigrants coming on their own accord from McNutt's home districts and other Ulster locales. On an interior wall of the Church of Ireland church at Glendermott, just outside Derry, the Nova Scotian connection is memorialized. A stone plaque reads: 'Susanna Stannus youngest daughter of Ephraim Stannus Esq of Windsor Nova Scotia Died Feb 23, 1819.' Windsor was part of the Irish – primarily Ulster – core at the head of the Bay of Fundy, and through the expansion of Canadian-born generations a sizeable Ulster district was maintained. It was not greatly enlarged by later emigration, for during the mass movements of the 1820s and 1830s Nova Scotia was largely bypassed because most of Ulster's links were determined by the timber trade from Quebec City and Saint John.

Although the areas around the Minas Basin received an early Ulster emphasis, the rest of the Irish districts in the colony were linked with the Gulf of St Lawrence trade and saw a much reduced Ulster component and a more significant contribution from the southeast of Ireland. The capital, Halifax, had accumulated large numbers of Irish from 1749 but especially from 1760 onward, many from Ulster and Leinster, and many others from Munster by way of the Newfoundland fisheries. A small, mixed Protestant and Catholic inflow became progressively more Catholic as immigration from the southeast predominated. Small fishing and farming settlements along Nova Scotia's Atlantic coast were similarly affected.

From the early eighteenth century Newfoundland had been a primary destination of young men from southeastern Ireland, but Newfoundland's meagre agricultural resources and limitations in its fishing economy led many Irish on the island to move on to Nova Scotia, New Brunswick, Prince Edward Island, and New England. These migrants established a strong link between southeastern Ireland and Cape Breton,[7] which was reinforced by direct migration from Ireland, with counties Kilkenny, Waterford, and Cork most prominent.[8] However, immigration from the southeast, which had in rare years reached 5,000,[9] had largely ceased by the mid-1830s, when the naval provisioning function of southeastern Ireland had declined. Its contribution to British North America, however, was considerable. It created around the Gulf of St Lawrence an Irish region quite different from those in New Brunswick and northwestern Nova Scotia, and in subsequent decades that region's isolation and social fossilization would make it even more distinct and unique.

Prince Edward Island was similarly affected by its location in the Gulf of St Lawrence. The timber trade linked the island's immigrants with those of the Miramichi and the north coast of New Brunswick, and the fisheries linked them with Newfoundland. As well, onward migration of Irish from Newfoundland naturally had an effect. Prince Edward Island formed an early cross-roads between Newfoundland and New Brunswick, and the origins of its settlers were among the most mixed of any Irish community in Atlantic Canada. Two-thirds of Ireland's counties were represented on the island, though the largest group was from Monaghan,[10] a region not as well represented in the Miramichi Valley or Newfoundland. A unique combination of chain migrations from Monaghan was intensified by a landlord priest promoting his island lands.[11]

Irish settlement was distinguished as well by the island's unusually attractive potential for agriculture. The well-drained and deep soils were quite anomalous in the Gulf region. Colonization of the island, however, resulted in landlord estates, reminiscent of arrangements in Ireland. Freehold land ownership was initially not possible, and tenancy was the norm for incoming immigrants intending to farm. That situation, set against freehold occupacy in most of British North America, led eventually to a 'tenant rights' movement[12] drawing its inspiration from Ireland. These characteristics made Prince Edward Island another unusual piece in a variegated set of Irish communities in British North America.

The geography of settlement and trade that made Prince Edward Island a cross-roads and gave Nova Scotia two contrasting Irish regions also divided New Brunswick. A heavily Catholic and Irish region, settled from the south of Ireland, centred on the Miramichi Valley and ranged along the coast of the Gulf. More Protestant and northern Irish settlements in the Saint John and Kennebecasis valleys, especially in Charlotte County on the Fundy shore, constituted a rather different region. We shall look at both regions in turn.

Along the Gulf, Newfoundland Irish had joined with other emigrants from the southeast arriving to serve in the lumbering and fishery ventures of Scots merchants. The Scots used Wexford and Cork as primary centres for provisioning and for recruitment of labour for overseas enterprises. As their lumbering operations extended inland into the great northern basin of the Miramichi, Irish farm settlements arose as offshoots, – in coastal centres, in the wake of the clearing, and in the scarce stretches of second-rate agricultural land. Little deliberate effort was made to develop agriculture: the merchants were interested in fish and timber, and the Irish were contracted labourers rather than independent farmers with families. However, permanent settlements did arise from this emigration. They were added to by some Protestant agricultural settlers arriving via the Saint John River and settling at the upper end of the Miramichi, away from the coast. From the 1830s few arrived there, a pattern of out-migration developed, and as a result the early character of the region became static. Peter Toner and William Spray have noted how this process made the Miramichi one of the most distinctively Catholic Irish areas in British North America.[13]

The Irish settlement along the 'New Road' to Cape Tormentine (Figure 7.3) was part of the Gulf shore Irish identity – almost exclusively Catholic and created well before the Famine by immigrants mainly

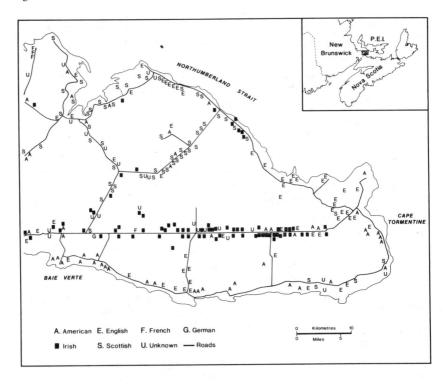

FIGURE 7.3
Ethnic background of residents, Tormentine Peninsula, New Brunswick,
1862

from the south of Ireland. In 1820 the government of New Brunswick
contracted the survey of an east–west line through the centre of
the peninsula tipped by Cape Tormentine. The road was meant to
encourage pioneering by immigrants who were then flocking into the
colony. Fifty parcels of land of about two hundred acres each were
marked off as free grants, and almost immediately Catholic Irish immigrants began arriving to claim them. In a very short time, a community
took form, built around numerous kin links, common origins, and
common experiences. By 1825 all the lots had been distributed. In 1826
a log building to serve as a church mission station was built, and in the
early 1830s a priest was sent over from Prince Edward Island to assess
the possibility of a parish. He reckoned there was insufficient means to

support a full-time priest. The Tormentine New Road settlement would be served by occasional visiting clergy from the large Acadian settlements to the northwest. In 1838 a proper church building was raised and the settlement given a permanent focus.

A Corkman, Timothy Lane, was the first to apply to the 'committee for settling emigrants' in January 1821 and was issued a 'location ticket' which gave him the right to occupy and make improvements on a 160-acre plot on the north side of the road.[14] His brother Aeneas was given a ticket for 190 acres on the opposite side.[15] Until their cabins were ready, the brothers boarded with their earlier-established neighbours, the Trenholmes, an English family.[16] A third brother, William, chose not to seek a land grant but acquired property nonetheless through marriage to widow Trenholme.[17] In late 1821, another Corkman, William Savage, a cousin of the Lanes, and a Kerryman, Michael Houlihan, were issued location tickets.[18] Houlihan had been in the colony for a year and a half before applying, Savage and his wife and child, a year. The following summer, Savage's brother John arrived from Ireland and arranged with Michael Houlihan to take over his location rights, notifying the authorities to that effect. In his letter to the settlement committee in 1823, John Savage explained: 'having emigrated to this Country in the year 1822 in order to look out for a small tract of Land to settle upon, I am induced, from a desire to live near my Brother, to apply to you, Sir for a quantity of Emigrant Land containing two hundred acres, situated at Tormentine, once located by a Michael Houlahan but surrendered to me. I have chopp'd down Three Acres on the same, and, god willing, intends to go on improving it, as I have a family of five Boys.'[19] Brothers Dennis, Patrick, and Morris Savage also acquired land nearby. Other immigrants trickled in – the Cross family from England,[20] the Dennis Murphy family and John Larsy from Ireland,[21] and the Irishman James Carroll from Newfoundland.[22] Dennis Murphy's wife was Catherine Savage, and they were rejoining that Cork family group. Dennis Murphy's three brothers went instead to Upper Canada. James Carroll came across from Newfoundland with his brother-in-law, John Kennedy.[23] Carroll's lot turned out to be useless, and he bargained for the location ticket and improvements of one Thomas Fox. Fox wrote to the government that he would 'Willingly give up ... the Lot of Land that my Ticket Specifies ... to [James Carroll] ... as his Lot is good for Nothing and he is married and I am single and am going to leave the Country.'[24] Single men could move on; married immigrants, having to fend for a family, were more likely to settle.

Figure 7.3 depicts the geographical arrangement and ethnic denomination of households on the Tormentine Peninsula in 1862.[25] The Irish were concentrated along the east – west alignment of the New Road, which followed not only the straight lines of compass bearings but the general trend of a natural ridge through the interior of the peninsula. Farming provided most of the livelihood for the Irish settlement, but the land was poor (although far from being the worst around), markets were local and small, and distant lumber camps provided seasonal work, barter, and perhaps a little cash. The Irish, by their interior location, were excluded from the fishery along the shores, where earlier arrivers had taken up suitable settlement sites. The Baie Verte shore was occupied first by American loyalists, among whom a couple of English families later arrived. English and Scots immigrants acquired most of the north shore and from there spread inland. The shoreline settlements, except for their French and Irish members, were started by immigrants arriving between 1783 and 1820. The French represented earlier movements, and the Irish were outliers of the New Road core.

Most of the Irish families were derived from people who arrived well before the Famine, a situation easily noted when the census was taken along the road in 1851. Then there were 167 Irish-born people left among a population of both immigrants and Canadian-born that numbered about 580.[26] The surviving immigrants were thus outnumbered more than two to one by the settlement's Canadian-born offspring. Of the 167 immigrants in the community in 1851, only 12 had arrived after 1844, that is, during the Famine period. Three of those twelve arrived in 1847 to join relations who had arrived in 1842; five arrived in 1848 from one family in which the father had come out alone in 1846 to prepare the way. While 'Famine emigrants' comprised only 7 per cent of all the immigrants living in 1851, they represented a much smaller proportion of the Irish immigrants who actually settled permanently along the New Road. By 1851, most of the early arrivals were dead and some had moved on. Within this Irish community of immigrants and Canadian-born, the Famine immigrants were an insignificant minority.

The localization of the Irish households within the settlement geography of the peninsula arose from the pioneer phase of Irish emigration, between the Napoleonic Wars and the Famine, when not only most of the Irish came, but few immigrants from elsewhere. The timing and exclusiveness of that emigration, and the prior settlement of other groups around the shores, confined the Irish to the interior land and farming. There was no anti-Catholic behaviour that excluded them from better resources and points of access; they were isolated because they were relatively late in arriving. Nor were their apparent isolation and confinement to the New Road any greater than the localization of earlier groups. Within the Irish settlement, non-Irish families mingled. By 1862, cases of intermarriage, both ethnic and religious, were numerous, and many settlers had moved on and had their places taken by neighbours, younger brothers and cousins, or newcomers. Three members of the Hickey family moved to Illinois, Richard Wall and his sister Mrs Heffernan returned to Ireland, and the Burns family moved a few miles away, to the north shore. Only one of the Savage brothers died in the settlement. Mobility, death, and emigration meant that the settlement was always in flux, and the situation depicted in 1862 was only one of innumerable temporary phases. Yet the settlement was basically as it had started in early 1821 – Catholic, voluntary, ahead of the church, and clearly pre-Famine. It does not belong within the American stereotype of the Catholic Irish but is a fine example of a common Canadian pattern.

The other part of New Brunswick's Irish geography, the Saint John River Valley, was created by a different history. There, Protestants were more prominent and Ulster ports combined with Cork as the main source of emigrants. In addition, agriculture was more important than in the Miramichi, although agricultural settlement proceeded in step with exploitation of the region's timber and most farm families participated in the wood trade. The County Donegal man David Moore, writing home to his brother in Carndonagh in 1840, urged him to emigrate to New Brunswick and join his relatives. From his home at Petersville in the lower Saint John Valley, David indicated that a third brother, John, was up in the Salmon River area, among many men from his home parish: 'John has lived most of the time since he came to the country in a place called Salmon River, a great place for getting timber for shipping home to Europe – there are great many acquaintances there from Malin who chiefly work at the timber trade. The part of the country where I have settled is different in some respects from what I have last mentioned, they do not grow large timber on this land, the timber that grows here is called hardwood, being of a hard nature and best for firewood, therefore the land where this hardwood grows is best for cultivation. – and most of the land in this settlement is equally as good as the Land about Carndonagh when it is properly cleared and put under Cultivation.'[27]

New Brunswick's variable environment gave rise to a very diverse

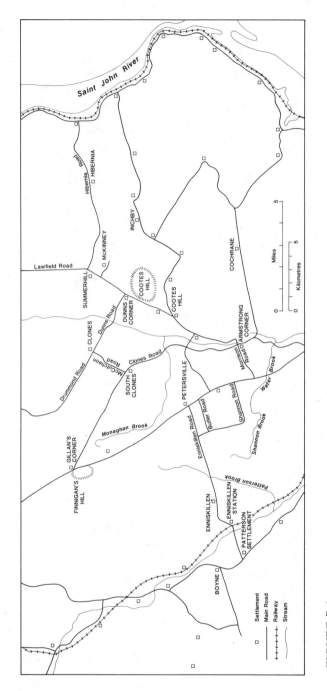

FIGURE 7.4
Irish place-names in the Petersville area of New Brunswick

economic character, and Irish settlers were found in all economic niches, from lumber camps to mixed lumber-and-farming operations or the fewer, exclusively agricultural districts. Along the Saint John Valley, the majority were Protestant and derived largely from Ulster and north Leinster.

Irish settlers arriving in the Saint John Valley created a very different society from the Miramichi's. They were seeking land and lacked the type of merchant patron who organized much of the labour in the Miramichi timber industry. They arrived via a route for paying passengers established by merchants in Cork, Belfast, Derry, and such Scots ports as Greenock and Paisley. The emigrants came largely on their own speculation to Saint John, hoping to get onto the land and re-establish lives as farmers. When the mass of the Irish arrived, some land was already cleared of timber and available for speculative sale to immigrant farmers, and those with some means got a head start. In the valley they took their place among and behind the riverside tier of earlier agricultural settlers from New England and the middle American colonies.

The geographical pattern set up by the Irish in the Lower Saint John Valley is illustrated by the Petersville area (Figure 7.4).[28] The map highlights places with names of Irish origin, most of them behind the riverside loyalist Americans. Settlements along the river generally lack Irish names, but seven or eight miles inland Irish names are common. Most names were derived from the adjacent counties of Monaghan, Fermanagh, and Cavan in south-central Ulster, the area so significant in early-nineteenth-century emigration. Ulster place-names Enniskillen and Clones and family names Dunn, Patterson, McCutcheon, Drummond, and Armstrong suggest also the importance of Ulster families in the original settlement of the area. A Protestant, Orange origin is also hinted at by the naming of Boyne Settlement, though 30 per cent of the area's Irish were Catholics.[29]

The community around the Petersville Settlement cross-roads and at the eastern end of the Enniskillen Road was settled by Catholic Irish, and Catholics were scattered in a few other localities, including Clones, which memorialized the local Catholic bishop's birthplace. In this area, the timing of settlement separated Catholics and Protestants. The Protestants had entered via the Saint John River before the Catholics arrived overland to the west. Both groups, however, hailed from the same regions of Ireland, a further consequence of the timber trade–related emigration that linked Saint John to north Leinster and Ulster. Saint

John's Cork connection is reflected in Cork settlements even further inland than Petersville, their greater distance from Saint John illustrating Cork's great role in Irish emigration later, during the 1840s.

Saint John tended to have a large fraction of Catholics in its Irish population. Among British North American towns, it was the most Irish, and the Catholic and Protestant components were of comparable size. In 1840 the city's Irish were probably equally divided between Catholics and Protestants, whereas in inland rural areas Protestants accounted for two-thirds of the Irish.[30] The city acquired this unusual character because of its role not only as the principal New Brunswick port for the timber trade but as a major junction on the cheaper passenger routes to the seaboard United States. Saint John received many emigrants destined for elsewhere and collected many people drawn by jobs, or immobilized by the cost of further journeys, and in need of work. The port provided work. After all, it was among the largest ship-building centres in the British Empire, and its hinterland offered many opportunities for work in logging camps. Through its timber and ship-building roles and its stop-over functions, Saint John became home to an Irish population more Catholic than its valley hinterland. During the Famine period, Catholics became about 60 per cent of its Irish population,[31] and Saint John became even more anomalous in its half of New Brunswick.

In Atlantic Canada, distinct phases of Irish settlement are discernible. The southeast of Ireland was linked through the fisheries to Newfoundland and subsequently the Gulf sides of Nova Scotia and New Brunswick. Ulster was linked first, in the late eighteenth century, with Nova Scotia, and then Ulster and north Leinster were connected in the nineteenth with Prince Edward Island and the Saint John Valley. On the Gulf sides of New Brunswick, Ulstermen were less common; in Newfoundland they were virtually unknown. The geography of Atlantic trade and the timing of the emigration impulses conspired to create a diverse set of Irish regions, the result of which prevents rigid typing of the Irish emigration and settlement experience.

CENTRAL CANADA

Although the Atlantic colonies had been a main focus of Irish immigration after the Napoleonic Wars, the region itself became progressively an area of out-migration. Increasingly, it also tended to be bypassed by newcomers. Irish movement to the Atlantic region in the years 1831–7 was only half that going to Lower and Upper Canada, and for the period 1838–45 the figure dropped to one-third that going on to the central provinces.[32] Upper Canada, because of the good land available there, had the greatest attraction for emigrants, and the geographical dominance of the Irish was apparent. Throughout most of Upper Canada the Irish comprised at least 20 per cent of the population, and they were particularly dominant in the back counties north and west of Lake Ontario (Figure 7.1), areas settled mainly in the 1820s, 1830s, and 1840s, when the Irish were most numerous in the flow of immigrants.

The Irish cores in the province had been established early: the British government's colonization schemes created small nodes of settlement that then acted as magnets for subsequent settlers. In 1823 Peter Robinson took 571 Cork people to settle on military reserves in the Rideau country (Figure 7.5) and two years later he repeated the project with 2,050 people to the Emily and Douro districts.[33]

Earlier, the neighbouring townships of Monaghan and Cavan had been set aside at the request of James Buchanan as the destination of the mainly Ulster emigrants he was directing there from New York. In 1817 Buchanan, British consul in New York, initiated a policy of dissuading 'loyal subjects' from settling in the United States, encouraging them instead to go to Upper Canadian settlement districts. He later reported: 'The first body of emigrants I forwarded were chiefly from Monaghan and Cavan and through the influence of Dr. Baldwin of York, Upper Canada (now the city of Toronto) two townships were laid out by the Lieutenant-Governor for those I should send, and were named Monaghan and Cavan.'[34] Most of the Irish he assisted were Protestants from Ulster, and by the time Peter Robinson's Cork settlers arrived in 1825 an Ulster Protestant presence was already in place in the bush. A few of Buchanan's emigrants went farther west to lands beyond York (Toronto), where two local place-names, Omagh and Boyne, memorialize the Buchanan connection. Omagh was the town of his birth in County Tyrone, and Boyne recalled his involvement in the Orange Order. As in the Monaghan and Cavan districts, Omagh and Boyne continued to draw Protestant Irish emigrants in the following decade.

Richard Talbot's Tipperary emigrants established other cores. They split on arrival in 1818: a third of them settled on a land grant in eastern Upper Canada, two families remained in Montreal, and the rest continued west to London township, north of Lake Erie.[35] From those bases, and through continuing chain migration from Ireland and within

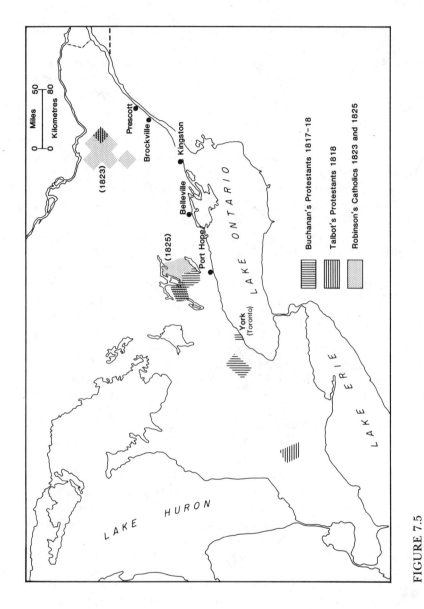

FIGURE 7.5
Locations of Buchanan, Talbot, and Robinson settlers in Upper Canada, 1817–25

Canada, the Tipperary settlers created an extremely extensive geography which has been well documented by Bruce Elliot.[36]

Buchanan, Talbot, and Robinson were instrumental in creating the
early cores of Irish settlement in the colony, but they were only acting
within a larger emigration process over which they had no control. The
numbers of Irish emigrating would have resulted in settlements north
of Lakes Ontario and Erie without these organizers. The three men
were responding to opportunities created by the popular mood for
emigration arising in Ireland.

Irish regions in Upper Canada evolved from the early cores. Figure
7.6 provides a township-by-township distribution of the Irish ethnic
group, immigrants and Canadian-born, in the southern, settled part of
Ontario in 1871. The cores of settlement established by Robinson in
Peterborough County, Buchanan in Peterborough and Peel, and Talbot
and Robinson in the east are very evident. Subsequent chain migration
to these cores by friends and relatives of the early arrivals allowed
expansion into three recognizable dense concentrations. Along the
Rideau Canal axis, between Ottawa and Kingston, Irish immigrants,
lumberers, farmers, and canal workers had filled in around the Robinson and Talbot settlements. Similarly, a concentration had developed
in the Peterborough area and had extended northward along the river
valleys that the lumbering industry followed and the colonization roads
developed to promote permanent agricultural settlement. Northwest of
Toronto, the original core of Buchanan settlers had been augmented
soon afterward by others seeking farm land. In addition, the creation
of Catholic churches in Toronto, Gore, and Adjala townships on the
Colborne land grants attracted other settlers. From these beginnings
there emerged the Irish concentration in Peel and south Simcoe counties. It was through this area that Wilson Benson and his compatriots
passed on their way northwest to Grey County in the 1850s. Overall,
the greatest contiguous zone of Irish settlement in Canada was in
Ontario, east of a line running from Hamilton northwest to Lake Huron.

Most of the Irish districts were the natural outcome of a voluntary
movement of tenant farmers and emigrant labourers seeking work and
especially land. In Upper Canada in the first half of the nineteenth
century, land offered the only reasonable security. Canal projects and
road clearing or other similarly labour-intensive public works attracted
immigrants initially but with few exceptions could not hold them in
place. Lumbering was likewise a volatile, temporary basis for settlement.
Unless agricultural land was available to provide the possibility of a

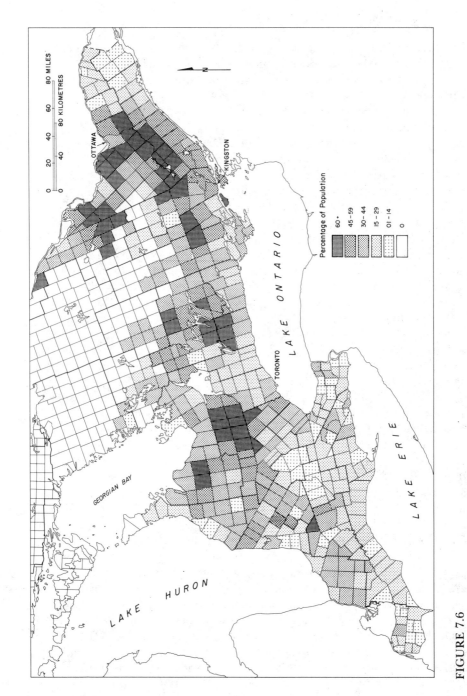

FIGURE 7.6
Irish as a percentage of the population of townships in Ontario, 1871

secure food supply for permanent family occupation, canals and lumber camps had transitory effects. It was therefore immigrants with some means, usually brought with them rather than obtained in the New World, who established the core of most Irish districts. Upper Canada could provide work for single and poorer people, but permanent settlement was more clearly equated with the obtaining of land.

In the southwestern region, between Lakes Erie and Huron (see Figure 7.5), land had been the primary attraction. In some parts close to the Lake Erie shore, the Irish had been preceded by loyalist refugees and other immigrants coming from the United States, and for the later arrivals the chance of getting land there was slight. The area formed a natural migration route from New York state westward across the Niagara Peninsula, a route used first by loyalists in the 1780s and later by Americans drifting westward in search of frontier land. Subsequent settlement along the Lake Erie shore was limited by this earlier movement, and communities there were likely to be of much more mixed origin than the back counties, away from the shore. In the back counties settled from the 1820s onward the Irish were important because of their large share of the immigration streams feeding into this zone. Into these areas came such families as the Carrotherses in London and the Whites in Goderich. Early arrival allowed children, the first Canadian-born generation, to extend the Irish base. The third generation being formed in the 1870s would extend those bases even further, eventually into the distant prairie regions of the western interior. By that time, however, that was not an Irish but a Canadian phenomenon.

As the Ontario society matured and its economy became more complex, towns and cities began to outgrow their primitive frontier origins. In 1851, the principal city of Toronto had about 30,000 residents, but in the next twenty years it almost doubled in size. Kingston, the second-largest city, had a population of only 12,500 in 1871. In all, 20 per cent of Ontario's population in 1871 could be described as urban,[37] and among the Irish in the province a similar percentage applied. Earliness of arrival and the overwhelmingly rural nature of Ontario had created for the immigrant Irish there a settlement geography that differed greatly from that of their highly urbanized fellow immigrants in the United States.

Toronto's Irishness was very recognizable in 1871, as a consequence of both the immigrants in the city and the numbers of the second generation who had been born there or moved in from surrounding Irish districts. Irish immigrants comprised 18 per cent of the population, the Canadian-born generation 25 per cent; they were fairly evenly divided between Catholic and Protestant. The Irish were widely distributed throughout the city, and although immigrant communities, clustered around churches and in cheaper-rent districts, were a feature of the city's geography, they represented only part of the Irish pattern in Toronto. The Irish could be found in pockets of poverty, in working-class clusters such as Cabbagetown and Corktown, and middle-class row-housing in better neighbourhoods. They also owned some of the finest mansions. The dispersion of the Irish throughout Toronto would be expected, given their numbers, a half-century of immigration, and the wide-ranging socio-economic niches that immigrants and Canadian-born filled.

In the last third of the nineteenth century and the opening decades of the twentieth, the geography of the Irish in Ontario was characterized by continuing growth in Toronto and industrializing centres and by extension northward into the mining and resource towns of the Canadian Shield. There, the Irish worked as miners, mill workers and railway gangmen, teachers, managers, and entrepreneurs. However, in northern resource towns, among a population of British, other European, and French-Canadian newcomers, the Irish were much less prominent than they had been in the earlier, agricultural phases of colonization. Slowly, inevitably, without massive immigration to renew and enlarge the Irish population, its relative size declined as immigrants from new sources, largely English cities, offset old balances. Settled rural areas, losing population through out-migration and rapid ageing, remained unaltered in their ethnic proportions, but growing places changed drastically. Toronto, which had been 43 per cent Irish in 1871, was only 18 per cent Irish in 1921. Despite that change, the city could still be perceived as an Irish place, a sort of Belfast, so much had the early citizens coloured the city's culture. Large stretches of the Ontario countryside would remain Irish, not just in image, but in fact.

The widespread significance of the Irish in nineteenth-century Ontario stands in stark contrast to the relative localization of the Irish in Quebec, especially in the port cities Quebec and Montreal. The Irish presence in Quebec antedated the British conquest. Irish soldiers from the early seventeenth century had been a component within the French army, and many eventually were stationed in the garrisons of New France. Some eventually obtained land grants within the seigneurial system and engaged in fur-trading and agricultural activities. It has been asserted that of the 2,500 families resident in New France at the close of the seventeenth century as many as 130 were of proven Irish origin. Other families of less evident Irish origin were also to be found. Time and assimilation had transformed names such as Teague Cornelius O'Brian into Tec Cornelle Aubry and so disguised their ethnic origin.[38] In the aftermath of the conquest, Irishmen were again to be found in the army and in the bureaucracy of the new colonial administration. The celebration of St Patrick's day was recorded in the *Quebec Gazette* as early as 1765.

Quebec City's port and customs administrative function meant occasional arrivals of officials and traders from Ireland, but early-nineteenth-century immigration generated large Irish communities. Quebec City, the main port of entry, and Montreal, the main distribution point for migrants heading to Ontario or the United States, retained some of the immigrant Irish inflow. Quebec City's Irish were mainly Catholic; Montreal's were more evenly divided. In 1825 Montreal's population of 25,000 included 3,000 Irish,[39] and in Quebec City five years later there were 7,000 Irish among a population of 32,000.[40] The dedication in 1833 of St Patrick's Catholic Church in Quebec City, the centre for a huge French Catholic community, underlined the strength of the Catholic Irish in the city and emphasized St Patrick's function as an ethnic institution for the newly arriving immigrants.[41] By the time of the Famine the Irish were the largest immigrant group in both Quebec and Montreal. In Montreal they outnumbered the English-speaking Canadian-born population, and, by two to one, English and Scots immigrants combined.[42] During the Famine the Irish populations in the ports were enlarged considerably, but structural limitations in Quebec City's economy cost that port its early leading position, and Montreal began to emerge as the primary metropolitan centre for the Irish in Quebec.

In rural Quebec, Irish settlements were scattered. Communities were formed first in the rural hinterland of Quebec City, and in 1821 the local seigneurie de Fossambault was renamed St Patrick's Mission.[43] In the Quebec City market-place, high-quality Irish linen, produced in a settlement south of the St Lawrence, was offered for sale.[44] And to the east, Irish communities were to be found in the emerging fishing settlements of Gaspé. Immigrants had also been able to found firm communities further inland, along the Ottawa River, west of Montreal. The timber industry in particular had attracted emigrants and demobilized Irish yeomanry[45] early in the century, but the main groups arrived in the 1820s and 1830s, as canal development and commercial timber companies began to seek labour and local farm produce and made possible permanent settlement throughout the Ottawa Valley.

Elsewhere in Quebec the Irish formed much less contiguous settlement, for although the St Lawrence River was the primary route into the heart of British North America, they were largely excluded from settling along its banks because of the prior settlement of the French. Immigrants were relegated to the agricultural margins on the slopes of the Laurentian hills north of the river, at places with such Irish names as Rawdon and Kildare. To the south of the river, in the Eastern Townships, Irish districts were sandwiched between French St Lawrence Valley settlements in the north and American settlements to the south. The appeal of the Eastern Townships, despite efforts to encourage settlement, had not been great. The Famine influx led to some increase, but afterward, as before, little of the effort to get Irish settlers there saw much success.

The case of John Cummins's expedition to Britain in 1859 to attract settlers to the territory of the British American Land Co. near Sherbrooke exemplifies the obstacles to extensive Irish settlement in the Eastern Townships. Despite his glowing accounts of the area's potential, he was unable to attract immigrants. He described the company's lands as being

in the nearest portion of Canada available for settlement being approachable by rail from Portland or Quebec at a cost of 12/6 Stg. Their Lands are not surpassed on the American Continent in fertility or salubrity yet they offer them at prices infinitely less than those demanded for similar lands in Western Canada. The Eastern Townships wherein their lands are situated are very well watered, beautifully undulating and entirely free from Lake Fever as well as from ague so common throughout the entire Western Country. Every grain and root crop which either Ireland or Western Canada produces flourishes there particularly turnips which latter are so difficult to obtain in the west that few grow there. Maize is a certain crop and yields largely. The soil and climate are particularly adapted to flax. Wheat from good seed yields twenty to twenty five fold. Copious showers succeed the early Hay Harvest thereby giving a rich aftergrass, a yield unknown in Western Canada. All these advantages as well as proximity to the markets of the Manufacturing States and of Quebec and Montreal, certainly point to the Eastern Townships as the most desirable portion of Canada for settlement. The low price of Lands is no mean boon to a settler.[46]

However, the geography of the Irish emigration and the timing of his efforts militated against success.

Cummins's efforts to forge a chain of emigration were nullified by the general decline in Irish (and other) emigration to British North America and by the much stronger link the Famine had created between Ireland and both the United States and Australia. When Cummins set off to find buyers for the company lands he did not know there would be only five more years of enfeebled flow to all of British North America. Of the great transition in Irish emigration well under way in 1860, Cummins was unaware. In addition, the Eastern Townships were unlikely to receive many immigrants, for they had been to a large degree missed at the outset. When the westward momentum of emigration had been created in the 1820s, the British American Land Co. had not been organized. Furthermore, its lands were not to be on the principal emigrant route, and the greater emigration flow passed them by. Cummins claimed that the region had been bypassed deliberately by 'agents of the Steamers,' who gained more profit by getting settlers to go far inland. In his view, and one consistent with the process of emigration, the first inland settlers 'urged their friends to follow them. The tide thus set in a particular direction has continued to up to the present day.'[47]

Quite simply, the emigration process, once in full motion, could not be easily altered, especially not at such a late date. In addition, the company, by its emphasis on getting English emigrants in the 1830s and 1840s, had effectively cut its lands off from much of the Irish inflow. The Eastern Townships of Bury, Lingwick, Weedon, and Alynwick were not clearly outlined on the Irishman's emigrant map of British North America, and they would remain ill-defined forever. Nor could the region compete with the United States and the Antipodes, which had become increasingly attractive. Cummins was unable to expand the settlements built earlier by such immigrants as the Fallonas from County Down and the Kellys from Mayo – both of which families had arrived in the 1830s, acquired lots from the British American Land Co., intermarried, and gave their names to localities near Sherbrooke.[48] Most Irish people interested in land preferred Ontario to Quebec or chose the United States over both. In all, the Irish were a minority in rural Quebec.

Despite minority status, place-names in Quebec suggest the local importance of Irish settlement, though they also show how place-names can be misleading. An example of this is given in Figure 7.7. The St-Sylvestre area, south of Quebec City, forms the meeting place of two

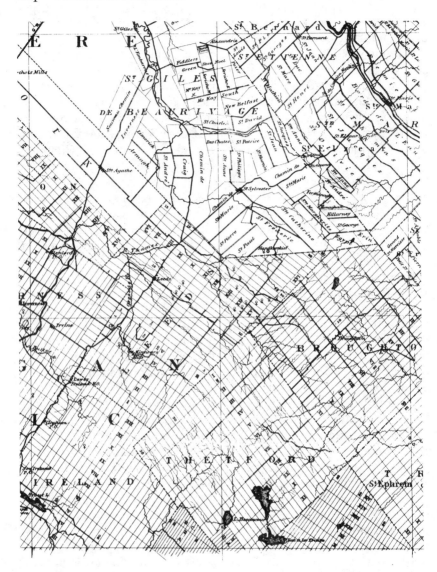

FIGURE 7.7
Cadastre of the St-Sylvestre area of Quebec

distinctive survey systems: in the north, a French parish subdivision arrangement of rectangular rangs of variable size and, to the south, a British system of numerically named concessions within square townships of approximately equal size. The area is also the meeting place of two Irish districts, a set of mainly Catholic settlements in the French parish zone and a set of mostly Protestant settlements in the townships.

Most of the Irish names are in the French area, among names memorializing saints. The Irish saint, Patrice, has a place with St-Pierre and St-Louis as well as Erin, New Belfast, Armagh, Killarney, Limerick, Fermanagh, and Monaghan. However, the places named did not have the degree of Irishness their origin suggests. Irish settlers began arriving there early in the post–Napoleonic Wars emigration, but by any measure these hilly lands that came to bear Irish place-names were of inferior agricultural value. Killarney, Monaghan, and Fermanagh were practically useless for agriculture and may not have been settled. Their timber was undoubtedly cleared, but farm settlement was unlikely, and most of the rest of the names similarly were statements of hope and expectation on the part of colonial authorities rather than descriptions of a successful Irish farm settlement in the Eastern Townships. To be sure, there were Irish intermingled among the French in the zone depicted, especially in the village of St-Sylvestre, but Irish settlers were relatively thin on the ground.

A few miles to the southwest, other Irish settlements, mainly Protestant, had developed in the townships marked by place-names such as Kinnear's Falls, Broughton, and Leeds, names much more British and not suggestive of Irish origins. The Irish names were allowed by the parish system of nomenclature but were discouraged in the townships by the British system, which highlights the name of the whole township and plays down, because of its numerical nomenclature, the chances of localities being named on such maps. Rural communities existed as localities, not townships, and thus the British system helps to obscure their legacy. Were place-names the sole evidence available, it could be estimated that the French area around St-Sylvestre was home to the Irish, and they were confined as Catholics within a familiar Catholic (albeit French) milieu. The Protestants in the French area would have been overlooked, and likewise the Irish of Kinnear's Mills and Leeds would have been unknown.[49]

The pattern of Irish settlement exemplified in Ontario and Quebec highlights the relationship between the timing of arrival of the Irish and

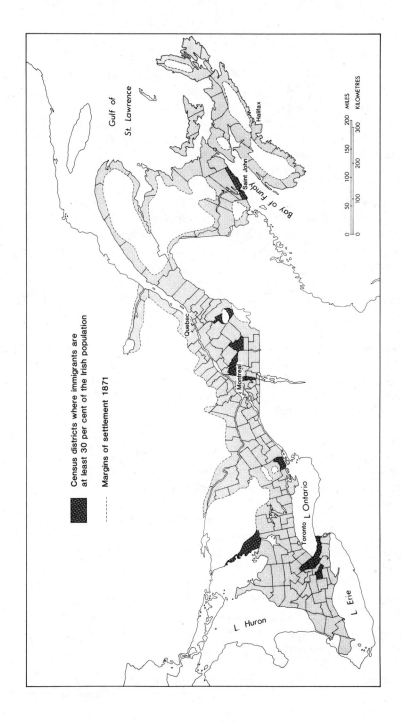

Census districts where immigrants are
at least 30 per cent of the Irish population

Margins of settlement 1871

FIGURE 7.8
Census districts in Canada where immigrants constituted at least 30 per cent of the Irish population, 1871

other groups. The Irish settled in behind the loyalist and American settlements and were able, especially in Ontario and along the Ottawa Valley, to create extensive communities. Where there was little settlement before 1820 the Irish became the primary group. But where, as in French Canada, they were preceded by others, the effect of their settlement was minimal. They were more easily associated with urban life in Quebec City and Montreal. The settlement geography of the Irish in British North America had been firmly established before the Famine, and its broad outlines were not altered by the influxes associated with that trauma.

REGIONAL GEOGRAPHY OF THE FAMINE IRISH

The impoverished arrivals of 1847 found only limited opportunities in the new land. There were few developed urban industrial centres to offer employment, and the dearth of free land grants excluded most from a stake in rural communities. Casual dockside labouring encouraged many to congregate in the ports of arrival of Saint John, Quebec City, and Montreal or in smaller ports along the St Lawrence. Begging and charity from local aid societies allowed some others to exist, but the majority were relentlessly pushed on. In Upper Canada immigrants moved from urban centres to rural areas in search of work on farms, only to be repelled by lack of work and residents fearful of disease. They then began the second stage of emigration, to us cities and railway projects. Comparable events in the Saint John region made Boston and New York the Famine emigrants' subsequent stops. Peter Toner has determined that in Saint John, the prime landing place for Famine emigrants on the east coast, no more than 15 per cent of the Irish there in 1851 had arrived in the Famine period, 1845–50.[50] This is an unusually small number and indicates the great weight of pre-Famine immigration – and the short-lasting significance of the Famine influx. While only a minority of Famine refugees may have chosen Canada, not all who arrived were hopelessly impoverished. The usual complement of voluntary emigrants and the earlier patterns of migration continued. Such arrivals, often sustained by kinship networks, were absorbed into the new society, just as others, stricken by the Famine and lacking kinship networks, were excluded.

Figure 7.8 depicts the geography of Irish immigrants from 1845 on who remained in British North America in 1871. It shows areas of

Canada where more than 30 per cent of Irish stock had been born in Ireland. It highlights areas where migrants of the previous twenty-five years probably congregated. In most districts of Canada, Irish-born constituted 20 to 25 per cent of the Irish ethnic group. The oldest settled areas of Nova Scotia had percentages as low as ten, indicating both the relative inconsequence of immigration around mid-century and the length of indigenous development of the North American communities there. Thirty per cent Irish-born is an extremely high value, and it provides a rough but reasonable measure of where the Famine and post-Famine impact was greatest.[51] In the Maritime provinces, only Saint John is signified on the map. Elsewhere in the Maritimes, second- and third-generation Canadians predominated among the Irish populations, indicating the importance of pre-Famine migration. A similar pattern is evident in Quebec, where only Quebec and Montreal and pockets of marginal land and small railway towns in the Eastern Townships had retained large numbers of Famine and more recent migrants. Although the majority of arrivals had been directed westward to Ontario, that province's Irish community remained dominated by pre-Famine arrivals and their offspring. Only Ottawa and the immediate vicinity of Kingston, in eastern Ontario, had more recent Irish settlement, along with the urban centres of the Niagara Peninsula, Brantford, and London. Likewise, the colonization area on the edge of the Shield in Muskoka, and further north in the mining districts of Algoma, revealed labour-oriented economies and recent settlement. Throughout agricultural Ontario, however, the early geography of Irish settlement had been unchanged by the Famine. The same was true for most of Canada's rural areas.

The relative unimportance of the Famine phase of emigration in the Irish settlement distinguishes the experience of Canada from that of the United States. We do not deny the depths of agony or the panic to which the Famine reduced much of Ireland, or the misery and degradation to which individuals were put. Grosse Isle, Partridge Island, and fever sheds through Lower and Upper Canada were sanitaria of indescribable misery. Centretown Famine hovels of British North American cities were heinous. But for British North America the Famine was an Irish event of limited long-term geographical and social consequence, submerged in the experience of those Irish who filled the colonies before its outbreak. So horrific was the event, however, that it remains the clearest image in the collective memory of the Irish immigration.

THE WEST

The Irish settlement geography of eastern and central Canada was distinguished by its early creation and by the preponderance of the Irish group among the total immigrant influx. In those facts rest the reasons for the Irish prevalence there. To the west, however, the Irish were minor. Settlement of the western interior and British Columbia was the final major phase of the expansion of Canada. It stretched from 1870 to 1920 and saw no coincidental influx of Irish. The 1850s had broken emigrant links, and social changes in Ireland had diluted the emigrant drive for land. Dreams of betterment focused on cities and industrial work, and peasants hopes for propertied independence sank amid growing prejudice against rural life and agricultural existence.

No mass movement from Ireland to Canada's west occurred. The full impact of the Irish in the west would need to be viewed in terms of the westward expansion of native-born Irish-Canadians rather than in terms of an immigrant pioneering society. It could also be viewed in terms of some 'great men' whose key roles in the colonization of the region exemplified that generational dichotomy. Capt. John Palliser of Waterford provided an early assessment of the resources of the western interior, John Macoun of County Down propagandized the lands for the railways, and Clifford Sifton, Canadian-born son of the first Tipperary settlers in Upper Canada, designed and effected the national policy that brought immigrants there.

In 1870, the much-desired northwestern territories of the Hudson's Bay Company were formally transferred to the new Dominion of Canada, and over the next fifty years the Canadian government strove to attract settlers to the world's 'last best west.' In the process were created the prairie provinces of Manitoba (1870), Saskatchewan (1905), and Alberta (1905).[52] The challenge was enormous, for the new lands of the west were separated from the established communities of central Canada by one thousand miles of rugged swamp and forest on the Canadian Shield, most of it useless for farming. At the outset, access to Manitoba was possible only through Hudson Bay (open to shipping for only two months a year because of ice) or by a combination of lake transport to Fort William, at the head of Lake Superior, and thence overland by the tortuous Dawson Trail, or via Minneapolis and the United States. The isolation was reduced when Winnipeg was linked to central Canada by railway in 1883. Subsequent settlement was facilitated by railway companies, especially the Canadian Pacific. Being the work of the late-nineteenth-century industrial era, settlement was more rapid and more organized in the west than in eastern Canada. By the mid-1880s Manitoba, which had had heavy in-migration from 1870, was becoming developed. In comparison with the newer, raw, frontier conditions pertaining further west, in what was to become Saskatchewan and Alberta, the new province of Manitoba, with its 'railroads and proven agriculture, its comparatively dense settlement and established communities, ... already appeared staid.'[53] The settlement of Manitoba established a model of colonization that was repeated a generation later further west.

In all the prairie provinces the majority of settlers were Canadian – of English, Scots, or Irish origin – and few were immigrants. The Canadians had come primarily from Ontario and the Maritimes, and Quebec provided some settlers from its English-speaking districts. The gradual westward extension of the frontier and the role played along it by the Canadian Irish are well exemplified by the history of the Carrothers family.[54] In 1889 John, Nathaniel Carrothers's son, migrated some two thousand miles westward from Ontario to become a pioneer rancher east of Edmonton. The land he settled was on the northern margins of the agricultural zone and suffered from a short growing season and inadequate rainfall. He subsequently left it in favour of Regina, a growing railway junction town and capital of the original North-West Territories. Two of Nathaniel's daughters also went west, Amelia to Innisfail, NWT, with her Canadian doctor husband, and Teresa, with her English husband, seeking a new life in Langley, British Columbia. Through the migrations of Irish Canadians like the Carrothers family, the new western hinterland was firmly joined to the established realm of English Canada.[55] Such an outcome had not been anticipated.

At the time of Confederation of Manitoba in 1870, the province contained a majority of French-speaking Catholics, and it appeared to many that the eventual settlement would reflect the English and French, Protestant and Catholic, duality of the Canadian nation. It was not to be. Canadian expansion, dominated by Ontarians, came to be defined in terms of an imperial drive, in which the social, moral, and political values of a British-Canadian society were paramount.[56] In that expansion, the Canadian-born Irish of Ontario were major contributors to the founding phase, but they would not attain the numerical prominence attained by their ancestors in the east. By 1901, the west had 66,000 Canadian-born Irish (Figure 7.9), about 16 per cent of the population,[57] and by 1921, they comprised almost a quarter-million people.[58] In time

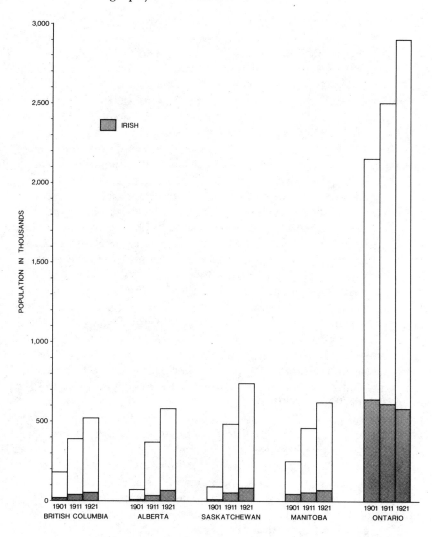

FIGURE 7.9
Populations of Canada's five westernmost territories / provinces, 1901, 1911, and 1921

and space their links with Ireland were attenuated, but they carried with them the traditions of a migrant society seeking social advancement through geographical mobility.

The transfer of Irish-Canadian values into the prairies can be exemplified in the role played by Orangemen in western colonization. This first became apparent in 1870, when followers of Louis Riel, the Metis leader of a local Manitoba rebellion, executed Thomas Scott, an Ontarian. Scott's death roused passions across Ontario, and he was soon enshrined as a martyr in the cause of anglophone-Canadian expansion. His execution focused the anti-Catholic animus of Protestant Canada. Scott was an Orangeman and an Irish immigrant, son of a tenant on Lord Dufferin's estate at Clandeboy, County Down.[59] For Protestant Canada he became the symbolic innocent murdered by the Catholic forces of insurrection.

Among the volunteers sent to put down Riel's rebellion were a number of Orangemen, including one Thomas Hickey of the First Ontario Rifles. Hickey carried in his knapsack an Orange warrant from the Canadian Grand Lodge authorizing formation of a lodge, and on 18 September 1870, the first Manitoba Loyal Orange Lodge, Number 1307, was convened at Fort Garry (Winnipeg).[60] Within a year the lodge had 110 members – from a local population of no more than 500. The bulk of the membership was made up of soldiers, local functionaries, merchants, and tradesmen, but there were also four members of Parliament. So popular was Orangeism in the new territorial addition to Canada that the lodge had to carry out initiations twice a week, and some 250 attended the first Twelfth of July parade in Winnipeg in 1872. The Order spread rapidly from this base, and, by 1900, 150 lodges and 25 Orange county jurisdictions existed in Manitoba. In many respects the imperial aspirations of the fraternity had been fulfilled. The grand master of Ontario East, in assessing the Manitoba situation in 1871, had noted: 'It seems to me a thing to be hoped for and wished for that a large Protestant emigration from Ontario may pour into that country and that of the emigrants, Orangemen shall not form the least proportion.'[61] He was not to be disappointed.

Ontarian settlement in Manitoba came frequently into conflict with the Metis, and many settlers squatted on Metis land early in the colonization process. For example, a group of Ontarians at Rivière aux Isles de Bois seized the land of Metis who were away on a hunt. In the debacle that occurred when the hunters returned, it is recorded in local lore that the Ontarians were led by one Sam Kennedy shouting: 'This will be the second crossing of the Boyne,'[62] a rallying cry hearking back to

William of Orange's victory at the Boyne River in Ireland in 1690. Neither side would yield, and the matter was decided by the province's lieutenant-governor, who rendered in favour of the Orange Ontarians.[63] The river was subsequently renamed the Boyne, and an Orange lodge, LOL 1514, flourished in its valley.

Compared with the emigration of Ontario's Irish to the west, few Irish responded to the opportunities on the prairies, especially relative to the waves of immigrants that had flooded eastern Canada half a century earlier. In an effort to resurrect an Irish inflow that might be directed west, Prime Minister John A. Macdonald sought to win the support of Archbishop Lynch of Toronto by proposing a Catholic settlement tract. Such groupings were becoming an important element of Canadian prairie settlement policy. Although Lynch had long opposed Catholic Irish emigration because it usually ended up in North American cities, he yielded in 1881 on rural settlement and went west to assess the possibilities of the northwest frontier.

The Canadian government was willing to offer free land, subsidized passages, and provisions to would-be settlers, in a scheme reminiscent of Peter Robinson's projects of the 1820s. Lynch was impressed by the terms and the situation and noted how the Catholic Irish both could be served by the church and could redress a denominational imbalance. He wrote: 'The Catholic emigrants can be placed in one locality where they can form congregations and have priests, churches, and schools – the Archbiship of Boniface, and the Bishops of the North West British Territories are most anxious to have Catholic emigrants in their dioceses and parishes – 12 years ago the Catholics were in the majority in these regions but as soon as the Protestants of Canada found out that Manitoba was so fertile a country tho very cold they flocked into it and now outnumber the Catholics as ten to one.'[64] As a result of his visit, and struck by the role of the Catholic church in colonization ventures in Minnesota and Iowa, Lynch threw his support to a movement to attract Irish Catholics to the new region.

In 1882, at the behest of Macdonald, Lynch visited Ireland for several months and consulted with the Irish hierarchy and the Irish Land Commission. From the latter, he hoped to obtain some of the funds designated for emigration by the Irish Land Act of 1881. He was instrumental in founding the North West Colonization Society, formed by leading Catholic laity and bishops:

Seeing that Companies were formed chiefly by Protestants, to undertake to introduce Emigrants into this country, as it is so fertile, The Most Rev. Dr. Tache, myself and a Mr. Foy, a very respectable barrister of Toronto, and a good Catholic formed ourselves into a company, with the approbation of the Government, and got assigned to us tracts of land in the most fertile and convenient part of the country, upon which to place Catholic Emigrants. Other Companies or Syndicates, as they are sometimes called, sell the land to their people and gain by their transactions, but we have no such object in view. We wish to help Catholics, first to live comfortably and practice their religion, and raise up their children in the fear and love of God, and thereby spread the true faith throughout the world.[65]

The archbishop's altruism was not devoid of practical considerations, and in a private letter he warned the prime minister of the need to attract the best sort of immigrant: 'There is one evil to be avoided, the Emigration of Paupers. The Poor Law Commissioners in all parts of Ireland are anxious to get rid of their poor people and would be glad to send them out in thousands to us by paying in advance on the expense of their voyage. Of course Ireland would be the gainer by this, but would Canada?'[66] Evicted tenant farmers and unemployed labourers were the people to be sought, he advised.

Despite Lynch's involvement, and the intentions of the Canadian government, the scheme was never realized. The British Treasury refused an outright grant to aid emigration, and the Canadian government balked at borrowing the requisite funds from the Irish Land Commission, repaying them with interest.[67] Also, emigration from Ireland had been minor for a quarter-century. Even if the scheme had gone ahead, probably few would have responded – the United States was the overwhelming draw.

Irish emigration to Canada in the latter decades of the nineteenth century was on the average less than two thousand per annum and during the 1890s was below one thousand (see Figure 2.4). The early twentieth century saw a perceptible upswing, and by 1905 just over two thousand again were leaving. From 1910 to 1913 about five thousand per year embarked for Canada. Some were destined to join the Canadians and Europeans enticed through the policies of Clifford Sifton to become agricultural settlers on the prairies. In 1911 a Belfast emigrant wrote home from Saskatchewan: 'I expect this will be the best year Regina ever saw. I suppose you have no notion of hiking out here. I see by the papers that they are coming out in their thousands now. We have 3 or 4 train loads landed in Regina already this spring straight from the old sod. Men. women and children, young and old, rich and poor, all classes and connections of people. Regina is going to be quite a city after a while.'[68] Many more arrivals from Ireland, however, became urban dwellers in Toronto and central Canada, and overall the Irish immigrant contingents were submerged and barely recognizable. Rarely did they establish Irish communities west of Ontario.

The Irish in British Columbia were likewise in a minor position. Some arrived in the 1850s among the northward rush of California gold miners into the lower Fraser Valley, but the principal pioneer in-migration occurred in the last quarter of the century. British Columbia was not a place where agricultural land provided the basis of settlement. Rather, salmon fishing, lumbering, and mining of both base and precious metals were the primary staple industries, and in them economic prosperity depended. Only 4 per cent of the province's territory was suitable for agriculture, and even then arable farming was rare. Ranching was extensive, and fruit growing a localized specialty. The resource base and the timing of its development necessitated large capital investment to instigate economic production, and the province developed as a consequence more of company investment than of individuals' small-scale independent efforts.[69] Most immigrants became employees, unlike the stalwartly independent pioneering farming and lumbering generations that had settled eastern Canada.

Some of the problems of settling in British Columbia are exemplified in the story of the County Down man Alexander Robb. He participated in the early waves of the gold rush to British Columbia, and over the course of a decade there he sought his fortune in gold mining and then, being unsuccessful, endeavoured to extract a living from labouring and ranching.[70] The great size of the province and the scale of investment needed precluded success through manual efforts. Coping with the isolation and dangers of a remote existence in a region as far from central Canada as central Canada was from the British Isles demanded an uncommon adjustment. Indians, the object of contemporary American fear, outnumbered white settlers and posed a new challenge in the history of Irish settlement. Mountainous terrain limited access and necessitated great effort to forge a network through which goods could be taken out and settlers and provisions brought in. Mule tracks, wagon roads, steamers, and eventually railways penetrated in the space of a few decades one of the last great areas of what was to become the Canadian ecumene. Men like Robb laboured in those endeavours. Missionaries, many from Ireland, were also a common feature of the settlement process, and in the police force and civil service an educated elite from Ireland was especially prominent.[71]

By 1901 there were 20,000 people claiming Irish descent in British Columbia, and twenty years later some 54,000 out of half a million people traced their ancestry to Ireland (see Figure 7.9). Notwithstanding the several thousands of Irish stock, the proportion of the population claiming Irish ancestry was lower than all in other provinces except Quebec. As with the prairies, immigrants coming directly from Ireland were rare, and the bulk of the Irish group was Canadian-born. North American – born Irish families, such as the O'Keefes and the Moores from Ontario,[72] both of which founded great ranching enterprises, provided exemplary instances of an otherwise limited Irish impact. By the time Canadian colonization had reached the Pacific, the energy behind Irish emigration had dissipated.

RELIGIOUS DIMENSIONS

In the Dominion of Canada in 1871, 60 per cent of the Irish were Protestants. That Protestant majority is diminished somewhat, but not overturned, if Newfoundland and Prince Edward Island are added;[73] the Protestant fraction of the Irish in all of British North America would still have been about 54 per cent. The easterly areas were more Catholic than areas further inland. Figure 7.10 illustrates the religious composition of the regional Irish populations. At one extreme is Newfoundland, almost completely Catholic. The other extreme is Ontario, by size and denominational proportions. Ontario, the demographic, social, and economic hub of English-speaking Canada, played a great role in determining the Protestant imbalance of Irish Canada. In Ireland, Protestants made up about a quarter of the Irish population. In British North America they constituted just over half, largely because of Ontario. The province was home to two-thirds of the Irish in Canada, and three-quarters of Canadian Irish Protestants. It was the most Protestant region, but not alone in having a significant Protestant population. Newfoundland was the anomaly. New Brunswick, with about half of its Irish Protestant, was much closer to Ontario. Nova Scotia, too, displayed denominational balance. In Quebec the Irish population was the mirror opposite of Ontario's: one-third of the Irish were Protestant, and two-thirds were Catholic.

The Catholic character of Irish settlements in Newfoundland, eastern Nova Scotia, and the Gulf side of New Brunswick, as well as the more

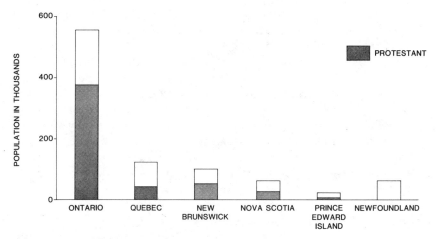

FIGURE 7.10
Estimated size and religious composition of the Irish populations of British
North America / Canada, 1871

TABLE 7.1
Protestants and Catholics (%) among the Irish in Ontario and Quebec, 1871

	Ontario			Quebec		
	All	Rural	Urban	All	Rural	Urban
Protestant	67	72	51	35	44	16
Catholic	33	28	49	65	56	84
Total	100	100	100	100	100	100

SOURCE: Estimated from Census data by the authors

Protestant character of Irish settlement in the Saint John Valley and
Bay of Fundy areas, can be explained largely by the regional origins
of trading links to Ireland. Economic class factors probably favoured
Protestant settlement in the Saint John Valley, the Protestants being as
a group better-off, and thus better able to acquire agricultural land;
farm land was much more important to settlement there than elsewhere
in the province. However, in explaining Quebec's Irish being more
likely Catholic and Ontario's more likely Protestant, regional bias in
shipping and economic links are less convincing. For both provinces,
Quebec City was the port of entry, and thus Quebec and Ontario had
the same pool of emigrants for their Irish populations (see Table 7.1).

All things being equal, Ontario and Quebec should have had comparable Protestant and Catholic fractions in their Irish populations. Table 7.1 indicates a very different pattern.

Quebec's Irish population was two-thirds Catholic, Ontario's two-thirds Protestant. Ontario's rural Irish population was the most Protestant and Quebec's urban population the most Catholic. Why these patterns arose can only be guessed at, but a number of hypotheses are possible. The timing of the emigration and the early movement to Upper Canada of better-off Protestants, who chose to avoid the French-speaking province, may have set the die for subsequent emigration. The upper province had the best land, and the most land, and those circumstances were known to the well-informed first movers in the emigration. The migration process would have served to maintain the Protestant character of emigration there. From the perspective of Protestant emigrants, Upper Canada, with its communities drawn mainly from Protestant districts of Ireland, may have offered a positive lure in the form of networks of friends and relatives. Not only the French language but the prominence of Catholicism in Quebec may also have worked against more of the Protestant Irish staying in Quebec, while providing encouragement for Irish Catholics. A cultural filtering process may have operated in combination with timing and economic factors, but definitive answers must be sought in comprehensive studies of emigration agents, relief agencies, and especially the economic classes of the Irish passing through Quebec.

The denominational contrasts between Ontario and Quebec were only part of a larger, variegated pattern. That pattern for the whole country is revealed in Table 7.2, wherein samples of the Irish populations of the four original provinces in 1871 have been separated into their principal denominations. In every case, Catholics are more prominent among the Irish-born, that is, Irish immigrants, than among those who claimed Irish ancestry. The larger Catholic fractions among the more recent Irish-born cohort reflected the shift in emigration within Ireland from an initially restricted set of origins to an all-Ireland source during the 1840s. Consequently, the Irish-born surviving in 1871 were more likely to be Catholic than were the Canadian generations born to parents from the earlier, more Protestant emigration. That situation was most marked in Nova Scotia, the earliest among these destinations, and the first to experience the decline of Irish emigration.

However, the shift was not sufficient to overturn the denominational identities of the provincial Canadian Irish populations established

TABLE 7.2
Denominational characteristics of the Irish population, 1871

Denomination	Ontario		Quebec		New Brunswick		Nova Scotia	
	Ancestry	Born	Ancestry	Born	Ancestry	Born	Ancestry	Born
Catholic	30.9	39.0	60.5	65.3	41.9	52.7	49.0	66.4
Protestant	68.9	60.8	39.5	32.7	58.1	47.4	50.9	33.6
Anglican	25.0	23.8	19.9	19.2	18.1	16.2	11.2	13.7
Methodist	22.6	17.7	9.2	6.6	10.0	10.1	7.0	5.2
Presbyterian	16.4	16.7	7.2	7.2	15.8	16.2	20.0	12.6
Baptist	2.9	1.3	0.9	0.3	13.5	4.1	12.5	1.7
Other	2.0	1.3	2.3	1.4	0.7	–	0.2	0.4
Total	99.9	99.9	100.0	100.0	100.0	100.0	100.0	100.0

SOURCE: A. Gordon Darroch and Michael D. Ornstein kindly provided us with previously unpublished tabulations from their study of the 1871 census; see their 'Ethnicity and Occupational Structure in Canada in 1871: The Vertical Mosaic in Historical Perspective,' *Canadian Historical Review*, 61 (1980), 305–33.

before the 1840s. Through the Famine and post-Famine years, each province maintained its own peculiar balance of Protestant and Catholic and its own distinctive mix of Protestant denominations. And, contrary to popular notions, Irish Protestants were more likely to be Anglicans or Methodists than Presbyterians, another consequence of diverse emigration sources. There were, however, differences between the Atlantic provinces, where the early Presbyterian consequences of the McNutt emigration had been reinforced by subsequent Presbyterian emigration through Derry and Belfast, to Nova Scotia, New Brunswick, and the St Lawrence Valley regions, where Irish Protestants were headed by the Anglican group. Quebec's Irish Protestant community was the most Anglican.

Methodists were important, much more so in Canada than in Ireland: they were probably overrepresented in the early emigration because of the contingents then of Palatines and Methodists from Fermanagh, and in the new country's pioneering areas Methodist circuit riders were more effective at conversion than their Presbyterian or Anglican counterparts. The greatest conversion of Irish Protestants (and a few Catholics) to Methodism occurred in the Ontario settlements. In New Brunswick and Nova Scotia, Baptist congregations were the striking result of a comparable conversion movement. Clearly local circumstances helped to mould new Canadian communities and a new kind of

Irish Protestantism. Diversity and denominationalism were enhanced in the New World, but fundamental Protestant values remained unaltered. Among provincial Irish populations, remarkable denominational variety showed how combined Canadian and Irish regionalism could create quite distinct Irish communities. The regional diversity that marked the country also marked its Irish component, and the question 'Who were the Canadians?' may be asked also of the Irish in the country. They are not easy to type.

Within the broad regional pattern of Irish settlement there existed a patchwork of Protestant and Catholic districts. Geographical fragmentation was apparent at the scale of provinces, where varying migration streams had affected different regions. For example, New Brunswick contained the mainly Catholic Miramichi and the mainly Protestant Saint John Valley. It was also characteristic of local communities. In the Petersville Settlement area of the Saint John Valley, for example, the Irish Catholic core was surrounded by groups of Protestant compatriots. At the head of the Miramichi, Ludlow parish was a remote Methodist outlier in a Catholic valley. Likewise, in the Eastern Townships of Quebec, Catholic and Protestant cases of Irish settlement could be found within the wider matrix of French-Canadian, English, and American settlers.

Much of the separation was the voluntary response to group identities and associated desires for territorially based communities, but some may have been the by-product of administrative decisions. The agent of the British American Land Co. in 1859 noted his willingness to keep Protestants and Catholics separate:

I fancy that in our exclusively Protestant towns of Bury and Lingwick we have sufficient disposable lands of excellent quality for [the Protestant converts from the west of Ireland]. Whilst to Catholics we can offer as comfortable a portion in Weedon where if there be a single protestant I am unaware of it.

Whilst I trust I am as free from bigotry as possible, I will own that my experience goes to show that in small communities parties professing opposite faiths should not be brought into proximity altho the attention within the bounds of a [?] may be [? ly] advantageous. I therefore am glad that we are in a position to offer to the protestant, neighbors of his faith with schools and churches such as he would desire and at the same time to the Catholic the same advantages, according to his views.[74]

In 1871, Ontario − more than 85 per cent Protestant and with the

Irish only one-third Catholic – had a few distinctive areas where Irish-Catholics formed islands of local majorities. Among the more than 450 settled townships in rural Ontario in 1871, Catholics predominated among the Irish in only 50. Although Catholic settlement was just as widely spread as Protestant, areas with a marked Catholic Irish identity were few, disparate, and small.

Figure 7.11 highlights southern Ontario townships with substantial Irish population and where either Protestant or Catholic Irish made up 30 per cent of the population. These Irish concentrations are set within a larger geography of other, numerically strong ethnic groups, mainly Scots and English. At the township scale, no unit was exclusively Irish. In most areas of heavy Irish settlement, as might be expected, Protestants were in the majority. Townships where Irish Catholics constituted 30 per cent of the population and Irish Protestants less than that were very few and concentrated mainly in the late-settled, northern-fringe districts of the Canadian Shield. The seven townships in which both Catholics and Protestants each comprised at least 30 per cent of the population are all in the older, early zones of Irish settlement – Biddulph, near London; Adjala, northwest of Toronto; the Peterborough district; and the eastern Perth district. They all reflect the early parallelism of the Catholic and Protestant streams of emigration. As shown in Figure 7.11, the Catholic islands occupy little space. They contained but a small minority of Ontario Irish Catholics, who were usually enmeshed within, rather than segregated from, the matrix of Protestant settlement.

Figure 7.12 provides a cadastral outline of landownership in the Ontario townships of Mono and Adjala.[75] The area had a combined population of 7,000 in 1881. About 1,600 were Irish Catholics, some 3,300 Irish Protestants, the remaining 2,100 Protestants of English and Scots extraction. As a unit, Mono and Adjala townships constituted a micro-geography quite representative of Irish Ontario, and similar counterparts could be found in all the other provinces, though not in singularly Catholic Newfoundland. The area included a full range of typical Protestant and Catholic settlement patterns. There were examples of individual Catholics being surrounded by Protestants and likewise individual Protestants surrounded by Catholics. There were large blocks of farmland occupied only by co-religionists, and there were variations between both extremes. Although Mono was extremely Protestant, a small Catholic community had formed in the northwest, and another, much less coherent, was aligned approximately along the Hockley Valley, which cut diagonally across the rectilinear geometry of

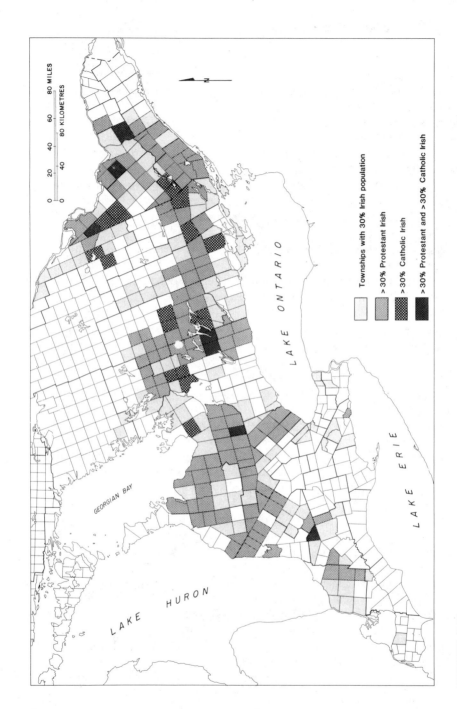

FIGURE 7.11
Ontario townships with high concentrations of Irish in 1871

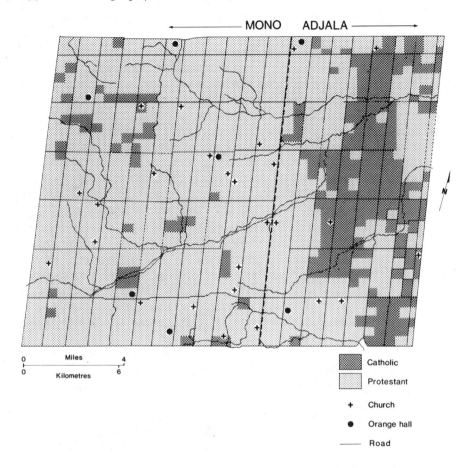

FIGURE 7.12
Catholic and Protestant occupancy of land in Mono and Adjala townships,
Ontario, 1881. On Figure 7.11, Adjala is dark rectilinear block located
between southern tip of Georgian Bay and Lake Ontario.

roads. In the southeast, a few Catholic families represented the edge of a settlement in the neighboring township. In Adjala township the Catholic settlement represented one of the main Catholic islands in Protestant Ontario. Catholics occupied a broad, fairly contiguous zone of farmland that was broken only in a few places. The pattern had developed from the first stages of settlement in the early 1820s, and its final outlines had been determined by the location decisions of the pioneers.

The communities were well served with social institutions. For the 7,000 people there were twenty-six churches, five Catholic and twenty-one Protestant, and Protestant congregations ranged from the majority Anglican to the Methodists, Presbyterians, and a few Congregationalists and Baptists. The multiplicity of Protestant denominations was not unusual, and the large number of churches reflected both that multiplicity and the effect of distance in a thinly settled territory. The average population density was a mere forty per square mile, a vast difference from their Irish homeland, even after the Famine exodus. The five Catholic churches provided an infrastructure for the district's 1,600 Catholics and for several hundred parishioners beyond. Four were outlying daughter-churches to which priests travelled to celebrate mass. The resident clergymen were located at the mother-church, St James, at Colgan, on the easternmost line of Adjala. In the Protestant areas, besides churches, seven Orange halls were scattered and, like the churches, served relatively small localities. This institutional geography summarized the transferred culture of the Irish immigrants and the patterns of their Old World milieux.

In Mono and Adjala, the settlement patterns revealed reconstituted communities, built by the slowly accumulating population of immigrants. The physical crudity of frontier life in the early stages was softened, even made bearable, by the immigrants' duplicating social organizations of the Old World. They had set about reconstituting their society as soon as they arrived in the early 1820s. At first, houses and fields had been places of worship, but in the mid-1830s purpose-built churches were erected. The Church of England missionary Rev. Mr Adam Elliott, on a pastoral visit to Mono in 1833, recorded: 'having arrived in Mono, I performed Divine Service on Friday, March 29th, at the home of Mr. Cobean, who resides on the 7th Concession. The hearers were very numerous and attentive. Many persons attended from the Township of Adjala, which is situated immediately to the east side of Mono. I baptized 18 children on that occasion. In Mono the people are principally Protestants, one half of the inhabitants of Adjala are Roman Catholics. The members of the church in these townships are exceedingly zealous, and are very solicitous for a resident clergyman. The frame church was raised last summer in a central situation, but without aid from some source it will be long, I fear, before they can accomplish their undertaking.'[76] In Adjala, the first Catholic church was built in 1833, after the bishop obtained land from the government.[77] Mono got its first Catholic church in 1837.[78] The early buildings were rudimentary log-and-frame structures and served generally less than a generation before being replaced by larger, formal structures in the vernacular of an increasingly sophisticated society.

In both Catholic and Protestant communities creation of churches was a central aspiration. Both townships had been settled at approximately the same time by streams of Protestant and Catholic immigrants from Ireland and other Protestants from Britain, and the settlement had evolved as an obvious consequence of their separate identities. The broad pattern of segregation was the result not simply of religious antipathies but of an emigration process that followed lines of information provided by kin, neighbours, and friends. Those conduits were naturally divided by religious distinctions, and as a consequence, at a scale below that of the township, clustering of minority communities was common. More the product of kinship links and parish organizational needs, these clusters thus reflect persisting distinctive identities.

FROM THE GENERAL TO THE PARTICULAR

The geography of the Irish in Britain's North American realm had been firmly established by the second quarter of the nineteenth century. Both ends of the country had significant Irish communities. Newfoundland's Irishness was unique, the fossilized social product of a localized set of emigrant origins in the southeast of Ireland. Elsewhere, the Irish districts were less homogeneous. They involved a variety of culture and experience arising from the mixing of the two principal elements of Irish culture – Protestant and Catholic. The regional blending of Irish emigration patterns and Canadian development that had gone on from 1760 to 1855 had created a diverse geography that would withstand the second century of Canada's history.

By 1855 the main Irish episode in the immigration history of Canada had been largely concluded. Henceforth the immigrants from Ireland represented only a trickle, and never again would the Irish-born be as important as in the four decades before 1855. In the second half of the nineteenth century the English and Scots dominated immigration from the British Isles, and those two groups would be especially prominent in the emerging cities of industrializing Canada and in the frontier territories of British Columbia and the prairies.

Yet, while the Irish communities in Canada ceased to be renewed by large-scale infusions of immigrants, their earlier contribution to the settlement geography of eastern and central Canada did not atrophy and disappear. By dint of their sheer weight of numbers at an embryonic stage in Canada's development, the Irish had made a great impact, and the surviving members of the pioneering generation and their Canadian offspring continued the mixing of Irish traditions into the new Canadian society. These traditions, whether in the form of material culture, or more generally in the realm of institutional, social, and ideological transfers, were, in the main, collective contributions. Individuals certainly distinguished themselves, but it was the size of the Irish contingents, the extent of their settlement districts, and the variety of their pursuits that allowed them to put such a stamp on rural Canada.

To this point this volume has explored the aggregate response and experiences of the Irish pioneers in generalized terms, but ultimately the pioneering experience represented a personal encounter with the new land. The following three chapters provide a balance by presenting the personal histories of four immigrants.

The personal histories presented below constitute researched biographies and are accompanied by letters written home by the emigrants themselves. The letters allow us to observe how the immigrants saw and interpreted their own migration and settlement. These personal stories therefore provide a different and complementary perspective from that already presented. They have been selected for a number of reasons. They were written from Canada, and thus Canada is generally the subject of discussion. They also comprise sets of documents rather than single personal items and thus can either relay the whole period of an individual immigrant's experience in Canada or exemplify especially well some facet of the immigration process.

The documents, which are all held in the collections of the Public Record Office of Northern Ireland, have been verified and expanded through other sources, and so the wider historical and geographical context of the material and the writers' lives can be determined. We know where these immigrants came from in Ireland, where they landed in British North America, where they went, and how they progressed or failed. The letters reveal what is usually not seen: pieces of life behind the anonymity of the ordinary immigrant. Although the documents provide evidence of typical experiences of people caught up in the emigration, they are not to be considered representative of all the people involved in the events. None of the collections is from the Maritimes or prairies, although single letters pertaining to those regions have been employed elsewhere in this volume. Not all parts of Ireland are represented. Significantly, too, the writers all are Protestants, because for Canada, as for the United States and Australia, preserved letters from Catholics are exceedingly few.[79] The necessary documents from which an appropriate sample could be culled do not exist. However, the documents presented here illustrate many experiences that were common to large sections of the pioneering generation.[80]

Above all, it is hoped that, whether considered individually or collectively, these writings will help dispel the notions of stereotypical Irish-people in Canada. Like all other mass migrations in Canadian history, the Irish were not a homogeneous group; yet more than most groups the Irish have been labelled with an unquestioning and simple image of unskilled, impoverished refugees whose fractious behaviour disturbed the tranquillity of their new homeland. Many immigrants did conform to this image; the great majority did not.

Part Three
Lives and Letters

CHAPTER EIGHT

Nathaniel and Joseph Carrothers: Upper Canadian Pioneers

In the Pond Mills burying ground of suburban London, Ontario, are marked the graves of seven emigrants (Figure 8.1), grandchildren of Edward Carrothers of Farnaght, County Fermanagh.[1] Edward had twenty grandchildren, of whom seventeen emigrated to Upper Canada between about 1835 and 1847.[2] Two of them, Nathaniel and Joseph, wrote home occasionally to their brother William in Lisbellaw, County Fermanagh (see Figure 8.2). Their letters were kept in the back of a bureau in the family house at Farnaght and brought out only when kinfolk abroad wrote to the home farm in search of genealogical information. Thanks to that historical interest, the family in Ireland prepared a typescript for the relatives in Canada.[3] A copy made its way to the Public Records Office of Northern Ireland in 1951.

The Carrothers letters provide invaluable descriptions of settlers coming to grips with the New World. They provide information on matters spanning a period from when their new land was but a forest to when oil was discovered. Most of the material is without much detail, and the reader is left to put flesh on the bones. Neither man wasted words, but with thoughtful reading we can read in their spare language the basic elements of their settling experience. Reading the letters aloud can also provide wonderful insights into Ulster patterns of speech.

From the letters the major elements of the emigration and settling process can be gleaned. The building of a house, the birth of children, the death of family members, and the visits of friends are relayed. The rate of land clearance and the type of farm economy followed are described, and though there is not the degree of detail necessary to

FIGURE 8.1
The Carrothers section of Pond Mills cemetery, Westminster township,
Ontario; photograph by authors

draw precise comparisons with other settlers, a bounty of personal
material and tone enlivens bald facts. Only Joseph relates aspects of his
voyage to North America in the summer of 1847, and his controlled
and deliberate prose shows that the experience was comparable to the
worst described by other survivors. He probably never fully recovered
from it. Family members died, shipmates were put into quarantine at
Grosse Isle, everyone was sick, and recuperation was very slow.

Some aspects of life in Canada are never discussed. For example, the
Carrothers families were dyed-in-the-wool supporters of the conservative political cause and renowned in their locality for being able to get
out the vote.[4] Not once is an inkling of that political activity given.
Perhaps it was automatically assumed within the family.

The brothers emigrated under very different circumstances. Joseph was
fifty years old and reluctant to go, his decision coming at least a decade

FIGURE 8.2
The resting place of William Carrothers, the brother with whom Nathaniel and Joseph corresponded, Derryvullan, County Fermanagh; photograph by authors

after the decisions of three brothers and thirteen cousins. He was the last of his generation to go, forced to take the emigrant route, probably under the duress of family needs, for his sons in time would have surely left without him. While Joseph had put off the inevitable, Nathaniel did not. He went as a single man, in 1835, a couple of years after the marriage of his younger brother William, an event that probably signalled William's rights to the family's lease of the farm. The farm was not to be divided, a condition of the lease,[5] and only one Carrothers could hold it. Nathaniel, Joseph, and the other brothers, Samuel and Thomas, all emigrated to Upper Canada. Nathaniel never regretted his decision; in 1836, and a mark of the finality of his emigration, he was joined by his betrothed, Margaret Kirkpatrick.

Nathaniel emigrated with his brother Thomas, and the two immediately bought a 200-acre lot of wild land on the Fourth Concession of the township of Westminster. Each took a hundred acres. Shortly afterward, a third brother, Samuel, and five cousins arrived, and a further 300 acres were purchased.[6] By 1860 Nathaniel owned 187 acres, and the Carrothers clan had title to a total of 1,200 acres of prime agricultural land.[7] Although Nathaniel purchased land on arrival, he did not become an agricultural pioneer immediately. Instead he applied his skills as a carpenter. In the village of London he worked on the building of the palisade and barracks at the fort erected in the aftermath of the 1837 rebellion, and he speculated on the building of two houses on King Street.[8] His bride joined him at one of the houses; see her lengthy postscript to his first letter below, written from London in 1839.

A few years later Nathaniel and Margaret moved to the farm lot in Westminster township and commenced pioneering. Over the next thirty years Nathaniel cleared land and built fences, and they created a farm from this acreage of virgin forest. He died in 1881 in the farm-house they had built and where their family of four sons and three daughters had been raised. The first of his four extant letters to William from the farm in Westminster township was sent in 1853, and the last in 1867; appended is a letter of 1863 to William's sons, who were preparing to emigrate to Canada.

Nathaniel's brother Joseph came late to Westminster township. Joseph did not leave Ireland until the Famine. Years before he had moved out from the family farm at Farnaght to a cottage at a neighbour-ing place with the suggestive name of Tanhousewater. His family counted three sons, including the eldest, Paul, who had gone to Australia before Joseph committed himself to British North America. Joseph's other two sons were seven and fourteen at the time of the family's departure. They arrived in Upper Canada in 1847, and Joseph began work as a carpenter, apprenticed with a wagon-maker in London. He remained at the trade of wagon-, implement-, and window-maker throughout his life. He never owned land. Rather his Irish-born sons eventually became pioneers. In 1860 the older of the two, William, bought land in the township of Bosanquet, about fifty miles west of Westminster, and Joseph and his other son, James, followed a year later. Joseph died in Bosanquet and is buried among his branch of the family in a cemetery near Widder Station. His twelve surviving letters to William, written between 1847 and 1870, appear later in this chapter.

Nathaniel and Joseph were carpenters as much as they were farmers, and both of them made their start abroad with their artisanal skills. Their example contradicts a stereotype of the Irish as unskilled farmers and labourers. Carpentry was a common trade in Ireland, and their family had made an early transition to the craft needs of a semi-industrial society. In late-eighteenth-century Ireland, factory development and the effect of the agricultural revolution on housing and stabling created demands for lumber and skills for fabricating such items as sash windows, fitted doors, wooden floors, rafters, and runners to hold slate roofs.[9] Rural areas had great demands for spinning-wheels, complex looms, and new types of farm implements. Wood was imported, first from the Baltic and then from British North America. New woods, new forms, and new structures meant new skills and more skilled carpenters. At Farnaght, the Carrothers family had built a saw-pit where a manual gang-saw cut boards and scatlings to be used in building. Nathaniel and Joseph were among the new breed, farmers' sons who were carpenters – workers in wood as well as tillers of the soil – the very sort of people that pioneering in the bush demanded. Ironically, they had probably worked with North American wood before setting foot in the New World, and though they may have brought little skill in felling trees, they certainly were experienced in the use and care of timber.

They had quite different personalities. Nathaniel appears a fairly no-nonsense type with clearly defined standards. Joseph appears more pensive and brooding. Both were very religious Protestants and yet quite tolerant of religious differences. Their Ulster sentiments about 'Catelickes' were certain and staunch, but not severe. Religious affairs were of more interest to Joseph, and he imparted a piety and heightened sense of religiosity in his letters. He was closely involved in the founding of the local Victoria Methodist Church, a role that gave him great personal pride. The church, its windows, and its pews stood as testimony to both his own handiwork and the family's honour. While Joseph attended his Methodist church, Nathaniel kept to the Church of England[10] and a much less active church life.

The denominational difference between the two was personal and had been established in Ireland. Joseph had adopted Methodism in Ireland and had been a regular member at the meeting house in Lisbellaw.[11] His brother William, to whom he wrote, was also a Methodist, as were his brothers Thomas and Samuel, but most of the cousins in Westminster were Church of England people. The denominationalism that characterized Irish Protestant families is well represented here. In the seventeenth century the Carrothers family had been Presbyterian. It converted sometime in the eighteenth century to the Anglican creed and then divided in the early nineteenth into Methodist and Anglican factions. In the twentieth century, the family at Farnaght returned full-cycle to Presbyterianism.

The age difference between the two men, the decade between their emigrations, and their own personal characters meant that their lives in British North America would contrast, and therein rests some of the fascination of their letters. The nuances of their individual lives are evident, and the experiences of the two brothers typify the different outlooks that existed among migrants. Joseph came too late to get land and too old to offer his life to pioneering. Many arriving during the Famine period were shut out of the farming economy. The Famine itself did not lessen access to opportunities; rather, in a much more developed society the value of land had risen remarkably.

Both Joseph and Nathaniel understood well the critical importance of being there at the right time. Joseph had seen on arrival that the success of people varied with the time spent in the country: those who arrived early had done well. However, he could not have been aware of the numbers who had not succeeded and who had been forced to move on. Nathaniel had more evidence of the significance of early arrival in taking advantage of opportunity. In his letters he opined that in the early 1840s it was still possible to get started in farming, but he was much less sure of the possibility for the 1850s. He wrote home in 1853: 'the land is getting dear in this section of the country it is worth from 20 to 30 doullours an acre and I would not take that amount for mine; there is no chance for a poor man getting a farm in this neighbourhood he will have to go back to some of the new townships where he may get it from 2 to 5 doullours an acre.' The clearing already done where Nathaniel lived precluded ordinary newcomers from pioneering there. In his view, if a judicious choice of location were made, pioneering could lead to success. To be successful, it was best to be at the outer edge of settlement. Joseph also recognized that factor but seemed unable or unwilling to act on the knowledge.

Despite the differences in their relative success, both men estimated that on the whole emigration had been beneficial. Although Joseph ventured no feeling of success on his own part and maintained but grudging acceptance of the new country, he was sure from the outset of the well-being of his cousins and brothers. In his first letter from Westminster he described various parts of the extended family as either 'well off' or 'in a fine way of doing,' and he was sure that for the cousins from the County Fermanagh townland of Bracky 'It was good hit the left Breaky.' Those sentiments remained through his letters, and despite his own qualms he never suggested that any one of the family had done poorly.

While Joseph gave faint recognition to how the Carrothers families had improved their lives, Nathaniel was unequivocal: 'To make a long story short all my Brothers and friends are well and have bettered their condishion by coming to america far beyont what it was possible for them to have done had the stopped in Ireland.' No hesitation there: emigration to British North America and industriousness had solved the family's Irish dilemma. Even the reluctant Joseph 'never was so well ... and could save some money if he likes.' Nathaniel was a confirmed Canadian. His letters are redolent with unspoken praise for the country as well as regrets for remaining so long at home before deciding to emigrate. He commiserated with his brother William in Fermanagh for having to pay the rent on Farnaght and give over to a landlord the profits of his labour. Nathaniel revered independence. It shows clearly in his willingness to help William, the last scion of the family in Ireland, to come to North America. William did not emigrate, but two of his sons accepted Nathaniel's offer (see letter, below, of 1863).

By 1860 members of the clan had established good farms. They had a good eye for land. Most were married and had large families. They were not rich – few farmers in Upper Canada were – and they maintained a significant vestige of collective occupancy. James and Christopher occupied fifty acres as bachelor brothers, and a spinster sister, Ann, kept their house. In the early stages, Mark, David, and Michael had taken together a 200-acre lot and subdivided it into three equal parcels.[12] Their sister Rebecca kept house for them until her marriage, and it seems that the men cleared and worked the land in common until they built their own homes and married. This form of land tenure represented a transferred Irish trait. Kinship also helped Joseph get started. His brother Thomas gave him some potato land and space for a house. Aid was offered whenever it was needed, and of course communal tasks were frequently undertaken.

Most family members lived close together in Westminster (see Figure 6.2, above), suggesting the strength of kinship bonds. Two other members lived in separate parts of Upper Canada: Noble Carrothers had settled in the Ottawa Valley, where another branch of the family developed, and Mathew pioneered near Forest, about sixty miles west of Westminster. In Westminster, Nathaniel's 100-acre lot formed the cen-

FIGURE 8.3
Carrothers land, Westminster township, Ontario. Three brothers settled
here: *left*: concrete silo marks ruins of Nathaniel's farmstead; *right*: farmstead
established by Thomas; *right foreground*: possible location of Joseph's Irish
cottage. Silo and large barn were built by the third generation. Photograph
by authors

tre of the family group, and around him were located the farms of
Thomas, Mark, David, James, William (son of the late George), and
Robert (who had come up from Ohio to join the group).

Nathaniel and Thomas chose to have their houses far back from
the road and shared a common track running between their orchards
(Figure 8.3). The houses of the rest of the group were all located
at virtually the road's edge. Joseph's house, described in the letters,
was built somewhere near the west front of Thomas's lot, across from
William Routledge's acreage and only forty rods from Mark's house.
Their houses were not exceptional, except for the mud-and-stone cottage Joseph had built. Nathaniel's was a wooden-frame single-storey
cottage, with a large open fireplace in the kitchen at the back end.

Mark's was also a timber-frame structure, but a bit larger, being one and a half storeys. The houses of the others were similar, except for David's, which was built of brick.

Although not rich, the Carrothers families were well set. Around their houses each had an orchard with apples and peaches, as was the pattern in the district. They also kept substantial gardens from which produce was taken to the London market. Their gardens were known for being highly ornamental. Nathaniel's pride in his garden was focused on the beds of flowering plants and shrubs. Joseph tried to replicate his Fermanagh garden, creating a kind of memory walk where, among his plants and shrubs, his mind might be transported home. Having fine gardens was a homeplace trait. Farnaght was a veritable herbarium and arboretum. There, a two hundred-year-old oak served as a boundary marker, beeches lined the lanes, and a wide variety of wild and domestic plants had protected shelter along hedgerow banks. Two orchards produced an assortment of eating and cooking apples, not unusual, given the tradition for fruit trees in Ulster. The farm at Farnaght, however, was special as a repository of species with medicinal value and a mecca for medics employing herbal remedies.[13] The botanical interest among the Carrothers family in Ireland was transferred intact to the New World – perhaps partly to maintain continuity in the face of the disturbance emigration represented – but in the main it was simply a family interest.

The Carrothers letters provide many clues about family, kin, and neighbourly migration chains that held together much of the new Irish world.[14] Nathaniel and Joseph noted, in addition to the family members mentioned in the letters, twenty-seven other individuals known to them in Fermanagh, all emigrants to western Upper Canada, mainly to the Toronto, Goderich, and London areas. A few were single people, but most were members of families and generally part of greater chains. The Stuarts were in Brantford and Goderich, the Rutledges and Batys in Westminster and Toronto, the Gregstons in London, and the Trimbles in Westminster. Newcomers sometimes married other immigrants from their home places. In the letters we are informed that George Stuart in Brantford married a Maguire from Magheraboy. Mathew Carrothers married a Dane from near Churchill, County Fermanagh, and Letticia Mason married John Watkin, 'nevew to Frank of derybrusk.' All the people named had originated from or lived within ten miles of Farnaght – indeed, in three small localities within that area. The

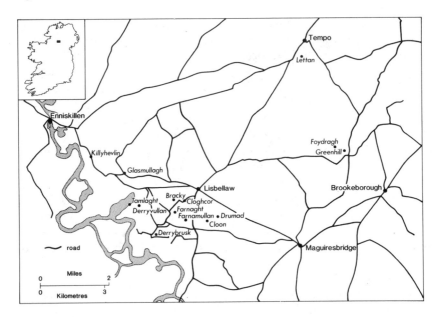

FIGURE 8.4

County Fermanagh place-names mentioned in the letters of Nathaniel and Joseph Carrothers

name of Tempo, one of the local places in Fermanagh, was transferred to the London district.

The map of Fermanagh places named in the letters (Figure 8.4) illustrates the limited geographical extent of the world from which the network of emigrants had been spawned. The networks extended to North America and Australia. Paul Carrothers, Joseph's eldest son, had gone to Australia, and so had a son of James Clegg, occupant of the house that Joseph's 'Breaky cousins' had left when they emigrated to Westminster. Houses in Ireland were emptied by emigration and refilled by others involved, one way or another, in the same process of emigration. The Carrothers world may have been very wide, but it was bound by intensely local social ties.

If we imagine the number of links the twenty-seven people mentioned in the letters may have had with other Fermanagh people, we may be able to conceive of the contact points the Carrothers family had in the New World. Not only was the family large, but the network of old-country people with whom the brothers and cousins could be linked numbered in the hundreds. They knew the whereabouts of many people well beyond Upper Canada, and the story of John Watkin chasing off to the United States to marry Letticia Mason and bring her back to Toronto reflects many and varied widespread contacts beyond the immediate core community. Although far from their own place in Ireland, they were not separated from their people. Emigration had not uprooted single individuals, dumping them willy-nilly into an unknown place and leaving them adrift in an emigrant limbo. Rather, emigration as a geographical process, involving chains of people, led to the development of far-flung social collectivities. Social ties remained unchanged – family, kin, and affinity with place of origin.

The Carrothers family had emigrated to Ireland from Scotland in 1602. Slowly, in generational steps, they made their way to Brookeborough in County Fermanagh. In 1769 Nathaniel and Joseph's grandfather, Edward, left Brookeborough, established two of his sons on a farm at Bracky, and in turn established himself and two other sons in neighbouring Farnaght. The next generational moves were those of seventeen of Edward's grandchildren to Upper Canada. Subsequently, the westward trend to the Pacific continued. The letters of Nathaniel and Joseph suggest, and the family's history confirms, that the children of the emigrants to British North America continued the patterns of their parents' pioneering and migratory life. Many of them took part in the westward move of Ontarians after 1870. Two of Nathaniel's three daughters migrated just after marriage. The third daughter remained close to home until she was widowed and then late in life migrated to spend her last days with a married daughter in Alberta.

Nathaniel's son John married in 1860 and moved immediately to the second Concession of Adelaide township, about fifty miles west of Westminster. John left behind for his younger brother the Westminster farm lot that Nathaniel had purchased in the expectation they would remain together. Twenty-nine years later, in 1889, John moved again, this time with his twelve children (aged from six to twenty-eight) some two thousand miles west to be pioneers on unbroken land near Buck Lake in the North-West Territories, later Alberta. In the latter move he went as his father had, with kin. John's family was accompanied by his wife's brother and family of seven children, aged ten to twenty-five. John spent only six years as a pioneer in the Buck Lake area, left part of his family there, moved back eastward with the younger children to the new town of Regina, and there passed the last years of his life as a flour and feed merchant. In subsequent years his progeny all moved to the cities.

In Joseph's household, the two sons became migrant pioneers. As noted above, his son William pioneered in Bosanquet township. Joseph went to join him and in the process thereby left his brother Nathaniel but re-established the cohesion of his own family. In addition, his new Bosanquet home was near the lot his brother Mathew had pioneered years before, and Joseph thereby re-established an association that had been broken by the initial emigration of the Carrothers families in the 1830s. Numerous others in the extended families also participated in the Ontarian westward migration and the eventual inrush to cities and suburbs.

The story of Nathaniel and Joseph Carrothers in Upper Canada is but a short generational episode in a pattern of movement that had gone on for centuries.

LETTERS OF NATHANIEL CARROTHERS TO
WILLIAM CARROTHERS

London December 25th 1839

Dear Brother,

I take this favour of writing to you leting you know we are all well thank god for all his merces; with every expetation this may find you and Mrs. and Children and all my friends in like maner; I received your letter brought out by Mr. Bredon for which I feel greatful to you for the information it contained both of your own circumstances and the many changes that has tacken place in many of my my old acquantances but I greatley fear that so large a some of money as you have to make up yearley will be to many for you I pray the lord to prosper you in all your under tackings. We have had a fine summer and a plentyful harvest provisions of all kinds in abundance flower is worth 15S per hundred pork from 25S to 30S per hundred beef much the same potates 2S per bushel butter from 7d to 9d per pound all in your money hay is very Dear in this place it has been sold at 3 per ton this is owing to so many miletery been in this place we have the 73 and 85 Regments each a bout 700 strong and a Compeney of horse artillery of 60 men and 60 horses besides 100 volintere Cavlery as I

mentioned in my last letter that the goverment was bilding very large
barrickes in London the are nearley complate the bildings and yards
occupy 20 acres of ground the are enclosed with a picket fence of
ceder timber cut in 12 foot lenths each pice from 6 to 10 inches in
diamiter A trinch being dug 4 foot deep the were sharpt at the top
and set in the trinch as close as the coud stand so the stood 8 foot
above the surface this made a good fence I still am working at the
bildings Carpenters has 6S-3d per day in the summer and 5S in the
winter or 10S Newyork Corency in the summer and 8S in the winter
bisnes of every kind is good London is nearley as large again as when
I came to it I still am well pleased with this country and with this part
of it as I am sure there is no better in it the climate good and land of
a most excellant quality and I may say I never wrote anything of this
country but the truth and I am sorry at nothing so much as that I did
not come sooner to it Thomas and I has bought 200 acres there is not
better land in the manner of Carrick Thomas and Sammuel is living
on his farm they have above 20 acres cleared and stock in proporsion
Mark and brothers has 200 acres more the are doing well the have
cleared 50 acres the sowed 13 acres of wheat this harvest the are all
well and is a bout writing home and the will spake for them selves the
manner of cleering the land you have hard so often that I need not
say any thing of it I have got 5 acres cleared this harvest and sown
in wheat the farmer is the most independant in this country as the
can have everything with in them selves to make life comfertible the
make their own soap and candles and sugar in abundance Thomas
made 400 weight of sugar last spring it was as good a quality as 8d
or 9d sugar the mapel from which this is extracted is in abundance
in this part of the country; the make sugar trakel beer and vinegar
out of the mapel in abundance the make those in the spring from this
tree and in the harvest cut it down and take out of it 50 or an 100
wheight of honey if it happens to be an hollow tree where bees can
hive this is not an uncomon case as the are plenty in the woods bees
do thrive and multiply in this country far better than with youes I
have counted 73 hives at a farmers place the honey is not so well
tasted as with yous I think it is owing to the wild state of the country
all is pace and quitenes this winter as yet and there is every prospect
of this country becoming far better than ever it was; there dos arong
nosion of this country prevail with yous that is that a person coming to
this country 15 or 20 years ago had a much beter chance of doing
well than those coming now I say the had not near so good the had

many diffulcultyes to encounter which has pased by I have had a
slight tuch of ague in September last but is quite well this distemper
alltho avery bad one is looked on much as the tooth acke for harley
any dies with it James Stuart wrought in this place last spring and
was macking money fast till June when he went to godrich and got
maried to a doughter of Robert bacoms and I hear he is working in
the same hous with him he could have saved money fast here; shomk-
ing is a good trade here and I fear he has ingered his futuer prosperity like others of the fameley by to earley a marage I had a letter from
Robert Carrothers he is still in the State of Ohio and spakes of
coming here Mathew is in this provence about 60 miles from here
and I hear he has got married to a girl the name of Dane from near
Churchill I had a letter from Henery Rutledge Toronto a few days
ago he is in a store and the are all well and in a fare way of doing
well he makes mention of Lettica Mason having got maried to John
Watkin he is nevew to Frank of derybrusk she is his third wife the
masons had gon a year ago to the states and he went after hur and
got maried and returned to toronto Alixander was coming with hur
flitting through the state of Ohio with the intension of stoping and
took ill in the City of Cleveland and died in a few dayes with out one
he ever saw near him he died in the morning and the beried him in
the after noon when he took sick he wrote to his brothers and James
folowed him but he was dead and beried some dayes before he came
on to Toronto with the doleful newes;

Dear Brother Mrs Kerk speakes of coming out to this country in
the spring I want you to get me some gras seed one kind I want
which I dismember the name of but it is the softest and lightest of all
the gras kinds I remember us to have it sown on the narrow strip of
meadow below the kill the have it in many parts of the country I think
Andrew mongomery can eisley get it for you only one pound of it I
want let it be very Clean it is jenerly sown on bottoms so you cant
mistake it; it produces very soft and light hay I want you to try the
seed shopes in eniskilen if the have got any of the Italian rye grass
seed and if the have get me a pound of it likewise it is sown and
cultivated in england and scotland and far preferible to any other
gras; gather me allso a pound of common gras seed of your own
stabel loft letting it be clean possible marking the name of each kind
on the enclouser we have the timethey and rye gras here the grow
well put I dont like them as the dont produce any after groth and

send them by hur and you will oblige me very much; give my best
rispects to my brother Josef and famely and sisters and fameley and
all enquiring friends and neighbours and I remain Yours

Nathaniel Carrothers

Let me know if ever Nobel Carrothers wrote home and if he did send
me the directions so I me rite to him and Robert wants to know so
he may send for him to come to this part of the country so the may
settle down together If you or any of my old acquantance wants any
Information of this country let me know in your next and I shall
gladly give it as far as my nollage of it goes and that truly; one thing
I can tell you that this is a better country for to emigrate to than the
united States I am glad that I did not stop in them I have had an
opportunity of conversing every week for the last three years either
with English Irsh or Scosh who had been in the states and the all
prefer Canada to them; and another strong proof of it is that a great
number of the inhabetants of this part of the country is americans many
of them sold large possessions in the united states and came to Canada
and the are coming fast thes last six months more espasialy old
country peopel who has tired of their republick goverment The goverment here has reduced the price of land you can by yield land for
eight shillings per acre and the are about macking it cheaper to
encourage emigrasion and all who come can do well if it is not their
own faults.

To Mrs Kirk of Maguiresbridge – I take this opportunity of letting
you know that I sent you the sum of £11 this money we gave to a
merchant that was going to Newyork to get a check on the bank of
Ireland but he got one on the bank of england which he enclosed
in a letter we sent with him directed to you in september last but he
should have got 2 checkes so that we might have had two chances of
sending it to you but hoping that you have received it; and thinkes
well of coming out to this country in the spring by quebeck is the
cheapest way it cost Eliza £6 to come to London for sea store plenty
of oaten bread well harned and plenty of mail to make gruel; some
bacon butter and eggs and a few herrings on sea is very good you
need by no biscuit and for cooking you tensils you can buy them at
any of the sea ports Eliza had plenty of provisions you have acquan-

tance in nearley all the towns you pass trough in Canada who will give you free quarters for anight and when you come to Toronto there you will have Mr Rutlege from thence to hammilton that is 80 miels from London and land carrage there you will have to look out for the cheapest way of travling as by stage is very dear and as I am determined to bild on my ground a frame hous earley in the spring it is on the upper end of king street as you come in to London there you will find us; and may the lord god who has been our kind protecter acros the reaging sea be Yours amen. [Margaret Carrothers writes:] Dear Mother I am just returned from the post office and there is no letter yet as I am every day expecting an answer to my letter of September I feel verry uneasy about it for fear that it should be lost or delayed so as to prevent you of coming out this spring as we are very anxious for you to come I think we shall send to New York and get another check and forward it to you as soon as possible, if you come this Spring I should like you to bring me some patterns of the newest fashion Capes and Sleevs and Cloaks and Silk Bonnet pattern if you can bring some straw plat with you let it be the best half Dunstable as it is verry dear here I have seen fine Straw Bonnets sold as high as 7 Dollars and Tuscan for 12 Dollars Dress of every kind is worn the same here as with you only much richer and gayer you have always the first of the fashions as the come out from England here this has become a verry fashionable place you would see more silks worn here in one day than you would see in Maguiresbridge in your lifetime and could not tell the difference between the Lady and the Servant Girl as it is not uncommon for her to wear a Silk Cloak and Boa and Muff on her hands and her Bonnet ornamented with artifical flowers and vail and can well afford it wages is so good. I have nothing more to say to you except that if you come the worst thing you have is good enough to wear on sea Mr. Oliver and Eliza is well she has got another Daughter 28th of October last she sends their love to you and Mary Jane and the children little John is getting a fine boy he speaks quite plain Nathaniel and I desire to be remembered to all friends and acquaintance in the kindest manner particulary to Sister Mary Jane and my Brothers when you come to Montreal enquire in some of the Straw Manufactory how plat could be bought and also in Toronto no more at present but remains your affectionate Daughter

M. Carrothers

Westmineister December the 5 1853

My dear brother I take up my pen after the lapse of a few years to
write to you and many of my old friends and neighbours who seem
to be anxious to know how I ame and what I have been doing in
America this informasion I have got in the letter you sent to Brother
Josef from his son Paul in austrilea and we were all glad to hear of him
being on the land of the living and doing well; likewise to hear of your
self and fameley at present thankes be to the giver of all goodnes for
all his mercies to me and fameley; dear Sir I shall commence by
restaiting some of my former statements that is shortley after my
arrivel in this Country I bought two half acre bilding lotes in the town
of London and likewise that I and brother Thomas bought two
hundred acres of land in the township of Westmineister; on my lotes
in the town I bilt two houses one to live in and a leser one to rent
this house rented at twelve pounds a year; nine years agoe I thought
I would go to the Country and improve my farm as there I intended
to spend the better part of my life be my years many or few; so we
removed to the Country there I have been cutting down timber and
burning it in the clearing of the land as much as would make a man
rich if it was in Ireland as you have heard so much a bout the clearing
of the land in Canady that I need not trouble you with a discripsion
of it after a few years in the countrey I thought it better to sell the
house that I lived in London and invest the price of it in buying more
land and improving the farm that I live on; so I have bought 87
more acres 30 of it cleared and fenced this farm corners the one I live
on; I have got 66 acres cleared on the farm that I live on which makes
me owner of 187 acres of land with 96 acres improved free of any
incumbrance as we hav no rent Collectres coming half yearley to
our door to a noy us no end to my leas; we pay a tax yearley which
goes to the improvement of the roades my tax is this year 8 dollours
or 2 pounds; I have got a good deacent frame house deacentley
fineshed and barn with other stabling for my cettel the barn is 50
feet long by 30 feet wide and 16 feet high in the side; in thisg i store
my grain as it comes of the harvest field this saves a grat dale of
trouble in the stacking we trash our grain all trashed by mashenery;
the one most in esteme in this part of the country is a two horse
tread mashene the two horses that workes the mashene drawes it

wright into the barn as our barns is so bilt that we can drive right
through with a span of horses and wagon with any load for the
convenicency of storing the grain; the floor is in the center this
mashene trashes and separates the straw from the wheat and the
wheat pases into the faning mill and comes out clean fit for the mil
or market this costs me four doulours per hundred bushel; and the
will trash from 100 to 150 bushels per day; the dwelling house and
barn I have ensured for two thousand dollours that being two thirds
of the supposed vallue of them this amount I would get if the were
destroyed by fire; or supposed a part of them was destroyed I would
be paid in proporsion to the amount of dammage done this costs me
three dollours a year; I planted out a bout an acre with fruit trees
such as apples pears plumes peaches cherries these all do as well in
this country as I ever saw them in Ireland if not better our verieteys
are very good the trees groo quick and bear soon I have had about
60 bushel on mine this season I allso carry on a flour and vegible
garden all of which do well in this country we have a great many
kinds of both that woud not grow in Ireland; farm stock of all kinds
do well in this country and is very healthey I have had none that
died of bad health in nine years that I have been farming in Canada
onley one pig and 2 sheep my flock of sheep number from 40 to 60
and pigs a bout 20 I keep a span of horses mostley maires from these
I raise foales this payes well as horses sell wel I keep also yolk of
Bullockes these are the best on a new farm my stock of other Cettel
are 12 in number. my heard is smal when compaired with some of
my neighbours we fat our pork on peas as we sow large fields of them
I sold 22 hundred of pork last winter at 30 shillings per hundred
and expectes to do the same this winter; we destroy a large quantity
of flesh in this country as we can raise it and not under the necesety
to sell it for the rent there is nothing but kill slay and eate mutton
beef and pork and fowls in any quantity as the do well and is easey
raised; I went 16 miles after a pair of pea fowl these are scarce in this
part of the country; our eighting and drinking are very good in this
country when compaired to that of the farmers in Ireland; this is a
fine country for growing wheat we have had an abundant crop this
harvest we sow two kinds the one in the harvast that is in the fore part
of september this we call fall wheat the other we sow in April or the
fore part of May this we call spring wheat and it will be ripe in

agust of these there are a great many verieteys; I plant a bout an acre
of potates every year Chiefley of Cups and pink eyes this gives me an
increase of 3 or 4 hundred bushels there has been a failour in this
country in the potatoe crop to some extent but I never had any I have
as good potates this year as you ever had in farnaugh; this has been a
very dry and warm summer hear; farming produce of all kinds sell
well this fall wheat is worth one doulour to one and a quarter per
bushel of 60 pounds and other grain in proporsion if prices would
continue for a few years the farmers would be all rich here in a little
time; you have hard so much about our summer heat and winter cold
that I need say littel and that is that the are not near so intence as
the are generely represented; this is a fine country for a man to live
in an indousteres man that Cannot make out a good living hear
need not go to the gold mines of Caleforna or Austrilea; there never
was a better time for emegration here wages of all kinds is good
mechanickes get from a doulour to one and a half a day; the are giving
a doulour a day to all the labours on the great westren railroad
which is maiking through this part of the Country it runs through
London; London has become a large and fine place since we came
to this Country there is a great many fine Churches, and merchant
shops and whole sale ware houses all of breek; the land in this part of
the country is very good I can raise as many potates as I wesh without
any dung; the land is getting dear in this section of the Country it
is worth from 20 to 30 doullours an acre and I would not take even
that amount for mine; there is no chance for a poor man getting a
farm in this neighbourhood he will have to go back to some of the
new townships where he may get it from 2 to 5 doullours an acre;
Dear Brother If you had onley plucked up courage and come to
America a few years agoe and got a good farm in this part of the
country before the land got dear you would have had no cause to rue
it and I ame sure your children woud ever bless the day that the
came to Canady; I never was sorry for comming, but ever shall be
that I spent so many of my dayes in Ireland many a wish the breakey
ones gave that you were hear; the old shoemaker stands it wel and is
making lots of money; Brother Josef seemed to be discontent when
he came and to murmer after I know not what but as he has kept
writing to you he has given you his opinion of this Country; suffice
it for me to say that he never was as well at the tanhousewater and

could save money if he likes; wel now to make a long story short all my Brothers and friends are well and have bettered their condishon by coming to america far beyont what it was posible for them to have done had the stoped in Ireland; with the exception that Gorge Carrothers is very ill and not expected to recover; Dear Brother I have often woundred that you did not send me a letter I would have wroute to you often onley knowing that Josef kept writing to you and that he gave you all the newes that was needed with out me troubling you; I hope you will write me a letter and fill it with a brief account of how many of my old friends and neighbours and acquantance are; and how the are doing in Ireland; if any of them shoud want any information about this Country and write to me I shall give it truly according to my knowlige of it give my bests rispects to sister Eliza and husband and fameley; and to gorge Carrothers of foidragha and wife and fameley; to Noble Graham and to the Blackes and many more to numerous to mention as my sheet is full;

I remain truly
Nathaniel Carrothers

I forgot to mention that we had got six children 3 boyes and 3 girls the two eldest ar boyes and the next two are girls and the youngest is a girl we have had none that died for none of them has had any sicknes we never lost an our of sleep with them yet I belive Children are fare more healthey in general than the are in Ireland gorge trimble and wife and sister have arrived here and are well; I hear Thomas Stuard has come to goddrige and that he left the wife behind him you will be pleased when you write to mention some pirtucalars conserning it; give my bests respects to Bessey and the Children and I remain your ever affecned brother

Nathaniel Carrothers

When you write direct your letter to London Canada West.

[To] Mr. William Carrothers / of Farnugh / near Lisbelaw / Countey Fermanaugh / Ireland
[Postage]1/2 1/4 Paid
[Postmarked] London u.c. de 6 1853 / Liverpool de 26 1853

Westminster June 15th 1858

Dear brother an opertunitey has offred its self of sendind you a few
lines by hand and a few small presents withe the bearer to you and
fameley in the way of keepsakes to keep you and them in mind that
such a person once lived and still Does live thank god for all his
mercies to me, these few lines leaves me and fameley in good health
hopping that the may find you and fameley in the same. All your
brothers are wel, and your Cousens allso; as I hav given you my opion
of this Country and my prospects in it allready it leaves me very little
to say in this epistol. I send you an essey or pamplet wrote by Mr.
Hogan; that will give you or any one desirous of informasion of this
Country information that can be relied on as correct; allso the bearer
of this letter can give you all the information a bout me and fameley
that you may desire – the bearer of this is Mr. James Oliver my sister
in law Elizaes husbant, who is going to Ireland for the good of his
health he is a man that is well of in this Country, and well rispected
he will call to see you and John Kirkpatrick if his health permites; and
if he should stop a Day or two with you any kindness you show him
for my sake shall be remembered by me for he is Deserving of it. I
would have wroute you a letter with Mr Gregston but he went a way
sooner than I thought he told me that he caled and saw you and that
you and fameley were well. Josef sent you a letter since and has got
no anser; he is very unasay to hear something of Paul, the past month
has ben the wettest that I have seen since I come to America; the past
year has been a year of much diffulcity with many of the merchants
in America Causing many feailours, farming produce sell for the
one half that it did last year give my best respects to all my old
neighbours that is yet alive; allso to Gorge Carrothers and fameley.
You will be pleased to send me a leter giving me a full account of all
my old neighbours that is worth retailing; margret and I join in love
to you and Bessey and Children allso to sister Eliza and husbant and
fameley.

Yours truley
Nathaniel Carrothers.

I send with the bearer my likenes and Margrets and that of my oldest

daughter taken the day Mr Olifer leaves London You will excuse
the scribl as it is Done in heast as I did not write it till I went into
London no more at present but remain

Yours
Nathaniel Carrothers

[Postmarked] Lisnaskea Jy 15 1858 E/Enniskillen M Jy 1658

~~~~~~

<div style="text-align: right">

Westminster January the 29th 1866

</div>

Dear brother

I once again take up my pen to write to you hoping that these few
lines may find you and famely in good health as the lave me and
famely at present thank god for all his goodnes; with the ecception
of my second son Josephf who has been in a state of bad health for
two years and dont seem to get beter it is a liver and stomack
complaint that eals him, he has tried three docters and none of
them seem to do him any good. Last spring we got every thing
ready to send him to Ireland for two or three months in the
summer, and when we told the doctor who is a Scochman he would
not hear of it; he said the climate in Ireland was to cold and damp
for his complaint and that it was sure to make him worse but he
advised us to send him north on our freshwater lakes avoiage; so we
sent him; he was a way two months and felt better when a way but
since he has come home I see no improvement in him. I see by your
letter to Joseph that times is better with youes, and that youes are all
hard at work to make money for your land lords; this is all write so
long as your famely stick to gether and is content. This has been a
very dry summer hear and the winter so far very mild; we have had
hardly any snow yet; the prices for every thing has been unusly dear,
the farmers will make well this year as the have not to hand their hard
ernings to the Landlord as with youes. I have sent youes som newes
papers so that you might have some Idea of the kind of aniables that
we raise; such as was shown at our Chrismas market. The provendisial
fair was held in London this year and was a large one it lasted five
dayes; and as many as forty thousand visited the grounds some dayes.

James Stewart and two of Edwards boyes came down to the fair and made us a visit. We had a young man a Mr. Armstrong son to Willey of the woods who came to see this country make us a visit last winter, he stopt a week with me, he coud tel me a good dale about my old friends and acquaintance a bought Greenhil, and he liked this country so well that the whole famely has come out this harvest, they have bought a farm of two hundred acres with a good breck house and other suitible buildings on it for seven thousant Dollars. I went to see them after the came the distance of 16 miels and we had jouvel time of it. The were stoping at the house of my old friend and acquaintence Mr James Armstrong of Latin, the are all delighted with this country. I have bought since I last wroute to you two hundred more acres of land for John and Joseph my two eldest sones, there is one of them 75 acres cleared and on the other 50 acres. John is maried and is living on his, the other I have rented to a man at 100 Dolars a year. The cost four thousand dolars which is something more than eight hundred of your pounds; so I have got 100 acres for each of my sones so that may liv comfertible with out toiling all their dayes to make the rent. I have been talking to a good many that lives on rented farms hear and the say that the woud rather live on one in this country than there; ther is a scoch man living on a rented farm near me and he has saved as much money as has bought him self a farm last year; I have been thinking had you come to this country when you were thinking of it with such a famely of sons how wel of you woud have been and how well it woud have been for them besides toiling all their dayes in Ireland. If you would send one of the boyes out to this country to see their friends and the country how the woud like it before the go renting a farm there and be not likin to live here and wishing to return, I will pay his passage home a gain and I am shure he wil be much the wiser after it; I have had strong nosions of going back to see the old country and you in times that are past, put I supose that I never shal now. There has been deaths and mariges a mong the friends hear since I wrout last. Brother Thomas has beried his wife and is maried a gain to a scoch woman, but I supose Brother Joseph has sent you al perticulars; we had a visit from Polwel gaham he was going from the easteren part of this provence to the westren to see his brother. You mentioned nothing about the fenians in Ireland in your letter to brother J but I see by the news-papers that you have trouble some times of it. The have large meetings in the states and make boistring speeches how the will invade Ireland and free it

from british rule and make it a republick of their owen, the allso talk
about taking Canada. There has been some feer that the woud cros
the lines this winter and rob and plunder and carry what the coud
a way with them, but I think the poor devils is putting their time and
money to a bad use as the never will be able to do either; the thing
that is causing the greates excitement in this part of the country is the
discovery of oil which is under the earth in large quantiteys in this part
of Canada which is going to become a sourse of welth as great as the
gold miens of Californa or Austrila; there has been hundreds who
has made a fortune of it the last year: this oil is caled rock oil and is
got by boring a hole into the earth to the come to the rock which is
from 40 to 50 feet and into the rock three or four hundred feet to the
come to the oil and when the strike a good vain the oil will rise to
the surface and flow over and run away; there is hundreds of such
wells and hundreds of them sinking this winter some of them yeilding
300 barrels a day it is worth 10 dolars a barrel there is severel wels
sinking in and neare Londond; write me a letter as soon as you get
this and let me know all you can about my old friends and neibours
and rememer me to all enquiring friends and neibours; and wife
and all the children and I remain

Nathaniel Carrothers.

March the 22th 1867

Dear Brother

I write these few lines to you hoping the will find you and famely in
good health as the leave me and mine at present thank god for all
his mercies to us. I wrote you a long letter in January 1866 giving you
all pirtuculars and my doughter Elizah Jane sent hur and hur sisters
potogaph to youes and I requested anser from you with all the newes
that you coud put in it, but up to the present I have go no anser to
it, and Brother Joseph sent you one last spring and you never have
ansered it neither; as I have sent you a great many long epistols
about that country I wil say littel in this one: as we can have the newes
of the day by the antlick Cable in the course of a few houres; I have
nothing in pirtuclar to mencion since I last wrout to you except the

death of my second son Joseph who died on the 15th of August last
Aged 25 years; he was in bad health for the last two years of which I
gave you anacount of in my last letter and I sent you a newes paper in
which his death was mencined the same week that he died. He died
very sudden alltho he had been complaining for along time, his
health seemed as good as yousial up to that morning and was in the
act of dresing him self when he drapt or fainted over and died in
about 15 minites; he was a very healthy boy till he was between 22
and 23 years of age and stout. When he began to complain and his
strenth fail he never kept his bed a day: Brother Joseph has moved
a way from hear, his son James has bought a farm in the same
township that his son William had settled in and close by and James
was determed to go on it last spring so the all moved to it; and I had
a letter from him last week and the were all well and he said his health
was very good; all the friend hear are well at present; this has been
a very mild winter hear some thing like an Irish winter the Country
is very prousperious at present only we are anoyed by the fenians
in the united states treatning to invade us, but if the come the will
soon have to go back again as the had last spring with their numer well
thined, as we are all loyel hear the will get no aid or assistance on the
soil of Canada. The have no simpothisers hear, the roman Cathelickes
hear are all loyal and our volintears are made up with agreat many
of them. The Cathelickes hear are quite different from what the are
in Ireland the are happy and content under the british Crown; but I
see the have been making a considerle rising with youes this month
and the have ben eisly put down; I have sent you some newes papers
during the last year in you see the market price of things in this
country; and you have done so likewise for which I feel thankful. I
got the Enniskillen paper with the account of your herticular show
in it and was glad to see that youes took so many of the prises. I got
the paper with the account of the loyal meeting in Enniskillen in it
and was glad to see that it was so wel attended: I allso got a good dale
of the local newes about Lisbellaw and its neighebroud from the
Carrols who came out last spring. There is one of them living with
me, the came a crose the ocien in 10 daye, the are all well: last
summer was the wetest that I have seen in this country. In some pars
of it the harvest was ingured on account of the wet, put in this secion
we had a good crop and got it wel saved mine was a god one; and
stock of all kinds sold well: I want you or some of the boyes to write
me a long letter with the account of all the friend and neighbours that

you can think of: there has been no deaths among the friends of mine on any side but that of Joseph since I last wrote to Yo William Gregston has gon Cresy and is in assilom; give my best rispects to all my friends and old neighbours. Margaret and I sends our best respects to you and Bessy and all the fameley and I remain

Yours Nathaniel Carrothers

Appendix: Nathaniel Carrothers to William's Sons

Westminister March the 20th 1863.

Dear friends your letter of the 18th of February was in London on the 7th of March but I did not get it to the 18th there being none of us in the City. I was glad to hear you and other of my friends were well as this leaves me and all friends hear thank God for all mercies. You ask me is there any choise time in coming and I say any time after the first of May as for which way I cant say which of them would be the best. The greater number of those that went home last year went and came by Quebeck and I heard no complaints. As for what you should bring with use I say bring nothing onley what is for your own use for it would not pay. As for your Carpenters tools bring all that you have that is good and buy none you might by a few extra plain irens and a few good hansaw fiels, as you can get any tools you would want hear a great deal better – all kinds of clothing are cheaper with use than hear and a decent supply of them will be of use to use; as for seed if you Cultivate any of the spring verieties of wheat you might bring a little sample of some of the choise kinds, a little bear barley and a littele of anything new. As for flowers we have nearly all the kinds that I ever new in Ireland and a great many more so that you need not bother your self with any; as for potates if you have got any choise kinds you might bring 6 or 7 of them; these you can put in the chest with your tools, you need not bring either the white rockets or the bloomers for I have had them and think them a worthles veriety hear. Mr. James Armstrong of latin was over three years agoe and brought them over and he let me have some of them. You might bring me A dosen of dinner knives and the same nimber of forke with carving knife and fork of a deacent qualitey; these you can put in the chest with your tools; as for the maiking of that dres for your ant you can bring hur 12 yards of the 3s–9d per yard as we think it the best, this you can put in the leg of your trowsers, that is some of those that will be folded in your chest or some other plase that you may think more safe; as this artical is liable to pay duty. When I wrote my last I had a mind to have troubled you with other things put I have altred my mind. When I come to this country we had some things that was liable to have paid duty for the never serched any of our chests. When we came to quarintine one of the revenue oficers came along and asked us to unlock our chests, so we did, he mearley lifted the lid asking what we had in them and he never removed any of the things. As our winters is much colder than yours you had better bring each of yous a good over coat of wheitey cloth not broad cloth. Light summer cloths are eiser bought hear than winter. My son Josef wants you to bring him out a wach let the price be as near 3 pound as you can get a good one for. I bought a new one for 3 when I come to this country and it is a good wach yet, this you can bring without any risk as one of use can ware it on your person, all this expenture I will pay you for when you come here. I remain your Uncle

Nathaniel Carrothers.

I will send you a copey of this letter next week least this might not come to hand and you be kept in suspence or weating for an anser, and you will be pleased to write me as soon as you are ready to start for this country letting me know the way that you are coming that we may know when to expect youes.

~~~~~~

LETTERS OF JOSEPH CARROTHERS TO
WILLIAM CARROTHERS

Monday 14th July 1847

Dear Brother

We are all well to the presn and bore with the journey thank God for his goodness. We are seventy miles from Derry since Saturday evening waiting to be Inspected by the Government Agent all hands busy putin the ship in sailing trim as the wind is fair expecting to sail this evening or tomorrow. We have the best ship that sailed from Derry and the best Capt. it is said by all that i have hear speak of her. Mr. Baird came with me from his office and took me through the ship and recommended a berth to me and sisters family Capt Hancock his Agent spoke to him to do something for me as I was a decent man this was uncilicited he is a very nice man and treated me very kindly Mr and Miss Alexander recved us very kindly the evening we came to Derry and we stoped with until next evening. With respect to our Enniskillen agent Mr Primrose he has done everything agreeable to our wishes and we will be benifited by his comeing to Derry with us. I have seen a Sabbath Day past such as I never expected to see and I pray God to send us better ones it was all confusion and Drinking as the Capt was not on board there was no regularrity, a few assembled at 12 o'clock and a man gave out a him and a good many gathered together for singing and prayers soo we have people that fears God with us. We had not time to get all the things we wanted such as Buistcake spirits wine but I have reason to think the Captain has got orders to supply me at moderate terms. Derry has left us with lighter purses. Give my respects to Docters Dane and Acheson you will likeway to Mr and Mrs Collum and to all my old Friends give respts to Mr C. Little as soon as you see him and show him this scrole as it is a Queer place to write at present

> I remain Dr Brt.
> Yours affectonatly
> Jos. Carrothers

[To] Mr. William Carrothers / Lisbellaw / Co Fermanagh / Enniskillen. [Postmarked] Moville, Derry, Monaghan, Enniskillen 15/16 July 1847.

October 18th 1847

Dear Brother,

I am yet spared to send you a few lines hoping they will find you and family in good health as the leave me and family in at present thank

God for his preserving mercy and care in our perilous journey which
was a tedious one. We went on board on Saturday 12th June and
sailed down the river that evening sd off on the 14th and after 8 weeks
arrived at Quebeck on 6th of August took the steam Boat for Montreal
at 4 o'clock that evening and from thence to Hamilton. We took a
team on the 12 and at 10 o'clock started for London 90 miles and
reached Brothers on the 14th at 4 o'clock in the evening. Brother and
cousins was rejoiced to see us all living; but on the 17th the child
Margaret died been worn out on the journey and up the country in
the boats and the waggon the most fatigueing of all. James was the
stoutest of us we were worn to perfect weakness I was sea sick all the
way, but my health is as good as ever and we are all doing well. I
thank you and Mr Copeland forwarding Pauls letter it was before me
Nat got it, in your answer you will let me know if any word from
him since and you will let me know how the crops has done with you
and if any changes in my old friends by sickness as it did prevail.
Sister Jane Died at Lashine 9 miles from Montreal and Thomas Stuart
Died since he came to Godrich Brother Thomas's eldest son Died
28th of last month of croop children are subject to it and it is generally
fatal George Scott was sent to hospital from the ship and some others
and I heard no word of him since. Our Captain was very good to the
passengers, and was very kind to me and family. Brother Nathaniel
and family is well so is Thomas and family and is well off. I am in a
house of Thomas's. Br Samuel and family is well and is in a fine way of
doing for his time, has crop and stock that I wondered to see. Next
comes the Breaky cousins the are well and well settled, the are in a
fine way of doing so far as the are cleared. It was good hit the left
Breaky. C. Mark is well but has got no wife yet, David and family is
well so is Mick and family, the have got good wives and is in a good
way of Doing. C. Rebecca and husband (Wm Webster) is well, they
have no children. All my friends has been friends to me, and mine.
You will remember us to Mr and Mrs Tailor and Miss Armstrong.
Margaret sends her word she met with friends she did not expect.
Remember us to Mr Wm McMullen and all my old friends in Clough-
cur and numerous friends in all the country

Remember us to Mr and Mistress and Miss Collum and to Dr Dane,
let me know if he has recovered his health. Give my respects to Dr
Acheson and to Mr and Mistress Michell. I hope by next month to
writ to those am under promise to. Let Robert Crawford know I

parted with A Crawford in Montreal I was 7s 6d out by bringing her that far she promised to write to me but has not. Give my best respects to Mr Charles Little. As far as I have seen of this country it is very fine land but grown with immence timber. Those that is settled for some years is well off. Markets is cheap Flour is 7S shillings per hundred, beef and Mutton from 1 1/2d to 2d per lb Butter 6d pr lb and other produce equally cheap. There is some rot in the puttatose in some places in this country this season. I stoped a month in Brother Nats until I was restored to strength and I am with a waggonmaker learning to make waggons at 20 Dollars pr month, so you see I have some of my trade to learn. I had the Yanky part of it. Next week ends my month. Lct Mr. Samuel Betty know I did not travel by Toronto and I got no word of Mr Wm his Brother the letters I
posted for their places. I parted with John Hilliard and family in Montreal in good health. I remain Dear Brother Yours affectionally,

Joseph Carrothers.

My plants and roots a great many of them is succeeding very well and part of the seeds I sowed is growing very well. If you can get seed of ground Ivy send me a little in the crease of your letter, paste them in the fold.

[To] Mr William Carrothers / Farnaught (Lisbellaw) / Co Fermanagh / Enniskillen / Ireland.
[Postmarked] Enniskillen Nov 18 1847 / Montreal L.C. Oct 23 1847 / London U.C. ... 1847

October 23rd 1848

Dear Brother,

I take this oppertunity after the lapse of another year of sending you a few lines to let you know I am stil and in good health as I have been since I arrived in this place and all my family thank God for all his kind mercies hoping the will find you and family in the same I received your letter of answer in due time I wrote to Miss R Armstrong but received no answer and I wrote to Mr Robert McFarland as I promised to do but received no answer I have received Mr James Copeland's News papers regularly for which I am very thankfull to him for his kindness I hope he and his Fathers family is in good health as the were when he wrote the few lines give my thanks to him in the most respectfull manner, and I hope he will continue his favours, Dear Willy I have been very busy this summer building a house and I am living in it now i have a neat Cottage House 30 feet by 20 the out walls 10 feet high of mud and inside walls of Brick It is well thought of in this country (stones is very rare in this place) I have a dislike to the timber Houses the are very cold in winter and very hot in summer and the are allways sinking and twisting. I got help from Brothers and Cosins but I was Brick layer and Carpenter my self the wondered I done the fireplaces so well your Brothers Samuel Nathaniel and Thomas and families are all in good health and lives well, Cosins James and George and Families are well the made a good change you could not think the are as well their stock and crop is so good George had 3 acres of Wheat he has 200 Bushels threshed of wheat and I cannot say how much oats the crops is very abundant in this part of the Country there has been a partial rot in the putatoe crop Cosin Mark is well he is my nearest neighbour about 40 rods from House to House David and Mick and families is well Mark is the Batchelor as yet (Cousin Becky) Mrs Webster and husband is well she has no family Margaret Gr.. otherways Mrs Harper lives at Toronto and is very well off we expe Mrs Betty (Mary Graham) up to see the old friends in a few days I have been advised to not mind settling on wild land and Thomas gave me an acre of land sowed in wheat on the 5th consession (that is the name the Government roads has that is laid out in survey of the lands it is the principal road from the east to London) and to try to live by the trade as the prospect is good in so thriveing a township. Opposite my House a Mr. Rutlege owns 200 acres of land and he gave me the liberty of it for 8 years until his son is of Age, to Clear and crop and pasture as I please for the time. I had betterthan half an acre of very fine pitatoes in Thomas' land. Thomas has been very clever with me, I wrote to Paul in December last but i got no answer let me know if John Clegg got any word in his letters of him, and when he writes he will please to

mention me to him and to his Uncle James and family, I gave some
plants of Balm of Gilead and Annagalis to William Graham and to Miss
Rebecca Collum and to Thomas Johnston you will oblige me if you
will make it your business to get some of the seed of the Balm of
Gilead & the Annagalis you will send them in your next letter You
will fold your letter first and then open it again and rub a little paste
in the crase and stick a row of the seeds in it and fold it up I have sent
seeds to Paul in that way. I gave plants to Miss Armstrong you can
get some of them put in to a corner of a newspaper by my Friend Mr
J.C. do not neglect it; remember us to Mr and Mrs Tailor and Mrs
Armstrong let me know who got Dr Dane's property and who lives in
Drimmad let me know how Edward Stuart and family is and how
he is doing remember us to Wm Mcmullin and Mr Collum and Mrs
and Miss Collum let me know if any of my old acquaintances came
out this last season and any Deaths that you would think I would wish
to know of, let me know if Anne Crawford wrote home and where she
settled for she did not write to me as she promised let me know if
Mrss Betty is well, and who she got to be her neibour, Margaret
wishes to know if her Aunt Tailor is living let Mr. Hugh Lunny of
Cloone know I am living and well remeer us to Mr and Mrss Thomas
Betty and all my old friends – this is a very fine country for all kinds
of grain crop the Old settlers is very well to live the only thing against
the Farmer he has a cheap market to sell his produce in but he dose
not want much money; when he has got his Deed there is no further
demand of him only a small tax once a year wheat is from 2s 6d to 3s
sterling pr Bushel of 60 pounds putatose 2d pr stone (but the are
sold by the Bushel) Apples 6d pr Bushel and peaches 2s 6d pr Bushel
this has been a fine fruit year there is a kind of cherry in the woods
that bear fruit in like manner as the currants the grown very large
trees from 2 to 3 feet thick and upward of 60 feet high and quite
strait, the timber is beautiful and very durable Flower 2 Dollars pr
hundred of 100 pounds beef 1d to 1 1/2d pr pound Mutton the
same, all the money is counted York money or Currancy money
Currancy money is the the lawful money of the country that is one
pound stn is one pound five currancy one shilling stn is 15d currancy
four Englus is one Dollar and is S Currancy (Hallifax) our 6d is a
York shilling (York Currancy) Dear Brother answer this letter as soon
as it comes to hand and let me know how you are able to meet the

demands that is on you for I know the must be Great Margaret and the boys join me in love to you and your partner and children

I remain your affectionate
brother
Joseph Carrothers.

[To] Mr. William Carrothers / Farnagh (Lisbellaw) / County Ferma-
nagh / Enniskillen / Ireland
[Postage] 1/2 stg.
[Postmarked] London u.c. Oct 23 1848 / Enniskillen Nov 22 1848

~~~~~~

<div style="text-align: right">

February 19th 1852

</div>

Dear Brother

Once more I am spared to send you a few lines hoping the will find
you in Good health as they leave me and the family in at present
thanks be to God for all his kind mercies to us. Dear Willy I received
no letter from you since I received your letter of May last together
with Mr Copelands which I answered immediately after. I have
received no papers from Mr Jas Copeland since June last I hope he
is stil living and well and all the family give my respects to them. I
had a letter from Paul before Christmas last from the Town of San
fransisco in Callifornia he was well at that time but he had fever in
the summer (Panama fever) I hear his health will be bad in the country.
   He says it is a good place for making money if he gets his health.
Labourers wages from 4 to 5 Dollars pr Day, Carpenters from 6 to
8 Dollars pr Day, Masons from 8 to 10 Dollars pr Day. He says the
mines did not do well last summer for want of rain, the had no water
for washing out the gold. I wrote to him to come to this country. We
have the coldest winter that has been this Twenty years, the 15–16–
17 of December last and the 17–18–19–20 of January and the last
three Day of This month the were in the extreme. The people like
deep snow for it gives good slaeing and the drive like fury with all
kinds of loding. Our markets is very cheap, wheat from 1s 6d to 2s

3d pr Bushel of 60 pounds puttatoes is the dearest of our crop the are 2s pr Bushel. The rotted last July very like what I seen in Ireland. All provisions is equally cheap. All your brothers and families are well and so is your cosins. George is the only one in a delicate state he is broke down by his former hard labour. I am told George Stuart has got married at Brontford to a girl of the name of Maguire from Magheraboy — he is at the shoemaking in Brontford. Rebecca (Carrothers), Webster's husband died in November she had no children she was well off during her life. Jane Trimbles Daughters is to come out early this season the will come to their uncles, Robert lives beside me. Please to send 4 sions off the Bakeing Apple and 4 off the wine Apple take them of short shoots of last years with a little old wood. Send me 4 of the scarlit Thorn. James Graham will show you them at my old Dwelling. Roll them in oild paper and tye them close. Send me a pint of spring veches and a dosen of Long pod Beans. Send these with Miss Trimble she will come to this place. We do not crop here until the leaf is on the trees. Send me a letter with Miss Trimble and let me know how my friends are and all my old acquaincances and how you are able to meet the requirements of Mr Porter. I and the fammily send our best love and respects to you and your wife and children. I remain Dr Brother

Yours affectonately
Joseph Carrothers.

[To] Mr William Carrothers / Lisbellaw / Co. Fermanagh / Enniskillen / Ireland
[Postmarked] London u.c. Feb 20 1852 / Montreal l.c. Feb 23 1852 / Enniskillen Mr 18 1852

Westminister June 15th 1855

Dear Brother

I received your present the pamplet with that of Mr Copelands I am happy to know you and family is all in good health, and this leaves me and the family in the same thank god for his mercies to us, I can inform you that all your Brothers and familys and cousins and famlies are all living and in good health I have wondered you did not answer my last letter, You will please to answer this letter and let me know how you are able to live and meet the rent and taxes, as the are stil high and wages high, let me know the changes in my old neighbours, let me know how John Black left his property and how the others are doing, let Margaret know if her cosin Rebecca Armstrong is living in Lisbellaw and how her uncle Wm McMullin is let me know how sister Montgomery and family is, and let me know how Sister Tirzah is.

Dawson Dane Heathers visited London in his tour through Canada raising money to support the reformation in Ireland he got 120 pounds in London, I heard, I was in town soon after he arrived, his arrival not been made publick I had not the pleasure of seeing him he had good success In all the towns he visited he return on the 20th of this month for Ireland.

We had a more than usual cold winter and this month for so far is much colder than usual our Peach Trees are kild by the cold of last winter in this part of the country and to a great extent in the States I had six Bushel of Peaches last year I will not have a single fruit this year last summer was very warm but the winter was extreme cold. Our crops looks very promising at present, Winter wheat looks very fine. We have very good markets for all farm produce Wheat from 2 Dollars to 2 1/2 pr. Bushel of 60 llbs a Dollar is 4 British shilling or 5 shillings Currancy Oats 1/2 Dollar to 1/2 Do and sixpence of 34 llbs to the Bushel puttatose the same as the Oats pr Bush. Butter from 8d to 10d pr llb Wool from 10d to 12d pr llb all other things proportionally Dear.

We had a visit from the Reverend Mr. Caughey an Irish man by Birth in London last winter he is called the Apostle of the Day he stoped better than two months he held services in the new Wesleyan Church a very spacious building, in the Gothick Order of Arkitecture it cost upwards of six Thousand pounds, many were aded to the in the town and neighbourhood, and in this part of the country the flame was kindlid and some of the lost was found Among others Brother Sam has started again and Cosin David. Margaret, and William and James has been added to the number which makes our comforts more sweet, I had a letter in January 54 from Paul from Beechworth in Victoria Colony but none since, it is gratifying to me that I am retained in the breast of some of my old friends particularly Mr. Copeland, I send my best respects to him and his Father and Mother, at his convenience I hope for more of his favours, please to let Mr

Hugh Lunny know I am living and well let me know if he is alive, let me know if Mr Copeland got the Almanack I sent him in December last, I now close these few lines hoping you will remember me to all my old acquaintances, Margaret wishes to be remembered to Miss Armstrong, her Uncle William and Aunts she sends her love to them, we all join in sending our love to you and family

> I remain Dear Brother your
> affectanly,
> Joseph Carrothers.

[Postmarked] London u.c. ju 16 1855 / Paid Liverpool 1 jy 55 / Enniskillen j ? 1855

~~~~~~

> Westminster Township November 26 1856

Dear Brother

I once mor send you a few lines hoping the will find you and all the family in good health as the leave me and my family in at present thanks be to the God of all our mercies. Your brothers and all their families is well and so is your cousins and families and there is a yearly increase among them. My son William got married last year a Miss Willsie, her Father gave her eight Hundred Dollars, he has removed last month to the Township of Bosanquet 54 miles from this place Land being cheaper than here. Land is selling in this place for 40 to 50 Dollars pr Acre as it is improved, and some above that price.

Mr. Carrol and his amiable wife came to see us in this place. We have got a new Methodist Church Built this past Summer. It is 40 feet long by 30 feet wide, it was opened for service last month. It is on David Carrothers Lot one quarter of a mile from my house. I was the mover of it. Last June was a year I started a subscription and it took good through all the name and two Mr. Willses that is members of the society that meet in it. I hope it will be of use. Methodism is popular in this country, but there is more hearers of the Word than Doers. In answer to this letter let me know how William McMullen and sister is and Miss Armstrong and my sisters families and my old friends.

I received a letter from Paul, he gave me to know he would be leaving Australia in this month he said he would come by England and that he would go to see his native country so you will have the pleasure of seeing him, first he said he would be here in March. The Rail Road is in full operation from London to New York and from London to Montreal a distance of 600 miles, this is the Grand Trunk Line opened last month for travel. You will give him to know this, when he arrives in London to go to Mr. Strongs Hotell there he will see his old friend Mr Henry Strong, every Hotell Keep an Omnibus that attends the arrivale of every train. Mr. James Oliver, Nathaniel's Brother in Law, Mr. John Doyle married to another, and Mr. Robert Keneday that is maried to their mother all will be glad to see you and will send me word of your arrival. Let him know also there is a Mr James Armstrong from this part gone to Ireland (Nath. and his wife is well acquaint with him, I have seen him) he is the Lawfull Heir of Mr Harry Armstrong's property (Latin). He will be returning in March. He might be with him to London. This season has been remarkable fine, very little rain has fallen up to this since the fall. Wheat dose not look so strong as other seasons.

Please to let Mr Hugh Lunny of Cloon know I am living and I hope he is so too. Remember me to all my old acquaintances as you see them

Brother Thomas seen James Stuart in London last month he said the were all well at Godderich, he did not come to see us and I have not any more to say of them. All farm produce is on good demand and good price.

Please to give my best respects to Mr James Copeland and his family. If you can, let me know what part of America Mr Ralph Copeland is living in. If spared I will write to you before March next as I want to get some things with Paul if he arrives safe to you.

No more at present but remains

Your affectionate Brother
Joseph Carrothers.

[To] Mr William Carrothers, / Lisbellaw / Co. Fermanagh / Enniskillen / Ireland.
[Postmarked] London Nov 27 1856 / Hamilton Nov 27 1856 / Enniskillen Dec 16 1856

~~~~~~

August 18th 1857

Dear Brother,

I hope you excuse me for not answering your letter of April last, the reason was I hoped to have got some word from Paul in June or July as I used to get but to the present no word from him. I fear something has befallen him. I have not wrote to him as he bid me not to write to him as he would be on his journey before my letter would reach him

Dear Brother I feel thankfull that you and your family is spared life and health and hope these few lines will find you in the same as the leave me and family thank God the giver of all Blessings.

Your Brothers and their families are all well at present and so is your cosins and families. Brother Thomas had a little girl died in March last of six years old of Consumption. I see by your last letter there is many of my old acquaintances remove to there long home while we are in mercy spared, it is cause of thankfullness. I have been engaged this summer puting Pews in our New Preaching House which we call Victoria Chappel, it is within 100 yds of my House and I have to say the name has been the principals in its erection, I hope many of them will benefit by it. We have got our harvest over, that is the Fall wheat harvest and the Spring will commence in three or four days. Every kind of crop is very abundant. The spring was a little late by reason of wet weather and the summer has been somewhat wet but the crop is great in all its variety. Markets is fallen low beside what the were last year, and stock is fallen. Land is fallen, the speculators in Land purchase many of them is much disappointed those that was bying on borrowed money for money rose from 15 to 30 pr cent which made some leave this province and go across the line as the journey is not far and rail road travel is speedy. Business has been somewhat dull this summer and wages not so high as the have been these last three year owing to the rail Road work been completed in this part and the town of London has out grown its Trade.

You will please to answer this letter and let me know if you are all well, and let me know of how Miss Rebecca Armstrong is as she will not write herself. Let me know how William McMullin and sisters is. Let me know how Sister Eliza and family is and sister Tirzah if she is living and well. Let me know of all the changes that has taken place in my old acquaintance.

As soon as I get word from Paul I will let you know it. I believe I have nothing more to write to you.

> I remain Dear Brother Yours
> Affectionately
>   Joseph Carrothers.

[To] Mr. William Carrothers / Lisbellaw / Enniskillen / Ireland [Postmarked] London, Canada Aug 19 1857 / Hamilton c.w. Aug 20 1857 / America Paid, Dublin Sep. 6 1857 / Enniskillen Sep 7 57

~~~~~~

<div align="right">February 15th 1858</div>

Dear Brother,

I send you a few lines hoping the will find you and family in good health as the leave me and family in at present thanks be to God for all his loving mercies to us. Your Brothers and families are all well in health and so are all your cosins and families. I must mention them by wholesail for the are a numerous progeny. In a few weeks the will come up to 90 in name and number. Dear Br. I have got no word from Paul this last year, the last letter he said he would leave Australia, I am hoping to be spared to see him. My son Wm. lives about 50 miles from this place, he was seeing us six weeks this day, is well and wife and child. I am sorry I have to let you know of the Death of John Doyle, he Died in October last, a man much regretted by all that Knew him, and that was a vast number, for he was Town Clerke and was allowed the best in the Province, it was worth very near 300 pounds pr. year, he had a great deal of writing to do, for the Town Council sat every Day. We had a very mild winter until last week we got snow and the slays is in full run now. Our markets is very cheap, best fall wheat 3S pr Bishele of 60 pounds, Oats from 8d to 10d pr. Bl. of 34 pounds, Beef from 16S to 20S pr Ht. of 100 pounds, Pork from 18S to 22S pr. Do. I give the price in your money as you will understand it better. Stock of all kinds is more than one third in price cheaper

than last year and so is land. Many has run to ruin by speculation in
Land where the had to Borrow money, hire as the call it here went as
far as 30 pr. cent and in some cases above it which caused some to
cross the line, which the can do in a few hours by Rail Road. We
have got to of Mr Gregston's sons (formerly Printer in Enniskillen) to
London. There Mothr lives in Brooksborrow, and a Mr Scott who
is married to a Daughter of James Scott tanner of Enniskillen. They
are in partnership, the are very well liked. One of the Mr Gregstons
is gone to England for goods. You can let the Lunnys of Cloon know
I am a live and Mr Jas. Copeland as the have an Interest in my
existence. Let me know if the build the Church in Mulrod and pull
Down the old one. Let me know if my sisters are living and well, and
their families. You will remember Margret and I to Wm McMullen
and his sister and let us know if the are well, and to Miss Rebecca
Armstrong. Let us know how she lives, or is her in Lisbellaw. Remem-
ber me to Thomas Lindsay, I am glad to hear of his well doing.
Remember us to Wm Betty and all our Tamlaght old neighbours.
You will ask Mr. Jonny Clegg if he gets any word from his Uncle
James if he mentions Paul in them. Let me know how the Mr Blacks
is doing and all my old friends. I heard the Johnstons was left
Tamlagh, let me know whether or not. Let me know who is in Mr
Halls place in Derrybrusk and if Mr Lloyd is living in Drumard,
Who is in my old House. Dear Brother, you will answer this letter as
soon as it comes to hand and let me know the several things I have
asked of you. You will excuse me for troubling you in such a way, I
am so glad to hear from my old country. Let me know how the
Bettys of Farnamulln is, how John is doing. I must give up asking any
more off you and conclude

> Dear Brother I remain
> affectionately
> Yours etc. etc. etc.
>   Joseph Carrothers.

[To] Mr Wm Carrothers / Lisbellaw / Co Fermanagh / Enniskillen /
Ireland
[Postmarked] (London) c.w. Feb. 17 1858 / Hamilton u.c. Fe. 18
1858 / 7 Paid MR 10 1858 A / Enniskillen M MR 11 58

January 4th 1860

Dear Brother,

I am spared through another year all in good health thank God for all his mercies to us and I hope these few lines will find you and family in good health as the leave me and mine at present, we are now in our winter snow this three weeks but the last week of Last month was a cold week the Thermometer from 5 to 10 below Zero. Saturday last very many got themselves frozen some feet some fingers some ears and some noses it is not very bad if you notice it in time and rub it with snow until you bring out the frost, if in the feet off with the Boots and hose and run through the snow, if not it becomes like a burn or scald the skin comes off and it dose be long healing. Since September 1858 we have had frost in every month since, summer and Winter. The June frost left without fruit, it kild Apples, Plumbs, Peaches, Cherries, Vines, and the others small fruit. The Puttatose was kild one Inch under the ground, but the 4 of July we had a frost such as wass not known before. It kiled all the fall wheat that was shot out of the blade. Some mowed it down at the time others let it stand to ripen the straw but no grain never grew after. Clover and other grass was not ingered, but after all we have aplinty. The spring wheat was very good. Peas, and oats and Puttatose were very good. I think I have as good Crops as ever I eat. There is more vegetable crop raised now than was some years past such as Turnips, Beets, Carrots, Parsnips, Cabbages and all Garden vegetables which grow to perfection. Our Country man George Laird Died on the 6th of October last he had 4 hundred pounds of money to Bequeath to his Children. He left his son Robert Laird 50 pounds Currancy. He was living with Mark Carrothers these last two years on his Board. I have got no letter from Paul these last three years, let me know if James Clegg sends any letters if he would mention him in any of them. Let me know if it is James and Acheson Black and I that is the Lives of Mr James Copelands Lease. Let the Lunnys of Cloon know I am living and well and let me know if the are living in it. Let the Glasmullagh family know that Margaret and I are well and let me know how

the are. Remember us to Miss Armstrong and let us know how she is
geting on if maried. Your Brothers and Cosins and their families
are all well, the are all heads of large families. Last night David had
his 5 son Born, that is 5 sons and 5 daughters. My son William has two,
son and daughter, he is well. We get no word from the Stuarts how
the are Doing, the do not be down here and I cannot say anything
of them.

This country has suffered very much this last year by Speculators
men that run into debt bying property and Borrowing money to
pay for it, until money rose from 8 pr cent to it went in some instanses
to 25 and some above 30 such was the ambition of some there was
Farms sold two years agoe and the would not sell for the half now.
Purchaseing Ground and building in London was carried to such
an extent that nothing could equal it, their Tenants is gone and the
houses not worth the Corporation tax, and worse left others in bail
for them and the property not worth the ground rent. There was a
man went off three weeks agoe and he has left his Bailsmen in large
sums of Debt which will put them down. He left them near 100
Thousand pounds to settle with the banks. Such men has been the
ruin of the country, but the country will be rid of them very soon and
things will come to a balance.

I hope Dear Willy you will answer this letter and let me know of all
my old neighbours. If there is any seed on the Marchmallows that is
good, and on the Queens-cups send me a few grains in the letter, rub
a little starch on the paper in the crase of it and the will stick to it,
five or six grains of each. Remember me to all my old friends.

> I remain Dear Brother Yours
> affectonally
> Joseph Carrothers.

[To] Mr William Carrothers / Lisbellaw / Co Fermanagh / Enniskillen /
Ireland
[Postmarked] London u.c. Ja 5 1860 / Hamilton c.w. Ja 6 1860 A /
Dublin 1 A Ja 23 1860 / Lisbellaw Ja 24 60

October 10th 1862

Dear Brother Will.

Excuse me for not answering your letter in the proper time, I write these few lines to let you know we are all living and well and I hope the will find you and all the family in the same thank God for all his mercies to us. We expected the troubles with our neighbours would terminated before this time, but it seems at a distance yet, it would give us better markets particularly for our stock which we have in abundance of every kind. The war with the South prevents the trade with them. Farm produce and grain has been in good demand til of late, grain is fallen, wheat from 65 cents to 72 per Bishel, peas 46 to 48 cents pr Bu. Butter from 10 to 12 cents pr. pound. Apples from 12 to 25 cents pr. Bushel, all other produce equally cheap. You wish to know what I think of America. It is a place of Hard labour both summer and winter. Summer is the worst but wages is good and so is the Board and a steady man will make money. Clear farms of 100 acres in this place dose sell from three to four Thousand Dollars. The wild Land is from one Dollar to Two Dollars pr Acre that is Government Land. Nathaniel thinks the Boys could do well by coming to this country, it is healthy. Some men speak favourably of the climate of Australia who has been in it from this country. As for Carpenters there is plenty of them such as the are, and the get good exploiment. There is some very excellent workmen, there is a great dale of work done in Factories such as planing stuff, making Doors and sashes but it is not to be compared to work by hand. If the Boys should go to Australia, if Paul is yet alive he worked at the mines, him and his partners the last account I had from him his Address is P. Carrothers Oven's Mines Diggins, he did stop with a Mr Kensington, he kept a station house. You will please to let me know as soon as this comes to hand what the are decided on doing. Please to give my best thanks to Mr J. Copeland and family. I see the have not for got me the tokens of ther kindness came safe to hand which is a treat I think a great deal of.

Please let me know if Wm McMullin is living. Let me know if Mr Hall is living in Derrybrusk, and if Mr Paul Dane is living in Killyhevlin.

Brothers Samuel, Nathaniel and Thomas and families are all well so is Cosins Mark, David and Micael and families and so is the Cosins from Bracy all living but George and the Carrothers are a strong party. Please give my love to all my old friends. My son Wm. is well has four children two Boys and two Girls. James is still with me, he is a Hard Worker.

Dear Brother I cannot think at present of any thing that would be worth writing to you, but what I have said, so I send my love to you and your partner in this life and your family

Yours affectionately
Joseph Carrothers.

[Postmarked] London, c.w. pm Oc. 11 62 / Hamilton u.c. Oc. 13 1862 / Lisbellaw m Oc. 25 62 / Enniskillen d Oc. 27 62

~~~~~~

<div align="right">December 15th 1865</div>

Dear Brother Wm.

I have received your letter of the 13th November with great pleasure to hear you and your family are all well as these few lines leaves me and family at present, thank God for his goodness. In answer to this letter let me know the Flowers that took the prises that your son Wm got at the show and the vegetable roots and where you have Built the greenhouse. I have a few seeds I will send (if spared) before spring. If you can procure the seed of the Spruce Fir and the Silver Fir the are very fine for shelter and Ornament. The sell very dear in the Nurserys, half a dollar each tree that is 2 shillings British.

Marks sister Beck died in May last, Nathaniels second son Joseph is in bad health this last year it is a nervous complaint. All your brothers and Families are well. Cosins are well and there families. The Bracky men and the old shoemaker is well. We have had a very dry summer and fall. Water has been very bad and very scarce, very many of the wells is dry from 40 to 60 feet deep and now we have a hard Frost and Dry and many has to draw water two and some 3 miles. My son and family is well has 6 children 4 Boys and 2 Girls. James is well is unmarried and of course lives with us, I cannot promise to send Liknesses to Bessy, I do not like such foolish things there only for Young people.

Give my best respects to Mr James Copeland, I thank him most kindly for the Newspapers he sent me. I hope it will be his convenience to send me now and again others of the Illustrated News. You said you wanted a letter from me before you would Buy Cloon, I suppose you wanted to know if I am living, I have to let you know I am living and writeing these lines to you. I have good health and I am able to work well, but how long God only knows. You will please to answer this letter and let me know if you make a bargin about Cloon. Remember me to all my old acquantances

I remain Dear Brother
Joseph Carrothers

~~~~~~

<div style="text-align:right">

Bosanquet March 8th 1870

</div>

Dear Brother Willy,

I send you a few lines to let you know I am living and well hoping you and the family are in the same good health Thanks be to God for his manyfold blessings. We have lost one of the old Farnaghts, Mark Died on the 16th of January and left a wife and 8 children to lament his loss, for the will feel his loss. The were in comfortable circumstances. I had word from Brothers last week there are all well and so is the old Breakeys, the are wearing out well, Anne is stil dodging about. My son William and family is well, James has got married last November to a Miss Fitchet a fine clever girl of Canadian family, we all live together as yet. I have been very busy all the summer chiefly at looms and sasher. I have made Gothick sashes for several churches since I came up here. Slays in Winter when the snow comes and we have a good long winter this year and is likely to continue this month. I am making Dimond Harrows for spring, no day goes better with me than the day I am at work at the bench and I work steady. The people wonder that I work as I do being the age I am in the seventy-seventh year of my age. What plants you sent me in spring last I had very bad sucksess in them the were all dried up only the carnation, you rolled them in dry fine paper, you should

Oiled the paper. James and I got 8 premiums last Octr at the Township Show, One pair of sasher (Gothick) one Dimond Harrow and the other six for Flower and Vegetables. I will send you a few seeds in this packet.

Dear Brother

You will oblidge me by sending me (perhaps the last time) if convenient the following plants, the Double Polyanthus, Double Primrose, Varigated Thyme, PepperMint, Double Carnation Pink, and if you can get it without troouble send me a plant of the Large Strawberry (Ma ....) I intend to send you a plant of the Bleeding Hart on, Deletrie Spictabella Botanical name, but I cannot get it until the frost is thawed out. In packing the roots fill a piece of tough paper with oil, Hogs grease will do, put a few sprigs of Damp moss and roll them up tight, and strong paper over all to Bear the Address which is Joseph Carrothers, Bosanquet, Widder Station P.O. Ont. British America.

Please remember me to Mr James Copeland of Lisbellaw, I hope he is living and well and all the family relations. Let my old acquaintance know that I am living and well yet I suppose a great many of them are no more.

You will be particular to answer this letter and let me know how you are getting on in your family and family affairs. I hope the troubles in other part of Ireland dose not interfere with the peace of your part to, papers give account of bad work going on in some parts of it.

No more at present from your

Affectionate Brother
Joseph Carrothers.

CHAPTER NINE

Jane White: Townswoman in Upper Canada

Jane White was a proper young lady, an only child, suitably schooled in County Down in the late 1830s in the niceties and haughtiness of bourgeois respectability. She was eighteen when she waited with her parents for the medical examination at the Grosse Isle emigrant quarantine station. The family had left Ireland at the beginning of May 1849, toward the end of the Famine, 'the time of the potato rot' Jane called it, and they travelled in relative comfort as cabin passengers on the *Eliza Morrison* from Belfast. In their luggage was Jane's piano, and they were accompanied by a servant. The journey had taken eight weeks through gales and rough seas, but passengers and crew arrived safely and in generally good health. Their boat passed inspection, and Jane, instead of being isolated in quarantine – the lot of thousands of less fortunate people – was allowed to go ashore on Grosse Isle for a picnic and a ramble in the woods. She also found there the time and peace to write her first letter home to a friend, Eleanor, in Newtownards, County Down.

The Whites made their way inland from Quebec and across Upper Canada to Goderich, on the shore of Lake Huron. That town had been established as a base of operations for the Canada Co. in the Huron Tract, a one-million-acre grant that the company was responsible for subdividing and selling to settlers. The town had been laid out and planned by officials in York (Toronto), where the company had offices and from which it organized the remittance services discussed in Chapter 4.[1] Goderich was planned around a central octagon from which main roads radiated along the eight principal bearings of a compass. The layout placed a court-house in the central octagon, where the judicial order it represented would be apparent to all. Commercial blocks were to develop along the outer side of the circular avenue surrounding the court-house and also along the spokes of the arrangement. The result was quite odd in Upper Canada, although a similarly contrived plan was intended for the neighbouring Canada Co. town of Bayfield. Practically all other Upper Canadian centres fitted the simpler, rectangular geometry of the land survey system and as a consequence were rectangular in form and subdivided into rectangular lots and blocks. Goderich, because of its open, octagonal centre, circular main street, and short radial avenues, had a unique aspect. However, Jane White seems to have been oblivious to it, although she later had numerous things to say about the town's commercial and social development in five letters she wrote to Eleanor between 1856 and 1860.

We have little information about the Whites apart from Jane's letters, her father's will, manuscript census records, and land-transfer documentation. Jane's correspondence indicates that her father obtained rents from properties he owned in Goderich. Land records of the town confirm that between 1851 and 1852 Mr White bought directly from the Canada Co. three quarter-acre properties, lots 967, 973, and 974 of Newgate Street.[2] The lots would have represented marginal locations in the town; despite the Canada Co.'s octagonal plan, the town did not evolve from its intended core. Rather, the river was the main focus of settlement, and the town spread away from the river bank. When the Whites reached Goderich, the vacant lots they purchased, while close to the planned centre, were at the outer edge of the settlement. Jane's father rented out living and commercial space in the buildings, and this was probably his main source of income.

On Mr White's lot 967, a two-storey commercial building in the Classic Revival style was built. A shop functioned on the ground floor, and living quarters were on the second. From Jane's letters it seems unlikely that the Whites ran the store. She never discusses the shopkeeper's trade. On the other two lots at least three small, one-storey brick cottages were built in the early or mid-1850s. These would have been occupied by labouring or artisanal tenant families. The Whites may have had a house to themselves on the east half of lot 973. The rental properties would have provided a modest income, but the White family's level of prosperity was very far below that of the town's main families.

Mr White was a minor speculator in urban real estate, a position quite like that of Nathaniel Carrothers, before the latter became a farmer, and quite like that of untold thousands of other such immigrants before and since. White survived the speculative property boom of the Crimean War period, his buildings were erected in time to gain for him the advantages of rapid inflation, but he did not sell. He held on cautiously, dependent on the rents, and was thus able to avoid the potential losses arising from the subsequent crash in property values in 1857. To invest in these properties so soon after arrival in Canada meant that he must have brought considerable funds with him from Ireland. That is suggested as well by the family's passage in cabin class and their bringing along Jane's piano. It is also apparent from the tone and unusually literate gentility of Jane's letters that her father was most likely a merchant or small manufacturer, the sort of person with the desire and the funds to finance an education for his daughter. That education probably helped to isolate her, and her sheltered life may have confirmed the many prejudices revealed through the letters.

Jane's letters offer a rare glimpse at the unabashed and simple prejudices that marked much of the Protestant Irish bourgeoisie in British North America. She lived, but did not work, except as the unmarried daughter of elderly parents, in a frontier town. The rough nature of the town's development and the mix of immigrant residents frequently grated on her sensibilities and roused her ire. She liked neither Americans nor Catholics, and her love for the English was not much greater. Except for the Irish Protestant group to which she belonged, the other ethnic groups in the town fared badly under Jane's naive inspection and felt her acerbic tongue. Her views on the English exposed the social tensions between the English and the Irish evident in numerous sources written on both sides of that division. She also suggested an Irish empathy for Scots. Catholics received the greatest criticism, as she considered them bigoted and uncharitable. Americans were seen to be little better, being typed by Jane in the widely held notion that they were a 'proud mean aristocracy of money.' Contact with Americans resulted from Goderich's being a lake port and transfer point both for settlers heading west through the Great Lakes and for grain moving east. The railway from Buffalo arrived in 1858 and made the link with the United States even more firm. It was not something Jane relished. Jane fails to mention the many French-speaking Canadians in the town at the time. Her opinion of them can be imagined. All in all she did not like most of the people, she did not like the town, and she would have preferred to have been in Ireland.

Her six surviving letters contain fine examples of social honesty and the personal anxiety of an unwilling immigrant. In the last one, of December 1860, Jane is an unmarried woman of twenty-nine, and her friend Eleanor in Ireland has married. Jane talks dispiritedly of marriage, her loneliness, and being without the comforts of her class. Her anxiety and discomfort in Goderich were never reduced: she died in 1867, unmarried and survived by her parents. Her mother died in 1875, her father in 1876. His properties were bequeathed to Jane's Belfast cousin[3] Catherine Beaumont, mentioned as orphaned in Jane's letter of 27 August 1858. Catherine emigrated to Goderich and would herself, like Jane, die there unmarried and propertied.

JANE WHITE TO HER FRIEND ELEANOR

[29 June 1849, from quarantine at Grosse Isle, Quebec]

I am glad to inform you that we are so far on, in our long tedious journey. We are anchored at Grose Isle about 36 miles below Quebec. It is an island in the St. Lawrence; the quarantine station is here and I assure you the passengers all feel very discontented at being kept here. We have been detained since our arrival on Saturday evening and it is now Wednesday. We have had fever and smallpox on board so that is the reason. The sick persons were taken on shore in a boat to the hospital. There are a great many sheds erected in the island that have been very useful for sick persons. There was a doctor here on Sunday from shore who examined the ship and was convinced there was not any sickness among the cabin or poop cabin passengers, which is a very great blessing for us. My Mama's health is pretty good. She was very very ill since we left home greatly owing to the extremely severe heaving of the ship. No one could have any idea of the inconvenience but those who have felt it. One is so tossed about and sometimes cannot keep on their feet. There are two families from Co Antrim in the poop, besides ourselves. One room is boarded in so we are comfortable in that respect. There are two nice girls here who have kept me in company since I came here.

We have had many fearful days on our long voyage. It is eight weeks on Saturday last since we embarked in Belfast Lough. I could not describe to you all our perils, such fearful gales as we had, a constant succession of them I may say without erring much. One morning we had a narrow escape from being shipwrecked. There was a heavy gale set in from the northwest that carried away our bulwarks, cabin skylight etc. washing two of the sailors down the main hatchway and laying our ship for a short time under water nor was she ever expecting to rise. She did rise thank God and very shortly after we picked up the [?] crew of a schooner that the same gale had broken to pieces. She had her broadside actually driven in by the sea. Such gales are dreadful.

Our captain had been above 20 years at sea and confessed we had seen as much desperate weather as he had seen in his time, but I should not tire you with too long a description.

A great number of ships have been lost in the ice here early in the spring. One was wrecked in the gulf of St. Lawrence here during the gales. It contained four hundred passengers who all perished except one child who was picked up by a vessel passing the spot.

I can only say Eliza Morrison has been slow but sure. The weather is very warm. The scenery on the banks of the river is delightful especially at this season of the year, hill and valley and beautiful towns and villages slooping to the river's edge together with fertile islands, form the most beautiful landscape I ever saw. The houses are of wood and very white. The inhabitants are mostly of French descent and speak the French language. The Roman Catholic religion is established here.

I saw a very pretty steam boat on Sunday afternoon last which was St John's Day. It came passed here on a pleasure excursion from Quebec, full of people gaily dressed. They stopped here and came past our ship. They were accompanied by a [?] band and played The Trubadour, Garry Owen and other tunes. It was a very handsome sight. The day was very warm and the sun [?] bright but it showed a very bad respect for the Lord's Day. They are only to be excused on account of being Papists.

You would be surprised to see the number of brigs crowded here all full of emigrants from Britain trying their fortunes in America. We are all in good health thank God. I was scarcely sea sick at all but my mama was and Abigail was very sick the first week but is quite well now and has had the offer of two or three places already ... Hope your dear mama is recovered. Tell her I will ever remember her kindness. Please give my kind love to her and to Miss Orr and if you see Miss Harriet Dobson please to tell her I am safe arrived here and please say I will write to her very shortly and give her my very kind love.

I hope I will soon be able to send you my direction and if there are any questions you wish to ask me about the voyage, do so. I am writing but in a confused manner but I hope you will excuse me as I merely snatched the opportunity to let you know I am safely landed at last.

The land is near. I was over in the island today and had a nice walk through the trees with my mama and dad and two young ladies. Their servant man came along with a basket so we had a sort of a picnic.

Remember me to Miss Jane Gelston. Tell her I cannot give her much information about Canada yet but the time may come ... My dear friend yours ever sincerely and affectionately [Signed] Jane White.

~~~~~~

[1 April 1856, Goderich]

I received your kind letter of January 16th. I was glad to find you were all in the land of the living. We have had a tremendous winter of it but I hope it is nearly gone. We had no January thaw this year but a close constant winter all the time. We may reasonably hope for an early spring after such weather. I suppose we will have a hot summer after so much cold. So many persons have been frozen to death this winter. If they fell down in the snow they never rose again. I fancy there is a great likeness between the winters of Canada and Russia. We had great talk of war with the United States but it is no doubt nonsense. I hope it is a false report. A large military force will likely be kept in Canada for some time. I think surely the Americans would not be so mad as to make any fuss at present.

How do you enjoy your health I feel quite sickly at present but I suppose I will get strong again when the weather gets good, so as I can go out and have a walk. I wish I had you to walk with me. I would like one of those long walks with you up the Belfast road. Sometimes when alone and I begin to think I often wish for my old home and then change again in my notion and try to fancy myself happier here. We are never contented in this world it would seem. I do not have much society with the exception of some young ladies of course that is quite enough. My former acquaintance Miss Parke returned from New York last summer. That pleased me very much. She is the one who supplied your place to me since I came here so I like you better. Now do not suppose I am rubbing you with soft soap for indeed I'm sincere my dear Eleanor.

I received a newspaper from you this morning containing an

account of the reception of three young persons at a concert in Belfast. Such a scene is something new in that Protestant town, but still one does not like to condemn it so I would rather keep my liberty either as a married or unmarried person. The scene must have been very grand and imposing. The Roman Catholics seem an enthusiastic people. I never liked any I ever knew. I was slightly acquainted with a lady here of that persuasion. My mother advised me to drop the acquaintance. I did so and do not regret it, they are so bigotted and uncharitable.

If you could conveniently enclose me a little Mignionette [?] seed and a little wallflower seed you will do me a great favour. It would be time enough to sow it about the middle of May or even later in this place.

Mr Fred White is in Goderich still. He comes to see us sometimes. I told him I was going to write to you. He sends his respects and begs of you to let his sisters know he received a letter from them and intends to answer it soon. Do you often see Mrs Hill. I suppose she is as pleasant as ever. Please remember us to her. I think you never saw such a fuss as is made here about learning to play on the piano. Everyone who can manage it is getting pianos and such good instruments too. I fancy few of them will be any use to them as the difficulty is to find teachers. The only one competent to teach is a Mrs Charlesworth (I mentioned her name to you before) but she charges £4 per quarter. This some people think too much. I never would give any instructions of the kind to any one. I could do it just as well as her. I soon snapped anyone who asked me for lessons. Any person knows I have no occasion but I suppose they would give me the trouble for nothing but I give Miss Parke a lesson sometimes merely for friendship's sake.

Remember me to Mrs Harrison. Tell her I don't know when I'm going to get married. I am always expecting to hear of your's. You never tell me anything about it. I suppose you intend to do it quietly but do not be in a hurry. You and I have both plenty of time to wait and should not let ourselves be blind to our own interests but I do not say this to prevent you from marrying any time. How is Mrs Andrew Moore. Remember me to her.

The railway is further away from us than we thought. It has passed into the hands of an English company so we will not have it for two years it seems but it is bound to come now the Canadian company who had it before did not give satisfaction *as usual*.

I hope your mama is quite well. Give my kindest love to her not forgetting my respects to dada. How is Anne Dickson Does she go to your house now at all I suppose she is the same looking girl as ever. I never hear how Abigail does, but she lives in a wild far away place but the places in this part of the country are improving very much. She lives about 30 miles away I think. I will hope soon to hear from you. I am sorry I cannot send you a more interesting letter but trust you will take the will for the deed. With kindest love I remain my dear Eleanor ever sincere friend Jane.

PS. My mama sends her love.

~~~~~~

[22 September 1856, Goderich]

I received your kind letter. I would have answered it sooner but I thought I would wait a little as I knew your loss was fresh in your memory. At such a time a long worldly letter would only be an intrusion. Only time, dear Eleanor, heals our griefs. The greatest comforts of this passing world often are only the forerunners of troubles still greater but there is nothing but trouble promised to us.

I have not the same light heart I used to have. I do not know how it is. I just feel like an old woman. There is only happiness in childhood. My mother was very poorly during the hot weather. I was quite alarmed. She is quite recovered. It is amazing how well she looks but I am afraid winter will make her suffer from rheumatism.

The railway is progressing rapidly. There will soon be one line of railway through the whole of Canada. British America is said to be more improved in the last seven years that it ever was before especially Upper Canada. I expect seven more years will make Goderich a fine city. Some of the inhabitants will be very rich. My father is just as keen for the world as ever. We are all fond of gathering but do not know who will enjoy it in this changing world.

I was reading a part of the remarks of a French gentleman M. de Beloize [?]: who has been visiting Canada a short time since and made a tour in the two Provinces. He likes Lower Canada very much, likely because it copies the manners and professes the religion of the land of their forefathers France. He says in steady habits and quiet unassuming manners they are antipodes to the United States but he thinks differently of Upper Canada. He says there is exactly a restless

changing spirit as in the States. Indeed I must say Goderich is as much
changed lately as could well be imagined. It is becoming an abominably Yankiefied place being so near the States and such a remote
place in Canada all the correspondence of any importance is with the
States. The more we approach the manners of the old country either
British or Continental it is the more conciliating mild and gentle,
whereas the other is the reverse. I used to hear the Yankees were
nice people but I don't think so now. This proud mean aristocracy of
money is very revolting especially when they do not care how or in
what low way it is obtained so as the steam is kept up. Down about
Hamilton, Toronto and further down the manners of the people are
quieter and more polished. It is amusing to walk up near the lake and
see the Indian huts and wigwams down on the flats below. I suppose
they will soon be moving them all away on the approach of winter.
The air is getting occasionally frosty already. I do not like the
thoughts of winter.

Rents of houses in business places here are rising greatly, one
hundred pounds a year is considered not too much. I don't see how
money is to be made to meet all this. My father says if it was not that
he is totally independent of business he would not stand such work. He
would just walk off to Ireland again but he reaps the benefit of all this
being the owner of property. I often wonder to see persons coming
out to Canada so many times. I know one young man who has come
out from England this summer for the third time. All he has to do
is a little in the lawyer's offices or some other trifling matters. There
seems a fascination in it but I somehow think everyone is compelled
to follow their destiny.

I saw Elizabeth McMordie once this summer. I suppose you remember seeing her in N[ew] T[own]ards. She is a great stout immense
woman. I would not have known her. She did not know me but I
don't wonder at it as we never were much acquainted. She stays with
her parents in the country. She seems to have given up dress making
altogether. Do you ever touch the piano now There was a tuner up
from London this summer who pronounced my old piano the most
substantial one he had seen. It seems the pianos they make in this
country are flimsy in comparison. You know how old mine is. Do you
see Mrs Hill. Please remember us affectionately to her and to Mr &
Mrs Waugh. Tell Mrs Waugh I am acquainted with a lady here I am
very fond of; she resembles her so much in manner. I hope she is
better. You mentioned she was sick.

I am sorry this letter is so uninteresting but I do hope dear Eleanor you will take the will for the deed, and believe me there is no one who thinks more about you or feels more anxious for your welfare than I do. My letters to you never can be so interesting to you as yours to me because this being a strange place to you the news of it or the people in it could not interest you much to hear of. My mother sends her kindest regards to you and your father and cousins in which I join her and believe me to remain ever your sincere friend.

Jane

PS. I will anxiously expect a letter from you. Do you ever see Anne Dickson now I hope she is quite well. Will you ask her if she knows anything of our old g[?] nanny Paisley. I often thought of asking through curiosity and still forgot until just now.

[27 August 1858, Goderich]

I think that it was more than time a month ago to reply to your kindest of letters. I was very glad to hear you were living and well. I received another letter at the same time that surprised me announcing the death of my aunt. Poor Catherine is in great trouble. She was so fond of her mother. I really thought my aunt was getting better. I thought perhaps I might see her sometime but perhaps we'll meet in a better home where I hope we will all meet. I was sorry to hear of Mrs Waugh's death. I am sure Mr W[augh] will feel it severely; she was a very nice person.

I did not like to write to you on indifferent subjects until your grief was mellowed down a little. I was thinking lately of what your mama said to me one day she was sitting beside me when she used to take me over to Bangor. She said for me always to rest upon the merits of our Saviour and give my thoughts wholly to him for everything earthly would pass from me. How truly we find it so.

I was surprised to hear of the death of Dr Whitlaw. Perhaps you would tell me something about them when you write. I never hear anything about N[ew] T[own] Ards except what you write unless when Mr Milliken favours us with a letter. I hope he and Mrs M[illiken] and family are quite well.

The railway is completed about two months ago or more. There were great excursions to Goderich of both Yankees and Canadians. On the celebration on the 8 July at the opening of the line the town was so thronged many had to leave same day because they could not be accommodated with lodgings, so many thousands persons. There were two brass bands up from Stratford and Brantford. The firemen's torchlight procession was pretty. The fireworks were very inferior to expectations. The Governor General Sir Edmund Head was up. There was dinner and ball. The town was decorated with flags, such a number I have not seen before. There were triumphal arches decorated with green mottoes such as 'success to the railway', 'Welcome American friends', 'Reciprocity etc.'. The plank sidewalks were finished for the occasion. There was a flag to be hoisted on the courthouse, a dangerous place from its great height. A man went up and did it for the sum of 3 15s. od. so that money was no object that day. The Signeaw [?] came by the Lake.

Goderich is bound to be a stirring place being a terminus but I hear that the towns down along the line are nearly ruined, the trains passing through spoils business, but strangers coming here would find this the poorest, coldest most profitless place they could come to unless some person particularly fortunate. A family arrived the other day from Westmoreland Street, Dublin. They talk of school teaching I hear. A number of music teachers keep coming up, all females. The Miss Caldwell I mentioned to you and her sister left for Philadelphia more than a week ago. She is married by this time to some person from Coleraine. I hear they intend settling in Goderich. I don't know whether she has married well but I hope so; she is a nice person.

I suppose you heard the telegraph (the submarine) is completed. It is surely a wonderful invention, scarcely credible.

This has been the queerest summer I ever seen, no rain scarcely no thunder, the ground parched and crops scanty. I fear there will be a hard winter upon poor people. The mechanics and labourers are badly off here at present.

There is to be another election next month. This is the country for elections. This is for the Upper House. They have made it elective now. It is for eight years with a large income for that time. There are four candidates in the field but it is expected the run will be between ex-Commissioner Jones and Donald McDonald of Toronto. I suppose Donald will walk in by a sweeping majority because the voting is in Huron and Perth much the same as the old election some years ago between Cayley [?] and Malcolm Cameron. Perth put in Cameron, being a Liberal. The same persons will likely put in McDonald for the same reason. Mr Jones is a High Tory I believe but I do not think it is any matter which goes in. No one here about seems to care about it. They are tired of fussing about elections. They are so expensive.

Dr Hamilton of this town died lately suddenly in Toronto from the effects of a sunstroke. It is melancholy how many have died from the same cause this summer. It has been the hottest in the memory of the oldest inhabitants.

How is Mrs Hill Please remember us to her and all enquiring friends but we have been so long away now I suppose we will soon be forgotten but I'm not the least afraid of you forgetting me. I received two papers from you yesterday but is Miss Bingham dead I am anxious to know. My father and mother join me in kindest love to you. I hope you will soon write and pardon me for being so long from writing. My mind was depressed mostly from thinking of my aunt's death and my cousins being left orphans but I feel easier now with kindest regards I remain your sincere friend

Jane

~~~~~~

[19 July 1859, Goderich]

I am late in replying to your kind letter. The weather is and has been so dreadfully hot one could scarcely walk. I do not know how people manage who have to work hard. It must be hard suffering. I never felt so knocked up with the heat any summer. Perhaps it is weakness of body. My mother complains dreadfully. I wish some cool weather would come and that would make us feel well again. The cool eve- nings are a great relief. We have beautiful moonlight nights. I think it can scarcely be better in Spain than here though the Spaniards go to bed in the heat of the day, I think the Canadians might do the same.

The 12th of the month was dreadfully hot. The Orangemen went down to Clinton and came home in the evening looking dreadful scare-crows with heat and dust. I hear in some towns below they celebrated the day with great spirit, but they have lost their prompter in this place since the death of Dr Hamilton so I suppose they will dwindle away. The rector is showing them such a cold shoulder. It used to be the reverse. He is so much in debt now and acts so queerly,

the people do not think so much of him as they did. He has a very
large and extravagant family who are for ever showing off their aristo-
cratic origin, and looking down on the congregation. This is quite
hurtful to the cause of Christ. One does not like to be too tight upon
their clergyman. He is a kind pleasant man withal. If they were an
English family I would have no mercy for them but seeing they are
Irish I would put up with their every fault because there will always
be a kind feeling remaining but I declare the English here would have
no objection to bore [?] the ears of the Irish through like the Bond
servants of old but they are not able for the Irish; they are too numerous for them. The Scotch too lean to Ireland most.

I suppose you were alarmed some days ago to hear about a French
invasion of Ireland. The same stories were flying about here and
that the lower Canadians were going to join the French in an invasion
of Canada but both Ireland and Canada are safe. Louis Napoleon has
his hands full and by the time his hands are clear of the Austrians his
funds will be too low for any more capers.

We have got six clergymen out from Dublin lately, some of them
very talented men. One who is placed at Clinton comes up to preach
sometimes, the Revd James Carmichael. He is very young and very
enthusiastic. He seems completely devoted, a little too theatrical but
a most attentive preacher. He carries the mind away until you would
think you actually saw what he describes. His Good Friday's sermon
on the crucifixion was startlingly vivid. He drew crowds from other
churches but they are more taken with a Mr Sullivan who has been
once or twice here indeed I think they are fidgetty. I have not heard
Sullivan yet. The name has a Popish sound with it.

I join with you in not thinking much of Roman Catholics. I have
known some of them here and think them deceitful. I would be
neighbourly with them but would not take them for companions,
their bigotry is too much.

Those revival meetings at home will surely do good. An impression
on the mind is often retained and recurs to the memory even after
being forgotten for a time.

The person I enquired about Mr Walker came to see us one day.
He came up to Goderich on some errand and enquired for us. He
has a farm about 30 miles away. I did not know him at first. I wonder
if you and I would know each other if we met on the street. You
would find me darker in the complexion I think.

The United States day is kept by some persons here. Some left for

Buffalo for the 4th July and it was celebrated here by [a] kind of a street masquerade.

How is Mrs Hill. Please remember us to her. Do you know where her sister Mrs McConnell is Would you ask her what part of Canada she is in. If still in Montreal. I suppose your garden looks well now. Ours is rather fading at present. The frost that comes about the 8 June did great injury. It killed our grapes and melon and cucumbers and a number of our annuals. The potatoes through the country were as totally withered as the time of the potato rot at home but they are all sprung up again. The bulbs threw up new shoots just the same with the dahlias in our garden. Would you take the trouble of sending me a few withered flowers of fuschias. Perhaps I could get some seed out of them. I cannot get any here. It is a hardy plant. I think it would grow here. I thought of begging a slip from you but I fear it would die before it would get this length.

The crops last year were a failure owing to the dryness of the summer. The people in Huron and Bruce are starving in hundreds. Bruce is worst being a new settlement. Some of the Highland Scotch up a Kinloss who depended on the cultivation of the new farms are subsisting on roots gathered in the bush. They could hardly be worse at home than this. A good deal of money has been raised I hear for them, some of them furnished with work. I hear the town council here have done a good deal.

The grain never looked better than it does this year. There is a prospect of an abundance of everything which should make every-one thankful. The other was a severe visitation. Every public business that could employ workmen is knocked up or broken down. Goder-ich is in a poor state at present. The people hide their wants the best way they can. My father gets his houses let amazingly while nearly everyone's houses are idle, owing to so many persons leaving the place but when times mend they will just throng in again so many of them owing property here induces them to come back. It is said down in London times are if possible worse than here but there is no loss without some gain. It has ruined the cheats and rascals; honest good people do not feel the times so severely.

I was surprised to hear of Mr Bell's death. He must have suffered severely poor man. He was a strong looking man quite like long life when I saw him last. I thought I furnished you with a nice story in the Signal [?] in 'one eyed Saul' [] but it turned out a very poor affair; such hunting about Ishmael [?] the wolf.

Please remember me to your cousin. My mother is anxious to know if the Revd H Moore is still in Newtownards. We heard there is another clergyman in his place is this so We were pleased to see the address to Mr Price in the paper you sent. We received another paper the same from Mr Milliken. My father and mother send their kindest regards to you. Please to accept the same from your much attached friend and hoping soon to hear from you. I remain yours most sincerely.

[28 December 1860, Goderich]

I suppose you will think I am dead by this time. I often thought of writing and fully intended it but when I received your kind letter I could not expect to hear from you sooner as you had not time to settle down before that. I sincerely hope the step you have taken will be always a happy one. I fully agree with you in saying matrimony is fate, so is a single life too. Everyone has their vocations marked out so if we do our duty well and choose the one thing needful it is all that is required. My friend Eleanor has done well and if anyone chooses to do better why let them try.

Christmas is far away now. We have had some very severe weather lately but it seems more like a moderate winter now. My mother complains of the cold but she is amazingly healthy. I often think what a kindness the Almighty confers on me by sparing my mother to me particularly in this strange country where I do not feel disposed for society as I would be at home. The people are not so good or simple in their habits as in Ireland, not the same humility.

I suppose you often heard me mention a Miss Parke to you. She has left her home and stops a week here or there as she finds convenient. She complains of ill usage from her father.

If she means stinginess of habit her father is unbearable in that way. My father confesses he never saw a more queer character and he puffs so much about his possessions! She is the only child he has though there may be faults on both sides; still it is a pity of the poor thing. If she had a mother living or even a step mother she would ...

CHAPTER TEN

Alexander Robb: Adventures in British Columbia

Alexander Robb, the fifth of a family of eleven children, was born at Ballybeen near Dundonald, County Down, in 1839.[1] There his family were well-to-do farmers, but like many of their type they experienced the emigration of the younger sons. Three Robb brothers went abroad. James, the second eldest, was killed in the American Civil War;[2] John, the third son, spent some time in the Australian gold fields before returning home to purchase a farm at Ballywalter, County Down;[3] and Alexander (see Figure 10.1), the fourth son and author of the twelve letters presented here, spent from 1862 to 1873 gold mining and ranching in British Columbia before he too returned home to settle.

The tradition of emigration among the Robbs had been established in the previous generation, apparently as the consequence of the legacy set down by Alexander's grandfather. Grandfather Robb provided for his second son with an inheritance that required him to emigrate. In his will, probated in 1852, he insisted: 'I leave to my son William the sum of fifty pounds sterling only on condition that he emigrates to the United States of America or to some of the British Colonies within six months from the date of my death and to be applied to that purpose and to no other by my executors.'[4] Whatever the reasons for the insistence that William emigrate, a pattern was started that other family members would follow. Alexander had gone on a whim with thirteen other young County Down men lured by the gold rush in British Columbia. His travels to British Columbia and his brother John's trip to Austra-

FIGURE 10.1
Alexander Robb, by Buchtel and Stolte, photographers, Portland, Oregon, on his way home to Ireland, c. 1874; courtesy Mrs Helen White, Westport, Ontario

lia were motivated by the lure and excitement of gold exploration. Theirs were intended temporary migrations of restless, adventurous youth, not conscious forsaking of home and family.

Alexander expressed well his keen attachment to the place of his birth in a letter to his father: 'Situated as I am in a wild country, with nothing but mere acquaintances around me, is it not natural that my thoughts should continually revert to those places where I was once so happy and that my heart should cling to the people whom I love and who I believe love me perhaps much better than I deserve.' That bond to family and place similarly distinguishes his various letters to his father, to his older sister, Eleanor, and to his younger sister, Susanna, all at home in Dundonald, County Down.

British Columbia, wherein Alexander Robb found himself in 1862, was one of the most isolated parts of the British Empire. Direct land communication between it and the rest of British North America did not exist. Contact was possible only by a long and hazardous two-ocean voyage, either around the tip of South America or along the route Alexander took via the Panama isthmus. White settlements on the Pacific rim were small isolated forts created by the Hudson's Bay Co. to oversee the fur trade of the region. They involved an inconsequentially small immigrant population, but they did serve to establish British sovereignty in the region. They were white outposts in a place whose native population numbered probably 100,000.

The first major influx of white adventurers commenced with the gold rush to Yale in the Fraser Valley in 1858 (see map on page 160). Twenty-five thousand miners arrived within a few months from the United States. The event represented a geographical extension of the great Californian gold rushes of a decade earlier, but its potential was much more limited. Three hundred miles north, in the early 1860s, a second gold rush to the Cariboo district drew seven thousand to that region.[5] Alexander Robb and his thirteen County Down friends who had arrived via Panama in 1862 were in the vanguard. The region was accessible only by river steamer as far as Yale, 100 miles upstream on the Fraser, and thereafter only a 300-mile-long trail led into the Cariboo mining sites. Alexander's journey along it in 1862 had to be done on foot, some of it with a ninety-pound pack on his back. He recorded that one part of the trail 'was awful up one mountain and down another for sixty or seventy miles,' while another section of 'only about fifty miles' made up what it lacked in length by its 'quality up one mountain and down another precipice sometimes up to your knee in water at other times wading through snow two to six or eight feet deep.' He spent six futile weeks in the Cariboo diggings before turning around and trudging back 200 miles to take a job as a labourer preparing a section of the Cariboo road north of Lytton for £8 per month. His thirteen friends had left with thousands of other gold-seeking strangers, but Alexander was left stranded in the ebb of the exodus. His disappointing encounter with gold mining was typical of the transient frontier society.

Subsequently, Alexander laboured in the vicinity of New Westminster, occasionally tried his hand at gold mining, and eventually tried ranching in 1868. First he undertook for an Irish friend, John Clapperton, some settlement duties on Clapperton's free grant lands, and shortly afterward Alexander joined a partner in claiming his own 160 acres of potential ranch land near Nicola Lake. There, he was one of a small minority of white men. As he noted himself about his arrival at Nicola Lake with Edwin Dalley, a young English immigrant: we 'were the two first white men who came to this district.' Although he had learned some of the native language, Alexander would remain insecure in this milieu. By 1872, however, his adopted region in the remote area had begun to fill up with settlers, and he noted the changes: 'Three and one half years ago there was not one white settler within forty miles. Now there are twenty-five within less than half that distance and we expect a further influx next summer. A good many too of the settlers have got wives and young families which gives the place something of a home look.' It had taken a decade for Alexander to regain the social familiarity of 'a home look.'

The social geography of the British colony on the rim of the Pacific Ocean was for Alexander alienating. It was a region of single and youthful people, mainly men, drawn there from America and from Europe, half-way across the world, in search of gold. Robb and his friends arrived in the colony when it was still a territory unsurveyed and largely unknown to whites. Tracks led through the major valley and mountain passes, but traffic along them was mainly on foot, and only slowly were these corridors elevated to the status of roads for stage-coaches and wagons. As acknowledged by Cole Harris, 'Means of transportation easily imposed on gentler, more proximate lands penetrated this wilderness at enormous cost.'[6] One of the earliest and most famous efforts to penetrate that wilderness was the Cariboo Road, which allowed wagons to pass from Yale, on the Fraser River, to Barkerville, in the Cariboo Mountains gold country. It opened in 1865. Robb had arrived three years before the opening and knew full well the significance of the road in promoting access to the wild place. He had travelled the Cariboo route when it was but a trail unfit for mules, and he had been forced to labour to exhaustion making that same trail fit for wagons.

Robb's years in British Columbia as miner, labourer, and rancher spanned the genesis of permanent white occupancy in the interior; it would be difficult to find a more likely candidate for the name of BC pioneer. The ranch he started was located in the semi-desert area of the interior plateau, on open range land where bunch grass grew wild in tufts scattered across open, exposed soils. In an average year only ten inches of rain might fall, making irrigation necessary for any improvement of pasture or cultivation. Such irrigation projects as those young Robb enthusiastically described to his father in 1868 required investment capital. The wanderer had none and began to accumulate debts, mostly owed to his partner. His dreams for the future agricultural greatness of the area were shared by many other immigrants from Britain who strove to turn the parched land into a veritable 'garden of Eden.' Like Robb's, many of their enterprises were destined to fail. Although his cattle thrived in the first years and his butter found acceptance, Robb, like most of his neighbours, suffered from the lack of available markets and the declining yields of the natural pasture. Beef on the hoof had to be driven down to the United States, or butter might be traded locally to incoming gold seekers, settlers, and road gangs.

Markets were scarce, and expectations for a developing market, raised by British Columbia's entry into Confederation in 1871 and the concomitant promise of a railway, were unrealized. The Canadian Pacific Railway was not completed in time for Robb to benefit, and neither settlement nor markets grew to the extent he needed to make his labours worthwhile. In 1873 he wrote to his father: 'Times are very dull here this summer and farm produce when it comes to market is likely to be very cheap even if it can be sold at all which I greatly doubt. We were expecting the Canadian Pacific Railroad would be started this summer which would have made things quite lively but the way things look now it is not likely to be started for a year yet if then, and everything has fallen in consequence.'

Economic swings from boom to bust and the alternating moods of euphoria and depression would characterize British Columbia's history. Dependent on natural resources of fish, timber, and metals, remote from the world's markets, and without the possibility of a solid and extensive agricultural base, British Columbia was at the mercy of international market trends. Robb's fate was similarly determined, and Confederation, heralded as the solution to the economic woes, did not greatly ameliorate the early manifestations of those conditions in which he found himself mired.

The extremes of climate and the hard work of ranching had all affected Robb's manner, and even more debilitating had been the isolation of frontier living and lack of close friends and family: 'There is not within some thousands of miles of where I sit tonight one solitary individual who would care two straws if I were dead and buried tomorrow,' he complained to his sister, Eleanor. In an earlier letter he had implored his family to send him out a young lady who might make a suitable wife: 'I need hardly say how much I have been grieved and disappointed that neither you nor father could see the propriety of sending out some young lady for a wife for your hopeful brother. Surely among so many female friends as you have got you might find *one* who for your sake, if not for mine, would be willing to travel eight or ten thousand miles to find a husband in the person of your brother. As I told you before I am not particular to a shade one way or the other.' Single, marriageable woman were rare in the colony.

Slowly, inevitably, Robb succumbed, as youthful optimism gave way to lonely bachelorhood and mounting private desperation. That personal descent can be interpreted easily in a chronological reading of the letters to his sister. Their expressiveness and plaintive loneliness are a striking comment on the effects of separation from family and on the sentimentality and romantic idealism in Robb's character.

For eleven years (1862–73) he had lived as gold miner, labourer, and cattle rancher but failed to make a fortune in the New World. Indeed, much of his activity there seems to have centered on clearing the debts he incurred, and only through the sale of his ranch in 1874 did he realize the respectable sum of $4,000, the net proceeds of eleven years in search of an eldorado. The ranch was sold because Alexander was required to return to Ireland. His two brothers on the family farm had died, and his father requested he come home to take charge.

Lacking personal ties and disillusioned with the opportunities of the New World, Robb returned to his native land, where his family provided him with a new beginning and the success that had eluded him as an emigrant. In Ireland he married a local woman, fathered seven children, and attained a position of social, political, and financial security (see Figure 10.2). He served several terms on the Castlereagh District Council, and at the time of his death he held the post of justice of the peace.[7] For almost forty years he was a member of the Royal Ulster Agricultural Society, the meeting place of privilege and position. He campaigned for land reform, and in 1907 he was invited to join the staff of the Department of Agriculture in Dublin. Aided by family connections and sus-

FIGURE 10.2
Alexander Robb with his wife and their seven children at the family home,
Balbybeen House, County Down, c. 1897; courtesy Kathleen Robb,
Dundonald, County Down

tained by his accumulated experiences, the youthful wanderer was a
paragon of social respectability back home in Ulster.

His life abroad had been unusually disoriented. Born into a society
of stable family relationships and intense social interconnectedness,
Robb in British Columbia was adrift. Although suffering the normal
complement of pioneer misfortune, his own sufferings were magnified
by lack of friends and separation from family.

Alexander Robb had arrived in British Columbia in the enthusiasm
of a boom and departed in the midst of a depression. His accounts
of these early years of the colony's history and unfolding settlement
geography document a particularly volatile period in the genesis of the
region. His experiences were typical of many. Society was highly mobile
and driven by a combination of personal recklessness, ambition, physical
courage, and youthfulness. Many gave up the struggle after a few years

and either returned home or sought more remunerative and stable regions elsewhere in North America. Many others remained adrift in search of their eldorado.

LETTERS OF ALEXANDER ROBB TO HIS FAMILY

[1862, probably April, near Panama; to a sister]

... Tell Uncle Crickard that I bought as good a pineapple as ever he grew (and that is saying a good deal) for ten cents. Cocoa nuts at 5 cents each and other fruits in proportion. We changed vessels there and the next morning sailed for Aspinwal. We had a beautiful run [   ] of four days down to the latter place and on Sunday March 20th arrived there. There is no third class on the steamboats that run from St Thomas to Aspinwal so we got second cabin berths and were in every way a[s] comfortable as we could have wished to be. We stopped on board the steamboat all Sunday afternoon and night and on the next day took the railway cars for Panama. I wish I could give you the faintest idea of what we saw on that ride of 48 miles. The whole way it is as beautiful as an Eden but it is an Eden turned into ...

... Were just about entering that port. Well we got in the next morning about five o'clock. I will try and give you an idea of what the place is like. Imagine yourself then entering Belfast from the Queen's Island and fancy yourself surrounded by high hills rising very nearly perpendicularly from the sea with the town stretched out right before you on the only level bit of land in the Island and this will give you an idea of what it is like. We stopped there for about 24 hours. Most of the passengers went on shore myself among the rest. But such a place and such a heat. Why you would literally [have] thought you were breathing fire. Up on the mountains it is not so bad but in town where the heat of the sun is reflected back from the hills that tower almost above the city (?) it would almost roast one ...

... and write me a long letter about everything and you can direct it to the care of Mr Kyle who has promised to forward it to me by his me[n], a letter two or three months sooner than I [   ] and I am very anxious to hear from home. Perhaps [you] would enclose a little bit telling me how [   ] is getting on. The post starts for New York [   ] time so I must now quit. Give my love to [   ] Aunt Ellen, Uncle Crickard, Frank, son (?) and B[   ] ... know who I mean and all the rest of my fr[iends] believe me dear [   ] you aff[ectionate brother] [Signed] Alexander Robb

P.S. The whole of us are in health and as the accounts from ... are very good of course we are [in] good spirits.

~~~~~~

[10 August 1862, Nicola Lake, BC; to his father]

I suppose you will be thinking by this time that I am either dead or have forgotten all about home else I would have written long ago. I can assure you however that this is not the case for I am as well as ever I was and as for the forgetting part it will be a very long time indeed before that time comes.

You will most likely have heard from some of the other boys what kind of a trip we had up to Cariboo. For fear you should not I will give you a slight sketch of it. We left Victoria in Vancouver's Island about the 1st May and after about six hours sailing landed in New Westminister a small town about twenty or thirty miles up the Frazer River. When there we learned that it was quite too soon to go up to the mines and we stopped a week there. From thence we proceeded to a town called Fort Yale about sixty miles farther up the river. The current, was so strong in the river that it took us two days to go this distance. From Fort Yale all communication by water ceases and the rest of the distance has to be done on foot. I wish you had seen the thirteen of us starting our packs, we all pretty heavy and the trail none of the best so you may be sure for the first few days we did not make very big work. The trail after the first 15 miles was awful up one mountain and down nother for sixty or seventy miles until we got to a town called Lytton after which it improved. At Lytton we met Alexander McWha. He keeps a small store about three miles from a place called Van Winkle Bar and I believe is doing very well. We stopped there one day or two I forget which and then started again. Our next halting place was to be Quesnel City a town situated at the headquarters of the Frazer River and about 200 miles from Lytton. The trail however is pretty good. It took us 13 days to accomplish this distance but our packs were very heavy at starting as we had bought as many provisions at Lytton as we calculated would carry us through. When at Quesnel we learned that there was no use going to the mines without carrying plenty of provisions with us so we invested all our money in flour, beans, picks, shovels etc. Then came the tug of war. I started with ninety pounds on my back and over such a trail it is only about 50 miles long but what it wants in length it makes up in quality up one mountain and down another precipice sometimes up to your knee in water at other times wading through snow from two to six or eight feet deep. I will live a long time before I forget that journey. This brought us to Antler Creek the first part of the Cariboo mines. The distance you see we have walked was about 400 miles.

When there the very wisest course we could have pursued would have been to have sold our provisions and have turned right back again but like blind fools we were we did not do so although it was then the first week in June. I do not believe there was more than six claims in all Cariboo working at all and these were only making preparations to take out gold of course then there was no chance to get any work and as for prospecting to get a claim for oneself that was out of the question. The snow was melting on the top of the mountains and the water was so high that you could not work more than a few feet any place until you were 'chocked' out of it with water. The rest of the boys all went away one party after another first Henry Stewart, William McDowell, J. Greenfield and the two Pattons left. Then John Dempsey, P. Moore, W. Boyd, John Robb and the two McCreery boys went away until at last there were none of us there except Robert McCance and myself. I heard before I left that he had went down also but whether he did or not I cannot tell as he was in a different part of the mines from where I was. I hung on for six weeks like a drowning man catching at straws always hoping that something would turn up that I might make a living at and perhaps make a little money.

I am sure that brother John will think it cowardly in me to give it up but in fact I could do nothing else. It came to be a question to either go down or starve. Just fancy the price of provisions when I came away. Flour when you could get it was selling at 5s. a pound, beans about the same, pork 6s., salt, sugar and everything else a little dearer. A single meal in a boarding house costs 10s. and for a small cup of bad coffee without any milk I paid 2s. Had I not got a little work occasionally and half starved myself all the time I could not have lived there so long for at the lowest calculation it cost one pound per day to live there.

I came with Mr Wightman's son. You may suppose that I was greatly surprised to see him in such a place. He only stopped a few days and then came down. I parted two weeks ago. He was going to San Francisco [as the winter is so severe*] and I to get work where I could. I have been fortunate to get work here on the road about 50 miles above Lytton. I am engaged for three months at £8 per month. I just got the work in time as I had only about two pounds of flour and one sixpence left. When my time is expired I think I will go down to San Francisco as the winter is so severe here that nothing can be done. Whether I will ever go up to Cariboo I do not know. I do not think I will.

There are three great objections to that country. In the first place provisions are and must continue to be too dear. In the second place the season is too short. One can only work three months and then unless you want to be frozen to death down you must come and the third reason is it takes a small fortune to open a claim there. Had I time and room I could tell you the reason of this but this is my last sheet of paper so I must be saving of it. I must now finish and it may be a very long time before I have another opportunity of writing. The nearest post office from this is 50 miles off and it is by a mere chance I can get this one sent. I would [have] liked to have sent a longer letter than this but as I have neither pen nor ink and as [I] am writing in a tent with eight or ten men talking round me and nothing but the floor to write on this will do at present. In the meantime do not be uneasy about me. There is always some way I can make a living and all the world is not so bad as Cariboo. As a specimen of what it cost to open a claim in Cariboo I may mention that Bill McWha and 8 other men had been working 8 weeks at his claim before I came away and it would take at least 3 more to open it. You may fancy how much money it will take to do this where living is so dear. In the meantime dear father keep writing to the care of Mr Kyle. Tell me how the farm is getting on and in fact everything. Nothing will be uninteresting. Give my love to all brothers, sisters, friends and believe me dear father your loving son [Signed] Sandy Robb.

[*Phrase deleted]

[15 February 1863, New Westminster, BC; to Susanna Robb]

My dear little Sister,

I don't know that this is a proper address for a young lady of seventeen but somehow I can hardly think of you as anybody else than the dear little girl who used to climb on my knee an comb my whiskers. Indeed I believe I would have continued in this state of blissful ignorance for I don't know how long had I not received your letter. The moment I read that my dream was dispelled for I at once knew that no little girl with short petticoats could write such a beautiful letter. Never make any excuses about letter writing any more for I declare to you that it is a very long time indeed since I received a letter either better written or better expressed. Remembering that I expect you to correspond with me regularly after this and I will never forgive you if you neglect to do so. You gave me also a great deal of news that was very interesting to me and which I could not expect Father to think about. You may be sure that I was glad to hear that Nellie and Lizzie were so well and so happy. May God bless and prosper them both. I think they have been blessed in choosing good kind husbands and that is everything for a woman more perhaps than even a good wife is to a man. For my part I hardly ever expect to be blessed by a wife but that can not lessen my preference for the married state in preference to any other and my greatest wish is that if I ever reach home I may see my brothers and sisters filling that station which God and nature has pointed out as the proper one for all human beings.

You wish to know you dear little simpleton if I get my washing and mending done for me comfortably. Of course I do and my cooking into the bargain and all by the one person. I mean myself. Of course it is all well done expecially the mending. 'Tis true the stitches are sometimes long and not very even but what is that where there are no woman to critizise ones appearances. As for baking I think I can beat any woman in the Parish of Dundonald giving us both the same materials. I mean flour and water. With these I can make bread that would make Barry Hughs hide his diminished head and blush for very shame. I find though that I am getting into a regular [ragmarsh] so I must draw to a close promising you to write you a decent letter the next time. So with Love to Mary, Andrew, Sam and Frank.

> I remain dear Sister
> Your affect brother
> Alexander Robb

~~~~~~

[15 February 1863, New Westminster, BC; to his father]

Dear Father,

At last I have received your letter. You can have no idea how anxiously I have been looking for them and how sick at heart I have been when mail after mail has come in without bringing me any word from home. I mentioned in my last letter that I had written to Mr. Kyle to have them forward to me here. My letter to him must have been detained as it was two months after I wrote until I got an answer. At last however they did come and I believe they were all the more welcome from being so long coming. I was very sorry to hear that you had such an awful summer as you describe. I can just imagine what an amount of trouble you must have had. In this respect if in no other I had the advantage of you. British Columbia (or at least the part of it that I was in) enjoys perhaps one of the finest if not the *very* finest Climates in the world. It is warm without being oppressively hot and from the first of May until the middle December only a few slight showers fell. The sky too is blue all the time and the atmosphere is so clear that mountains that only look two or three miles from you are probably twenty or thirty miles distant. This does not refer to the district of Cariboo in which blessed region rain thunder and lightning seems to have established their head quarters. As regards the rest of the Country I believe a better healthier climate cannot be found. However, as there is no rose without its thorn so even this country is not without its drawbacks. I do not refer to the wild animals although, bears, wolves and [?] are pretty plenty [?] to the reptiles though rattlesnakes are plentier than five dollar pieces. These you can avoid or kill but there is another thing that you cannot avoid and where you kill one, one thousand arises to avenge his death. I mean the musquitoe – This is decidedly *the* pest of British Columbia. I cannot

describe to you the horrible torments they inflict upon one. They
creep up ones arms they crawl round your neck they settle in hundreds upon your face and in fact wherever there is a bare spot of
flesh upon you these pests make it their business to leave a blister.
About the middle of August the nights commence to get a little chilly
and then the mosquitoe begins to loose part of his fierceness and
shortly after dies away all together. He leaves as is successor a little
black gnat that though not so large is quite as bad as the other. Each
has it own peculiarities. Mr. Mosquitoe is a spanish gentleman of
rather dissipated habits. He loves to get up early in the morning
(about two or three oclock) and as he no doubt thinks this is a virtue
that ought to be shared by all creation he takes particular pains that
you should not sleep either. When the sun gets warm he gets drowsy
and goes to sleep until about four oclock in the afternoon when out
he rushes with renewed energy and continues his orgies until about
twelve oclock at night when too drunk even to fly he reels under a
blade of grass and no doubt dreams of his *nip* in the morning. The
gnat on the contrary is rather a lazy kind of fellow. He wont get up
until the sun is high in the heavens and goes to bed exactly at sunset.
To do him justice however he improves his time most wisely and
judiciously while awake. Unlike the mosquitoe who is not particular
where he lets your blood flow Mr. Gnat is a dainty fellow and his most
dainty morsel is extracted from the corner of your eye where they
settle in clusters and there they will stay do you best. This is an
overdrawn picture for there are places in this Colony where strong
horses have been killed dead in the night by the mosquitoes. I have
seen men from the Canadian swamps from the Mississippi plains
from Australia and in fact from every part of the world and all agree
that British Columbia beats them all hollow. It is said that they are not
so bad on one after the first year and I am sure I hope so for nothing
but a young Irishman strong and healthy *could* have gone through
such a course of surgery as I have suffered this year. I have been
rather prosy on this subject as I have little to write about and when
I did commence about these things my feelings got the better
of me –

Dear Father I have but little news to tell you. I am in my usual good
health. Tell Eleanor that I am sorry I cannot send her my likeness
as there is no artist in this town. I believe however that I am stronger,
stouter and I flatter myself looks better than ever I did in my life before.
I have got all the money I wrought for and am able with some little

work I do to pass the winter very comfortably. There is no cold line and in fact this is just

[Rest of letter missing]

~~~~~~

[4 June 1863, New Westminister, BC; to Eleanor Robb]

My dear Sister,

I received your letter dated March about three weeks ago. I could not answer it any earlier for the simple reason that where I was then I could neither get pens ink or papers. I was then working on Burrows Inlet an arm of the sea that comes in about 8 miles from here. Three other parties and I took the contract of cutting a water ditch for a saw mill about eleven weeks ago and we only got it finished last week. We made pretty well of it averaging nearly 12 shillings per day and board which is considered good wages in this part of the country. I just wish you could see what kind of a place we had to run it through. Of course it was all through the woods 'and such woods'. You may remember a little song that commenced 'Some love to roam through the dark sea foam Where the wild winds whistle free But a chosen land on the mountain land And a life in the woods for me Now Eleanor you may just put it down for a dead certainty that the fellow who wrote that song was either a fool or had never saw any more woods than is contained in a gentlemen's park. You can have no possible idea what a forest is in its primitive state. In the first place the trees grow almost as thick as they can stand, and such trees. Why the largest I ever saw at home were mere walking sticks in comparison. They run from three to five, ten, and very often 15 and sixteen feet in diameter and from two to three hundred feet in length. I think it is Sam Slick who says that it is impossible to look at the falls of Niagara without thinking of a cotton mill and I am sure I cannot look at one of those monsters without thinking of David Grainger. Then fancy that those fellows have been tumbling down for centuries and are lying in every stage of rottenness someplaces three and four deep add to this a thick growth of underbrush and you can just fancy what pleasure one would have with 'a chosen land' in such a place. Why three miles walk is enough to tire one thoroughly for two days. You may guess its pretty bad when A.R. cares, even Canadians who I sometimes think are born with an axe in their hands [?].

I think it very singular that you have not had a letter from me before you wrote as I wrote to you immediately after I came down country. The week before Christmas I think it was and also once since that. I had a letter from John the day before I started for the Inlet. it was the first intimation I had of the death of poor James it also told me of Uncle Whites death. I meant to have written to John immediately after I went there but could get not an opportunity. John will think it very ungrateful of me and I would not like to have him think so as he is a man whom I esteem and admire as much for a friend as I love him as a brother. You can just tell him that I will write to him in about three weeks from now. I also mean to write to Frank McRoberts at the same time. Tell Frank I expected a letter from him before this and if he has not written to do so immediately on pain of my heaviest displeasure. The same mail that brought your last letter also brought one from E. Murdock enclosing one from Alex Robb. I was very glad to get them especially Ellen's. I write to her by this mail. Dear Sister I don't think that I will go up country this summer as I am afraid I will not have enough money to do so with any prospect of success. The four of us however who are in company are thinking of sending up two of the party to prospect a claim for next season. The two that remains below to give an equal quantity of money and work down here and try and make as much as will keep the others next winter in case they should come down broke. Two of the party are Californian miners and very decent steady men so of course it will be them will be sent. Whether this arrangement will stand good or not I cannot tell but I think it will. In the meantime I am going out to the Inlet to work for a month or two and then I mean to cut hay plenty of which grows on the banks of the Frazer and for which a good market can be had in Victoria. I don't know that I have anything more to say although I am almost ashamed of my short letters after getting your fine long ones. Give my best love to Father. Tell him I expect a letter from him in your next. To Lizzie, Mary, Susanna, Andrew, John, Martha and the rest of them at home. Give my love to Aunt Ellen and tell her I would sometimes like to spend a Saturday night with her. To all my old friends I need not mention their names for you know them.

> And believe me dear Eleanor
> Your affect brother
> Alex Robb

~~~~~~

[10 May 1868, Nicola Lake, BC; to Susanna Robb]

For a long time my conscience has been telling me that it was time for me to write home and when I got your dear kind letter it's voice got too strong to be any longer disregarded. You cannot tell how much your letter interested me containing as it did so much news of things and people whom I am still very much interested in. You are perfectly right in your conjecture that I never received the letter containing poor Lizzie's likeness. I am going to send down to New Westminster for it. In future if you would simply direct your letters to Lytton British Columbia I would be sure to receive them. By directing them to New Westminster Lytton they are just as likely to stop at one place as some to the other and the two places are about 150 miles apart.

Would you believe it, the first intimation I had that John and Martha had a little daughter was by the mere accident of her being sick and you mentioning it. I never before heard that ... there was such a being in existence as Jennie Robb.

I am very sorry that I cannot comply with your request about the likeness. I think though, that when you hear my reasons you will be satisfied that [it] is not my fault if I don't send it to you. In the first place, I don't think there is a single photographic artist in this colony or at least there is none nearer than Victoria, and that is nearly 300 miles from here, and in the second how far do you think I would have to go by the most direct road to visit my nearest white neighbour You would never guess, so I will just tell you. I would have to travel as nearly as I can judge (for the track has never been measured) between 45 and 50 miles. I have heard indeed that two men have settled about eight or ten miles from here, but I have never seen them.

And now I think I hear you say 'What on earth can you be doing in such a place'? Well I am just starting a ranch or farm for a friend of mine who wishes to commence farming and stock raising here and I will most likely stop here a year at least if not longer. I have never seen a place in my life so admirably adapted for both pursuits as this is. There is a valley here about seven miles long and from one to two [miles] wide, mostly of the very best kind of prairie land. It requires neither draining, clearing or any other improvement to grow the best kind of wheat barley oats or vegetables of all kinds for years to come. What would they think at home of land that would grow wheat or oats ten or twelve years in succession and the last crop be as good as the first, and yet I have seen within this last month thousands of acres of such land.

According to the land laws of this country any British subject may take up 160 acres of land in any place in the country by merely paying the registration fees which is only ten shillings and settling on it. After he has done a certain quantity of work on it you get what is called a 'certificate of improvement' which is in face neither more nor less than a government title to the land. This you may sell or otherwise dispose of as if it were your own land. In fact it is so only that when the land comes to be surveyed (which may not be for years) you or your successor have to pay government one dollar per acre for it. There is a wonderful difference between this and paying twenty pounds or so per acre for leave to farm a patch of hungry land from which one may be turned out by the mere caprice of a landlord.

But this is not the only advantage connected with this valley. On each side of it, for I don't know how many miles, rise a succession of gently rising hills. These, though unfit for agriculture, afford in summer the best run for stock I ever saw. They are covered with a kind of grass which I think is peculiar to this part of the world. It is called bunch grass from its growing in tufts or bunches. These tufts are sometimes two or three feet apart while in other places they grow quite close to one another, the spaces between the bunches being quite bare. It grows from about 4 inches to 2 feet in height, and I saw anything in the world that appears to agree with animals so well as it does. In one month after it commences to grow in the spring cattle or horses which can scarcely walk will be rolling fat. As a general thing animals do very well in the winter by what they can pick up over the hills, but it is safer to make a little provision for them in case a very deep snow should come and last a long time.

It is true that there is no market nearer this than 50 miles, but in a very few years all this valley will be settled up and a good road made to it. Until that time most of a farmers' dependence will be in his stock which he can drive any place but there is a sure fortune to be made out of them by any one who has capital enough to buy enough of them to get a start with.

I forgot to mention that there is a young man along with me here a partner of the person for whom I am making the farm. However uninteresting these things may be to you my dear sister I mention them because in the first place I have no news to tell you and in the next I want to show you that I am not half so much to be pitied as from the way you and Eleanor writes you appear to think I should be. No person is to be pitied in a new country who has got good health and knows how to work. The only thing that I regret about leaving home is the leaving those that I love behind me and could I only see them once more (which I hope yet to do) I would be perfectly satisfied to end my days in this country.

Give my best love to father. Tell him I will write to him in a short time, to Andrew Mary and all the rest, and believe me dear Sukie [Susanna] your loving brother [Signed] Alexander Robb.

p.s. When you are writing to Eleanor tell her I received her letter and will answer it shortly. [Signed] Sandy.

~~~~~~

[14 December 1868, Nicola Lake, BC; to his father]

Dear father, I have been reproaching myself for some time for not answering your last kind letter which I received in the latter end of October. 'Tis true that I have been very very busy, but still I might very well have spared enough time to write to you.

When I last wrote I told you that I had come up here and that I was much pleased with the looks of the country. In fact it would be impossible to be otherwise than pleased with it for it is beyond comparison by far the best part of British Columbia I have yet seen. It lies in what is called the dry belt of British Columbia, and indeed it may be well called so for a shower is rather a rare occurrence. In summer it is warm and dry and in winter it is cold and dry. Of course it would be impossible to grow any kind of crop without artificial watering so when any one is looking out for a farm he has got to look out for a place near a creek where the water can be easily got on the land one wants to cultivate. The irrigation of the land is done by making small water furrows about three feet apart after the land is harrowed and rolled. Into these furrows the water is conducted by a large ditch or drain and allowed to run until the land is pretty well saturated which generally takes from twelve to twenty four hours according to the nature of the soil. The operation has to be repeated three or four times during the season and altogether it is a very tedious job requiring a great deal of patience in the person who conducts it. There is this advantage in it that one can generally control a crop and there is always beautiful harvest weather.

I think I told you in my last letter that a young Englishman and I were the two first white men who came to this district. When we came here our nearest neighbour was from 40 to 50 miles from us. Since then quite a number of settlers have located in the valley making it much more pleasant and safe to live in.

I do not think that there was any real danger at any time and the Indians have been very quiet and civil, but still one feels a little more secure from having a few neighbours around. I think that I am a little of a favourite with the redskins. I have managed to pick up enough of their language so that I can understand what they say, and when I promise anything to them I always keep my word and these two things go far to get one in the good graces of the savages.

Most of the Indians round here are well off, nearly all of them owning more or less horses, some of them cattle. One man (a chief) has nearly 200 horses and 20 or 30 cows. As a general thing the more wealth an Indian has the more wives he keeps. One old fellow who is the grand chief of the district has no less than seven wives and thirty five children living besides twelve children and I don't know how many wives dead. He is not more than 50 years old yet and if he only keeps on he bids fair to rival Brigham Young.

I don't know whether this yarn about Indians will interest you very much. If I thought it did, I could write you enough about them. Perhaps you would rather hear of what I am doing myself. As I told you in my last letter I came here to work for a friend of mine who wished to start farming here. I wrought for him until a month ago when I quit and took up a place about 7 miles farther up the lake. I have gone into partnership with another man a Canadian named Frank Mickle, I believe an honest decent man. We took up our 320 acres of land and I think that if you only saw it, it would please you. It is nearly all quite as level as the levellest part of your holms without a solitary stick on it. Neither is there on the whole lot a stone as large as a hen egg. The soil is a deep black loam and I will be greatly disappointed if it does not in time make one of the finest, if not the very best farms, in British Columbia. As for grass there are thousands of acres of it of the very best quality on the rising ground adjoining the flat on which we are located. We have also got 40 head of cattle and 5 yoke of work oxen. These last we intend to sell as soon as we get through our spring work.

You need not think, dear father, that I had money enough to buy these cattle and what implements we require besides food for a year without going into debt. So anxious however was my partner that I should go in with him (he being a blacksmith and not knowing much about farming) that he lent me money enough to pay my share and promises to wait for it until I can pay him. It is the first time I ever have owed a dollar in this country and I hate the idea of it as bad as I hate poison but I am so heartily sick and weary of working for other people that I am willing to take my chance however desparate so that I may get quit of it. I would not be a bit afraid but that I could soon make enough to put me out of debt if there was either a road or a market here but there is neither one or other and it costs as much to pack produce on horses or mules to where there is a market as it is worth when it gets there. However I hope for the best and at any rate I can do no worse than I have done these last six or seven years besides having a great deal more comfort. A man with a small amount of capital saved from £500 to £1,000 could make himself independent in a very few years by raising stock for which this country is peculiarly adapted.

The winter for so far has been mild and pleasant and I think is likely to continue so. Last winter was the coldest ever known in the colony. For six weeks in Lytton the thermometer was from 15 to 28 degrees below zero and a little way further up the mercury froze. You cannot imagine anything like such weather.

Tell Susanna that I sent to Westminster and got the letter with poor Lizzie's likeness but there was none of hers as she said there was. If she does not wish me to be very angry she had better sit down and write to me and enclose her likeness just as soon as this reaches you. Give my best love to her and all the rest and to John Martha and the little ones, and believe me dear father ever your affectionate son [Signed] Alexander Robb.

p.s. When writing direct to Nicola Lake, Spence's Bridge, British Columbia.

~~~~~~

[8 December 1869, Lytton, BC; to Susanna Robb]

My dear sister, I take the opportunity of Mr Alexander McWha's going home to Ireland of writing to you. I would have done so long ago but that I have not been at home all summer. You know that what I call home is a place called Nicola Lake, but unfortunately our crop this year was a failure owing to the scarcity of water. As soon as I saw that we were going to have little or no crop I left my partner to take care of the stock and place and started for Cariboo. There I stopped all summer and have only been down here about three weeks. I did not make a great deal up in Cariboo but still I done much better than by stopping down below and am very well satisfied that I went there.

Cariboo is much changed since I was there last in 1864. Everything is much cheaper than they were then and although perhaps fewer men accumulate large fortunes still the majority of miners live much better and are a great deal more comfortable than they were at that time. Mr McWha will be able to tell you all about the mines much better than I can as he has been up there for over six years so I will leave him to tell you anything you wish to know of them.

I hardly think that I will be likely to go up there again for some time but it is just possible I may do so next spring. In fact it all depends on what word I may have from there during the winter. I would like better to stop at the farm during the summer and attend to the ranch as it would pay me better in the long run. We have now about twenty five cows that we can milk and if I can only manage to make butter I can do very well. I could find a ready sale for all the butter I could make at two shillings per pound and as the feed of the cows costs nothing I think or rather I know that there is plenty of money to be made by the business.

The only trouble is whether I can make the butter good or not but I rather think I can. Do not you know of some decent girl whom you could send out to help me If you know of such a one just send her along as I think that a good wife would be the making of me just now. She may be of any age from twenty to forty, long or short, fair or dark, money or no money, but I would like her to be industrious, decent, tolerably intelligent and at least middling good looking. Seriously if I had only the means I would come home and get married but at present my circumstances will not permit me doing so. So if you know of any girl who will answer the above description and who wants to get married very badly tell her to come along and she will find a tolerably good husband in your big brother. I believe Mr A. McWha is going to bring his niece with him to this country and my intended can come along for company.

A good many of my acquaintances have left this country lately on visits to their friends in Canada and Europe. Amongst them is one who will be likely to pay you a visit. His name is Mr John Clapperton of Queens County, Ireland. He and I have been acquainted for over 7 years and during that time I have received many kindnesses from him. Any kindness you can show him I will consider as a personal favour, and I can confidently recommend him to your acquaintance. You will find him a cultivated man and a gentleman in every respect.

I am likely to stop here a month or six weeks before I go to Nicola Lake. William McWha is not in very good health and wishes me to attend to his business while he goes down to Victoria for a change of air. Bill has been a very good friend of mine and I cannot very well refuse to do this much for him although I would much rather be at home.

I have been in very good health this last year and feel better and stronger than I have done for some years previously. I do not know that I have anything more to add. Give my love to father. Tell Sam I got his letter ... and was very glad to hear from him. When writing to Eleanor tell her I also received her letter and that I am going to write to her before long. Love to all the rest and believe me, my dear sister your affectionate brother [Signed] Alexander Robb. p.s. Mr McWha has promised to bring me out any photographs you may send. Be sure and send yours and Mary's and the boys if possible. [Signed] Sandy.

~~~~~~

[17 September 1870, Nicola Lake, BC; to Susanna Robb]

I received your letter with the likenesses you sent out by Alex[ander] McWha about four weeks ago and it has taken me all the time since then to make myself sure that you have not been imposing someone else's likeness on me for yours and Sam's. Mary's I would have known very well. What a stupid ass I have been to be always calling you my little sister and my *little pet*. Why you are a woman now and although my reason told me long ago that you must be one still I had to see your likeness to convince me fully that you were anything else than the little girl I remember so well and I do not think it will make you too vain my darling (you see I cannot avoid pet names when I think of you) when I say that I think that you are a very nice little girl too and so thinks everyone to whom I have shown your likenesses but that is not many for it is not everyone in this country I would show my sister's likeness to. I can assure you that I am not a little proud of my sisters. I like Sam's likeness too. He has got a fine open honest look about him. I do not think that such a face could belong to a person who would be guilty of a mean action.

Many thanks my dear sister for the socks you so thoughtfully sent me. They will be a comfort to my soul or soles this winter. Socks are a thing it is very difficult to get good in this country. I pay from three to four shillings per pair for them and the average length of time they last is from two to three days without holes.

Tell Sam that I am much obliged to him for the knife he sent. It is almost a chest of tools in itself. Your last letter I received two or three days ago. It contained Aunt Ellen's likeness but I suppose you concluded not to send Frank's until next time. Be sure and do not forget and if you have got a spare one of Andrew's send it also. I want to have the whole family.

I need scarcely say how much I have been grieved and disappointed that neither you nor father could see the propriety of sending out some young lady for a wife for your hopeful brother. Surely among so many female friends as you have got you might find *one* who for your sake if not for mine would be willing to travel eight or ten thousand miles to find a husband in the person of your brother. As I told you before I am not particular to a *shade* one way or another so I think that the young lady you mention under the head of No. 3 would suit me to a niceity.

My partner got back from Canada in the beginning of summer and brought a wife with him. She appears to be quite a nice woman and I have been more comfortable since she came here than I have been before for a long time. We all live together for the present and most probably will do so all winter and I can assure you that it [is] quite a relief to me to get rid of cooking.

Mostly on account of my partner being so long in getting back from Canada but partly for other (?) reasons I could not get to Cariboo (?) this summer in time to represent my claim. On account of the severity of the winter all claims are laid over from the 1st November until the 1st May. Of course as I was not there at the latter time the ground was open for anyone. Well according to my usual luck my claim (that is the one I had last fall) has turned out to be one of the most likely ones for a big thing that has been in the Cariboo country for years and although not one dollar has yet come out of it nor will likely for months yet, four thousand dollars has been offered and refused for a half interest in it.

Mr Clapperton that I wrote to you about has returned to this country. He had not time to go north as he intended to do. I do not think that you would have thought him quite so nice as you did Jim Allen but I am sure you would have liked him very much. I liked Jim better than any stranger I have ever met. I think that he is not only nice but good. If any of you are writing to him give him my best respects. I am very glad to hear that Frank has got such a good situation. It is much better than emigration and if he only tries hard to do his duty and studies his business thoroughly he will not only come to like it but his employers will like him.

Give my best love to father and all the rest and believe me dear sister yours [Signed] Sandy Robb.

P.S. Whoever directs my letters in future will please not put Esq. to my name. It appears to be so very ridiculous [Signed] Sandy.

~~~~~~

[23 May 1871, Nicola Lake, BC; to Susanna Robb]

My dear sister, Your very welcome letter came to hand about three weeks ago and as I am going to start for Lytton (our Post Office) today I will take the opportunity of answering it. Just fancy, it will take me 3 days to go down and as many more to come back and yet this is the only way unless by a chance that we have of communicating with the outside world. We did expect to have a direct mail of our own before this time and the legislative assembly actually granted us funds for carrying mail, but it appears that the governor vetoed the vote as he had no money to spare for that purpose.

You may possibly have herd that by a vote of the parliaments of
Canada and this country we now belong to the Dominion of Canada
or will be as soon as the home government gives its assent to the bill
which we expect will be about the month of June or July. Great
benefits are expected by some people from the change, and although
I am not so sanguine as some are, still I have no manner of doubt
but that it will do some good. Among other benefits we expect to
derive from the confederation is that of having the full management
of our own local affairs, of which we are in a great measure deprived
under the present form of government. You see that our present
assembly or parliament is composed of only one third of what we call
popular members that is those who are appointed by the people,
while the remaining two thirds are what is called official members and
are appointed by the governor and are totally irresponsible to the
people at large. It is very easy to see to what abuses such a system is
likely to give rise. Of course where people have the voting of their own
salaries it is only likely that they will have good ones and the officials
certainly do rate their services at a very high figure considering what
they have to do while it is scarcely possible for any measure, however
necessary it may be for the good of the country to pass through the
assembly if it interferes in any way with the interests of these gentlemen. Under confederation we expect these abuses will be done away
with. *All* the members of the legislature will be elected by the people
and it will be our own faults if we do not get laws to suit ourselves.

Another benefit which we are to derive from joining ourselves to
Canada is that in the terms of confederation the government of Canada
binds itself to commence a railroad from Canada to the Pacific Coast
within two years and finish it inside of ten. Most people think that
the road will be completed in a little over half that time and I understand that a party of surveyors have arrived already from Canada to
look out for the best route for the proposed line. It is just possible
that they may bring the road through this valley and at any rate it
cannot miss us by more than fifty miles and we think nothing of that
distance in this country. Go where it will, it will be of immense benefit
to everyone as the very money which will be spent in it's construction
will be a big item among such a small population as this colony has
got while the stimulus it will give to industry of all kinds will be of
incalculable value to us.

I am very sensible, my dear sister, that this must appear to be a very
strange kind of letter to write to you but I really have not got anything

to say that I think would interest you. I am and have been in good health and with ordinary good luck I think that in two or three years more I will be not indeed rich or anything like it but at least out of debt and independent and you may be sure that the first use I will make of the first money I can get a hold of will be to take me where I can eat my Christmas dinner with you.

Poor Andrew appears to have had a narrow escape of it. I cannot tell you how thankful I am that he has got better. It would have been such a blow on father and all of you had anything serious happened to him. How is John The last letter I had from him he appeared to be very poorly but I think that some of you would have let me know had he not been any better. In your next letter be sure and let me know how he is. Many thanks for Frank's 'carte'. What a big fellow he has got to be. It makes me think myself quite old to look at him. I hope he is doing well and giving satisfaction in his present situation.

My object in going to Lytton now is to take down some butter and get things from the store. It is a very unpleasant trip at this season, as the snow is melting on the mountains and the creeks and rivers are very high. Fortunately there is now a bridge across the worst and largest river. Last year I had to ride my horse and make him swim across it and I do not care about taking such risks oftener than is necessary as it is both a wide and rapid river larger, I should think, than the Shannon (that is at this season; at other times it is quite easy to cross almost anywhere). Give my love to father and all at home also to all my friends and believe me my dear sister your loving brother [Signed] Alexander Robb.

~~~~~~

[24 February 1872, Nicola Lake, BC; to Eleanor Robb]

My dear sister, I received your long and very welcome letter three days ago and the same mail brought me one from Sam dated nearly two months later. Now Eleanor dear, if I could find in my heart to scold you I would certainly do so. What on earth could put into your head, if only for one moment, that I had forgotten you. It is very true that I have been very remiss about writing but I may well accuse you all of the same fault for from all the friends I have at home I do not believe I get on an average more than one letter in six months. You little know, my dear sister, what it is to be alone in the world or you would certainly never think of accusing me of forgetfulness. Don't you know Eleanor that one must love someone and what have I got to love but my father yourself and my friends at home. It is true that I have got lots of friends, as the world calls them, and I believe I may say without any vanity that I am generally regarded as not a bad sort of a fellow but I do thoroughly believe that there is not within some thousands of miles of where I sit tonight one solitary individual who would care too straws if I were dead and buried tomorrow. Do you think then that I am likely to forget those whom I know do care for me.

It now only wants three days of being ten years since I left home and I can safely say that during that time there has not been one day nor scarcely a waking hour I have not thought of home. Not that I am what is called homesick but as I said before one must love something. But enough on this subject.

I was extremely glad to hear such good accounts of all the young folks as you gave me (you see I am beginning to put myself on the old list, though *you* may possibly object to it). What a comfort it must be to father to see them all doing so well and keeping themselves so respectable. I myself feel almost as proud of them as if they were my own boys. You most likely have heard that I wrote to Sam asking him what his idea was about coming to this country. I believed and indeed was about satisfied that I could find him a situation, much better as far as salary was concerned than the one he is now in. However since the folks at home were unwilling that he should come I consider he did quite right in staying where he is. He is certainly much happier than he would likely be here and that after all is everything. I believe after all it was as much selfishness in my part as interest in Sam's welfare that induced me to write to him for I do long so to see someone of my own kindred.

I think I hear you say 'then why don't you come home and see them' But I am afraid that I must deny myself that gratification for some time to come. I am just now beginning to get my head a little above water and I am afraid if I were to take such a plunge as a visit to home would be, I would drown altogether. I am in hopes though that if God spares me I will before many years be able to see you all once more.

You can scarcely expect to receive such long letters from me as you are able to write to me, I have so very little to write about. I am well in health as indeed I always am. As to my worldly prospects why I am getting along about as well as I expected that is to say slowly but I believe steadily. You may be a long time in getting this letter as communication is very uncertain at this time of the year. I am going to write to Dundonald by this mail. Give my best love to John and the children. Do not let it be so long again before you write as it was the last time and with warmest love believe me dear sister your loving brother [Signed] Alexander Robb.

P.S. When writing direct to Nicola Lake, Lytton, British Columbia. New Westminster is 200 miles from here and I think your last letter must have been detained there. [Signed] Sandy.

[24 February 1872, Nicola Lake, BC; to Susanna Robb]

What can be the matter with you that I have not heard from you for so long. I had been waiting nearly all winter for a letter from you, always expecting one, and always being disappointed, and since I have heard that you are or have been so delicate I am and will be seriously uneasy unless I hear regularly from yourself. How I wish I could transplant you here for the next six months or as much longer as I could prevail on you to stop. Besides the comfort it would be to me to have you near me, I am satisfied that a few months in this high altitude and dry climate would completely restore your health, diseases of the chest being a thing almost unknown here. And what a comfort it would be to me to have you visit me if for ever so short a time! For I am afraid I am going to be very lonely now.

I may perhaps have mentioned to you that for these last eighteen months or so a brother of my former partner and his wife have been living with me. I have lately bought his farm and in a short time he and his wife will be moving to a place about twenty miles from here so I expect to be entirely alone. It is true that my old partner and his wife live only a little over a mile from here but I am afraid I will feel the want of company in the house. I will be very sorry too to part with Mrs Mickle (the woman who lives in the house with me). She has been as kind to me as if I had been her brother and I have come to like her almost as well as if she were my own sister. Her husband is gone now to put up a house on his new place and meanwhile his wife and a little girl are stopping here. I expect they will all leave for good in about two weeks.

This district is getting to be quite settled up. Three years and one half ago there was not one white settler within forty miles. Now there are twenty five within less than half that distance and we expect a further influx next summer. A good many too of the settlers have got wives and young families which gives the place something of a home look.

We have had a very severe winter here this year. It set in nearly a month earlier than usual and we have had more snow and more cold than I have seen for these last three years. On Christmas day the thermometer was down to 31 degrees below zero. You cannot fancy what such cold is, but it may give you an idea when I tell you that at 15 degrees lower mercury will freeze and strong brandy will become as thick as syrup. Had you such weather in your damp climate I do not believe anything could live but here we do not feel it so badly. It is however very lucky that even here such extreme cold is rare and never lasts longer than three or four days.

In spite however of the cold and snow cattle although they have neither any food but what they pick up, or any shelter but what they can find have generally done well. Some of mine are good beasts and now the weather is beautiful snow almost all gone and too warm to wear a coat.

Tell Samuel I received his letter 4 or 5 days ago and that I think he done quite right in refusing to come here, so long as the folks at home were unwilling he should come. The same mail also brought me one from Eleanor. I spent part of yesterday evening in replying to her.

We are all expecting to have a regular mail here next summer and I hope we will not be disappointed. We are, some of us at least, also expecting to have a road made but I am afraid we will be disappointed in this matter. At present everything has to be taken in and out of here on horses or mules backs.

Give my best love to father. I will write to him ere long, to Mary, Andrew, Sam and Frank and all my friends and believe me dear Susanna your loving brother [Signed] Sandy Robb.

~~~~~~

[8 July 1873, Nicola Lake, BC; to his father]

My dear father, last mail but one brought me 3 letters from home, one from Eleanor, one from Susanna and from yourself. I need not tell you how much I was pleased to hear from yourself directly once more but I suppose it is my own fault that I do not hear oftener as I know that I have been writing to my sisters much more regularly than I have to you.

You asked me, my Dear father, whether I ever think of home! If you had been as many years as I have been away from home you would not have thought it necessary to ask the question. Since the day I left Dundonald until now, there has never one day or scarcely an hour passed but I *have* thought of home and the dear ones who live there. Situated as I am in a wild country, with nothing but mere acquaintances around me, is it not natural that my thoughts should continually revert to those places where I was once so happy and that my heart should cling to the people whom I love and who I believe love me perhaps much better than I deserve.

For your kind offer to assist me in case I should think of coming to see you, I can only say that I am deeply grateful, and if I can manage it at all I will try and avail myself of it. I think it would make me feel ten years younger to see you all once more. I had intended to try and come home a year from next fall and with the assistance you offer me, I have no doubt that I could manage to do so but for one thing. The fact is that I am afraid I will have [to] go to Victoria this winter. I have not been so well as usual these 4 or 5 months and I am beginning to think that I want change of air. I have now lived 8 years in this high altitude and I think that I want a sniff of the salt water to put me to rights again. Victoria is the capital city of this country. It is situated on the seaside and enjoys a beautiful climate and I have no doubt but a month or so down there will make me all straight again. The only thing that I am sorry about is that it will take money which I had intended for a better purpose; I mean I meant to see you with it. I am almost sorry that I have told you anything about this matter as it may make you uneasy and I can assure that there is no occasion for feeling so, as I am actually not sick. I only feel not so robust as usual.

Times are very dull here this summer and farm produce when it comes to market is likely to be very cheap even if it can be sold at all which I greatly doubt. We were expecting the Canadian Pacific Railroad would be started this summer which would have made things quite lively but the way things look now it is not likely to be started for a year yet if then, and everything has fallen in consequence. Bullocks which last year would bring £12 cannot now be sold for £8, the few which are sold fetching not more than 2-1/2d. per lb. dead weight. This is quite different from the prices you mention in your letter but they would pay very well here even at that figure if we had only a ready sale. It cost little or nothing to raise cattle here and one can keep an almost unlimited number. Lots of people who started ten or twelve years ago with only a few head of stock have now from 1 to 4,000 each. It would do you good to see the stock in this valley now. Not that the breed is any extra but the condition is surprising and the abundance of feed makes them grow very large. I sold a two year old bullock last year which weighed between 900 and 1,000 lbs. of beef sinking offal and I never fed him 1 lb. of anything since the day he was calved.

We have had a very backward season for so far and very cold and what is more surprising a great deal of rain. This last week however has been fair and very warm and everything is growing very fast. The grass is better than I ever saw it and when I tell you there is about 70 miles long and 10 or 15 miles wide of it for a few hundred cattle to run over you will agree with me in thinking they are not likely to starve to death. Mine now can scarcely walk they are so fat.

I mean to start haying tomorrow. The hay we get here is a natural grass which we call rye grass. It is however nothing like the grass of the same name at home. It grows very tall from 5 to 8 or 10 feet high and it is awful hard work to mow it as the stems are almost as thick as pipe shanks and very hard and tough. It makes pretty good hay when cut in season and keeps cattle in the winter even if not cut as the stems are so strong that the snow cannot break it down and cover it.

Tell Susannah that I have not been getting any papers these last few weeks and that I am going to write to her and scold her about it. Supper is just ready so I must finish. Give my love to John, Eleanor and all at home and believe me dear father your affectionate son [Signed] Alexander Robb.

CHAPTER ELEVEN

Conclusion

Nineteenth-century Canada emerged as the by-product of European mass migrations. Although the ethnic character of the migrations altered as the century passed, the overwhelming majority of the immigrants were drawn from the British Isles, and through them the character of English-speaking Canada was firmly established. These charter groups were not without considerable internal social and cultural variety: religion, social class, and regional backgrounds all served to complicate what has often been interpreted superficially as a British cultural homogeneity. Language differences, offered in the form of Scots Gallic or Irish Gaelic, added to the mixture. Central, therefore, to any interpretation of Canada is an understanding of who the immigrants were and whence they came. Combined with this is a need to determine the variety in locations and types of settlement formed by the newcomers in a land that contained a great diversity of social and environmental challenges. For the study of these nineteenth-century migrants a regional emphasis, focused on their source areas and their chosen destinations, is of primary utility. It combines history very clearly with geography.

The forces causing the migration were many, and while ultimately each decision was the product of personalities and circumstances, the general patterns of migration owed much to established transatlantic routes and the localized traditions of emigration in Europe. The British colonies in North America were connected to Europe by a trading system that distributed basic staple products to a set of primary markets. Because of an imbalance in the volume of return trade, the cargo ships, faced with an expensive westward voyage in ballast, frequently sought fare-paying passengers. As a result, a symbiosis between trade and emigration developed in the eighteenth century and reached a peak during the first half of the nineteenth, before passenger liners took command of the emigrant traffic. Given Britain's extensive trading links and imperial ties with her North American colonies, it also supplied the bulk of early emigrants. The logistical possibilities for travel and settlement overseas created by the staples trade were augmented by a general sensitizing of the home countries to the notion of social betterment through emigration. These influences found their greatest response among communities located near ports, where increasing dissatisfaction with prospects at home heightened the likelihood of emigration. These conditions were most clearly met in Ireland, and it supplied the bulk of pre-1850 emigrants. Upward of 60 per cent of arrivals in the colonies were Irish, and this component was the primary distinguishing characteristic of pre-1850 migration, separating it decisively from the English and Scots-dominated movement of the second half of the nineteenth century.

In Ireland's case, the possibilities of emigration to British North America were allowed by trade in the staples of fish and timber, but the emigration was initially created by Irish conditions. The trade facilitated more than it caused the outflow. The controlling centre of the fisheries trade rested in the English West Country, and the two great centres of the timber trade were Glasgow and Liverpool. Fishing boats sailing from Poole in Dorset en route to the Grand Banks off Newfoundland called at the southeast Irish ports of Waterford, New Ross, and Youghal to take on water, provisions for both the trip and New World markets, and men for seasonal employment in the fisheries. Eventually the seasonal migrations were transformed into the permanent migration of both men and women, and there was thus forged one of the most striking cultural bonds linking a well-defined small hinterland in Europe to an equally well-defined overseas destination. The fishery and provision merchants availed themselves of a willingness to emigrate among the people of southeast Ireland. In the same way, timber merchants directed their westward-bound ships, temporarily outfitted to carry passengers, to call at Derry, Belfast, Dublin, Cork, and a host of other Irish ports to take on fare-paying cargo. Given the location of the ports and the nature of the shipping routes, it was not surprising that the bulk of the Glasgow and Liverpool ships should be diverted primarily to northern and eastern Irish ports. The populations of the northern counties responded with alacrity to the opportunities of movement and were greatly overrepresented among Irish arrivals in Quebec and Saint John. Trade and the tradition of emigration bonded distinctive regions on either side of the Atlantic.

In keeping with the emigration tradition of Ireland, the Protestant communities first displayed greatest willingness to seek their fortunes abroad: Catholics were initially more rooted, a function of heritage and generally lower socio-economic status. But even from the outset the sons of the better-endowed Catholic farmers of southeastern Ireland and the Catholic artisans and labourers recruited specifically for the fisheries participated in the outflow, and by the 1830s the disparity in the behavioural pattern of both religious groups had been much reduced. By 1845 emigration had acquired an all-Ireland dimension.

Nonetheless the early filters of religion and socio-economic status that operated among migrants served to consolidate among the Irish in the British colonies an identity different from that established by their US counterparts later in the century. At mid-century more than half the Canadian Irish were Protestant, although Ireland at the time was only about 25 per cent Protestant. Geographical selectivity was also apparent. Ulster, the adjoining border counties, in Leinster and Connaught, and Cork accounted for the bulk of Canadian Irish. The source regions of American Irish were more clearly located in the midlands and western counties of Ireland. Catholics rather than Protestants were also predominant in the American republic.

Apart from its impact on the identity of the emerging Irish community in Canada, the geographical regionalism in the early migrations also emphasized the complexities of the emigration process itself. Shipping links, mercantile activity, and, above all, prior emigration all served to channel emigration along distinctive regional lines. Information flows across the Atlantic and their corollary, family migrations, determined the geographical impact of emigration in Ireland, clearly reflecting the premeditative dimension of the exodus. The emigrants were not involved in a lemming-like abandonment of their native country. Their decisions were arrived at after careful consideration of economic prospects and logistical possibilities, and given the conditions of the time the emigrants possessed an impressive amount of information about their chosen destinations. Through private letters and the public press the crude outlines of a transatlantic geography were promoted among communities only too willing to respond to its lures. Having responded, the emigrant found himself or herself in an environment that was at once different yet redolent with familiar elements. Neighbours and kin, familiar institutions such as churches and lodges, and above all the seasonal rhythm of agriculture were consolations in a pioneering experience that implied personal and social dislocations of great magnitude.

The main thrust of the present volume has been to explore the regional character of Irish emigration and settlement in Canada and to shed, in particular, some light on the nature of the processes involved. Represented in these were the interests of merchants, shipowners, governments, land companies, emigration agents, landlords, and individual emigrants, and by their very nature the precise functionings of the various parties are difficult to unravel and not susceptible to easy typecasting. The Irish emigration and settlement experience in Canada had identifiable eighteenth-century origins, but it was concentrated in the four decades following the Napeolonic Wars. It included the Famine, but clearly it was not a Famine event. Notwithstanding the poignant silent testimony of the commemorative Celtic cross on Grosse Isle, only a minority of the immigrants experienced the horrors of that pestilential quarantine station: 'In this secluded spot lie the mortal remains of 5,294 persons who, fleeing from pestilence and famine in Ireland in the year 1847, found in America but a grave.'

Subsequent generations of writers and scholars have extrapolated the significance of Grosse Isle to characterize the whole of the Irish experience in Canada. The reality was otherwise. The majority of the Irish who settled in Canada lacked such epic origins: theirs was, more commonly, an experience of a voyage of hardship and discomfort undertaken willingly and in expectation of social and economic betterment. It was for most a voluntary migration, undertaken as part of a chain-migration process, and the participants, although not rich, were not the most destitute elements of Irish society. Most of the earliest arrivals were sons of small farmers and tradesmen, but during the 1830s and 1840s, as the regional limits and social breadth of the emigration field widened in response to intensifying crises in Ireland and declining costs of passage, there was a perceptible increase in the number of poor. However, at all times the emigration included a numerically small but highly significant group of gentry, administrators, politicians, surveyors, barristers, doctors, clergymen, and other professionals. In summary, the emigrants contained representative fragments of all classes in Irish society, but the group most commonly involved was the respectable but financially constrained small farming class.

When the religious composition of the group is considered, the complexity of the Irish emigration experience is further at variance with the simple stereotypes. Among the arrivals, Irishness was not synonymous with Catholicism. Slightly more than half of all the Irish settlers were Protestant, and among them Anglicans rather than Presbyterians predominated. The Protestant element was overrepresented in proportion to its relative demographic position in Ireland. What had been a religious minority in Ireland was transformed into a Protestant Irish majority in much of New Brunswick and especially in Ontario, where only one-third of the Irish group was Catholic. In contrast, Newfoundland's Irish population was overwhelmingly Catholic, and the Catholic group was well represented in the Miramichi Valley of New Brunswick, in Quebec, and in the emerging urban centres of British North America. By virtue of their religious composition, and mitigated by the regionalism of Irish identities, the Canadian Irish are distinguished from their counterparts in the United States.

The creation of an Irish-Canadian stereotype has been compounded by the invocation of an association between Irishness and urbanism. A small fraction of the Canadian Irish could be classified as urban dwellers in the mid-nineteenth century; the vast majority obtained a living from farming, lumbering, fishing, and labouring in rural areas. Given the early arrival of the Irish and the slow development of the Canadian urban system, the rural character of the immigration was to be expected. Only a minority could be accommodated in a Slabtown, Corktown, or Cabbagetown, the visible ghettos of cities ranging from Halifax to Hamilton. The inhabitants of those quarters were only part of a much more socially diverse immigration, and even among the urban Irish there were many whose contact with the immigrant slums was but ephemeral. For most, the farm lots of Ontario and the Eastern Townships of Quebec, the woodland clearings of New Brunswick, and the fishing villages of Newfoundland and Nova Scotia offered a non-urban alternative. Their settlement experience varied also according to the physical environment of their chosen region of settlement and according to the economic and ethnic contexts into which newcomers were inserted. Ultimately the settlement experience was highly personal.

The Canadian Irish are distinguished from their American counterparts by religious composition, settlement experience, and especially the temporal dimension of their migrations. Predominantly pre-Famine in origin, Canadian Irish lacked the cultural continuity that successive waves of new immigrants gave to American Irish communities. Attenuation of mass movement from Ireland to British North America in the 1850s implied curtailment of contact with the homeland, and that in turn affected the process of immigrants becoming Canadians. Moreover, that process in Canada occurred in an Irish emigrant community rent by regionalism and by varying settlement experiences.

There was no single ideal type of the Irish in the country. Two different regional situations – the one emigrants found and the one they left – combined to produce a complex and varied mixture in Canada, where no one Irish community developed just like another. The economic and cultural geography of Ireland affected the character of the migration. In Canada variations in natural resources, accessibility, opportunity for social mobility, and intermixing with other ethnic groups created different contexts in which the Irish settled. Though emigrants had a common strand in the mass transatlantic migrations that linked Ireland with North America, from the time of arrival they began to create diverse settlements in Canada. The accumulated effect of factors promoting diversity could be striking, even after a few generations. There is no doubt a marked contrast between an outport Newfoundlander descended from Waterford stock and a Torontonian of similar Irish roots but modified by generations of Canadian urban living. From the time of arrival an obvious difference would have existed between a Catholic farmer from Cork settling in New Brunswick and a Protestant linen-weaver from Armagh resettled in the Eastern Townships of Quebec. In the creation of Irish-Canadian diversity, the geography of places on both sides of the Atlantic mattered.

Notes

CHAPTER 1: Introduction

1 Ontario, 33rd Legislature, 3rd Session, 1987. Bill 88. An Act to Proclaim 1995 as the 150th Anniversary of the Arrival of Irish Immigrants in Canada. The authors wish to thank Derek Nelson for bringing this bill to their attention.

2 Joe Serge, *Toronto Star*, 16 March 1988

3 Wilson Benson, *Life and Adventures of Wilson Benson Written by Himself* (Toronto 1876), 17–18

4 Nicholas Flood Davin, *The Irishman in Canada* (Toronto 1877)

5 Kenneth Duncan, 'Irish Famine Immigration and the Social Structure of Canada West,' *Canadian Review of Sociology and Anthropology*, 1965, 19–40

6 John J. Mannion, *Irish Settlements in Eastern Canada: A Study of Cultural Transfer and Adaptation* (Toronto 1974)

7 William Baker, *Timothy Warren Anglin – Irish Catholic Canadian* (Toronto 1980)

8 Cecil J. Houston and William J. Smyth, *The Sash Canada Wore: A Historical Geography of the Orange Order in Canada* (Toronto 1980)

9 Donald Harman Akenson, *The Irish in Ontario: A Study in Rural History* (Toronto 1984)

10 Bruce S. Elliott, *Irish Migrants in the Canadas: A New Approach* (Kingston 1988)

11 Terence Punch, *Irish Halifax: The Immigrant Generation* (Halifax 1981); *Some Sons of Erin in Nova Scotia* (Halifax 1980)

12 Cyril Byrne, *Gentlemen, Bishops and Faction Fighters: The Letters of Bishops O'Donel, Lambert, Scallan and Other Irish Missionaries* (St John's 1984)

13 Brendan O'Grady, 'The Monaghan Settlers,' *Abgeweit Review*, 4, 1 (Spring 1983), 51–81

14 Marianna O'Gallagher, *St. Patrick's Quebec, 1824–1834* (Quebec 1981) and *Grosse Isle: Gateway to Canada, 1832–1937* (Quebec 1984)

15 Murray W. Nicholson, 'Ecclesiastical Metropolitanism and the Evolution of the Catholic Archdiocese of Toronto,' *Histoire sociale/Social History*, 15, no. 29 (1982), 129–56

16 Peter Toner, 'Ethnicity and Regionalism in the Maritimes,' *Social Science Monograph Series* (Saint John), 1985, 1–18; 'The Origins of the New Brunswick Irish, 1851,' *Journal of Canadian Studies*, 23, no. 1 & 2 (Spring/ Summer 1988), 104–19. See also his edited collection, *Historical Essays on the Irish in New Brunswick: New Ireland Remembered* (Fredericton 1988).

17 Robert O'Driscoll and Lorna Reynolds (eds), *The Untold Story: The Irish in Canada* (Toronto 1988)

18 William Spray, 'Reception of the Irish in New Brunswick,' in Cyril J. Byrne and Margaret Harry (eds), *Talamh An Eisc* (Halifax 1986), 228–49

19 Deirdre M. Mageean, 'Nineteenth-Century Irish Emigration: A Case Study Using Passenger Lists,' in P.J. Drudy, *Irish Studies 4. The Irish in America: Emigration, Assimilation, and Impact* (Cambridge 1985), 39–61

20 John Mannion, 'Patrick Morris and Newfoundland Irish Immigration,' in Byrne and Harry, *Talamh An Eisc*, 180–202, and 'The Maritime Trade of Waterford in the Eighteenth Century,' in William J. Smyth and Kevin Whelan (eds), *Common Ground: Essays on the Historical Geography of Ireland Presented to T. Jones Hughes* (Cork 1988), 208–33

CHAPTER 2: Emigrant Origins

1 T.W. Acheson, *Saint John* (Toronto 1985), 3

2 Kirby Miller notes that in the years 1700–76, 250,000–400,000 emigrants left Ireland for the North American colonies. See Kirby Miller, *Emigrants and Exiles; Ireland and the Irish Exodus to North America* (New York 1985), 137. Professor Maldwyn Jones claims that in the last quarter of the eighteenth century upward of 5,000 people departed from Ireland annually. Maldwyn Jones, 'Ulster Emigration, 1783–1815,' in E.R.R. Green (ed), *Essays in Scotch Irish History* (Belfast 1969), 50

3 The map is based on data provided in R.J. Dickson, *Ulster Emigration to Colonial America, 1718–1775* (Belfast 1966); and Audrey Lockhart, 'Some

Aspects of Emigration from Ireland to the North American Colonies,'
MLitt thesis, Trinity College, Dublin, 1971.

4 J.G. Leyburn, *The Scotch-Irish: A Social History* (Chapel Hill, NC, 1962)

5 David Noel Doyle, *Ireland, Irishmen and Revolutionary America, 1760–1820*
(Dublin 1981), 67

6 Ibid

7 John Mannion, 'The Maritime Trade of Waterford in the Eighteenth
Century,' in William J. Smyth and Kevin Whelan (eds), *Common Ground:
Essays on the Historical Geography of Ireland Presented to T. Jones Hughes* (Cork
1988), 218

8 J.J. Mannion (ed), *The Peopling of Newfoundland* (St John's 1977), 8

9 Mannion, 'Maritime Trade,' 216

10 J.J. Mannion, 'The Irish Migrations to Newfoundland,' *Newfoundland
Historical Society Lecture*, 1973, 1–12

11 Contemporary observors noted a trend of through-migration of Irish
from Newfoundland to Nova Scotia. In a public lecture delivered at St
Patrick's College, Maynooth, October 1984, Cyril Byrne typed these
people as 'two-boaters.'

12 *Belfast Newsletter*, 21 April 1761

13 *Dictionary of Canadian Biography*, v, 553–7

14 Data for the 1766 religious denominations were kindly provided by Dr
W.H. Crawford, Ulster Folk and Transport Museum. The originals of
those data are held in the Archives of the Church of Ireland, Dublin.

15 Ibid

16 Quoted in W.O. Raymond, 'Colonel Alexander McNutt and the Pre-
Loyalist Settlements of Nova Scotia,' *Transactions of the Royal Society of
Canada*, Section II, 1911, 80.

17 T.W. Freeman, *Pre-Famine Ireland* (Manchester 1956)

18 Ibid. Chapter 2 contains a discussion of seasonal migration to England in
the pre-Famine period.

19 The data for the period 1825–45 are to be found in William Forbes Adams,
Ireland and Irish Emigration to the New World from 1815 to the Famine (New
Haven 1932). The data for subsequent periods are to be found in *Reports
of the Commission on Emigration and Other Population Problems, 1848–54*
(Dublin 1955).

20 Cormac O'Grada, 'Some Aspects of Nineteenth Century Emigration,' in
L.M. Cullen and T.C. Smout (eds), *Comparative Aspects of Scottish and Irish
Economic and Social History* (Edinburgh 1976), 73

21 Letter of James Reford in Massachusetts to his mother in County Antrim,
Ireland, 9 June 1833, Public Records Office of Northern Ireland (PRONI)

22 Minutes of evidence of A.C. Buchanan in *Report from the Select Committee on Emigration from the United Kingdom with Minutes of Evidence, Appendix and Index, 1826* (404), 1, 170–1

23 Ibid, 170. Buchanan claimed that while a majority of arrivals remained in the Canadas, 'not more than half' of New Brunswick arrivals settled in the province.

24 For a discussion of the chronic out-migration from the Maritimes region, see A. Brookes, 'Outmigration from the Maritime Provinces, 1860–1900,' *Acadiensis*, 1976, 26–55.

25 Minutes of evidence of M.H. Perley in *Report from the Select Committee of the House of Lords on Colonization from Ireland*, 1847 (737) (737-II), VI, 18

26 For the Census of New Brunswick, 1851, residents were asked to state the date they arrived in the colony. Peter Toner of the University of New Brunswick has collated the information as part of his study of the Irish in that province. He has shared this result with us.

27 *Colonial Land and Emigration Commissioner General Report with Appendix, 1847–48* [961], XXVI, 17

28 Quoted in Marianna O'Gallagher, *St. Patrick's Quebec, 1824–1834* (Quebec 1981), 30

29 The figure of 160,000 is an approximation based on data from Census reports.

30 Based on data presented in Adams, *Ireland and Irish Emigration*

31 Determined from a comparison of the Census of the Canadas, 1851, with the Census of Upper Canada 1842 and the Census of Lower Canada, 1844

32 The data sources are given in note 19 above.

33 Report of the Toronto Board of Health, 2 February 1848, cited in G. Tucker, *The Canadian Commercial Revolution, 1845–1851* (Toronto 1936), 120

34 *Colonial Land and Emigration Commissioners General Report with Appendix, 1847–48* [961], XXVI, 16

35 Report of Emigration Commissioners, 1851, quoted in *Census of Ireland, General Report* part VI, Vol. XXXI, Sess 1856

36 Letter of John S. Cummins, Sherbrooke, to Richard Heneker, Sherbrooke, October 2, 1860, Public (now National) Archives of Canada (PAC) MG 24 154 Vol. 3, p. 480

37 T.R. Weir, 'The People,' in J. Warkentin (ed), *Canada: A Geographical Interpretation* (Toronto 1968), 137–77

38 Adams, *Ireland and Irish Emigration*, 1, 158

39 S.H. Cousens, 'The Regional Variation in Emigration from Ireland between 1821 and 1841,' *Transactions of the Institute of British Geographers*, 1965, 15–30

40 D. Fitzpatrick, 'Irish Emigration in the Later Nineteenth Century,' *Irish Historical Studies*, 1980, 131

41 Data from Quebec Emigrant Agents Reports, 1833–4 (PAC Sundries)

42 *Population of Ireland*, 1841 Census Report, xxviii

43 Minutes of evidence of A.C. Buchanan in *Report of the Select Committee on Emigration from the United Kingdom with Minutes of Evidence and Index, 1826* (404), IV, 170

44 The virtual absence of English emigrants among the arrivals at Saint John after 1820 is clear in the evidence from extant passenger lists, almshouse and work-house records, the 1851 Census manuscripts, and the newspaper accounts of ship landings.

45 Montreal Emigrant Society, Passage Book for 1832, PAC RG 7 G18 Vol. 46

46 The data were culled from annual emigration reports. Sligo has been included as an Ulster port because the natural hinterland of that north Connaught centre extended far into the Ulster counties of Fermanagh, Donegal, and Cavan.

47 A.B. Hawke, cited in Marianna O'Gallagher, *Grosse Isle: Gateway to Canada, 1832–1937* (Quebec 1984), 55

48 Department of Agriculture, Ireland, *Emigration Statistics*, published annually from 1876

49 Ibid

CHAPTER 3: The Emigrants

1 The Tithe Applotment records for County Armagh (Public Records Office of Northern Ireland – PRONI) in 1830 reveal that 70 per cent of farms in the county were less than ten acres in size.

2 A fragment of the manuscript record of the 1821 census exists for Kilmore Parish; PRONI.

3 Brenda Collins, 'Proto-industrialization and Pre-Famine Emigration,' *Social History*, 1982, 127–46

4 Graeme Wynn, *Timber Colony* (Toronto 1981), 79

5 The Ulster Custom was a leaseholding convention whereby an outgoing tenant could sell the 'goodwill' or his interest in the lease of a farm to an incoming tenant. In 1845 sums of £20 per acre were raised by this exercise of tenant rights. See *Digest of Evidence Taken before Her Majesty's Commissioners of Enquiry into ... the Occupation of Land in Ireland* (Dublin 1847), 435.

6 The will of Alexander Robb, cited in chapter 10 of this volume, is a fine example of a parent's legacy encouraging emigration.

7 See Wendy Cameron's 'Peter Robinson's Settlers in Peterborough,' in

Robert O'Driscoll and Lorna Reynolds (eds), *The Untold Story: The Irish in Canada*, 1 (Toronto 1987), 343–53.

8 See Oliver Macdonagh, 'Irish emigration to the United States of America and the British Colonies during the Famine,' in R.D. Edwards and T.D. Williams (eds), *The Great Famine* (Dublin 1956), 332–40.

9 Parliamentary evidence cited in William Forbes Adams, *Ireland and Irish Emigration to the New World from 1815 to the Famine* (New Haven 1932), 181

10 By the end of 1820, Buchanan had sent about 7,000 people to Upper Canada; H.J.M. Johnston, *British Emigration Policy 1815–1830* (London 1972), 24. About half of these have been assumed to be Irish, given the pattern shown in the extant records of Buchanan's emigrants in 1817 and given the majority position of the Irish among emigrants from the British Isles at the time.

11 'Passes Signed by British Consul, New York, for Emigrants from Great Britain, March 1817,' PAC, RG 5 A1, Vol. 37, 17227–578

12 James A.W.P. Buchanan, *The Buchanan Book* (Montreal 1911), 216

13 Buchanan's Orange connection is revealed by Hereward Senior in 'The Genesis of Canadian Orangeism,' *Ontario History*, 60 (1968), 14.

14 J.A. Edmison, *Through the Years in Douro, 1822–1867* (Peterborough, Ont. 1967), 11

15 Cameron, 'Robinson's Settlers'

16 See L.F. Gates, *Land Policies in Upper Canada* (Toronto 1968), 97.

17 The controversy over the best emigration strategy is reflected in the parliamentary debates, excerpts of which are to be found in P. Burroughs, *British Attitudes towards Canada 1822–1849* (Toronto 1971). See also Johnston, *British Emigration Policy*.

18 Edward Allen Talbot, *Five Years Residence in the Canadas*, 2 vols. (London 1824). This group migration is the subject of detailed analysis by Bruce Elliott in *Irish Migrants in the Canadas* (Kingston 1988).

19 Evidence of A.C. Buchanan given before the *Select Committee on Emigration from the United Kingdom, 1827* (237), 75

20 Report of A.C. Buchanan in *Emigration Commissioners Reports to the Secretary of State for the Colonial Department 1831–32* (724), XXXII, 20

21 Despite the appearance of poverty frequently commented upon by domestic observers and foreign visitors in Ireland, there was a considerable degree of modest wealth in the country in the early nineteenth century. A good account of the contemporary Irish economy is to be found in L. Cullen, *The Emergence of Modern Ireland 1600–1900* (London 1981).

22 Letter of William Hutton in Belleville, Upper Canada, to his wife in Ireland, 8 June 1834, presented in Gerald E. Boyce, *Hutton of Hastings*

(Belleville, Ont., 1972), 32

23 *Dictionary of Canadian Biography*, IX, 404

24 Boyce, *Hutton of Hastings*, 3

25 *Golden Jubilee, 1869–1919, a Book to Commemorate the Fiftieth Anniversary of the T. Eaton Co. Limited* (Toronto 1919), 73

26 St Patrick's College, Maynooth, was established as the Irish national seminary in 1795. All Hallows College, Drumcondra, was founded almost half a century later (1842), to ordain priests for foreign missionary service.

27 Kevin Whelan, 'County Wexford Priests in Newfoundland,' *Journal of the Wexford Historical Society*, 1985, 55–68

28 Wilson Benson, *Life and Adventures of Wilson Benson* (Toronto 1876)

29 Irish seasonal migration to Scotland is described in J. Handley, *The Irish in Modern Scotland* (Cork 1974), and T.W. Freeman, *Pre-Famine Ireland* (Manchester 1956).

30 See R. Bleasdale, 'Class Conflict on the Canals of Upper Canada in the 1840's,' Paper submitted to the Annual Meeting of the Canadian Historical Association, London, Ontario, 1978, 30 pp typescript.

31 Benson, *Life and Adventures*, 27–8

32 Passenger Lists, Saint John, 1833–4, Provincial Archives of New Brunswick (PANB)

33 Montreal Emigrant Society, Passage Book for 1832, PAC

34 Ordnance Survey of Ireland, Memoirs, County Antrim, Royal Irish Academy, Dublin

35 Return of passages furnished at the public expense to destitute emigrants at Prescott, from the opening of the navigation to 31st August, 1835, inclusive, PAC, Upper Canada Sundries, C-6887

36 William Hutton, *Canada, a Brief Outline of Her Geographical Position, Production, Climate, Capabilities, Educational and Municipal Institutions* (Toronto 1857), 5

37 Ontario, Commissioner of Agriculture and Public Works, *Annual Report*, 1870, iv

38 Ibid, vii

39 Passenger Lists, Saint John, 1833–4, PANB

40 See Elliott, *Irish Migrants*.

41 Deirdre M. Mageean, 'Nineteenth Century Irish Emigration: A Case Study Using Passenger Lists,' in P.J. Drudy, *Irish Studies 4. The Irish in America: Emigration, Assimilation, and Impact* (Cambridge 1985), 59

42 Abstracts of Emigration Reports, New Brunswick, December 30, 1840, PANB M7890

43 Montreal Emigrant Society, Passage Book for 1832, PAC

44 The problems of applying American models to the study of the Ontario Irish are well debated by D. Akenson, *The Irish in Ontario* (Toronto 1984).

45 Terence Punch, *Irish Halifax: The Immigrant Generation* (Halifax 1981)

46 Ibid

47 The authors wish to thank Peter Toner for sharing the raw data on which he based 'The Origins of the New Brunswick Irish, 1851,' *Journal of Canadian Studies*, 23, nos. 1 & 2 (Spring/Summer 1988), 104–19.

48 Brian Clarke, 'Piety, Nationalism and Fraternity: The Rise of Irish Catholic Voluntary Associations in Toronto, 1850–1895,' PhD thesis, University of Chicago, 1986, 28

49 W.E. Vaughan and A.J. Fitzpatrick (eds), *Irish Historical, Statistics, Population, 1821–1871* (Dublin 1978), 49

50 A.C. Buchanan, Minutes of evidence given in *Report from the Select Committee on Emigration from the United Kingdom with Minutes of Evidence, Appendix and Index, 1826* (404), IV, 175

51 Ibid, 176

52 Letter of James Humphrey, Highland Creek, Ontario, to his parents in County Londonderry, Ireland, 24 September 1824, PRONI

53 The varying proportion of Catholics among Famine immigrants is discussed by Kenneth Duncan, 'Irish Famine Immigration and the Social Structure of Canada West,' *Canadian Review of Sociology and Anthropology*, 1965, 19–40. See also Akenson, *The Irish in Ontario*, 346–7.

54 Lynch Papers, Archives of the Catholic Archdiocese of Toronto (ACAT), LAE07.01 1864.

55 Ibid

56 Ibid, LAE07.03 1864

57 Ibid, LAE07.02 1864

58 Ibid, LAE07.07 1873

59 Ibid, LAE02.38 1881

60 Ibid, LAE07.12 1881

61 Ibid, LAE07.13 1881

62 Ibid, LAE07.44 1882

63 Letter from Christopher J. Shiel, Ballinasloe, Ireland, to John O'Donohoe, Toronto, March 10, 1873, PAC MG 27 I E12 Item 17

CHAPTER 4: The Emigration Process

1 John Mannion, 'The Maritime Trade of Waterford in the Eighteenth Century,' in William J. Smyth and Kevin Whelan (eds), *Common Ground: Essays on the Historical Geography of Ireland Presented to T. Jones Hughes* (Cork 1988), 208–33

2 Rev. G. Vaughan Sampson, *Statistical Survey of the County of Londonderry, with Observations on the Means of Improvement: Drawn up for the Consideration, and under the Direction of the Dublin Society* (Dublin 1802) 367

3 Sholto Cooke, *The Maiden City and the Western Ocean* (Dublin [1968]), 48

4 Ibid, 49

5 The term *Dear Summer* comes from the folklore of Inishowen, County Donegal, as recounted marvellously by Charles McGlinchey, *The Last of the Name* (Belfast 1986), 77.

6 Cooke, *The Maiden City*, contains information on transatlantic fares. See also Terry Coleman, *Passage to America* (London 1972), 101–46.

7 Cooke, *The Maiden City*, 117

8 Ibid

9 H.J.M. Johnston, *British Emigration Policy 1815–1830* (London 1872), 25

10 Ibid, 51

11 Ibid, 62

12 Ibid

13 A summary of the log of the *President* from which this graph was created is presented in Cooke, *The Maiden City*, 85–7.

14 Papers of J. and J. Cooke, Shipping Agents, Londonderry, Passenger Books, 1847–71, PRONI

15 Joseph Carrothers, 14 July 1847. Letters used in the text and included in chapters 8, 9, and 10 will be referenced simply by writer's name and date of post.

16 Papers of J. and J. Cooke, Shipping Agents, Londonderry, Letterbook, 1839, PRONI

17 For a discussion of the role of the Canada Co. in land colonization see James M. Cameron, 'The Canada Company and Land Settlement as Resource Development in the Guelph Block,' in J.D. Wood (ed), *Landscape and Settlement in Nineteenth Century Ontario* (Toronto 1975), 141–59.

18 Cooke, *The Maiden City*, 50

19 An advertisement for Buchanan's ship, the *Halifax Packet*, indicates that L. Gault was an agent for the Robinson and Buchanan shipping company; *Londonderry Journal*, 4 August 1818.

20 James D. Stephens, 'Diary and Autobiography,' 1890, ms, Archives of Ontario (AO)

21 *Londonderry Journal*, 19 August 1817; Magee University College Library, Derry

22 *A Cyclopedia of Canadian Biography* (Toronto 1886), 464

23 Letter of James Buchanan, New York, to Lord Gosford, Quebec, January 6, 1838, PRONI, D2259/7/1

24 In 1826 A.C. Buchanan described his Canadian activities: 'I have erected steam saw-mills for cutting up logs into planks, in conjunction with my

brother William, and I am interested in shipping, and we are erecting grist and flour mills'; *Minutes of Evidence Given before the Select Committee on Emigration from the United Kingdom*, 1826 (404), IV, 171.

25 See *Dictionary of Canadian Biography*, IX, 97.

26 Letter of James Buchanan, New York, to Lord Gosford, Quebec, June 1, 1838, PRONI, D2259/7/6

27 Letter of Mary Duggan, Kingston, Upper Canada, to her sister in Dungiven, Ireland, 1847, PRONI

28 Letter of James Humphrey, Highland Creek, Ontario, to his parents in County Londonderry, Ireland, September 24, 1824, PRONI

29 *Enquiry into the State of Ireland*, 1825

30 Bruce S. Elliott, *Irish Emigrants in the Canadas: A New Approach* (Kingston 1988)

31 Unsorted Kirkpatrick family correspondence, PRONI, D1424/11-

32 Letter of Mrs. A.S. Woodburn, Ottawa, to her cousin in Belfast, November 6, 1897, PRONI

33 A.C. Buchanan, *Minutes of Evidence Given before the Select Committee on Emigration from the United Kingdom*, 1827 (237), 74

34 Letter of Sampson Brady, Montreal, to a friend, Miss Fanny Reford, Graystone, County Antrim, Ireland, September 17, 1832, PRONI

35 Letter of Captain Mitchell, Quebec, to his wife in Ireland, PRONI

36 Letterbook of J. and J. Cooke, 1837, PRONI

37 Canada Company Remittance Advice Book, January 1843–December 1846, AO

38 Nathaniel Carrothers, December 25, 1839

39 Thomas Moore's ballad was written in 1804, and Gerald Craig noted that most of the 'tourists' and 'travellers' to the Canadas in the first half of the nineteenth century were aware of it; Gerald M. Craig, *Early Travellers in the Canadas, 1791–1867* (Toronto 1955) xxvii.

40 The authors wish to thank Professor Peter Toner for providing this estimate based on data from the manuscripts of the 1851 Census of New Brunswick.

41 H. Belden & Co., *Illustrated Atlas of the Eastern Townships and South Western Quebec*, 1881, 13

42 Ibid

43 Ibid

44 A. Hoekstra and W. Ross, 'The Craig and Gosford Roads,' *Canadian Geographical Journal* (August 1969), 55

45 Gerald Tulchinsky, *The River Barons: Montreal Businessmen and the Growth of Industry and Transportation, 1837–1853* (Toronto 1977), 129

351 Notes to pages 99–108

46 Cited in W.S. Shepperson, *British Emigration to North America* (Oxford 1957), 188 note 36

47 See Thomas E. Appelton, *Ravenscrag: The Allan Royal Mail Line* (Toronto 1974).

48 Letter of John S. Cummins, Bury, to R.W. Heneker, Sherbrooke, 15 August 1859, PAC MG 24, 154, Vol. 3, 416

49 Letter of John S. Cummins, London, to A.H. Brown, London, 20 June, 1860, PAC MG 24 154, Vol. 3, 476

50 Circular printed on behalf of John S. Cummins, Londonderry, 27 January, 1860, PAC MG 24 154, Vol. 3, 440

51 Ibid

52 Ontario, Commissioner of Agriculture and Public Works, *Annual Report*, 1869, iv

53 Ibid, 1875, iv

54 For a discussion of the role of pamphlets in the emigration process see Dympna McLaughlin, 'Information Flows and Irish Emigration: The Image of America in Ireland 1820–1870,' MA thesis, National University of Ireland, Maynooth, 1983.

55 John Towgood, Journal of Tour to Ireland 17th March–23rd May, 1820, 53, PRONI MIC9B/17

56 Letter of William Hutton in Quebec to John McCrea in Ireland, October 20, 1854, PRONI

57 William Hutton, 'Letters on the Prospects of Agricultural Settlers in Upper Canada,' *British Agricultural Magazine*, 1835, 102–17

58 *Canada, a Brief Outline of Her Geographical Position, Production, Climate, Capabilities, Educational and Municipal Institutions* (Toronto 1857)

59 Catherine Parr Traill, *The Female Emigrant's Guide* (Toronto 1854)

60 Charles Foy, *Dominion of Canada: Emigration to the Province of Ontario* (Belfast 1873) (National Library of Ireland, Dublin)

61 See G.R.C. Keep, 'A Canadian Emigration Commissioner in Northern Ireland,' *Canadian Historical Review*, 34 no. 2 (June 1953), 152, 154.

62 Emigrant's letter home quoted in Foy, *Dominion of Canada*, 63

63 Ibid, 70

64 Ibid, 70–1

65 Ibid, 63

66 Ibid, 67

67 In *Passage to America*, Coleman discusses the application of regulations set out in the Passenger Acts.

68 Letter of William Campbell, Peterborough, Upper Canada, to his father in Templepatrick, County Antrim, Ireland, October 28, 1839, PRONI

69 Ibid

70 Wilson Benson, *Life and Adventures of Wilson Benson* (Toronto 1876), 20

71 Joseph Carrothers, July 14, 1847

72 Diary of an Irish Immigrant (Mrs Forster), PAC MG 55/27 No. 131

73 Letter of Lord Dufferin, Rivière-du-Loup, Quebec, to the Duchess of Argyle, August 3, 1872, PRONI

74 Letterbook of William McCorkell, 1828, PRONI

75 Letterbook of J. and J. Cooke, 1837, PRONI

76 Benson, *Life and Adventures*, 17

77 Letter of Mary Duggan, Kingston, Upper Canada, to her sister in Dungiven, Ireland, 1847, PRONI

78 John Towgood, Journal of Tour to Ireland 17th March–23rd May, 1820, 53, PRONI MIC9B/17

79 Joseph Carrothers, July 14, 1847

80 Letter of Edmund Letson, Haldimand, Ontario, to his parents in Glenavy, County Antrim, November 25, 1863, PRONI

81 A discussion of mortality rates is to be found in Coleman, *Passage to America*, chapter 9.

82 Irish University Reprints, *Colonial Land and Emigration Commissioners General Report with Appendix 1847–48* (961), XXVI, 15; *Papers Relative to Emigration to the British North American Provinces 1847–48* (932), XLVII, 385

83 Ibid

84 Letter of John and Eliza Anderson, Quebec City, to his family in Coleraine, County Londonderry, July 1, 1832, PRONI

85 Jane White, June 29, 1849

86 Letter of William Campbell, Peterborough, Upper Canada, to his father in Templepatrick, County Antrim, Ireland, October 28, 1839, PRONI

87 Letter of James Humphrey, Highland Creek, Upper Canada, to his parents and sisters, Moneymore, County Londonderry, September 24, 1824, PRONI

88 Jane White, June 29, 1849

89 Benson, *Life and Adventures*, 20

90 Letter of Lord Dufferin, Rivière-du-Loup, Quebec, to the Duchess of Argyle, August 3, 1872, PRONI

91 Letter of Sampson Brady, Montreal, to a friend, Miss Fanny Reford, Graystone, County Antrim, September 17, 1832, PRONI

92 Joseph Carrothers, October 18, 1847

93 Ibid

94 Letter of William Hutton, Quebec, to his brother-in-law John McCrea, Leck, Strabane, County Tyrone, September 17, 1853, PRONI

95 Ontario, Immigration, *Annual Report*, 1873, 43

96 Ibid, 1874, 15

CHAPTER 5: Settling In

1 Joseph Carrothers, October 18, 1847
2 Wilson Benson, *Life and Adventures of Wilson Benson* (Toronto 1876), 43
3 William Hutton, 'Letters on the Prospects of Agricultural Settlers in Upper Canada,' *British Agricultural Magazine*, 1835, 105–6
4 Cited in Harold W. Goodwin, 'The Humphreys and Richardsons of Scarborough,' *Scarborough Historical Notes and Comments*, 9 no. 1 (February 1985), 13
5 Ibid
6 Diary of Benjamin Crawford, 1800, AO
7 Benson, *Life and Adventures*, 40
8 Alexander Robb, May 10, 1868
9 Ibid
10 Robb mentions his role of proxy in his letter of 10 May 1868. That he was working for Clapperton is noted in Nicola Valley Archives Association, *Newsletter*, 1 no. 1 (December 1977), 7.
11 Hutton, 'Letters,' 116
12 Ibid
13 Nathaniel Carrothers, December 5, 1853
14 Nathaniel Carrothers, December 25, 1839, reported a winter wage for carpenters of five shillings per day. The same wage has been noted for New Brunswick by Wynn, *Timber Colony* (Toronto 1981), 80.
15 Wynn, *Timber Colony*, 79–82
16 *Papers Relative to Emigrations to the British North American Provinces, 1847–48* (50), XLVII, 69–70
17 Alexander Robb, December 14, 1868
18 Ibid
19 Joseph Carrothers, October 18, 1847
20 Joseph Carrothers, October 23, 1848
21 Nathaniel Carrothers, December 5, 1853
22 Gerald Boyce, *Hutton of Hastings* (Belleville, Ont., 1972), 175
23 Benson, *Life and Adventures* 40
24 Hutton, 'Letters,' 103–4
25 Ibid
26 Ibid
27 This description of the land was expressed to the authors by a Belleville resident.
28 Hutton, 'Letters,' 113

29 Ibid, 111
30 Benson, *Life and Adventures*, 38
31 Hutton, 'Letters,' 111
32 Ibid, 112
33 Ibid, 111
34 Benson, *Life and Adventures*, 42
35 Ibid, 46
36 Jane White, July 19, 1859
37 Wilson Benson managed to clear 33 acres in his first decade.
38 Hutton, 'Letters,' 112
39 Wynn, *Timber Colony*, 83
40 Benson, *Life and Adventures*, 46
41 Ibid
42 Alexander Robb, February 24, 1872
43 Nathaniel Carrothers, December 5, 1853
44 Letter of Ernest Cochrane, to Kitty Finlay, Holywood, County Down, Summer 1897
45 Ibid, December 8, 1897
46 Ibid, January 24, 1898
47 Hutton, 'Letters,' 103
48 Joseph Carrothers, February 19, 1852
49 Benson, *Life and Adventures*, 45
50 Alexander Robb, February 24, 1872
51 Peter Carr, *The Most Unpretending of Places: A History of Dundonald, County Down* (Belfast 1987), 144
52 Nathaniel Carrothers, December 5, 1853
53 Hutton, 'Letters,' 117
54 Benson, *Life and Adventures*, 48
55 Ibid, 44
56 Joseph Carrothers, February 19, 1852
57 Letter of Edward M'Cullom to Charles Foy, October 14, 1872, quoted in Foy, *Dominion of Canada*, 68
58 Hutton, 'Letters,' 116
59 Joseph Carrothers, November 26, 1856
60 Nathaniel Carrothers, March 22, 1867
61 Benson, *Life and Adventures*, 42
62 Census of Canada, 1871, manuscript for township of Artemesia, Ontario
63 Illustration taken from H. Belden and Co., *Illustrated Historical Atlas of the Counties of Hastings and Prince Edward, Ontario* (Toronto 1878), 65
64 Nathaniel Carrothers, December 5, 1853

65 Ibid
66 Ibid
67 Joseph Carrothers, October 23, 1848
68 Nathaniel Carrothers, December 25, 1839
69 Joseph Carrothers, October 23, 1848
70 Ibid
71 Benson, *Life and Adventures*, 40
72 Map taken from H. Belden and Co., *Illustrated Atlas of the County of Grey* (Toronto 1880), 24
73 Grand Orange Lodge of British America, Register of Warrants, Orange Archives, Toronto
74 Census of Canada, 1871 and 1881, manuscript for township of Artemesia, Ontario, AO
75 Land Records Index, entry for Wilson Benson, AO
76 Benson, *Life and Adventures*, 47–8
77 Letter of Richard Braithwaite, Cannington, Upper Canada, to his parents in Lisburn, County Antrim, October 1, 1849, PRONI
78 Nathaniel Carrothers, December 25, 1839
79 Nathaniel Carrothers, December 5, 1853
80 Benson, *Life and Adventures*, 37
81 Ibid, 47
82 Jane White, August 27, 1858
83 Letter of Lord Dufferin, Rivière-du-Loup, Quebec, to the Duchess of Argyle, August 3, 1872, PRONI
84 Letter of Mrs. A.S. Woodburn, Ottawa, to her cousin in Belfast, November 6, 1897, PRONI

CHAPTER 6: Social and Religious Life

1 The issue of transiency in nineteenth-century Canadian society is a central theme in David Gagan, *Hopeful Travellers: Families, Land, and Social Change in Mid-Victorian Peel County, Canada West* (Toronto 1981). See also Michael Katz, *The People of Hamilton, Canada West: Family and Class in a Mid-Nineteenth Century City* (Cambridge, Mass., 1975).
2 Katz, *The People of Hamilton*
3 Field investigation in the Markdale area, where Wilson pioneered
4 Wilson Benson, *Life and Adventures of Wilson Benson* (Toronto, 1876), 26
5 Ibid
6 See introduction to the Carrothers letters, below, chapter 9.
7 Nathaniel Carrothers, December 25, 1839

8 Nathaniel Carrothers, December 5, 1853
9 Joseph Carrothers, October 10, 1862
10 Nathaniel Carrothers, January 29, 1866
11 The garden at the family home at Farnaght was well known in the area for its variety of flowers and herbs.
12 Nathaniel Carrothers, December 5, 1853
13 Joseph Carrothers, October 10, 1862
14 Joseph Carrothers, March 8, 1870
15 Nicola Valley Archives Association, *Newsletter*, 1 no. 1 (December 1977), 6
16 Ibid
17 Ibid
18 Ibid, 7
19 Alexander Robb, May 10, 1868
20 Alexander Robb, December 14, 1868
21 The authors wish to thank Mrs Helen White of Westport, Ontario, for this information.
22 Francis Hincks, born in Cork, was a cousin of William Hutton and like Hutton a Unitarian. Hincks was founder of the Reform party, a political ally of another Corkman, Robert Baldwin, and served as premier of the Province of Canada from 1851 to 1854.
23 Alexander Robb, February 24, 1872
24 Letter of Mrs. A.S. Woodburn, Ottawa, to her cousin in Belfast, November 6, 1897, PRONI
25 Joseph Carrothers, October 23, 1848
26 Joseph Carrothers, June 15, 1855
27 Nathaniel Carrothers, March 22, 1867
28 Letter of Ellen Dunlop, Peterborough, Ontario, to Reverend George Kirkpatrick, Craigs, County Antrim, November 2, 1881, in unsorted Kirkpatrick letter collection, PRONI D1424/11/-
29 William Hutton, 'Letters on the Prospects of Agricultural Settlers in Upper Canada,' *British Agricultural Magazine*, 1835, 115
30 Alexander Robb, September 17, 1870
31 Margaret Carrothers's note is included in the letter of Nathaniel, December 25, 1839.
32 Jane White, April 1, 1856
33 Jane White, September 22, 1856
34 Charles Foy, *Dominion of Canada: Emigration to the Province of Ontario* (Belfast 1873), 67
35 Ibid, 73

36 A commemorative plaque outside St Peters Anglican Church at Erindale, Ontario, presents the story of James McGrath.

37 Letterbook of Bishop Strachan, October 6, 1841, AO

38 Jane White, July 19, 1859

39 Joseph Carrothers, June 15, 1855

40 John S. Moir, 'The Problem of a Double Minority: Some Reflections on the Development of the English-Speaking Catholic Church in Canada in the Nineteenth Century,' *Histoire sociale/Social History*, 4 (April 1971), 53–68

41 Byrne, *Gentlemen, Bishops and Faction Fighters: The Letters of Bishops O'Donel, Lambert, Scallan and Other Irish Missionaries* (St John's 1984), 34

42 Ibid, 217

43 Ibid, 20, 24

44 Kevin Whelan, 'County Kilkenny Priests in Newfoundland,' *Old Kilkenny Review*, 1986, 242–55; 'County Wexford Priests in Newfoundland,' *Journal of Wexford Historical Society*, 10 (1984–5)

45 Byrne, *Gentlemen*, 217

46 Ibid, 23

47 Ibid, 129

48 *Jubilee Volume with an Introduction by Archbishop Walsh, Diocese of Toronto, 1842–92* (Toronto 1892), 120

49 Ibid

50 Father Kelly's Notes, 120, ACAT

51 Charbonnel Papers, ACAT AB 1306

52 Letter from Lynch, Toronto, to Archbishop Leahy, Cashel, October 8, 1864, ACAT Lynch Papers, LAE07.06 1864

53 The authors wish to thank Mark McGowan, a doctoral student in history at the University of Toronto, for these data from his forthcoming thesis.

54 D.G. Cartwright, 'Ecclesiastical Territorial Organization and Institutional Conflict in Eastern and Northern Ontario, 1840–1910,' Canadian Historical Association, *Historical Papers*, 1978, 176–99

55 ACAT Lynch Papers, AD 04.53 1874

56 Ibid

57 *Jubilee Volume*, 78–9

58 Ibid, 82

59 Ibid, 101

60 Kelly Papers, Vol. A, Parish History, no date, no page, ACAT

61 Parish of St. James Colgan, Notes of Fr. McGivern, ACAT

62 Cited in Kelly Papers, Vol. A, Parish History, no date, no page, ACAT

63 *Methodist Missionary Society Reports*, 1846–7
64 Letter of Patrick Mee, Adelaide, to Bishop Power, Toronto, May 27, 1844, Power Papers, ACAT PAB1105
65 Cecil J. Houston and William J. Smyth, *The Sash Canada Wore* (Toronto 1980), chapter 5
66 Elements of the role played by Ogle R. Gowan and the Orange Order in administering local patronage in the early 1830s are described in D.H. Akenson, *The Irish in Ontario: A Study in Rural History* (Toronto 1984), 172–3.
67 William Archer, *The Marching of the Lodges: A Poem. Orange Melodies* (Dublin 1869), 121–2
68 Houston and Smyth, *The Sash*, 113
69 Quote from *Obligation of an Orangeman*; see Houston and Smyth, *The Sash*, 120.
70 Grand Orange Lodge of British North America, *Annual Proceedings*, 1848, 15 (Orange Archives, Toronto)
71 Grand Orange Lodge of Ireland, *Annual Proceedings*, 1858, 10 (National Library of Ireland, Dublin)
72 Grand Orange Lodge of Ireland, *Report of the Half-Year Meeting, Dublin, February 1871*, 50 (National Library of Ireland, Dublin)
73 C.J. Houston and W.J. Smyth, 'Transferred Loyalties: The Orange Order in the United States and Ontario,' *American Review of Canadian Studies*, 1984, 199

CHAPTER 7: The Geography of Settlement

1 For a good account of the geography of nineteenth-century Canadian industrialization see L. McCann (ed), *Heartland and Hinterland* (Toronto 1982).
2 See J.J. Mannion, 'Introduction,' in J.J. Mannion (ed), *The Peopling of Newfoundland* (St John's 1977), 1–15, and J.J. Mannion, 'The Irish Migrations to Newfoundland,' *Newfoundland Historical Society Lecture*, 1973, 1–12.
3 See John Mannion's biography of John O'Brien in the *Dictionary of Canadian Biography*, VIII, 658–9.
4 McNutt's colonization scheme in Nova Scotia is described in W.O. Raymond, 'Colonel Alexander McNutt and the Pre-Loyalist Settlements of Nova Scotia,' in *Transactions of the Royal Society of Canada*, Sec. II, 1911, 23–114.
5 A.H. Clark, 'Old World Origins and Religious Adherence,' *Geographical Review*, 1960, 321

6 *Dictionary of Canadian Biography*, IV, 553–7

7 A.A. McKenzie, *The Irish in Cape Breton Island* (Antigonish, NS, 1970)

8 Ibid and Terence Punch, *Irish Halifax: The Immigrant Generation* (Halifax 1981), 13

9 Arthur Young in *A Tour of Ireland 1776–1779* recorded: 'The staple trade of the place [Waterford] is the Newfoundland Trade; this is very much increased, there is more of it here than anywhere. The number of people who go passengers in the Newfoundland ships is amazing; from sixty to eighty ships, and from three thousand to five thousand annually. The ships go loaded with pork, beef, butter and some salt and bring home passengers or get freights where they can; sometimes rum' (406–7).

10 Brendan O'Grady, 'The Monaghan Settlers,' *Abegweit Review*, 4 no. 1 (Spring 1983), 51

11 Ibid, 55–7

12 See Ian Ross Robertson, 'Political Realignment in Pre-Confederation Prince Edward Island, 1863–1870,' *Acadiemis*, 15 no.1 (Autumn 1985), 35–58.

13 Peter Toner, 'Ethnicity and Regionalism in the Maritimes,' *Social Science Monograph Series* (Saint John), 1985, 1–18, and William Spray, 'Reception of the Irish in New Brunswick,' in Cyril J. Byrne and Margaret Harry (eds), *Talamh An Eisc* (Halifax 1986), 228–49.

14 Cape Tormentine, Emigrant Settlement in District of Westmoreland, Location tickets and records of sale to emigrants during the 1820s, New Brunswick Museum, Saint John, New Brunswick Historical Society Papers, Packet 11, Item 37

15 Ibid

16 The First President of the Anti-Profanity Society, *The Story of Melrose* ([Moncton, NB], n.d.), 6 (Mount Allison University Library, Sackville, NB)

17 Ibid

18 Cape Tormentine, Item 30; *The Story of Melrose*, 6

19 Cape Tormentine, Item 34

20 Ibid, Item 6

21 *The Story of Melrose*, 16

22 Ibid, 6

23 Ibid

24 Cape Tormentine, Item 15

25 The location and names of resident households were taken from H.F. Walling, *Topographical Map of Westmoreland and Albert Counties from Actual Surveys by D.J. Lake and H.S. Peck* (New York 1862) (New Brunswick Museum). The ethnic origin of families was based on the identity of male

heads of household listed in Census manuscripts, gravestone inscriptions, and local lore.

26 Wayne A. Gillcash (ed), *The New Brunswick Census of 1851: Westmoreland County*, 1 (Fredericton 1981).

27 Letter of David Moore, New Jerusalem, New Brunswick, to his brother in Carndonagh, Donegal, June 28, 1840; reproduced in Marion G. Reicker, *A Time There Was: Petersville and Other Abandoned Settlements in Queen's County, N.B., 1815–1953* (Queen's County, NB, 1984), 17–19

28 This map of Petersville is based on place-names found on topographic maps of the area. Professor Peter Toner of Saint John and Mr. Charles O'Donnell of Welsford, New Brunswick kindly verified the compilation.

29 The percentage for Petersville is an approximation based on the known figures for the neighbouring parish of Blissville from the 1851 Census of New Brunswick. The Census manuscripts for Petersville parish have been lost.

30 T.W. Acheson, *Saint John* (Toronto 1985)

31 Based on an unpublished compilation of Census manuscript data for Saint John by Professor Peter Toner, Saint John

32 Punch, *Irish Halifax*, 10

33 See Wendy Cameron, 'Selecting Peter Robinson's Irish Emigrants,' *Histoire sociale/Social History*, 1978, 29–46.

34 A.W.P. Buchanan, *The Buchanan Book* (Montreal 1911), 216

35 E.A. Talbot, *Five Years Residence in the Canadas*, 1, (London 1824), 100–65

36 Elliott, *Irish Migrants in the Canadas: A New Approach* (Kingston 1988)

37 Urban centres are those with a population of more than 1,500.

38 John O'Farrell, 'Irish Families in Ancient Quebec,' in R. O'Driscoll and Lorna Reynolds (eds), *The Untold Story: The Irish in Canada* (Toronto 1988), 1, 283

39 Raoul Blanchard, *Le Canada français* (Montreal 1960), 78

40 Marianna O'Gallagher, *St. Patrick's Quebec, 1824–1834* (Quebec 1981), 31

41 See ibid for an outline of the development of this parish.

42 Census of Lower Canada, 1844

43 *Ninetieth Anniversary of the Foundation of St. Patrick's Parish, Quebec* (Quebec 1923), 3

44 R. Vezina, cited in Fernand Ouellet, *Histoire économique et sociale du Quebec, 1760–1850* (Montreal 1966), 262

45 Cecil J. Houston and William J. Smyth, *The Sash Canada Wore* (Toronto 1980), 53

46 Letter of John S. Cummins, Cork, Ireland, to land agents in Ireland, 13 March 1860, PAC MG 24 154 Vol. 3, 449

47 Ibid, 450
48 The authors wish to thank Margaret Fallona of London, Ontario, for her kindness in providing this information.
49 For an introduction to the Catholic Irish community of the St-Sylvestre area see D. Aidan McQuillan, 'Beaurivage: The Development of an Irish Identity in Rural Quebec, 1820–1860,' in R. O'Driscoll and L. Reynolds (eds), *The Untold Story* (Toronto 1988), 263–70.
50 These preliminary results of Peter Toner's study of the Irish in New Brunswick were shared with the authors.
51 The highest percentages were those for Montreal and Quebec City, where respectively 41 and 40 per cent of the population that claimed Irish descent had been born in Ireland.
52 Manitoba became a province in 1870; Alberta and Saskatchewan attained that status in 1905.
53 John Warkentin (ed), *Canada: A Geographical Interpretation* (Toronto 1967), 79
54 Carrothers family history documents held by Mr Samuel Carrothers, Farnaght, County Fermanagh, Ireland
55 For a discussion of the role of the French in Manitoba see A.I. Silver, 'French Canada and the Prairie Frontier, 1870–1890,' *Canadian Historical Review*, 1969, 11–36.
56 Carl Berger, *The Sense of Power* (Toronto 1970)
57 Census of Canada, 1901
58 Census of Canada, 1921
59 Information obtained through personal communication from Andrew Harrison of the Public Records Office of Northern Ireland, May 1984
60 Houston and Smyth, *The Sash*, 58
61 Grand Orange Lodge of Ontario East, *Proceedings*, 1871, 15 (Orange Archives, Toronto)
62 Dr. T.J. Harrison, 'The Early History of Dufferin Loyal Orange Lodge No. 1514, Graysville, Manitoba, 1883–1959,' mimeo, 1959, 1. The authors wish to thank Professor John Merritt, Brandon, for bringing this document to their attention.
63 Houston and Smyth, *The Sash*, 61
64 Lynch Papers, Letter of Lynch to an unidentified cardinal, ACAT AE07.44, 1881
65 Lynch Papers, Letter of Lynch to the Bishops of Ireland, 18 April 1881, ACAT AE07.26. For fuller discussion of the northwest colonization episode see Gerald J. Stortz, 'Archbishop Lynch and New Ireland: An Unfulfilled Dream for Canada's Northwest,' *Catholic Historical Review*, 68 (1982), 612–24.

66 Lynch Papers, Letter of Lynch to Sir John A. Macdonald, 12 April 1882, ACAT AE07.45
67 Ibid, Correspondence between Lynch and Sir Alexander Galt, Canadian High Commissioner, London, 1882, ACAT AE07.16–29
68 Letter from 'Sam,' Regina, Saskatchewan, to a friend, 'Nick,' Belfast, 6 April 1911, PRONI
69 The depiction of British Columbia as a company province is given in Martin Robins, *The Rush for Spoils: The Company Province, 1871–1933* (Toronto 1972).
70 See the fuller presentation of Alexander Robb's emigrant life in chapter 10, below.
71 See Margaret Ormsby, 'Some Irish Figures in Colonial Days,' *British Columbia Historical Quarterly*, 1950 (Jan–April), 61–82.
72 Cornelius Okeefe was born near Fallowfield in the Ottawa Valley, and the Moores came from Bruce County.
73 Prince Edward Island joined Confederation in 1873; Newfoundland, in 1949.
74 Letter of John S. Cummins, Bury, Lower Canada, to R.W. Heneker, Sherbrooke, 15 August 1859, PAC MG 24 154 Vol. 3, 422–3
75 Derived from *Historical Atlas of Simcoe County, 1881: John Hogg's Map of Simcoe County, 1871* (AO); manuscript census data, church records, and records of the Orange Order (Orange Archives, Toronto)
76 Quoted in Pauline Roulston, 'The Urbanization of Nineteenth Century Orangeville, Ontario: Some Historical and Geographical Aspects,' MA thesis, University of Toronto, 1974
77 Notes on the parish of St James Colgan, Archdiocese of Toronto, ACAT
78 Fr E. Jackman, *The History of the Parish of Orangeville* (Toronto 1976), 26
79 The dearth of letters from Catholics among the many collections of emigrant letters may be discovered in the work of Patrick O'Farrell on Australia and Kirby Miller on the United States. Dr Brian Trainor, responsible for the fine collection of emigrant letters at the PRONI, has been keenly aware of the issue but is at a loss to explain it.
80 Other collections of Irish letters include: Cyril Byrne, *Gentlemen-Bishops and Faction Fighters: James Louis O'Donel, 1737–1811* (St John's 1984); Frances Stewart, *Our Forest Home* (1982); Louise Wyatt (ed), 'The Johnson Letters,' *Ontario History*, 1948, 27–52; Thomas Radcliff (ed), *Authentic Letters from Upper Canada* (Toronto 1953).
    For other aspects of the Irish emigrant experience, the following studies of Australià and the United States deserve attention: Patrick O'Farrell, *Letters from Irish Australia, 1825–1929* (Sydney and Belfast 1984);

The Irish in Australia (Kensington, Australia, 1987); and Kirby A. Miller, *Emigrants and Exiles* (New York 1985).

CHAPTER 8: Nathaniel and Joseph Carrothers

1 Cemetery visit; genealogical information provided by Carrothers family descendants; and the Pond Mills Cemetery Record. The authors wish to thank Mrs Margaret Fallona and Mr Clifford Carrothers of London, Ontario, and especially Mr and Mrs Samuel Carrothers of Farnaght, County Fermanagh, for their kindness and assistance.

2 'Genealogy of the Archibald Edward Carrothers family,' prepared by Edward C. Webster, 1980, 5; in the possession of Samuel Carrothers, Farnaght, Ireland

3 Edward Norman Carrothers, 'Irish Emigrants' Letters from Canada, 1839–1870,' typescript 1951, PRONI

4 Interview with Clifford Carrothers, London, Ontario, July 1985

5 Document in the possession of Samuel Carrothers of Farnaght

6 'Genealogy,' 5

7 Tremaine's *Map of the County of Middlesex*, 1860 (AO)

8 Lots 6 and 7N, King Street, London, AO, Land Record Index

9 Personal communication with Alan Gailey, architectural historian and keeper of the Ulster Folk Museum, May 1985

10 In the Census manuscripts of 1851 and 1861, Nathaniel and members of his family are declared to be members of the Church of England.

11 Family lore provided by Samuel Carrothers of Farnaght

12 'Genealogy,' 5

13 Information provided by Samuel Carrothers on a walk across Farnaght, June 1985. In the twentieth century the family's interest in plants was carried on by Edward Norman Carrothers, an eminent Ulster naturalist. See Kenneth Jamison, 'Edward Norman Carrothers (1897–1977): An Appreciation,' *Irish Booklore*, 4 no. 1 (1978), 5–6

14 John G. Mannion, *Irish Settlements in Eastern Canada*, (Toronto 1974), 43, offers a contrasting view in his assertion of individualism and lack of kinship bonds among the immigrants.

CHAPTER 9: Jane White: Townswoman in Upper Canada

1 The Canada Co.'s head office was one of Toronto's first corporate offices; see G. Gad and D. Holdsworth, 'Building for City, Region, and Nation,' in V.L. Russell (ed), *Forging a Consensus* (Toronto 1984), 274.

2 Land Records, Goderich, Ontario, Registry Office of the County of Huron, Goderich
3 Probate Will of Wm. M. White, 21 March 1879, Registry Office of the County of Huron, Goderich

CHAPTER 10: Alexander Robb: Adventures in British Columbia

1 Robb Family Genealogy, PRONI
2 Ibid
3 Ibid
4 Probated Will of Alexander Robb, PRONI
5 R.C. Harris and J. Warkentin, *Canada before Confederation* (New York 1974), 29
6 R.C. Harris, 'Moving among the Mountains,' *BC Studies*
7 Resolution of Royal Ulster Agricultural Historical Society on death of Mr Alexander Robb, J.P., PRONI

Index

368   Index